# THE FIRST WORLD WAR DIARY OF NOËL DRURY, 6TH ROYAL DUBLIN FUSILIERS: GALLIPOLI, SALONIKA, THE MIDDLE EAST AND THE WESTERN FRONT

edited by

RICHARD S. GRAYSON

Published by

THE BOYDELL PRESS
for the
ARMY RECORDS SOCIETY
2022

First published 2022

An Army Records Society publication
published by The Boydell Press
an imprint of Boydell & Brewer Ltd
PO Box 9, Woodbridge, Suffolk IP12 3DF, UK
and of Boydell & Brewer Inc.
668 Mt Hope Avenue, Rochester, NY 14620–2731, USA
website: www.boydellandbrewer.com

ISBN 978 1 83838 771 6

A CIP catalogue record for this book is available
from the British Library

The publisher has no responsibility for the continued existence or accuracy of URLs for
external or third-party internet websites referred to in this book, and does not guarantee
that any content on such websites is, or will remain, accurate or appropriate

This publication is printed on acid-free paper

Typeset by BBR Design, Sheffield

Printed and bound in Great Britain by
TJ Books Limited, Padstow, Cornwall

# Contents

# Illustrations

Drury was a keen photographer and took all of the photos shown here except those including himself and one of his brother. His own descriptions are those in quotation marks. Illustrations appear in a block between the Abbreviations and the Introduction.

# Acknowledgements

I would like to thank Tim Bowman for initially suggesting that I edit the Drury diaries for publication, and for his continued support throughout the process. Thanks are similarly due to Peter Johnston (then of the National Army Museum (NAM), now of the Royal Air Force Museum, Hendon) for securing the NAM's cooperation with the project and answering many queries along the way. The Drury diaries are held in the Templer Study Centre at the NAM and I am grateful to them for permission to reproduce the text along with the photos in the NAM's possession. Thank you to George Hay of the Army Records Society for his assistance, to the Society's copy-editor, Gillian Northcott Liles, for her professional support, and to Tom Davies for indexing.

Transcription of the diaries was largely done in 2019, when one could never have imagined the challenges which would soon face historical researchers needing to access archival material. However, much of my editing work, especially the addition of material from outside the diaries, was done during the Covid-19 lockdown. To that end I am very grateful to Aisling Lockhart of the Manuscripts and Archives Research Library at Trinity College Dublin for pointing me towards online information on Drury's enrolment at Trinity. Deirdre O'Connell of the National Archives of Ireland gave valuable advice on how to obtain a copy of Drury's will from a distance using a good old-fashioned cheque and combination of the Royal Mail and An Post. Keith Edmonds and Keith Roberts of the Salonika Campaign Society provided invaluable material in relation to Salonika maps and published material at a time when it was desperately needed. Peter Elliott, the archivist of the Mill Hill Foundation, provided information on Drury's school life. I am very grateful to Robert Fleming of the NAM for sending me digital copies of photographs from Drury's diaries having arranged for most to be photographed for me specially. I am grateful to The National Archives at Kew for enabling a bulk order of WO files once lockdown began to ease, which were crucial for individual biographies. Thank you to the Army Records Society's anonymous readers for their helpful suggestions on the manuscript.

I am very grateful to my Mum, Jannat Grayson, who read a full draft of the text, providing valuable comments, queries and corrections. Finally, I am grateful for the tolerance of Lucy and Edward Grayson as I explained to them why obscure aspects of Noël Drury's life were so fascinating to me.

# Abbreviations

| | |
|---|---|
| BGC | Brigadier General Commanding |
| CF | Chaplain to the Forces |
| CO | Commanding Officer |
| CRA | Commander Royal Artillery |
| DMP | Dublin Metropolitan Police |
| DSO | Distinguished Service Order |
| FGCM | Field General Court-Martial |
| GNR | Great Northern Railway |
| GOC | General Officer Commanding |
| GS | General Service |
| GSO | General Staff Officer |
| HE | High explosive |
| HMS | His Majesty's Ship |
| HMT | His Majesty's Transport |
| HQ | Headquarters |
| KP | Knight of the Order of St Patrick |
| KTS Ridge | Kiretch Tepe Sirt Ridge |
| MC | Military Cross |
| MG | Machine gun |
| MLO | Military Landing Officer |
| MO | Medical Officer |
| NCO | Non-commissioned Officer |
| OC | Officer Commanding |
| PRI | President of the Regimental Institute |
| RAMC | Royal Army Medical Corps |
| RC | Roman Catholic |

| RDF | Royal Dublin Fusiliers |
| RMF | Royal Munster Fusiliers |
| SAA | Small arms ammunition |
| TCD | Trinity College Dublin |
| VAD | Voluntary Aid Detachment |
| VC | Victoria Cross |
| WAAC | Women's Auxiliary Army Corps |
| YMCA | Young Men's Christian Association |

Figure 1    Second Lieutenant Noël Drury, taken at Carlow in 1915.

Figure 2    Part of a
Zeppelin at Salonika,
May 1916.

Figure 3    'Bunty visits
me at the 30th Stationary
Hospital', 24 July 1917.

Figure 4    Kenneth Drury,
France 1917.

Figure 5    Lieutenant Colonel
Patrick George Ashley Cox DSO,
Dudular Camp, 1 September 1917.

Figure 6    Major John Luke,
1 September 1917.

Figure 7    'Loading our camels after a halt'.

Figure 8    'Stuffer' Byrne at Rafa,
September or October 1917.

Figure 9    Drury (left) with
Lieutenant Guy Loveband at Rafa,
September or October 1917.

Figure 10
Captain F. Paine, Royal
Army Medical Corps,
at Rafa, September
or October 1917.

Figure 11   'Some of our prisoners', November 1917.

Figure 12  '10th Division artillery near Junction Station', November 1917.

Figure 13  'The Dome of the Rock, Jerusalem', December 1917.

Figure 14 'The Wadi Sunt', December 1917.

Figure 15 'Bethlehem showing Church of the Nativity (square tower) upper right hand corner', January 1918.

Figure 16 'Bristol fighter in which I flew over Bethlehem and Jerusalem', January 1918.

Figure 17 '"The Three Fusiliers" Captains HA Shadforth, J Gaffney, JM Tittle', March 1918.

Figure 18 'The Famous Green flag in Ajul Camp', March 1918.

Figure 19 Captain Noël Drury (right) with Captain Alan Beard (1st Connaught Rangers), at the Great Sphinx of Giza, Egypt, April 1918.

Figure 20    'Officers of 6th Battalion, The Royal Dublin Fusiliers', 30 November 1918. 'Top row, left to right: Lieutenant GE Larkin, Second Lieutenant McMillan, Lieutenant WO Parish, Second Lieutenant Young, Second Lieutenant Livingston, Lieutenant McGaghey. 3rd row: Second Lieutenant GT Swayne, Captain GY Loveband, Second Lieutenant Harney, Second Lieutenant WR Wade, Reverend JS Burns, Second Lieutenant Scales, Second Lieutenant PP Purcell, Second Lieutenant TJ Byrne, Lieutenant HJ Oliphant, Lieutenant AJ Carrig, Second Lieutenant CW Booth. 2nd row: Captain JI Watson RAMC, Captain RD English, Captain J Esmonde, Major V Vance, Lieutenant-Colonel WB Little DSO MC, Major AS Wodehouse, Captain HJ Hayes MC, Captain NE Drury, Lieutenant GF Unwin. Bottom row: Second Lieutenant J McCann DCM, Second Lieutenant Millar MC, Second Lieutenant Manley, Second Lieutenant Rooker, Second Lieutenant O'Hea.'

Figure 21 '6th Royal Dublin Fusiliers Band with Captain & Adjutant J Esmonde, MC', November 1918.

# Introduction

## Drury's Background and Peacetime Life

Noël Edmund Drury was born on 24 December 1883 in Upper Rathmines on the southern edge of the city of Dublin.[1] His first name probably came, as was often traditional, from the coincidence of his birth with Christmas. His parents, John Girdwood Drury and Frances Mary Drury (née Figgis), married just over a year before, on 30 November 1882, at Dublin's Adelaide Road Presbyterian Church. John was about ten years older than Frances. It seems likely that the house in which Noël Drury was born, Glen-na-Smoil, was his mother's family home, since she had been living there at the time of her marriage. On his marriage certificate, John Drury was described as a 'merchant' living at Kenilworth House. The fathers of the bride and groom were also merchants.[2] Specifically, John Drury's business was paper manufacturing, having taken over the running of the Swift Brook Papermill at Saggart, County Dublin, in 1880. Paper had been made on the site since 1785 by the McDonnell family, who had converted a flour mill, and the company which the Drury family would run at Saggart retained the original name: John McDonnell and Company Limited. The Drury family ran the business until 1926.[3]

---

1   https://civilrecords.irishgenealogy.ie/churchrecords/images/birth_returns/ births_1884/02703/1995399.pdf [accessed 21 April 2020].

2   https://civilrecords.irishgenealogy.ie/churchrecords/images/marriage_returns/ marriages_1882/10984/8015547.pdf [accessed 21 April 2020].

3   Mervyn Ennis, *The Story of Swift Brook Papermill* (Dublin: South Dublin County Council, 2016), 9, 28–34. This publication describes John Drury as having taken over the business in 1880 with his brother Noël, with the latter having become Managing Director and John being Secretary and Director. However, this seems to confuse the management arrangements in 1880 with those in place after the death of Noël's father, John. In the first place, the older John Girdwood Drury does not appear to have had a brother Noël, since there are no genealogical records for a Noël Drury other than the one born in 1883. Meanwhile, in 1882, John Drury was described as Managing Director

I

Noël Drury appears to have had two younger brothers and no sisters. The first brother was Kenneth Kirkpatrick Drury, born on 18 May 1885, by which time the family was living close to the papermill at Swift Brook in Saggart, County Dublin.[4] They were joined by the paternally named John Girdwood Drury, born on 9 January 1895 at Swift Brook House, who became known as 'Jack'.[5] Their mother died aged 41 in 1895 of a form of carcinoma.[6] Drury was sent away to school in England: Mill Hill School, on the north-west edge of London, in the third term of 1899, and Jack also later attended the school.[7] It had been founded in 1807 to provide a nonconformist alternative to the so-called 'public' schools which required those attending to be Anglicans, and was therefore an obvious destination for a Presbyterian.[8] At Mill Hill, Drury was a member of School House and left in July 1901. He was a Monitor (the name given to senior Prefects) and played in the 2nd XV (rugby) and the cricket 3rd XI. He seems also to have been the first Captain of Cycling.[9] Then, aged 17, Noël Drury enrolled at Trinity College Dublin on 2 November 1901.[10] It is not clear what he studied and he does not appear to have completed his studies, because although he is included in the college's

---

(*Irish Times*, 2 Nov 1882, p. 6), in 1902 the mill was described as being 'under the skilful management of Mr John Drury' (*Weekly Irish Times*, 18 Jan 1902, p. 16) and on his death in 1907, John Drury was described as 'managing director of the Swiftbrook Paper Mills' (*Irish Times*, 12 June 1907, p. 7). The book about the mill includes photos, which appear to be from a newspaper or other publication, of a Noël and John described as Managing Director and Secretary and Director respectively. However, the Noël pictured there is clearly the one whose diaries are edited here. Finally, the earliest sources found by this author referring to any Noël as Managing Director are after his father's death. See, for example *Weekly Irish Times*, 8 April 1911, p. 2.

4   https://civilrecords.irishgenealogy.ie/churchrecords/images/cert_amends/
    cert_1889/1918998a.pdf [accessed 21 April 2020].
5   https://civilrecords.irishgenealogy.ie/churchrecords/images/birth_returns/
    births_1885/02658/1980240.pdf [accessed 21 April 2020]. See diary entry,
    January 1919.
6   https://civilrecords.irishgenealogy.ie/churchrecords/images/deaths_returns/
    deaths_1895/05924/4682095.pdf [accessed 21 April 2020].
7   Email to author from Peter Elliott, Mill Hill Foundation Archivist, 1 Sept 2020.
8   https://www.millhill.org.uk/senior/our-school/history-of-the-school/
    [accessed 22 April 2020].
9   Email to author from Peter Elliott, Mill Hill Foundation Archivist, 1 Sept 2020.
10  Trinity College Dublin Archives, Admissions Records, 1877–1910, TCD MUN
    V, ff. 212v & 213r. Available free of charge online at: https://www.tcd.ie/library/
    manuscripts/collections/genealogy.php [accessed 22 April 2020].

'War List' there is no degree against his name.[11] Kenneth followed Noël to Trinity in November 1906, having previously attended Tipperary Grammar School.[12]

Their father died on 11 June 1907, aged 64, of intestinal problems.[13] Noël and Jack took over the paper business after the death of their father, but it is possible that they had become involved in it before then. At any rate, by 1908 Noël was connected to business beyond the family concern through the Council of the Dublin Industrial Development Association, and he later became part of the same body of the Irish Industrial Development Association.[14] By the time of the 1911 census (2 April), Noël and Kenneth were sharing a house in Saggart, with Noël described as a paper manufacturer and Kenneth as a medical student at Trinity College.[15] Jack was married and living in Frankfort Avenue in Rathgar and, like Noël, was a paper manufacturer.[16] Later that month, Noël and Jack hosted a visit to the mill by the Countess of Aberdeen.[17] The mill normally manufactured a particularly high quality of paper and that gave it a strong reputation. James Connolly's newspaper, *The Worker's Republic*, was printed on its paper. Later, so was the 1916 Proclamation of the Republic, although by that time, due to wartime restrictions on the use of linen in paper, that used for the Proclamation was a much lower standard than would have been produced in peacetime.[18] It was ironic that paper produced by the Drury family business would become iconic in Irish Republican history because Noël was also a magistrate and in that role was involved in the preparation of an address to the King and Queen on their visit to Dublin in July 1911.[19]

Kenneth does not appear to have been part of the family business. He graduated with a medical degree in 1914 and took posts first at the

---

11 University of Dublin, Trinity College, *War List, February, 1922* (Dublin: Hodges Figgis, 1922), 56.

12 Trinity College Dublin Archives, Admissions Records, 1877–1910, TCD MUN V, ff. 252v & 253r.

13 https://civilrecords.irishgenealogy.ie/churchrecords/images/deaths_returns/deaths_1907/05531/4550561.pdf [accessed 21 April 2020].

14 *Irish Times*, 23 December 1908, p. 6; *Weekly Irish Times*, 8 Feb 1913, p. 15.

15 http://www.census.nationalarchives.ie/reels/nai000016213/ [accessed 21 April 2020].

16 http://www.census.nationalarchives.ie/reels/nai000146446/ [accessed 21 April 2020].

17 *Irish Times*, 1 April 1911, p. 6.

18 Ennis, *Swift Brook Papermill*, 49–50.

19 *Weekly Irish Times*, 27 May 1911, p. 5.

Stewart Institute in Chapelizod on the edge of Dublin, then at the County Asylum in Warwick. That medical background influenced his war service as he joined the Royal Army Medical Corps in August 1914 and served in that throughout the war. He rose to the rank of Major by the end of the war and was awarded the Military Cross in June 1916.[20]

At some point before the war, Noël spent time in Edinburgh, for reasons which are unclear. This is apparent from references in his diary to the Lethem family, with whom he appears to have stayed, and especially William Lethem,[21] whom he encountered at Gallipoli. He knew the family well enough for them to send packages to him, and for him to spend some leave with them in September 1918.[22] In other areas of Noël's pre-war life, he was a Freemason,[23] and a significant pioneer of motorcycle racing. He came sixth in the twin-cylinder version of the 1908 Tourist Trophy, or 'TT', on the Isle of Man, riding a Matchless which he had built himself. He raced on the Isle of Man with one of his future commanding officers, Colonel W.B. Little. It was only the second ever TT race there, and he was only the second Irishman to compete, returning again to race in the next two years but not finishing on either occasion.[24] Later, he was involved with the Dublin and District Motor Cycle Club and both he and his brother, Jack, took organisational roles in the Motor Cycle Union of Ireland, while Jack took part in motor car trials.[25] However, Jack died of the Spanish flu at the end of the war.[26] His widow, Ida, survived him by more than 54 years, dying in March 1973.[27]

---

20  University of Dublin, Trinity College, *War List*, p. 56; *Supplement to the Edinburgh Gazette*, 5 June 1916, p. 998; WO 339/10955. See Figure 4.

21  Captain William Ashley Lethem, RAMC (WO 372/24/37610).

22  See diary entries, 20 Sept 1915, 24 Aug and 14 Sept 1918. For further information on the Lethems, see: http://www.ghgraham.org/marianmacintosh. html & http://smsec.rcpe.ac.uk/intimation-form/lethem-william-ashley [accessed 30 April 2020].

23  A certificate issued by Sir Charles Cameron Masonic Lodge in December 1918 records the war service of its members. See page inserted in the first volume of the Drury diaries [hereafter D1].

24  *Irish Times*, 23 September 1908, p. 5 and 29 May 1957, p. 3; https://www. gracesguide.co.uk/Noel_E._Drury [accessed 30 April 2020]; see also diary entry, 31 Aug 1918. Drury was pictured with a JAP motorcycle, probably the one he had ridden in 1909 in *The Motor Cycle*, 26 May 1910, p. 473. He rode a Chater Lea in 1910.

25  *Irish Times*, 7 October 1911, p. 4; 8 March 1912, p. 4; 31 March 1914, p. 4; *Weekly Irish Times*, 6 June 1908, p. 20.

26  See diary entry, Jan 1919.

27  *Irish Times*, 26 March 1973, p. 18.

# Diary Themes

If Drury himself took any overall message or purpose from his accumulated diaries it is perhaps embodied in his choice of words for a frontispiece for Volume One, a rendering of Pericles' oration from Thucydides, which points to the first overall theme of the diaries:

> They gave their bodies to the common weal and received, each for his own memory, praise that will never die, and with it the grandest of all sepulchres, not that in which their mortal bodies are laid, but a home in the minds of men where their glory remains fresh to stir to speech or action as the occasion comes by.[28]

The 'They' for Drury was probably the Royal Dublin Fusiliers in general because his pride in the regiment, and the extent to which he was telling a story which was part of its wider history, appear very clear. On the very first diary page he pasted an image of the regimental badge, which was followed by six pages of regimental history.[29] The final volume then concluded with a much more lengthy section on the same subject.[30] Drury seems to have wanted to add his own chapter to that regimental history by recording the story of the regiment's 6th battalion. Had there been a full regimental history of the Royal Dublin Fusiliers produced in the 1920s, when such works were produced on the other Southern Irish regiments, Drury might have been the ideal candidate to write it. Indeed, one might speculate whether his diary drafts were a prelude to some such kind of work, but there is no evidence in his papers that it was a prelude to a wider regimental history or indeed a publication on just his own battalion. Consequently, the works published on the regiment's First World War were limited to the regular (1st and 2nd) battalions and one company of the 7th Royal Dublin Fusiliers (and that only to the end of the Gallipoli campaign).[31]

---

28  D1, no page number, but immediately before p. 1.
29  D1, pp. 1–6.
30  D4, additional pp. 1–43.
31  H.C. Wylly, *Neill's Blue Caps*, vol. III (Aldershot: Gale and Polden, 1925); H.C. Wylly, *Crown and Company, 1911–1922: The Historical Records of the 2nd Batt. Royal Dublin Fusiliers* (London: Arthur L. Humphreys, 1925); Henry Hanna, *The Pals at Suvla Bay: Being the Record of "D" Company of the 7th Royal Dublin Fusiliers* (Dublin: Ponsonby, 1917).

At any rate, Drury did leave a lasting testament to his pride of having served in the Royal Dublin Fusiliers, shedding some insight into what it meant to be an Irish Protestant officer in the British Army. In the first place, for Drury as a Presbyterian, the war brought him closer to the Roman Catholic Church than he had been previously. He attended a Mass on St Patrick's Day in 1915,[32] having little knowledge of Catholic practices, and later in the war he saw close at hand how important the work of the Catholic Chaplain was to the men under his command. It certainly caused him to reflect on divisions at home.[33] Meanwhile, Drury held a strong appreciation of the traditions of his regiment and did all that he could to make it clear to his comrades that they were serving in part of a regiment which could claim to be the oldest in the British Army.[34]

A second theme of the diaries is that since they cover fighting in four different theatres of war, they allow comparisons of the nature of fighting, showing how, for example, the relative absence of allied artillery dogged the war effort at both Gallipoli and Salonika compared to the Western Front.[35] If we see the static nature of trench warfare at Gallipoli and Salonika, we can also see a mobile war being fought in Palestine in early 1918 and then on the Western Front in the summer and autumn of that year.[36] Drury's experiences in those latter two theatres show how successful allied command was towards the end of the war, while the problems his unit faced at Gallipoli tell a different story of poor planning. His damning verdict on the landing there was that 'we went to Gallipoli without any orders, and without any maps'.[37]

All of this points to a third theme – that experiences of fighting and trench life could be relatively limited. As such, the diaries form an antidote to popular myths of the war in which men lived in trenches for four years, unless they were sent 'over the top' and inevitably mown down by machine-gun fire. Even as an early volunteer, and one of the first batch of Irish volunteers sent to the front (as part of the 6th Royal Dublin Fusiliers), Drury did not leave Ireland until the last day of April 1915, and was not sent from England until July, not being deployed in action until early August, a year after the war had begun. In each of his first three deployments, at Gallipoli, Salonika and Palestine, his

32  Diary entry, 1915.
33  Diary entry, 26 Sept 1915.
34  Diary entries, 19 Oct 1915 and 14 Nov 1918.
35  Diary entries, 11 Aug 1915 and 8 Dec 1915.
36  Diary entries, 5 Jan 1918 and 9 Oct 1918.
37  Diary entry, 7 Aug 1915.

battalion saw major action on only a few occasions: at Gallipoli on 8–12 and 15–16 August,[38] several engagements over a week in early December 1915 at Kosturino,[39] and then on 10 March 1918 at the Battle of Tel 'Asur in Palestine.[40] Their most sustained engagement with the enemy came following deployment to the Western Front, when they saw rapid movement over 7–11 October at Le Catelet during the Battle of the Hindenburg Line,[41] and then on 17–18 October at Le Cateau during the Battle of the Selle.[42] Of course, the 6th Royal Dublin Fusiliers were regularly in front line trenches and holding them in the face of enemy fire, but often there was little happening. Instead, daily life was often monotonous and with little going on. Drury trained, dealt as Adjutant with much battalion bureaucracy, and had a surprising amount of time for tourism. His biggest concerns were often water, food and warmth (or a lack of them), while on other occasions excessive heat was a bigger challenge. For Drury personally, malaria and eye problems were a major feature of the war, seeing him spend a year away from his battalion from July 1916 to July 1917. His experiences of treatment in Casualty Clearing Stations and General Hospitals are a fascinating insight into this aspect of the war.[43]

## After the War

In the post-war years, Noël Drury continued to support motor sports as he had done pre-war, for example being a contributor to the costs of running the Irish International Grand Prix in 1930.[44] It is not clear if he continued to compete on a motorcycle, but he did take up yacht racing in the 1920s.[45] He was part of the Royal Dublin Fusiliers Old Comrades' Association, at least in the early 1930s.[46] Kenneth Drury married Martha Elizabeth Tomb in Willesden, Middlesex, on 5 July

---

38  Diary entries, 8–12 Aug 1915, 15–16 Aug 1915.
39  Diary entries, 6–11 Dec 1915.
40  Diary entries, 9 and 16 March 1915.
41  Diary entries, 7–8 Oct 1918.
42  Diary entries, 17–18 Oct 1918.
43  Diary entries, 18–27 July 1916.
44  *Irish Times*, 7 Sept 1929, p. 6.
45  *Irish Times*, 3 June 1922, p. 4; 7 July 1923, p. 10; 16 July 1923, p. 9; 17 Sept 1923, p. 8; 18 June 1930, p. 4.
46  *Irish Times*, 5 Dec 1932, p. 2.

1918 and left the army in 1919. It is not clear if Martha was the 'Bunty' referred to in his brother's diaries, and to whom Kenneth was clearly close during the war. When Kenneth died aged 95 on 9 August 1984 in a nursing home in Burnham-on-Sea, Somerset, his death certificate described him as a retired medical practitioner. His death was notified by his son, partly named after Drury: Dennis Arthur Noël Drury, who lived then in Aylesbury, Buckinghamshire.[47]

From the mid-1920s, it is not exactly clear what Drury did for an occupation. He returned to the papermill after the war and was still managing it in September 1925,[48] but due to a post-war slump in the paper trade, business was difficult. The mill closed in February 1926 and was put up for sale in March but no buyer was found. At that point, the *Irish Times*, said, 'The village of Saggart was almost entirely dependent on the mills, which employed from 80 to 100 hands.' With a sale secured in December 1927 the mill reopened in January 1928, at which point it was the only papermill in the Irish Free State.[49] What Drury did for employment after 1926 – or whether he even needed to be employed, perhaps living from the proceeds of the mill sale – is unknown. At any rate, any business activities he might have had did not feature on the pages of the *Irish Times* as they had once.

Drury died a few weeks before 92nd birthday, on 5 December 1975, at his home, Suncroft, in Foxrock, County Dublin.[50] He had been living there since at least July 1964 when he made his Will. When the home last sold, in 2016, it was described as being 'designed at the turn of the last Century by Sir Richard Orpen from the Arts and Crafts style'.[51] It was a large house, but there is no evidence of Drury having married or having had children. When he wrote his Will in 1964, his cousin, Florence Winifred Drury, was named in it as residing at the same address. His *Irish Times* death notice, which referred to him as 'Captain', only otherwise described him as 'eldest son of the late John Girdwood Drury'. His Will left a series of small bequests (£50–£100) to a nephew, niece, God-daughter, and a

47  WO 339/10955; copies of marriage and death certificates in possession of author.
48  *Irish Times*, 23 Sept 1925, p. 3. The report refers to him as Captain E.M. Drury, but the initials are likely to be a mistake as there is no other evidence of an E.M. Drury.
49  Ennis, *Swift Brook Papermill*, 35; *Irish Times*, 20 March 1926, p. 11; 22 Dec 1927, p. 8; 19 Jan 1928, p. 5.
50  *Irish Times*, 6 Dec 1975, p. 20.
51  https://www.myhome.ie/residential/brochure/suncroft-mart-lane-foxrock-dublin-18/3599195 [accessed 23 April 2020].

Richard Eaton of Rathmines, along with specific items (mainly books) going to the Royal Irish Yacht Club in Dun Laoghaire and the Benevolent Order of the Friendly Brothers of St Patrick. The books mainly related to the First World War, some specifically to the Royal Dublin Fusiliers, and appear to have been special to him. The residue of his estate was left to the cousin with whom he was living in 1964, and given her middle name, she might have been the 'Miss W Drury' who donated his diaries to the National Army Museum, along with a prismatic compass, in 1976. He left nothing to his brother, Kenneth, other than 'the Drury Family Vault in Mount Jerome Cemetery', saying that Kenneth 'may either retain or abandon it as he thinks fit. I do not wish to be buried in it as I consider it a Pagan and un-Christian method of burial.' Instead, he was buried at Deansgrange Cemetery, with his gravestone describing him as 'Captain Royal Dublin Fusiliers'.[52] His last home at Foxrock was approximately 15 miles east of Saggart, and only 6 miles south of where he was born. Drury had travelled far, but 'home' had always been the area just south of Dublin city. That, and his final rank in the Royal Dublin Fusiliers, defined him to the end.

## Sources and Editorial Method

Drury's diaries began almost immediately after he volunteered for war service on 1 September 1914. He continued to keep a diary throughout his service which would see him journey to Gallipoli, Salonika, the Middle East and then finally the Western Front. Four volumes of diaries now rest in the National Army Museum.[53] The four volumes total over 620 pages and come to approximately 200,000 words. In addition, there are another few hundred pages inserted containing items ranging from divisional Christmas cards to newspaper cuttings. Drury was a keen photographer, and he included many photographs, some of which have been reproduced in this edited edition.

---

52  *Irish Times*, 6 Dec 1975, p. 20; copy of Will in possession of author, obtained from National Archives, Dublin; Ennis, *Swift Brook Papermill*, 48; email to author form Peter Johnston, National Army Museum, 18 June 2020.

53  The diaries are held in the museum's Templer Study Centre, with two volumes viewable online: https://collection.nam.ac.uk/detail.php?acc=1976-07-69-1 & https://collection.nam.ac.uk/detail.php?acc=1976-07-69-2 [accessed 23 April 2020].

Volume One of the diaries covered the period from Drury's enlistment to the 6th Royal Dublin Fusiliers' withdrawal from Gallipoli. Volume Two is about Salonika, while Volume Three covers the Middle East, and Volume Four relates to the Western Front. Volume One was typed until the day Drury landed at Gallipoli. From then on it is handwritten, as is Volume Two. Volumes Three and Four are typed, apart from the opening page of the latter and a 43-page historical sketch of the Royal Dublin Fusiliers.

It seems very unlikely that any of the pages are original versions, written exactly at the time to which they relate, while Drury sat in a dugout at the end of the day. The opening page of the first volume says: 'Copied from original diary and various other notes and embodying various orders, etc., of which the originals are in my possession.' This is below a heading 'MY WAR DIARY, 1914–1918', so those words would appear to relate to the entire diary, not simply the volume in which they appear. However, there is a hint in Volume Two that at least parts of the diary were written up during the war: on one page Drury appended a note about an individual under a heading of 'Added after the war'.[54]

It is clear that the surviving diaries do not reflect all the material that Drury had at some point written. At the start of Volume Three Drury noted, 'My rough diary is somewhat incomplete owing to the loss of sheets and pages sent home separately. The blanks have been supplied from various copies of operation orders, 'phone messages, etc. which survived. A good many ships with mails were torpedoed.'[55] Volume Three appears to have suffered especially from the loss of material. Between the entries for 26 December 1917 and the week ending 29 December, Drury noted 'My diary from 27th December, 1917 onwards was lost on the way home and the following has been made up from various orders, rough notes, maps, etc. which survived.'[56] Unfortunately, it is not clear whether he meant 'the following' to mean only the remainder of that volume, or everything that followed until the end of the war. We can be sure, however, that Drury continued to look at and tweak his diaries well after the war. In a typed entry for the week ending 13 October 1917, a handwritten note by the name of Philip Chetwode says 'made Field Marshal on March 3rd 1933'.[57]

---

54  D2, p. 103.
55  D3, p. 1.
56  D3, p. 119.
57  D3, p. 49.

In editing the diaries, their contents have been cut down here to approximately 100,000 words, which is around half their full length. The focus has been on selecting material which enables a clear narrative of the 6th Royal Dublin Fusiliers to emerge. In places, especially at Salonika, the battalion's daily life became monotonous, and extensive accounts of that have been omitted, while still making it clear how far such routine daily life continued over long periods of time. Drury wrote extensive 'tourist' accounts of the places he visited, and a selection of these have been included to give a flavour of how new sights appeared to an Irish officer, but much such material has been omitted. In addition, the length was greatly reduced through the excision of most of the lists of names that Drury often included (although some of his lists are reproduced here as appendices), and through omitting full transcripts of orders which Drury often wrote up. Drury broadly wrote very well and there has been no 'copy-editing' of his own phrasing. However, occasional spelling and grammatical mistakes[58] have been corrected as would have been the case if Drury had found a publisher himself, while numbers have been stand-ardised (Drury used many different formats mixing digits and letters). British Army ranks have been produced in full, and regimental names have been altered so that they are in full, except for the Royal Dublin Fusiliers and the Royal Munster Fusiliers. The former are obviously mentioned very often. Drury used different abbreviations such as Dublins, RDF, R.Dub.Fus., R.Dublin Fus. and others, sometimes with or without full stops after shortened words. These have been altered to either RDF or the full name as seemed appropriate for the situation. The same applies to RMF for the Royal Munster Fusiliers, for whom Drury used a similar range of abbreviations. Overall though, the approach has otherwise been to reproduce the diaries exactly as they were written by Drury.

As regards place names, complications arise for the Salonika Front and the Middle East with names often having changed since the war. For both, the diary entries have been standardised so that they refer to the names in use by the British Army at the time, but notes have been added with current names so as to enable modern readers to identify the places mentioned.

Each chapter of this volume begins with a brief introduction, explaining the background to the events in which Drury was involved, and

---

58  For example, Drury periodically used 'comming' instead of 'coming' and 'cant' instead of 'can't'. He sometimes had a full stop after etc. and sometimes did not. This is corrected as etc. with a full stop.

summarising the key points of each chapter. Numbers in square brackets within those introductions refer to sequentially numbered diary entries. In the footnotes, the following references appear occasionally: D1, D2, D3 and D4, followed by a page number or other place identifier. These refer to parts of the original four diary volumes where the relevant section has not been included in this edited volume. Biographies are included at the end of the volume for those who are mentioned frequently (more than five times) in the edited volume. For those who appear less frequently than that, but were still key figures for Drury, brief identifying material is included in footnotes, along with explanations for men whom it has not been possible to identify.

Part of the value of the Drury diaries is that they do not come from a well-known figure. Drury was (and remains) relatively obscure, with significant chunks of his post-war life a mystery. But that is partly why this is an important set of diaries which are worth a wider reading than is possible when they remain only as archive material. The diaries were the subject of a chapter specifically called 'The Drury Diaries' in a book by Myles Dungan, which was a very significant publication in opening up a new wave of historiography on Ireland's war and included some lengthy extracts.[59] The diaries have also been used throughout this editor's own book on Dublin,[60] but beyond that they have not been greatly used by historians. Dungan's verdict on Drury was that his writing displayed 'all the snobbery, prejudice and bigotry of his class and "race"'. But he also said that Drury 'was an honest, conscientious, hard working, brave man who possessed in abundance what Napoleon required of his generals, luck'. This is because while men standing beside him were hit by rifle fire or shrapnel, and while his own kit and uniform were often hit, he avoided injury (if not serious illness) himself.[61] As such, his relatively unremarkable war makes the breadth of his diaries unusual and deserving of a wider audience.

59  Myles Dungan, *Irish Voices from the Grear War* (Dublin: Irish Academic Press, 1995), 85–102.
60  Richard S. Grayson, *Dublin's Great Wars: The First World War, the Easter Rising and the Irish Revolution* (Cambridge: Cambridge University Press, 2018).
61  Dungan, *Irish Voices*, 102.

# 1

# Volunteering and Training, September 1914–July 1915

All those who joined the British forces in Ireland during the First World War did so voluntarily. There was never any conscription, as there was in Great Britain from early 1916, although the government tried and failed to introduce it in the spring of 1918. Across the war as many as 210,000 Irishmen served in the British forces. When war broke out, around 21,000 were already in the British Army, especially but not solely in the Irish infantry regiments. They were rapidly supplemented by 30,000 reservists from the Special Reserve or Army Reserve who were called up to the 'Regular' 1st and 2nd battalions of each regiment. The city and county of Dublin made a particular contribution to the war effort. Pre-war, with a population of just under 11 per cent of the island as a whole, Dublin supplied around 30 per cent of the army's Irish recruits. In August 1914, as many as 6,500 of the Irish regulars and 6,900 of the reservists could have been from Dublin, and towards 40,000 Dubliners served across the war. The peak month for army recruitment across the UK and also in Dublin was September 1914 when 3,091 enlisted. By mid-December 1914, one-quarter of Dublin's total wartime recruits had enlisted. By the end of the war, Dublin's total recruits for the army represented around one-fifth of Ireland's total of 123,724, almost twice its share of the population.[1]

Irish voluntary recruitment was focused on three divisions: the 10th (Irish), the 16th (Irish) and the 36th (Ulster). The latter two were political and sectarian in their composition. The infantry battalions of the 36th were initially formed from the Ulster Volunteer Force, the Unionist

---

[1]   Grayson, *Dublin's Great Wars*, 13, 37–8.

paramilitary group established to oppose Home Rule. The Unionist leader, Edward Carson, secured War Office agreement to transfer their ranks en masse to the British Army from early September 1914. Soon after, the Nationalist leader, John Redmond, did a similar deal and the pro-Home Rule National Volunteers joined the 16th (Irish) Division, especially its 47th Brigade.[2] Because of the political context, the 16th (Irish) and 36th (Ulster) divisions had the highest profile of the New Army divisions. Each 'side' of the divide had interests in promoting 'their' own activities. Yet the first New Army division formed in Ireland, on 21 August 1914, was the 10th (Irish), a non-political formation which recruited across the island.[3] It was this division in which the bulk of Noël Drury's service would take place.

There has been much academic debate over why men enlisted and why they joined certain units. One of the most significant contributions is David Fitzpatrick's article on the 'logic of collective sacrifice'.[4] He challenged ideas that economic factors offer the primary explanation of Irish service in the British military, and argued that 'The readiness of individuals to join the colours was largely determined by the attitudes and behaviour of comrades – kinsmen: neighbours, and fellow-members of organizations and fraternities.'[5] This is based on the fact that enlistment tended to be highest where economic insecurity was lower.[6] Fitzpatrick's work has recently been convincingly challenged for downplaying the importance of politics and religion in Irish recruitment,[7] but his case does fit some enlistment to one part of the 10th (Irish) Division: the 7th Royal Dublin Fusiliers, and especially its 'D' Company, which was formed initially by members of the Irish Rugby Football Union, including Ireland internationals. The glamour bestowed by such sporting prowess ensured that the 'Pals', as they became known, would receive much more media coverage than any other Dublin unit throughout the war.[8]

---

2   Grayson, *Dublin's Great Wars*, 24–5.

3   Stephen Sandford, *Neither Unionist nor Nationalist: The 10th (Irish) Division in the Great War* (Sallins: Irish Academic Press, 2015), 11–15.

4   David Fitzpatrick, 'The Logic of Collective Sacrifice: Ireland and the British Army, 1914–1918', *Historical Journal*, XXXVIII (1995), 1017–30.

5   Fitzpatrick, 'The Logic of Collective Sacrifice', 1030.

6   For a review of this debate, see Keith Jeffery, *Ireland's Great War* (Cambridge: Cambridge University Press, 2000), 18–20.

7   Timothy Bowman, William Butler and Michael Wheatley, *The Disparity of Sacrifice: Irish Recruitment to the British Armed Forces, 1914–1918* (Liverpool: Liverpool University Press, 2020), 236.

8   Grayson, *Dublin's Great Wars*, 34–6.

For the 10th (Irish) Division as a whole, evidence of the impact of fraternal factors is less conclusive.[9] However, they did offer a way into the army for Drury. He was not a member of the Officer Training Corps at Trinity College Dublin prior to the war, but his path to the British Army was through joining it on 1 September 1914. In that month he took part in night and route marches and also attended training lectures. He applied for a commission precisely a month later but heard nothing for several weeks so applied again. In mid-November Drury used a personal connection to put him in touch with General Sir Bryan Mahon, who was commanding the 10th (Irish) Division, and learned that his name had been put forward for the Connaught Rangers. In early December he was notified that he would be posted to the 5th Connaught Rangers. Standing at 5'10" and weighing just over 12 stone, Drury would have been taller than most of his men, and his thick moustache might have been imposing to some if in keeping with fashions of the time.[10] After arranging kit and paying bills, 'There was a nice little ceremony at home when I was presented with a beautiful sword, suitably engraved, and belt, by the work-people. It was awfully kind of them and I was very proud of the sword.'[11] However, in late December he was ordered to join a different battalion, the 6th Royal Dublin Fusiliers, at Beresford Barracks, Curragh Camp. There he met fellow officers with whom he would serve much of the war and took part in training which initially included parades, drills, much exercise, and practice in bayonet fighting. The effect of so much physical work was initially weight loss, but, fed well, Drury soon put on a stone.[12]

From early 1915 training focused on field work such as practice attacks. Drury himself gained an extra responsibility as the battalion Signal Officer, which meant leaving the battalion for special training at Carlow Barracks.[13] There were frustrations for the battalion. Drury noted, 'Everyone has been grousing at not being sent to the Front, saying that the war would be over before we could join in', although he added, 'recently, the battle of Ypres showed that the system now used would probably prolong the war'.[14] However, some political divisions seemed

---

9   Sandford, *Neither Unionist nor Nationalist*, 35.
10  The National Archives, Kew [hereafter TNA], WO 339/32747: NE Drury.
11  D1, p. 7. Note: there are contradictory numbers on some pages; those used here are the handwritten ones at the top right of each page.
12  Diary entry, Dec 1914.
13  Figure 1 was taken at this time.
14  Diary entry, 1915.

less important than they once had. Writing of St Patrick's Day 1915 when the battalion had marched to a Roman Catholic service, Drury noted, 'What a change the war has brought over things to be sure. If anyone had told me a year ago that I would have marched to a R[oman] C[atholic] chapel to a rebel tune, I would have said they were potty to say the least of it.'[15] During this time, speculation began to mount as to when and where the battalion would be deployed for active service, but before that could happen, it was sent to England for further training. Leaving the Curragh at 1pm on Friday 30 April by train for Dublin's Alexandra Basin, the battalion sailed to Holyhead and then travelled by train via Crew, Birmingham, Oxford and Reading before reaching Basingstoke around noon the next day. There they camped under canvas and used Lord Curzon's estate, Hackwood Park, for training.[16] On leaving the Curragh, Drury reflected on the complex and varied motives men had for joining up, feeling that for him, 'shame must have been the deciding factor; how could one stay behind when every letter, every article in the papers, every dispatch, called urgently for help for our men in France, apparently with their backs to the wall'.[17]

From Basingstoke, the 6th Royal Dublin Fusiliers carried out rather more expansive training manoeuvres than they had at the Curragh, around the Hampshire/Surrey border, and also continued musketry training. One of Drury's major concerns at this time appears to have been when he could get a warm bath, but his free time was enhanced by having his car sent over from Dublin.[18] A highlight of the battalion's time at Basingstoke was an inspection by the King, followed a few days later by a visit from Lord Kitchener.[19] Eventually, in early July, a hint of their destination was found in the issue of light drill clothes and helmets, which suggested a warmer clime, and on 9 July the battalion entrained for Keyham,[20] part of the Devonport Dockyard.[21] Drury noted that as the 6th Royal Dublin Fusiliers left Basingstoke, 'a big crowd cheered loudly and for the first time since joining the Service I felt really proud of going off to help the stout fellows at the front'.[22]

---

15  Diary entry, 1915.
16  D1, pp. 30–1.
17  Diary entry, 1915.
18  Diary entry, May–June 1915.
19  Diary entry, May–June 1915.
20  Diary entry, 6–9 July 1915.
21  D1, p. 38.
22  Diary entry, 6–9 July 1915.

# December 1914

I was met at the door by Lieutenant GA Watt,[23] a horsey-looking youth whom I found was Transport Officer. An elderly-looking major came in just then and, addressing me in a very peculiar drawling voice, asked who I was and invited me to come in and have some tea. I found this was Major JG Jennings, 66th Punjabis, Indian Army, attached RDF. He was very kind and told me a lot about the Regiment and sent out to get me a suitable servant. This turned out to be Private Costelloe from Cork, a decent old chap who also looked after several other officers of A Company. I took a walk around after tea and went to the Orderly Room but there was nobody about except the orderly officer, who had a pug nose, red hair and an amiable disposition. He was Lieutenant JJ Doyle.[24] I found my room was in the CO's house (for his use if married) and changed for mess.

Major Jennings met me in the ante room and introduced me to two or three officers who were there. Felt awfully nervous and "green" to everything, but a nicer a lot of men could not be met. The Major made me sit next to him and, beside me was another Indian Army officer of the Carnatic Rifles, Captain PTL Thompson,[25] also Captains WH Whyte and AJD Preston. Was very much taken with Preston – he seems to remind me of Captain Power in "Charles O'Malley"[26] with his cheery manner and keenness on the Regiment.

Next day, Sunday, I spent looking round with two other subalterns, AA Cullen and DB Gilmore,[27] and, in the afternoon, we borrowed horses and rode across the Curragh. I hadn't been on a horse for years and nearly fell off several times. In the evening, I was so stiff I could hardly walk. All the other officers who had been on week-end leave turn up at mess

---

23  Gerald Allingham Watt, born in 1888, had previously trained with the Royal West Kent Regiment when he volunteered in Sept 1914, giving a Londonderry address as his home. Appears not to have travelled to Gallipoli with the whole battalion, instead departing in Sept 1915. Contracted typhoid in Dec 1915 and was invalided out in Nov 1916. His July 1917 application to be re-commissioned was rejected. See WO 339/20588.

24  John Joseph Doyle, born in 1893 at Clontarf and living there when he volunteered in Aug 1914, while an engineering student at University College Dublin. See WO 339/13039.

25  WO 372/24/61598.

26  Charles Lever, *Charles O'Malley, the Irish Dragoon* (Dublin: William Curry, 1841).

27  Later Captain in Tank Corps (WO 372/8/24412).

except the Colonel who was on a visit to the front. Introduced myself to Captain HA Shadforth, the Adjutant. I was told he is much younger than he looks and is about 21 years of age only. He has a rather off-hand manner and a low, quiet voice, rather hard to understand. He told me to report officially at 9am at the Orderly Room the next day. There was a very remarkable officer who put me through a rather intimate cross-examination in the ante room. He was about 6'2" high with enormous shoulders and a very small round head with jet black hair. His eyes seemed all one colour, both pupil and iris, jet black, with a queer glitter in. He had a cold and had lost his voice so he could only speak in a whisper. It seemed so weird to hear this thin horse whisper coming out of so big a body that I felt inclined to laugh but somehow I didn't like that glitter in his eyes and I fancied I saw a pretty fiery temper lurking behind them.

Next day, I found I was appointed to C Company commanded by Captain John Luke and an orderly guided me to the Company lines. I was surprised, but hardly pleased, when I found that Captain Luke was my herculean friend with the black eyes. However, he was very kind and took me out to the Company, who were on parade, and introduced me to the officers and the Company Sergeant-Major, and told me to take over No 10 Platoon, Sergeant Mangan[28] in charge. The officers were Charlie Martin, whom I knew before, RW Carter[29] and WC Nesbitt,[30] who looked rather elderly for a subaltern. This morning, I felt, was the ordeal by fire. I could feel the men watching me and sizing me up and wondering what sort of a chap they were to serve under. I surveyed them hurriedly and the feeling came over me 'Here's good material to go soldiering with if handled properly.' The Sergeant and I walked along the two ranks which he had opened for me, but I did not see any men I knew. I said a few words to them but hardly know what. They took it well and there was a sort of 'sucking of the teeth' sound which conveyed to me, even if not so intended, that so far they were satisfied. Fortunately, I was fairly

---

28  Probably either 16540 P.J. Mangan or 13553 W. Mangan (WO 372/23/140527 &24/97965).

29  Robert Wellington Carter, born 1889, volunteered in Sept 1914, while a member of the educational staff of the Royal Hibernian Military School in Dublin. Wounded in Sept 1915 and returned to the UK, but later served in the 2nd Garrison Battalion of the Royal Irish Fusiliers and in the Machine Gun Corps. Ended the war as a Lieutenant. See WO 339/25769.

30  William Charles Nesbitt, born in 1875, and living at Booterstown, Co. Dublin, when he volunteered and applied for a commission in Nov 1914. Killed in action 15 Aug 1915. See WO 339/4895.

well up in ordinary drill and did not disgrace them, as we marched out of the lines to do 'Sweeds'[31] on the square. All of us, officers and men, stripped off jackets, etc. and braces, and did 'Sweeds' for a solid hour. I did not realise how soft I was till then, the sweat fairly poured off me in spite of the cold, but I saw many others in the same plight and was duly comforted.

I found Company Sergeant-Major Murphy[32] a smart NCO and a very good athlete. He had been lately in charge of gym and sports at some school near London. I had many bouts at bayonet fighting with him and also with the gloves in the Gymn[asium].

For several weeks, we did nothing but arms drill, company drill and 'sweeds' with aiming practice and miniature range practice. An amusing incident occurred one morning at company parade. A battalion order had come out a few days before that all men must know the officers by name so that they could deliver messages, etc. without delay.

As soon as Captain Luke came on parade, he walked over to the first platoon and with the steely glitter in his eye which I knew meant he was not in a humour to be trifled with, asked the first man he stopped at, 'Do you know my name?' 'Yezur' replied the man promptly. 'What is it[?]' asked Luke, 'Johnson, sir' was the reply. Luke winced a bit at this but, saying nothing, walked on a bit and repeated his question getting the same reply. After this had happened two or three times, he was fit to be tied, and turning to the Company Sergeant-Major, told him to come into the Company Office. He asked him what the blazes the men meant by calling him Johnson and fairly let off steam at the CSM who seemed to be more inclined to laugh and otherwise. The Sergeant-Major then explained that, before the men knew his name, he had been nick-named 'Jack Johnson'[33] as they saw a likeness to the boxer. New recruits coming in had never heard any other name used and thought it was his own name. By bad luck the men he happened to ask were comparatively new and knew no other name for him. John Luke took this as a compliment, I think, and later on, in the Gymnasium, showed some of them that he could show some rights to the nickname when he donned the gloves.

Our day was employed something like this, –

---

31 Short for 'Swedish Drill', part of the gymnastic training carried out by the army.
32 13190 Henry Murphy (WO 372/14/151787).
33 John 'Jack' Johnson (1878–1946), the first African-American heavyweight world champion, which he held from 1908 to 1915 (*The Times*, 11 June 1946, p. 3).

Reveille was at 6 am

6.30 – 7.30 drill under the Adjutant on parade ground.

7.45 – 8.15 breakfast.

8.30 – Company Orderly Room in the Company "bunk."

8.45 – Battalion Orderly Room.

9.0 – Companies parade for various kinds of work.

12.30 – 2.30 lunch-time, writing notes, etc.

2.30 – 4.0 drill, Swedish exercises etc.

4.0 – 4.30 tea.

4.30 – 6.30 gymn[asium], bayonet fighting in barrack rooms.

7.15 – mess.

8.30 – 10.0 Lectures by Adjutant, Brigade Major or Machine Gun Officer.

We generally were finished about 4pm on Saturdays and leave was freely given to officers and about 20% of the men got away each week-end. Second Lieutenant JJ Doyle, for some reason which I never heard disliked going away at the week-ends, and always volunteered to do duty for the subaltern whose turn for doing orderly officer fell on Saturday.

The result of all this hard work in the fresh air was that I began to lose weight at first, but one's hunger seemed unappeasable. We fed really well, lashings of good, well-cooked food was always served, and the mess bill was extra ordinarily small, viz, about 2/6d per day, which included hire of piano and some furniture and membership of the club. Compare this with 4/6d in the 4th Hussars' mess. After a while, I began putting on weight again until I weighed no less than 13-st[one] 8-lbs or nearly a stone over my usual weight, although I was as hard as nails.

A few days after I joined, I heard that Colonel Cox was back from the Front. I was very anxious to meet him. I have heard a lot of our first commander, Colonel Loveband,[34] who was known by all ranks as 'the little man' and very much loved by everyone, and comparatively little about Colonel Cox, so that I felt, somehow, that he was still on trial, as it were, and I almost expected to see some sort of ornamental figure-head. I was agreeably surprised that evening when, on entering the ante-room, I found a man of about 50, or perhaps a little less, about 5'6" high, lithe and active in appearance, with beautifully fitting clothes. He was full of animation, chatting to several of the senior officers standing round the fire. Luke took me over and introduced me. Colonel Cox gave me a

---

34 Arthur Loveband.

quick look over, shook my hand, and, smiling genially, gave me welcome. I quite took to him. After several weeks at the Curragh, I came to the conclusion that we were almost as good as a Regular battalion. There seemed very little of the 'Kitchener crowd' about us. We were very lucky to have such a big proportion of officers who were either Regular soldiers or who had soldiered before.

Colonel Cox had been in the Rifle Brigade, now retired.
Major Jennings belongs to the Indian Army.
A Company     Captain Preston officer serving RDF.
A Company     White had served in RDF.
A Company     Luke had served in RDF.
A Company     Thompson belongs to the Indian Army.
A Company     Lennon[35] belongs to the Royal Irish Constabulary.
C Company     Captain MacDonnell had served with RDF –
Africa (South).
A Company     Carrell belongs to Royal Irish Constabulary.
A Company     Newton had served with RDF.
Captain Shadforth, Adjutant, belongs to RDF serving officer.
Lieutenant & Quartermaster Byrne, belongs to RDF serving officer.

The Regimental Sergeant-Major, J Campbell,[36] was an old Dublin Fusilier and a typical example of the old Regular NCO, quiet, impertur[b]able, knowing everyone and everything, exacting obedience and respect from all, without bullying, but by example and character. He had the most uncanny understanding of the feelings of the subalterns, and many's the time he has whispered a word of advice or warning about some hasty action one of us was about to take. He has never lost his Scots accent and I have often been amused at CO's Orderly Room parade to hear him giving the advice in a stage whisper to the malefactors lined up, when the CO was approaching, "Staund steady. Staund steady."

Four or five of the NCOs in each company were also either serving soldiers or time expired men rejoined, as were a lot of the privates.

---

35  William Sherlock Lennon, born in 1880 and joined the Royal Irish Constabulary, working as a Second-Class District Inspector on applying for a commission in Nov 1941. Lived in Dublin and ended the war as a Major in the Egyptian Army. See WO 339/13484.
36  Probably 13507 John Campbell (WO 372/4/1740).

After a few weeks, I found it inconvenient to have a servant belonging to another Company so I got a batman from C Company named GE Thomas, a taciturn pallid-looking Welshman, with a thin black moustache, and a rather piratical appearance generally. I knew, of course, of the historic attributes of the 'Taffy' but I didn't mind whom he robbed, if he looked after me all right. I found him a very good fellow, neat and clean and he always kept my gear in good order, and was most thoughtful in bringing me a coat out to the rifle ranges if it came on wet and such like attentions. We never became friendly somehow, there was always an invisible barrier over which neither ever climbed but once, and that was on the day we left the Curragh. He came to me as I was packing and, after much hesitation, produced a picture postcard of himself in marching order and said he would be proud if I would accept it. I was delighted to have it and gave him one of mine in return. It was a very good likeness indeed of him. A great character, whom I didn't meet for a considerable time, as he was married and didn't live in the mess, was our quartermaster Lieutenant RC Byrne. He was Regimental Quartermaster Sergeant at the Depot in Naas, when war broke out, and was given a commission within a few days and was practically No 1 of the 6th (Service) Battalion RDF. In my ignorance of regimental life and work, I never dreamed for many a month to come, of the hard work skilfully and accurately done by Byrne, or 'the Stuffer' as he is usually called. He is ready to help everyone and seems able to produce almost every requirement on demand. He was a great athlete and runner in the regiment some years ago but is now somewhat aldermanic in appearance.

## 1915. The Curragh, Carlow and Basingstoke

[…] When the men had become quite good at platoon and company drill and had done their miniature range firing, we started on the Curragh ranges teaching them to shoot. I enjoyed this period very much. The weather fortunately was fine and fairly warm after a bitter winter, and, being quite a decent shot myself, I hoped to get my platoon good enough to top the list. I did not get the chance, however, as will be seen later.

We now started field work and were allotted an area at Dunmurray Hill where we practised all sorts of attacks. It took us an hour and ten minutes to march there and we therefore used to parade at 8.30 and get back about 1.30. It was nearly always possible during this period to get to leave from Saturday evening to Sunday evening, and I got my car

(20.1 Horse Power Talbot) down to the Curragh and used to keep it in the courtyard of the CO's house covered with a big tarpaulin. When we were finished on Saturdays, I could nip away quickly without waiting for the train. I generally had at least two others with me in the two-seater and used to go by Athgarvan and the Woolpack road which was in good order and entirely free of traffic. Used to do a great scorch into town trying always to beat the time of the previous run. The best I ever did was from the Gough Barracks mess door to Jammet's Restaurant in Suffolk Street in 46 minutes exactly. Captain Joe Carroll[37] had a two-seater car (French make, I think) but he could never get near this time.

One day I was sent for to the Orderly Room and told that the authorities had said 'Let there be signal officers' in each battalion and that I had been appointed and was to go off at once to the 10th (Irish) Division Signal Company Royal Engineers at Carlow Barracks for a course of instruction. I drove down next day and reported to Captain Smithers who commanded. I found that there was no room in the Barracks for me so I stayed in the Royal Hotel, Dublin Street, and was very comfortable […]. […]

This change in my arrangements didn't altogether please me. It meant giving up my platoon with whom I was getting on well and taking over a lot of men belonging to each of the companies who were really under their own Company for discipline, clothing and rations, and only under me, when being trained or on duty. As well as this, it meant my being attached to headquarters and I felt that I would be in a sort of backwater. […]

Brigade field days were great fun as the men and junior officers had not much to do, these excursions being intended more for staff training. Our Brigade Major Alexander was a very stern, harsh sort of man but knew his work from end to end and I always enjoy his lectures very much, and I learned a lot about outpost duties, flank and rear guards, etc. He also gave us some wonderful accounts of the earlier movements in the war, illustrating his remarks by models in the sand bath. He was very keen on the proper use of machine guns and was evidently much impressed by the German methods. […]

One of the events of the spring was a full parade and inspection of the Brigade by Lieutenant General Sir BT Mahon, DSO and other officers. We mounted Canon McLean and Father Murphy on staid old horses and begged them not to fall off. Mahon and his party came mounted on the

---

37  J.J.T. Carroll. See *Monthly Army List*, Nov 1916, col. 1551.

most beautiful horses, Mahon in particular. He looks a born horseman, with a fine seat. […]

Everyone has been grousing at not being sent to the Front, saying that the war would be over before we could join in, but, recently, the battle of Ypres showed that the system now used would probably prolong the war. […]

On St Patrick's Day, it has always been the Custom in the Regiment for <u>all</u> the officers to go with the men to the RC Service at mid-day and, this year, we kept up the custom. Good Presbyterians like myself paraded and marched off to the tunes of the 'Boys of Wexford' and 'A Nation Once Again' and went to Chapel for the first and, probably, the only time in our lives. What a change the war has brought over things to be sure. If anyone had told me a year ago that I would have marched to a RC chapel to a rebel tune, I would have said they were potty to say the least of it. It was rather disconcerting to find oneself standing up or sitting down at the wrong time through ignorance of the ritual but nobody seemed to mind.

We got up a great concert in the evening of St Patrick's Day, and a lot of good talent was discovered among the men and officers. […] Altogether it was a great evening, with a good long interval for the men to go out and have a drink to wet their parched throats. […]

I had one or two rather interesting signalling schemes assisted by, or, rather, run by Tony Shadforth. Whenever there was sunshine, we had several heliographs out, one on Dunmurray Hill, one on top of the water tower in the Curragh Camp and one on the high ground east of Athgarvan. We also worked out similar schemes at night with lamps. We have some beautifully made electric ones made by Lucas Ltd and also the old out-of-date oil-burning Begbie. Sergeant Johnston is the only one who can keep these wretched old things lit. They have a series of shutters on one side like a Venetian blind and they are nearly useless if brought near the 'enemy' as they can read the loud 'clack' of the shutter at several hundred yards distance. […]

An order came in sometime in March that we were to hand in all the web equipment and drawing new, dark green coloured, leather stuff. Both officers and men were to be equipped and all dismounted officers were to carry packs and regulation haversacks the same as the other ranks. This leather was rotten stuff and stretched badly when wet, upsetting the hang of the equipment and the distribution of weights. We did curse that leather. All our buttons, too, had to be painted over dull so that nothing would be left to make a glint in the sunlight.

Rather a lot of fun used to be got out of some of the officers like Lennon, nicknamed 'Lenjohn' and old MacDonnell ("Mack"). One night some of the 5th Connaught Rangers ('The Common Dangers' is their nickname), led by 'Peeler' Burke[38] the Detective Inspector of Naas and assisted by some of us drove some sheep in to the mess and into Lennon's room, locking them in, and leaving the key on the outside of the door. We did this also with Joe Carroll. They slept through the ceremony, apparently, and it was only the next morning when their batmen arrived and asked what they 'wanted with them sheep' that they found out the trick. They never found out who did it.

We have two very nice padres attached to the Brigade. Canon McClean was Rector of Rathkeale, County Limerick, and joined up as temporary Chaplain. Father Murphy[39] is a Regular Army R[oman] C[atholic] Chaplain and has been attached to us since the Brigade was formed. Neither of them lives with us, but they come over to mess occasionally. I haven't seen much of the Canon, but I have seen a good deal of Father Murphy and like him very much. He is a broad-minded, kindly, man of middle age and seems quite different from priests I have met hitherto.

The change in the appearance of the men since they joined up must be seen to be realised. Many of them had never had any systematic exercise in the open air, and, as is unfortunately usual in the poorer classes in Ireland, never had really good, well-cooked, meals. They turned up here during the winter looking dirty and ill-clothed, and ill-fed in many cases, but now look at them! They look well-fed and seemed to have grown in every way. They throw out their chests on parade in a way that makes your heart warm. On the whole, they are very well-behaved, although a few hard old cases do get tight at the week-ends and overstay their leave.

We had a big mess meeting one night to decide about messing when we go to France, and it was finally decided to divide up into five messes – Headquarters and four companies – and to buy a fitted box for each containing plates, knives, forks, cups, etc. and holders for tea, sugar,

---

38  It has not been possible to identify this man.
39  It has not been possible to identify any details about this chaplain. Only one Catholic Chaplain with that surname was serving at this time, with the initial W, but he was only appointed on 30 Aug 1914, so was probably not a Regular army chaplain, though might have been prior to the war and had stepped back to be a cleric outside the army. See *Monthly Army List*, Sept 1915, col. 1794 and WO 372/14/155915. A series of WO 339 and WO 374 files were checked for men with other initials, but the men were either the wrong denomination or serving at the wrong time.

salt, etc., and big enough to put in some potted meat, candles, etc. Some different patterns were secured by Captain Whyte, Mess President, and were on view. One type was finally fixed on and an order was sent for five of them, payment being made out of the mess fund which was considerably in credit at the time.

In April, orders came that we might slow down the training somewhat from the strenuous time we had been having as everyone was a bit stale, and the hours have been a bit too long, particularly for the officers. Consequently, the early morning parades were dropped and games were played as fancied in the afternoons. We had a bit of free time to visit about the neighbourhood, and we often went to tea at the Greers, Kennedys, etc. or played tennis at the Club.

Everyone believed that this was a sure sign that we were soon going out and were correspondingly elated [...] and, in the end, it was found that the whole Division was to concentrate in Hampshire about the beginning of May. We found that we were to go in two lots, one half on Friday, the 30th of April, and the other on the 1st May. [...]

There was great dashing into town to say farewell during the two remaining days, but our martial ardour was somewhat damped when we learned that we were to entrain at the Curragh sidings and go straight by rail to the North Wall. We had fondly hoped that we would exercise the old right of the RDF to march through the city with fixed bayonets and show ourselves off a bit to the delight of the onlookers and our own secret satisfaction. We thought ourselves devilish fine fellows and forgot that pride goes before a fall. Stuffer Byrne told us an amusing yarn about the 1st Battalion entering at the Curragh sidings for South Africa. He swore it took 100 men two days to clear up the broken bottles after the regiment left.

The last good-byes were said but no exact time could be given for our departure as we didn't know. It was going to be a silent folding of tents and quiet stealing away, without anyone to see us off. I call this damned bad policy of the authorities. The battalion had been formed at the Curragh and had stayed at the Curragh ever since, so the men's wives and friends had never seen it as a unit. It would have been worth 100 recruits at least to have marched the first service battalion of the first Kitchener Division through the city with bands playing, but no, we sneaked off unsung in pours of rain, everyone looking rather miserable. My feelings were somewhat mixed, I admit – hard to put on paper. It was natural to feel a kind of satisfaction that at last we were to put to the test all we had worked so hard to learn and what, in fact, we had joined up for, but, at the same time, one wondered whether we would come back safely out of the turmoil.

I remember asking myself why I had joined up – why had all the others joined up? None of us knew much about the causes of the war and anything we had heard was all on our side and we knew nothing of the other side's view. Was this, indeed, a vital struggle for our country? Could my individual presence do any good anyhow? Couldn't I stay at home out of it? I wasn't a Regular soldier, few of my friends or relatives have been soldiers, why, therefore, couldn't I stay where I was[?] These and other questions, I suppose were subconsciously answered but I think shame must have been the deciding factor; how could one stay behind when every letter, every article in the papers, every dispatch, called urgently for help for our men in France, apparently with their backs to the wall. No matter how they found themselves in this position, they at least had done nothing but obey orders, had done nothing to be ashamed of, and they wanted help. That was it, they wanted a hand in a tight corner, and they mustn't cry in vain. One would be ashamed to stay. I don't know whether others felt the same way. Some like young 'Fritz' Cullen seemed sort of fire-eaters, who wanted to let off steam by 'doing in' Bosches, others, who had fought before, seemed to take it all in the day's work. Outwardly, at least; but who knows what they really felt. [...]

## May–June 1915. At Commons Camp, Basingstoke

Our work at first consisted of route marches intended to accustom the men to the hot damp climate here (so different to the bracing Curragh) and rough roads. The latter are very bad indeed, being covered with loose stones and flints to a depth of several inches.

We soon started manoeuvres against armoured divisions, mainly the 11th. The first place visited was Odiham where I slept in the bath in a small but clean, hotel. Next day turned out very wet and, after fooling about until 2 o'clock, we proceeded back to Camp via Upton Grey, roads deeply flooded in places. Everybody felt very miserable and could not get dry nor warm. Loud cheers greeted the sun next morning about 10 o'clock.

Next, we went to Aldershot to do a musketry course at Ash Ranges. We had a very heavy march about 30 miles on hot dusty roads, halting for 45 minutes in a wood two miles east of Odiham. A good many men fell out in the last three miles. The camp we took over was an old standing camp and filthy dirty and dusty. Started the next morning at 4.30 for the ranges and got back to camp at 6.45pm. We had a very good scrap near Hartfordbridge Flats against 13th Division, [and] did a lot of wood fighting. Came across one of the enemy's telephone wires and put an instrument on. Heard their HQ call and many others. Cut the wire and sent directions to their gunners to proceed to Blackwater, using their HQ call. This got rid of their artillery and enabled us to advance and capture the position. Billeted two nights in very nice country house in Hartly Row for this scrap. Two elderly ladies – very nice. Good bath and plenty of hot water and served with a magnificent dinner, a butler in attendance.

(2nd and 3rd June) Did another scheme near Newbury. Billeted in empty house, men in a brewery. Bad place with very slippery narrow steep stairs. Would take a long time to get a battalion out in case of fire. Next day finished up at Ladle Hill and bivouacked on top of the hill. This was the first time I heard a nightingale singing. It was enthralling in the still night with bright moon overhead.

This was our first decent scheme of signalling, had two lines of enamelled wire laid out to two outpost companies and had a lamp station working 2½ miles to the Brigade Headquarters. Everything went like clockwork.

Had another day starting at Mortimer and clearing all the woods north of this right up to Aldermaston. Bivouacked at Upton Green for the night and made an attack at dawn on Beenham Hill.

Alton was our objective on another occasion. We marched there in four hours, starting at 5.30am to avoid the hot sun. Bivouacked in the field next the gas works, and strawberries for the first time. Next day, fought all round near Borden, Haslemere and Farnham and, in the evening, marched back to the same field in Alton. Started for home early the next day.

I had the car sent over to me from Dublin and kept it in the lines near my tent, and had good value out of it, taking fellows for a breather in the evenings and sometimes going to London to see a show.

We have been practising bombing in Hackwood Park but have no proper bombs. We have been making home-made ones out of jam and milk tins. I wonder we don't get blown up with the beastly things.

[…] We played a joke on the 6th Royal Munster Fusiliers, whose lines were beside ours in Camp. They (like the rest of us) had a sort of Regimental flag, not official colours, of course, with their crest on it. It consisted of a tiger and a conventional grenade in gold on a green ground. We used to call this the 'Cat and the Pineapple'. Some of our lads got a cardboard model of a pineapple and a cardboard cat of terrible aspect and, climbing up their flag-pole one night, unrove the halliards and nailed the fake cat and pineapple at the top of the flag-pole.

Great was the rage of the RMF when they came to hoist their flag next morning. We had to move our quarter guard tent and put it against our flag-pole in case they tried to reciprocate. They never caught us out, however, and we remained fast friends.

It is an interesting fact that our battalion, officers and men, are far more chummy with the 6th RMF than with our own sister battalion, the 7th RDF but so it has been since the start. It reminds me of the 'Chummy Ships' in the Navy.

We had a great review towards the end of May of the whole division by the King. It was held in Hackwood Park in magnificent weather and the turnout was a great sight. We had never seen our own artillery before and the size of the whole complete Division surprised most of us. The great number of molehills made it very difficult marching in line, and the armoured cars lurched about badly. The King and staff were superbly mounted and Mahon was said to have got all the horses over from Ireland for the occasion. Lord Kitchener could not be there, and it is supposed that the King gave him such a good account of the First Kitchener Division that we had to repeat the performance on the 1st of June for K. of K.'s benefit. Everything went off splendidly, better even than on the first day. (The other way around! K of K came first and gave the King such a glowing account that he came down three days later to see for himself. Kitchener's review held Tuesday 1st June. King's review Thurs, 3rd.)[40]

I arranged to sell the car to Kenneth[41] when we left, and I was to leave it in the station yard under care of the station-master to whom Kenneth would show my order whenever he had a chance to come and collect it. [...]

# 6–9 July 1915. The March Out From Basingstoke

After a strenuous time clearing up things and fitting out the men with light drill clothes and helmets, we practically marked time on the 6th, 7th and 8th July, waiting for final instructions. Old soldiers earned quite a decent sum showing new hands how to fold their puggarees on the

---

40  This text in brackets was a marginal note added by Drury.
41  His brother.

topees, or doing it for them. Rumours as to port of embarkation and the boat we were to sail on, were floating round. [...]

Strange sensations these few days – delight at being about to be put to the test at last, mingled with regret for the hard lines of those who have to stay behind and think, also a vague wonder whether we would see them again.

At last, we got orders to entrain at Basingstoke at 6.05pm on Friday, 9th July. Two trains were to take us. [...] We paraded at 4.15pm, everyone's kit and equipment minutely inspected. Men in great form. Some of my men who are old soldiers, Sergeant Johnston, McGinn, Booth, etc. quite unmoved, others in great excitement and heartily glad to see the last of Commons Camp, Basingstoke. The band played us to the station and I led the signallers at the head of the column. The men marched out splendidly, swinging along singing 'Tipperary' and 'Are we down-hearted? No.', also the Dublin Fusiliers' song written at the time of the Boer War, –

> Bravo, the Dublin Fusiliers,
>     You're no craven mutineers,
> Bravely stormed up the Glencoe height,
>     Put five thousand crafty Boers to flight,
>     It was a grand and glorious sight,
>         Bravo, the Dublin Fusiliers.

We had a great send off, the people of Basingstoke being sorry we were going, as the men behaved very well during their stay and made many friends. In the market square, a big crowd cheered loudly and for the first time since joining the Service I felt really proud of going off to help the stout fellows at the front. [...]

## 2

# The Voyage to the Dardanelles, July–August 1915

The 10th (Irish) Division left England not knowing exactly where they were to be deployed. However, the decision had already been taken to deploy them to the Dardanelles because successive phases of the campaign there had failed. Initially, the British and French hoped that a naval bombardment from 19 February 1915 would destroy Turkey's defences along the Dardanelles passage at the entrance of the Sea of Marmara which led to Constantinople. Then, through a mix of land and sea power the Turkish capital would be seized and the Central Powers would lose a key ally. However, no such breakthrough took place and on 25 April 1915 an amphibious operation began at Cape Helles (on the Gallipoli Peninsula's south) and at an area which became known as Anzac Cove (on the west). The troops who landed there were highly trained Regulars but they soon became bogged down.[1] Over May to July 1915 discussions led to a decision to try to break out of Anzac Cove while also deploying two New Army divisions, the 10th (Irish) and the 11th (Northern) to secure a winter harbour at Suvla Bay. These fresh soldiers would work with the Australian, Indian and New Zealand units already there.[2]

The 6th Royal Dublin Fusiliers left Keyham in Plymouth at 3.30pm on Saturday 10 July 1915 on the former Cunard liner the *Alaunia*. With them were the 7th Royal Dublin Fusiliers, 31st Field Ambulance and parts of the 6th and 7th Royal Munster Fusiliers and the 5th and 6th Royal Inniskilling Fusiliers. Battalion strength was a total of 952: 29 officers,

---

1   Jenny Macleod, *Great Battles: Gallipoli* (Oxford: Oxford University Press, 2015), 11–44.
2   Macleod, *Gallipoli*, 52–4.

6 warrant officers, 45 sergeants, 8 lance sergeants, 34 corporals, 42 lance corporals and 797 privates.[3]

The voyage was a leisurely one, despite early rising. Drury worried that 'we will all get fairly soft by the time we land, as we don't get much exercise and we eat a lot more than in camp'. However, there was some opportunity to exercise on deck and use rudimentary gym equipment.[4] Drury's main responsibility was censoring the letters home which men hoped to post when they put ashore.[5] Within five days, the men had much to write home about as they had seen first the Rock of Gibraltar[6] and then had sight of the North African coast, which would have been new to most of them.[7] Yet one man resorted to making up heroic war stories 'to cheer the old woman [his wife] up a bit', describing 'how he often had two of the enemy on his bayonet at one time', despite not having been in action. Drury gave him 'a good telling off'.[8]

Putting ashore at Valletta in Malta on 18 July gave Drury the chance to take part in some tourism, which he was often to do as he visited new places. His diaries carried extensive accounts of how places looked to someone who had not left northern Europe before, and were replete with descriptions of people, buildings and customs.[9] Two days later, Drury had his first experience of Alexandria where he unsuccessfully tried to bathe,[10] and the battalion stayed docked there until the evening of 22 July,[11] reaching Lemnos on Saturday 24 July.[12] As they anchored at 'Mitylene Island' (Mytilene, another name for Lesbos) a day later, Drury offered a typical reflection of the classically educated officer: 'This is where the poetess Sappho lived. "Burning Sappho lived and loved."'[13] Encountering local people ashore the next day, Drury noted, 'The people are curious, coming round and listening to what is said. They are very kindly, however, and courteous. […] They grow olives, figs and many other fruits that we failed to catch the names of.' At the village of Perma, Drury and his fellow officers 'caused great amusement by trying

3  D1, p. 44.
4  Diary entry, 16 July 1915.
5  Diary entry, 13 July 1915.
6  Diary entry, 14 July 1915.
7  Diary entry, 15 July 1915.
8  Diary entry, 16 July 1915.
9  Diary entry, 17 July 1915.
10  Diary entry, 20 July 1915.
11  Diary entry, 22 July 1915.
12  Diary entry, 24 July 1915.
13  Diary entry, 25 July 1915.

to buy a melon using Attic Greek to the moderns, whose Greek bears little resemblance to the old tongue'.[14] As the men soaked up the sun and experienced new sights and smells, frustration began to set in. On 4 August Drury noted, 'This day last year the war started, 365 days and we have done nothing yet, it's disgusting, and the delay is doing the men no good, besides, everyone is getting flabby after so long on board doing no hard work.'[15] Two days later the waiting ended as the battalion received orders to head for Gallipoli as part of the Mediterranean Expeditionary Force and set sail in the afternoon.[16]

---

14   Diary entry, 26 July 1915.
15   Diary entry, 4 Aug 1915.
16   Diary entry, 29 July 1915.

# Tuesday, 13 July 1915

Up at 5.45am and visited all the sentries on ammunition, water taps, passages, etc. Slacked on deck till 8.30. Breakfast. Saw several whales spouting. […] After lunch, the Captain gave a lecture on various methods of making life-saving rafts and telling us where we could get doors to pull off their hinges and ropes to lash spars together. Started censoring letters at 3.30. Tremendous job as a rumour got round the ship that we were going to have a tender meet us at Gibraltar and that mails could be sent. Letters were most amusing, showing three principal features, (1) recording the state of writer's health, (2) remarking on the fine grub and quarters on ship and (3) cursing the censor. Fancy a pile of, perhaps, 1,000 letters, scrawled addresses in pencil – the envelopes, and especially the flaps to be licked, filthy, dirty through being carried in the pocket.

These letters have to be examined to see that no information is given that might be useful to the enemy should he get hold of the letter. The censor has to sign the letter and replace it in the envelope and seal it down, afterwards stamping the censor's number on the envelope. Worked at this from 3.30 to 10pm except for dinner. Saw first sight of land at 6.30pm – a faint outline of some low mountains, probably near Trafalgar.

# Wednesday, 14 July 1915

Got up at 5.30am and found we were just coming in sight of the Straits of Gibraltar. Tremendous keenness to see the famous Rock. The morning was lovely, hot sun shining down from a cloudless sky on to the blue sea. There was a fresh breeze from the east which prevented the ship getting too hot. The Straits were being controlled by several small torpedo boats, some of them looked in the distance like French ones.

We steered a very zig-zag course, and for some time were in doubt whether we were to stop. However, we dropped anchor outside the breakwater and a tender came off with orders for the Captain and to get any letters from the ship. Everyone had turned up in pyjamas and nobody started dressing till after we left 'Gib.' A large Italian steamer *The Principe Umberto* of Genoa had arrived shortly before us packed with Italian reservists going home from, we heard, South America. They left just before us and as they sailed past gave us a tremendous reception, cheer upon cheer coming over the water to us and responded to by our fellows with equally hearty cheers for the Allies. Many guns were to be seen on the Rock but I think they must have been dummies, as no modern guns would be placed in such an exposed position. A very large wireless station with two tall masts is placed low down near the sea-level. Masts appear about 200 feet high. Telephone or telegraph wires run all over the place in very exposed positions – funny. Altogether it is a wonderful sight and I wish I could visit it. We stayed about half an hour at 'Gib' and then steamed off eastwards. The clock rapidly picked up the time it lost while running down from England. The mountains running inland from 'Gib' seem fairly high probably 3,000 feet, not much vegetation, trees stumpy. [...]

We had a concert in the lounge from 5 to 6pm and it proved very pleasant. The sunset now takes place at about 7pm and there is very little twilight but the colours in the sky, after the sun has gone down, are wonderful. The portholes must all be shut at sundown and the ship gets very hot in the evening. It is quite usual to see people at dinner perspiring on their foreheads as if they had been exercising hard. I think we will all get fairly soft by the time we land, as we don't get much exercise and we eat a lot more than in camp. I suppose this is due to the fine sea air and reminds me of a trip to Norway on one occasion.

[...]

## Thursday, 15 July 1915

[...]

About 1 o'clock pm, we passed Algiers about seven or 8 miles off, rather hazy with the heat and therefore could not see very much with the glasses. There is a large lighthouse on the head near the town and there appear to the many large warehouses near the harbour. We could also see the railway trains. We have been steaming all day within sight of the coast of Africa and I noticed that although the vegetation generally is scarce, still there are many trees and woods to be seen, even right up on top of the hills inland.

## Friday, 16 July 1915

Another lovely day. Going along in sight of the African coast all day. There seems to be a very fine system of lighthouses all along this coast.

They are generally small and stumpy like those on the Norwegian coast and many of them have a small tower close to them which we could not see the reason for. They may have been old lighthouses now disused. We passed one headland with a lighthouse high up on it, probably 200 feet above sea-level and beside it what seemed like a wireless station.

[...]

Had a busy day censoring letters to be sent away tomorrow at Malta. Nearly 3,000 including officers' letters. Most of the men contented themselves with a short letter saying they were well and enjoying themselves and hoping their wives were 'in the pink as it leaves me present' but one or two others, evidently 'old soldiers' groused at everything and swore at the NCOs by name, one fellow even damning Captain Thompson to heaps.

There was one letter from a C Company man giving a most blood-curdling account of the battles he had been in and telling how he often had two of the enemy on his bayonet at one time and had to shove them off with his foot. He ended up by saying 'The rule out here is "Die dog, and eat the baynit"'. I stopped the letter and had the man up before the CO at Orderly Room. His only reason for writing such lies and nonsense was that he wanted to 'cheer the old woman up a bit'. He got a good telling off, but I don't think even now he sees anything wrong about it.

[...]

We had a boxing tournament during the afternoon but I was too busy to go to it. There is quite a good little gymnasium on board with patent bicycle, exercises and a rowing machine, also several Sandow exercisers.

[...]

Nights are very hot indeed – no air in the cabins, as we can't open portholes. I sleep now lying on the bed using no bedclothes at all, and, even then, I often get up in the middle of the night and have a cold bath.

[...]

## Saturday, 17 July 1915

Got up at 4.30am to see the sunrise. Very nice but did not strike me as any finer than it does on land, at home. Perhaps not as fine, as there are no wispy mists to be dispersed. Sighted Malta at 4.45, delighted at prospect of getting ashore. There did not seem to be much vegetation to be seen, the general tone of the Island being a baked light brown. There seemed to be a tremendous lot of houses scattered all around, not gathered into villages as at home. Noticed a windmill with six arms, which I think is rather unusual. One very big mosque stood out prominently with a big shining white dome.

[…]

Valletta is a most wonderful place. From the harbour it looks uninteresting and seems nearly all forts, guns or barracks, but, when one learns and takes one of the little rickety fiacres[17] with canopy and the veteran driver, it makes one feel something of the glamour of foreign courts that is pictured on the mind when reading books of travel.

There are a lot of priests about wearing black fur hats with wide brim. They are often the most part dirty and unshaved. One of them tackled us as we stepped on the pier, asking asked for donations for his monastery. He got nothing from me.

We took a fearful-looking 'shandradan' or small victoria with a white canopy over it. The horse was a wretched-looking animal, its chest was only about a foot wide. We drove up a winding and steep street to the top of the town and got out at the Bank of Malta or some such name where they cashed a cheque on McGregor without question. Valletta is one of the most charming towns I have ever been in. Most of the streets are very narrow, almost too narrow for two vehicles to pass. The houses are very high, having windows built out on little balconies with wooden sun-blinds. These blinds are painted every colour. The houses remind me somewhat of those in the High Street, Edinburgh.

The streets are kept very clean, in fact, the whole town and the houses looked clean. There is a tremendous glare from the white limestone streets and foot paths and, after being in a shop out of the sun, it is almost impossible to open the eyes for a few minutes after leaving. Many of the people wear smoked glasses or green ones when out.

My preconceived ideas led me to expect that most of the people in Valletta would be English but I was surprised to find the native element so predominant. They are of Arabic origin and somewhat resemble the Italians. They speak, I hear, an Arabian dialect. Every house seems to be a shop of sorts and the owners are very importunate, running after one down the street asking one to buy things.

---

17  A small, horse-drawn carriage.

They do it in such a nice way and behave so nicely over it that it is really impossible to take offence at it. One cabby followed me down several streets asking me to hire him. 'He would drive me to see the town, only one hour.' No, thanks. 'He would drive me to see the Governor's palace,' No, thanks. 'To the lace factory, then.' 'Ah, yes, far too long walk for M'sieur.' No, thank you. 'He would drive me to see a beautiful girl.' No, thanks.

I bought one of the native scarves or wraps of a sort of mercerised cotton but beautiful and soft. I also bought a pair of smoked glasses.

Tobacco has no duty levied on it here and we bought for 3/– per 100 cigarettes that would cost 6/6 or 7/– in Dublin. A first-class cigar can be bought for 8/– per 100.

I've never forgotten the look of the sea, intensely blue, when getting a peep of it at the end of a long steep street.

[…]

There is an electric tramway system running from the outskirts of the town into the country [and] also a narrow gauge railway.

It is very quaint to see the herds of goats being driven through the streets, and the men stopping them to give a pennyworth of milk to some one. Cullen got a snap of a man milking a goat on the footpath of the main street and a girl reaching out a glass from a window for her pint.

We had an iced drink on the square outside the officers' club. One is constantly being approached (not pestered, as at home) by boys to buy matches, postcards or have one's boots polished. We didn't mind these picturesque little urchins, but Sammy O'Carroll,[18] having no imagination apparently, bitterly complained of them.

Our few hours were all too short and we had to get back to our good ship. I won't forget my first visit to Malta in a hurry. It was splendid.

[…]

We left the harbour at Malta on Saturday evening at 6.30pm onwards for Alexandria. A good many people came out to see us away and the gun teams stood to their guns on the batteries as we passed out.

---

18  This could be a nickname for Francis Brendan O'Carroll as there was in officer of that name in the RDF and indeed no Samuel O'Carroll has been found as an officer in the entire army. F.B. O'Carroll was born in 1895 and lived in Dublin. He attended Shrewsbury School and volunteered in Sept 1914. Killed in action in Sept 1915. See WO 339/25819; https://www.cwgc.org/find-war-dead/casualty/689412/o'carroll,-frank-brendan/ [accessed 19 April 2021].

# Sunday, 18 July 1915

Got up at 8.15 and breakfasted off melons, apples and coffee. Very hot day. Church of England Service at 11.30, afterwards ship inspection by Captain. We stayed a most erratic course all day, sometimes N[orth] then E[ast] and often N[orth] 30 E[ast]. Twice we turned about and steamed for ten minutes in the opposite direction thus facing the wind and making a good draught down the ventilators. This was getting absolutely necessary for, on account of the following wind, the men's quarters were getting fearfully hot. The manoeuvre caused some excitement on board, as it was thought to be done to avoid a submarine. The machine gunners got very alert and working to show what good shooting they could do.

[…] In the afternoon had a tug-of-war competition.

5th & 6th Inniskillings v. RAMC (Officers only)
RAMC v. Details (Men)
7th RDF v. 6th RDF (Officers)
7th RDF v. 6th RDF (Men).

[…]

# Tuesday, 20 July 1915

Arrived at Alexandria about 7.30am. A magnificent harbour consisting of two parts. The outer harbour where ships are loaded from lighters and the inner where this method is used as well as the piers and wharves. The biggest steamers can come alongside.

We had the usual parades in the morning and were allowed ashore from 1.30 till 8pm. Whyte, Preston, Lennon and self went ashore in a sailing boat and sailed round the inner harbour and went ashore. Here we took a carriage and drove through the town to the other side (east). We then got on a tram and went to St Stephano where there was a big hotel and Casino and bathing place when Preston and Whyte were there with our first Battalion six or seven years ago. We found the hotel turned into a Red Cross Hospital and divided between the French and Indians. The bathing place was also closed. We met several French officers who gave us most elaborate salutes which we all returned. Finding our hopes of a bathe here disappointed, we went by tram to Stanley Bay and had a most delightful bathe, staying in about an hour. What a very warm, probably nearly 60°, nice big swell coming in. Some nice Greek ladies also bathing – very fine looking women. We then returned to Alexandria past Mustapha Barracks and race-course. Preston and Whyte had to meet the C.O. so I and Lennon knocked around the town, first of all going to the Savoy Palace Hotel to write some letters. We had a lemon squash each (the waiter called it Squotch) for which I paid 1/– each. [...]

We had some tea in the 'Piccadilly Tea Rooms' where we were presented with a copy of the words of 'Tipperary'. Oh, when will we escape from this wretched ballad. A notice on this cafe stated that ices, cakes, pastries and everything else provided on command, adding that it was a high-class cafe and stayed open till 3 in the morning.

We got back to the ship at 19.30 and found that we were to remain for another day, at least, and that we were to move into the harbour for coal at the quay.

## Thursday, 22 July 1915

[...]

We sailed from Alexandria about 6pm for some destination unknown to us but guessed at – the Island of Lemnos and Mudros Bay.

## Saturday, 24 July 1915

[...] about 5 o'clock, we sighted Lemnos Island and soon saw the narrow entrance into Mudros Bay opening in front of us. The entrance is narrow and very carefully protected by various methods such as nets, etc. No ships are visible when entering the harbour, but when we got inside, an enormous harbour appeared, nearly as big as Queenstown[19] and probably better, as there seemed to be deep water all round. The Island did not appear to have any grass growing on it nor trees, except in two spots where a little village was situated. There were many camps, on the surrounding hills, very dirty and dusty they looked, after our Commons Camp. Saw several submarines. One came into harbour in the evening and was cheered by the warships' crews as she had carried out some fine exploit.

[...] I stayed on the bridge till 12.30am looking at the stars through the telescope [...]. Saturn looked very well, the rings and four moons

---

19   In Co. Cork, now called Cobh.

being clearly visible. A really beautiful night with the full moon, making a silver path across the water. It was hardly possible to realise that our fellows were having desperate fighting only 40 miles away – little more than an hour's run on the Talbot, were there a road.

## Sunday, 25 July 1915

Weighed anchor about 10.30am and […] soon a rumour went round that we were not bound for the Peninsula but for Mitylene [*sic*] Island. We had a southern course during the day and soon sighted land on each side of us. One island had a very high mountain which looked four or five thousand feet at least.

About 2.30pm we came to the Island and sailed down close to the coast. The northern end has very little vegetation but as we went further down we saw olive groves and some beautifully situated little villages at the feet of ravines, where there must have been water, as quite green grass was to be seen. We passed the narrow opening into one bay and, after an hour's run, were stopped by a patrol boat and given orders. Just now, we were opposite a small bay with an island in the centre. We swung round the back of this and saw a narrow opening like a river. To our astonishment, this huge ship went straight to this, and, reducing speed, sailed up a tortuous channel, so narrow in places that one could almost have jumped on shore, but the lead was being used and never less than nine fathoms was reported and this only in one place at a bend. There was a fortified island halfway up the channel to protect the anchorage inside. We could not imagine what sort of place we were going to, when suddenly we rounded a bend and there was a large battleship lying anchored, (HMS *Canopus*), a little further on, another (HMS *Euryalus*) came in sight, and, finally, a huge harbour called Yera, or closed-in arm of the sea, came into view. It must have been four miles across and five long, something like a tennis racquet in shape, the water is very deep right up to the sides, as we anchored only a few hundred yards off the shore. This is where the poetess Sappho lived. 'Burning Sappho lived and loved.'

The hills surrounding the bay vary in height up to 3,500 feet, and all the smaller ones are covered with olive trees, carefully planted at regular intervals, and well looked after and pruned. The whole place reminded me of the upper end of Loch Lomond.

There was no wind blowing in the evening and it was very hot but an order came out that the portholes were not, or, rather, need not be shut.

The moon rose about 8.30 over the hills and the scene was delightful. I could hardly believe that we were not many miles from where our fellows, good men and true, were fighting hard.

## Monday, 26 July 1915

After the usual parades in the morning, leave was given to go sailing, or walk ashore. I went with Joe Carroll, Lennon and Sammy O'Carroll, for a sail across to Perma, a small village opposite the entrance to the harbour. Here we went ashore and caused great amusement by trying to buy a melon using Attic Greek to the moderns, whose Greek bears little resemblance to the old tongue. We got three large melons for 1/-.

The streets of the village are only rough paved paths, something like the Wynds in Edinburgh. The people are curious, coming round and listening to what is said. They are very kindly, however, and courteous. We walked through the village up the hillside and found that hidden away in the trees were numerous houses and little villages. They grow olives, figs and many other fruits that we failed to catch the names of. The houses were nearly all square blocks and had huge verandahs built out over the door and going out twenty yards from the front of the house. This verandah was composed of a light wooden frame with vines growing all over it. This gave pleasant shelter from the hot sun and the grapes could be picked by reaching up for the clusters which hung down in great quantities. We saw an enormous waggon about twenty feet long on four tiny wheels, probably only two feet diameter, being driven by bullocks. The waggon was painted in fancy colours and ornamented by the owner's name and address in Greek on the sides.

Went back to our boatman and sailed out about a quarter of a mile and let down the anchor and had a swim. The water, as at Alexandria, was very salty indeed and hurt the eyes when the water was rough. [...]

Several officers from the French cruiser *Latouche Treville* and from H.M.S. *Canopus* (which the men call 'The Canny Puss') came over to dine with us. They all seemed very nice fellows. We had a jolly evening sitting on deck in the moonlight, sipping iced drinks and smoking some of our famous Malta cigars. Broke up about 11.30 pm.

# Thursday 29 July 1915

[…] In the afternoon, leave was given for six officers to go to Mitylene [*sic*]. I went with Cullen and walked over the hills. The road is beautifully engineered and although the summit must be nearly 1,000 feet over sea, in no place is the road steeper than about one in 20. There are many hairpin bends and the road surface on the whole is good. When passing along one stretch of road where there was no wall at the side, one could look nearly straight down to the bay and the ships lying peacefully at anchor. The view reminded me very much of the road from Sally Gap to Roundwood, high up over Lough Tay in County Wicklow.

When we arrived at the summit, we found ourselves right on the top of a sharp ridge, and when sitting alongside the tiny inn drinking iced lemonade, we could see Yera harbour and Mitylene town at the same time. The view was magnificent as we could see the town of Mitylene with its quaint old castle and tiny harbour, down at our feet and ten or twelve miles away there was the Asiatic shore of Asia Minor. We saw the smoke of what we were told were burning villages belonging to Greeks who had been driven out by the Turks and taken refuge in the Island of Lesbos to the number of 85,000, we were told. We then started to descend the hill to the town and saw the fine villas built along the sides of the hills by wealthy Greek merchants.

I saw the first case I ever witnessed of ploughing with oxen. The ground seemed nothing more than rocks and stones, with the tangled roots of a few weeds. I could not understand from the man what they were going to plant.

[…]

The road was well designed and had a good camber to throw the water off into the huge deep channels cut in the rock at each side of the road. They evidently get big floods in the rainy season, as the water channels and the bridges were all very big indeed, although at this time of the year not a drop of water is to be seen. We walked rapidly down the long hill to the town, passing a children's school on the way. Here all the kids rushed out on the road plucking at our coats and begging for pennies. […]

The town of Mitylene is a well-built place with very narrow streets, paved with enormous blocks of granite about two feet square, and having many holes and bumps. The principal street is a sort of quay running in a semi-circle round the bay, from the Gardens at one end to the British Consulate, and the post office at the other. We were astonished to find three Ford landaulettes for hire. They looked so out of place bumping over the awful paving on the quay.

I called in at the 'English Hotel' to see if there were any one I knew staying there. [...] Saw a copy of the *Times* of July 15th, first paper I have seen since 8th July. [...]

Had some dinner in a queer cafe on the front. Proprietor could not speak any English but he conducted us into the kitchen and showed us all the dishes and we made our choice. It would have been the same if I hadn't chosen, as the dishes were all native ones, in which they use a lot of olive oil for cooking. There is not much water for cooking during the hot part of the summer, nor for drinking either, so they make use of the plentiful supply of olive oil from the numerous factories on the Island.

The Cafe man seemed very surprised and interested when I started writing down in Greek letters the English names of the things on the table. We paid two drachmas 50 lepta for dinner.

Saw several pastors of the Greek Church (Orthodox). They let their hair grow long and have it stuck in a little bun on their necks like a woman, they wear a sort of tall silk hat without a brim, and having a flat top which projects out an inch or more beyond the sides of the hat. Dirty, unshaven looking chaps they were too.

Great variety of uniforms about. Some of the Greek officers were very smart in tight light blue breeches, riding boots, spurs and white starched linen tunics with tight collars. They all carry swords and enjoy clanking them along the streets as they walk.

One man I met – Captain Gonadas, was a very fine looking fellow and very nice. He spoke no English but was a good French scholar. Some of the Greek Tommies wear khaki much the same colour as our Home Service stuff but they look very sloppy and only half fed. This, I heard afterwards, was the case.

The police wear a steel grey tunic with the Greek baggy trousers and they all looked very smart.

[...]

After dinner, we strolled through the town. There was nothing of great interest in the buildings architecturally but they were all clean-looking and well-built, with red tiled roofs. Many of the houses had big, heavy double hall doors with heavy brass knockers and handles much like those seen in London. Of course, they were all fitted with the close-fitting sun-blinds, as the sun in the middle of the day and early afternoon gets exceedingly hot.

We strolled along to the public gardens for dinner about 8.00pm and found a small band-stand surrounded by numerous small tables and plenty of chairs. It was quite the Continental style. Every family seemed to be there. Many Greek officers came in and we exchanged salutes. I sat with Captain Gonadas and a cousin of his of the same name, who was a refugee from Asia Minor, having been cleared out by the Turks. It occurred to me that they might be spies (of whom we were warned) so I was particularly careful of what I said to them. Young George Gonadas spoke English fluently, having been for a couple of years in London. He was a most gentlemanly fellow and most amusing.

[…]

## Wednesday, 4 August 1915

This day last year the war started, 365 days and we have done nothing yet, it's disgusting, and the delay is doing the men no good, besides, everyone is getting flabby after so long on board doing no hard work. […]
In the afternoon took two boats' crews out to practice rowing. Good job we weren't torpedoed coming out, as no one had the least idea how to handle an oar, and, as all the ships' boats are huge, clumsy things like a big canal barge, with about three feet of freeboard, our progression caused much amusement.

## Friday, 6 August 1915

Got orders in the morning to start as soon as possible for Gallipoli. During the forenoon the SANIA and the FAUVETTE (General Steam Navigation Company Bordeaux Service) came alongside and we were very busy getting stores and kits transferred to them. […] HQ with C and B companies are to go on the FAUVETTE and Major Jennings with A and B companies on the SANIA. We sailed away from the *Alaunia* at 15.30 and the SANIA went at 18.00.
We had our last meal on the *Alaunia* at lunch and toasted the ship's officers. Drank success to our undertaking.

3

# Gallipoli: Landing at Suvla Bay and the Next Ten Days, 7–17 August 1915

The landing of the 10th (Irish) Division as part of IX Corps[1] commanded by Lieutenant General Frederick Stopford[2] at Suvla Bay was a part of a renewed effort to consolidate and break through on the Gallipoli Peninsula. While Australian, Indian, and New Zealand forces would break out from Anzac Cove, the 10th (Irish) and the 11th (Northern) divisions would secure a winter harbour at Suvla Bay.[3] The 11th (Northern) Division led the landings and were ashore before midnight on 6 August. The 10th (Irish) Division, including Drury's 6th Royal Dublin Fusiliers, followed the next day. The battalion was put ashore around 06.00 on steel barges and faced only light gunfire from Turkish positions. The landing was therefore relatively easy, but there were no orders about what to do once they had established a beachhead, prompting Drury to note 'we went to Gallipoli without any orders, and without any maps'. At one stage

---

1    https://www.gallipoli-association.org/campaign/order-of-battle-mef/
     oob-august-offensive/ [accessed 17 April 2020]. For details of the 10th (Irish)
     Division as a whole at Gallipoli, see Bryan Cooper, *The Tenth (Irish) Division in
     Gallipoli* (London: Herbert Jenkins, 1918); Philip Orr, *Field of Bones: An Irish
     Division at Gallipoli* (Dublin: Lilliput Press, 2006); Sandford, *Neither Unionist
     nor Nationalist*, 83–96; and Jeremy Stanley, *Ireland's Forgotten 10th: A Brief
     History of the 10th (Irish) Division 1914–1918, Turkey, Macedonia and Palestine*
     (Ballycastle: Impact Printing, 2003).
2    Lieutenant General Sir Frederick William Stopford (1854–1929) (*The Times*,
     6 May 1929, p. 23).
3    Macleod, *Gallipoli*, 52–4.

the battalion commanding officer 'was looking around for someone to give us our orders but no staff were to be seen'. Drury was also critical of the 11th (Northern) Division for not being where he believed they were meant to be, a theme to which he would return during his time at Gallipoli.[4] The next day, the battalion was again without any sense of direction. They were attached temporarily to 33rd Brigade in 11th (Northern) Division and were ordered to make a short move towards Chocolate Hill (taken by the 7th Royal Dublin Fusiliers on the evening of 7 August) but were soon sent back and Drury noted, 'I cannot understand the delay in moving inland. There has been no fighting all day and the Turks haven't fired a shot and are probably moving up reinforcements and digging new trenches. The men are all talking about the waste of valuable time.'[5]

On 9 August, the 6th Royal Dublin Fusiliers finally got orders to take part in an advance from Hill 50 towards Ali Bey Chesme. This was Drury's first real action and he recalled, 'The firing was worse than I imagined it would be and I felt very scared', with snipers hidden in trees a particular problem. The attack failed and Drury attributed that to 'the failure by the staff to work out any proper scheme at the beginning while there was a chance of our getting there without much opposition' and also 'the extraordinarily bad behaviour of the 11th (Northern) Division troops and some of the 53rd'.[6] Casualties for the 6th Royal Dublin Fusiliers were heavy: 11 officers and 259 other ranks, with 6 of the officers turning out to be dead, which necessitated some reorganisation of the battalion.[7] The battalion spent the next few days digging in, struggling to find water but on 12 August were reattached to their own 30th Brigade and sent to a 'rest camp'.[8] Drury felt there was a 'subtle wit' at work in naming this a rest camp, noting 'Anything less like a Rest Camp you couldn't imagine. It was a bare slope, cleared in the scrub and having tracks of a "hay" crop of hard wiry burnt grass. The sun was beating down with a heat such I have never felt before. There was no shade.'[9]

However, the 6th Royal Dublin Fusiliers' stay there was short-lived as they were ordered back to the front line in the afternoon to the Kiretch

---

4   Diary entry, 7 Aug 1915.
5   Diary entry, 8 Aug 1915.
6   Diary entry, 9 Aug 1915.
7   Diary entries, 9 and 11 Aug 1915.
8   Diary entry, 12 Aug 1915.
9   Diary entry, 13 Aug 1915.

Tepe Sirt, which they labelled 'KTS Ridge'.[10] As the men dug in, Drury got his first proper sleep since landing a week before, and post arrived, the first for over a month.[11] On the morning of 15 August, Drury managed to get to the sea and had his first bathe for ten days, but the battalion was ordered into action that afternoon in an effort to capture the whole crest of KTS Ridge. Although initially held up by snipers, the battalion took the top of the ridge just before 6pm when 'we charged and reaching the top drove out the Turks with the bayonet sending them rushing down the other side', while machine gun fire from Jephson's Post took a heavy toll on the enemy.[12] The command structure of the battalion was further weakened with two more officers killed and two wounded that day, and one more killed and two wounded on 16 August.[13] Deaths on the 16 August came in a Turkish counterattack, but the 6th Royal Dublin Fusiliers held their ground.[14] As the responsibilities of the battalion's officers were reorganised, Drury became Adjutant, which in future would give him a greater insight into liaison between his unit and both 33rd Brigade and the 10th (Irish) Division.[15]

---

10  Diary entry, 13 Aug 1915.
11  Diary entry, 14 Aug 1915.
12  Diary entry, 15 Aug 1915.
13  WO 95/4296: 6th RDF.
14  Diary entry, 16 Aug 1915.
15  Diary entry, 17 Aug 1915.

# Saturday, 7 August 1915

We found the FAUVETTE in a perfectly filthy condition and the smell below was like nothing else. The cushions in the cabin and saloon were stuck to the woodwork and were alive with vermin. The boat was packed from stem to stern and there was hardly room to sit down. There was no food on board and hardly any water and all the stuff I got was two breakfast rolls and fourth of a bottle of champagne! The armament consisted of two 12-lb quick-firing guns on the fo'castle in case of submarine attack and there were naval ratings in charge. I slept in snatches beside one of the guns on the starboard side as I couldn't stand the state of affairs below. I also kept my valise on deck so that it shouldn't get infected. Strict orders were given that no lights were to be shown – no smoking on deck, and no loud conversation.

So we started off for the great adventure. I felt very nervous, as I am sure the others did, about how I would get on when real fighting started, and I think the responsibility of leading the men well, weighed on us.

The men didn't seem a bit worried but just lay all around either sleeping or chatting in low tones. One of the men remarked to his pal alongside him, when we were passing Helles, 'Eh, Mick, is this the War at last?' and the reply came in a sleepy voice 'I suppose so, and it seems a terrible noisy place'.

During the evening the Colonel [Cox] told me to come up to the Bridge with him to see about our orders. He had been led to believe that orders would be handed to us by the Naval officer in charge of the ship. When Paddy Cox asked him for orders he replied 'What orders?' and when we told him we wanted our operation orders he said he had none for us. Paddy then asked him what <u>his</u> orders were, and he replied 'to dump you on a lighter there (pointing to the chart) and then get away for more troops'. The Colonel then said he must get on to Mudros by wireless, but was told wireless must on no account whatever be used tonight as it might give the show away, and the landing cease to be a surprise. So we went to Gallipoli without any orders, and without any maps.

About 02.00 we passed Cape Helles and could hear gun and rifle fire that seemed to me very heavy as if an attack were being made. We could see innumerable little pinpoints of light all over the place where shells and bombs were bursting. Several Naval vessels which I couldn't see were firing towards the land, making a tremendous noise. This scene was very beautiful with star shells going out, and the loom of the early dawn with the beautiful lemon-coloured flash of the naval guns. As we passed further up the coast the outline of the hills became visible and as we approached Suvla Bay I was able to identify Lala Baba from the Captain's chart. There was a salt lake marked, but I could see no sign of it, although the land for a couple of miles inshore looked very flat. We reached a headland called NIBRUNESI point, about daylight and I could see steamers sailing in from every direction. It is marvellous how the Navy have managed to bring all these troops together at the same time from places varying from twenty to 120 miles away and on steamers whose speed probably varies from ten to eighteen knots.

The *Fauvette* anchored about half a mile from shore inside a line from NIBRUNESI point on the south to SUVLA point on the north of the bay. I recognised the SANIA near us with the rest of the Battalion on board, by her one very flat funnel.

Soon two big steel barges came alongside to ferry us ashore, and the 7th RDF started disembarking on the starboard side of the ship and we 6th RDF did the same on the port side. The barges or 'BEETLES' as the men promptly christened them are very interesting and look as if they were specially designed for this work. They are made entirely of steel, are about 60 feet long by about fifteen feet beam and have a heavy oil engine right in the stern. The engine is a single cylinder something like a Bollinder in the fishing boats, and the boat is steered and engine controlled from a little shelter on the engine hatch. The speed is about five or six knots. In the bow is a ramp eight or ten feet wide normally held vertically by chains to two Samson posts but capable of being let down onto the beach landing the troops. It is possible to pack in 500 fully equipped men, and the ammunition, tools etc. are carried on the deck. I had to sit on the top of the pile of tools and other gear and I felt very bare and unprotected, and hoped I wouldn't get sniped as we landed. I nearly had a bad accident at the start as the nails in my boots slipped on the steel deck, and my legs went down between the lighter and the ship just as they were swinging together. Someone gave me a pull up just in time to prevent my legs getting crushed.

The 6th RDF landed about 06.00 at a spot about 250 yards south of NIBRUNESI point and we rushed the men up the little beach to a low bank about six feet high and piled arms and took off equipment. We then started bringing ashore the tools, machine guns, ammunition, water and food. We had some gunfire but not anything like what I expected and there were very few casualties in the 6th RDF but the 7th RDF had more. One shell dropped in the water between the two lighters (6 ft apart) without hitting anyone, but soaking us to the skin.

The 6th Royal Inniskilling Fusiliers landed 100 yards south of us and also a field ambulance. There was also an aeroplane over dropping bombs but I saw no one hit, although I heard someone say that a steamer had been struck. While this was going on, the Colonel [Cox] was looking around for someone to give us our orders but no staff were to be seen. I could see no sign of Turks anywhere nor any trenches. After a long delay we came across General Hill, 31st Brigade, who told us we would not join our own 30th Brigade but would remain with his Brigade. I didn't hear the orders he gave but gathered that we were to move north and attack the high ridge we could see across the plain. We were told to follow the 7th RDF across the sea side of the hill to LALA BABA where we dumped the men's packs and left them in charge of the Company Quartermaster Sergeants. Then about 13.00 we started off in artillery formation to cross the spit of sand between the Salts Lake and the sea. This isn't usually a lake but a sort of marsh in which the salt water has dried up leaving a coating of glistening salt shining in the sun.

We had a good deal of shrapnel fired over us while crossing the spit but it was aimed too high and most of the bullets fell in the sea. There were a couple of barges stuck on a sandbank a few hundred yards from the shore and I think a lot of the shells were aimed at these. When we came to the 'Cut' or entrance to the salt lake we found that the Turk was firing salvoes of high explosive shell into it at regular intervals, but we got the men safely over in small parties by timing the shells. There seemed to be a very large number of troops near us along beach to the N. of us who were doing nothing except lie about sleeping. There did not seem to be any fighting, but the Navy was shelling a high KTS Ridge with 6″ shells. I sank over the knees in stinking rotting vegetation and many of us were covered by the filth thrown up by the shells. We got some shelter under a low hill or mound near the beach on the North side of the cut [...].

The 7th RDF, 6th Royal Inniskilling Fusiliers, and the 5th Royal Irish Fusiliers passed and turned east along the north side of the Salt Lake, leaving us in Brigade reserve. The Battalion stayed here for the rest of the day, helping to land stores and ammunition. The weather is fearfully hot and I have a fearful thirst, but everyone has been warned that water is very scarce. There were evidences all round of fighting this morning by the 11th Division who landed about midnight. Turks and British lying about everywhere, many of them bayoneted. A burial party under Captain J LUKE C Company had anything but a nice job, and to make matters worse the scrub was set on fire by Turk shells and many bodies were burned the smell being nauseating. I examined some of the Turkish arms lying about, with interest. There were old Martini rifles converted to charger loading and having a 5-round magazine. I also saw Mauser rifles and bayonets, and hand grenades like an apple, held to a hook on the belt by a short piece of brass chain.

During the day there was a heavy cannonade going on over our heads by the Fleet. The big Monitors we saw leaving Malta, HMS HAVELOCK and RAGLAN, with 14.2″ guns […] were there, also the CANOPUS, EURYALUS, TRIUMPH and CHATHAM which were firing broadsides of 6″ guns. These smaller naval guns make a terrific sharp noise which actually hurts us on shore. I found them much more distressing than big guns.

During the day a curiously shaped ship came up close behind the fleet, having all the fore part apparently covered with a light yellow canvas cover. Presently I saw this swelling up and realised it was a captive balloon of some kind. It was shaped like a sausage with a much thinner one bent round one end on the vertical axis. The observer is slung in a basket 50 feet below, and there is a long tail like a kite to keep it head to wind. I had my first dose of biscuit and bully beef today, but the latter I couldn't face it all. It turned out of the tin in a horrible slimy multicoloured mess.

There was a shower of rain in the afternoon which cools the air slightly for a while. This is the first shower I have seen since leaving England. During the day I was very busy carrying up ammunition for the 31st Brigade and we formed a dump in a hollow close to a well called ALI BEY CHESME […]. There are two small hills to the South of the well, one of which has had the scrub burned and is called CHOCOLATE HILL (53 metres) the other being Hill 50 (metres) sometimes called Green Hill. There was some fighting going on here, but I could see very little of what was going on, and I saw no units of the 11th Division who are supposed to be near here on the left flank. The 31st Brigade were on a line running about N[orth] E[ast] from the N[orth] E[ast] corner of the salt lake. There did not seem to be any troops on the left and there must have been a good many Turks there as a lot of rifle fire was coming from the left and left rear, causing a good many casualties. Our line seemed somewhat drawn back to deal with this fire. About 16.00 when at the well, there was heavy firing and soon afterwards a heavy bombardment of the top of the hill started and continued for a short time only. The 7th RDF are attacking with the 6th Royal Inniskilling Fusiliers on one right flank and the 5th Royal Irish Fusiliers on the other left. I felt dead beat in the evening as the heat all day was tremendous and we had to carry ammunition back over 5,000 yards through very heavy and rough going. About 19.00 I met a 7th RDF man who said they had captured Chocolate Hill and that Major TIPPETT and several other officers were killed. I don't think the Turks made any counter-attack, as I heard no particular firing. I didn't sleep much as I was too tired. My leg muscles are aching through being out of practice.

## Sunday, 8 August 1915. Hill 70

Just after midnight we got an order to move up to HILL 53 or CHOCOLATE HILL as everyone now calls it on account of its dark brown colour. I had to guide the Battalion up as I had been up and knew the way. We did not stay very long and got orders to move back to the 'Cut' before dawn. I don't know what we were wanted up for as no fighting was going on. I felt awfully tired once we got back as I had been on the go 24 hours, so I lay down for about an hour's doze, then breakfast about 06.00 of bully beef and a small cup of tea. The night was very cold in comparison with the heat of the day. Hard at work all the forenoon getting up ammunition, food and water for the 31st Brigade to Chocolate Hill. [...]

I cannot understand the delay in moving inland. There has been no fighting all day and the Turks haven't fired a shot and are probably moving up reinforcements and digging new trenches. The men are all talking about the waste of valuable time. We have had quite a lot of old soldiers who know a good deal about this sort of war and they are all grousing like blazes, saying we are throwing away our chance and will pay for it later. The whole place here near the Cut and across to HILL 10 is thick with troops of the 11th Division doing nothing but lying about sleeping or eating.

It seems we are now attached to the 33rd Brigade (11th Division) Brigadier General RP MAXWELL[16] and in the evening he ordered Lieutenant RONNIE KENNEDY and his two machine guns up to Chocolate Hill so it looks like some sort of move forward, but I don't like our machine guns going off and leaving us. We carried nearly 400,000 rounds of SAA[17] and a great quantity of stores to Chocolate Hill today.

---

16  Robert Percy Maxwell (WO 372/13/182954).
17  Small arms ammunition.

The heat during the day was tremendous and the smell simply awful. I shall never get it out of my nostrils. […] During the afternoon I had a squad of men helping the RAMC to load wounded men on to the ships' boats from the dressing station on the beach. I saw poor BRIDGE of D Company 7th RDF who was very badly wounded in the side and had been waiting with many others, since 22.00 last night for transhipment. He seemed awfully glad to see me, but could hardly speak. He wanted a cigarette but was too weak to smoke it. I'm afraid he won't stick it. There were some wounded Turk prisoners there including one fat little chap whose foot and ankle were shattered by a shell or bomb. Couper[18] amputated his leg at the knee during the night without any anaesthetic, and the fellow didn't seem to mind a bit. When I saw him this evening he was in great form, smoking a cigarette and smiling at everyone. There was another Turk there, slowly dying from an awful wound in the stomach. He absolutely refused to allow anyone to touch him or do anything to ease the pain. He seemed to think we would poison him or do something cruel to him.

There is a great shortage of water and stern measures have to be taken to ensure every man getting his fair share. It did one good to see our men giving up their few precious drops to the wounded men. The look on their faces was sufficient reward. We found a good way of cooling the water by soaking the felt cover in the sea and then evaporating it by swinging the bottle round and round. I have only had a bottle full for last night and today for all purposes. Making tea is wasteful owing to loss by steam.

There is a rumour that Sir Ian Hamilton came ashore for a while this evening, but I didn't see him.

## Monday, 9 August 1915. Hill 70

We paraded this morning at 02.30 and marched from the 'Cut' along the N[orth] side of the Salt Lake to the foot of CHOCOLATE HILL arriving there before dawn. Colonel Cox explained to the officers that the idea was to push out to ISMAIL OGLU TEPE or Hill 112 (some call it Hill W) […]. It seems a very long way and if the scrub is as thick as here it would take days to walk there even without fighting. Can't understand

---

18 Alexander Johnston Couper, deployed with 6th RDF as Medical Officer at Dardanelles. Later Captain in RAMC and Captain attached to the 7th Royal Horse Artillery. See WO 372/5/44939.

why this wasn't done yesterday or before. There was any amount of troops available, and when Chocolate Hill was taken more troops should have been pushed through them at once without allowing the pace to slacken. I went off to look for the 33rd Brigade HQ and found the Staff Captain who pointed out to me where their signal and report station would be.

The 33rd Brigade are to attack HILL 70 and HILL 112 with three Battalions in the line – 6th Lincolns on the left – the 7th South Staffords in the centre – and the 6th Border Regiment on the right. Simultaneously the 32nd Brigade are to attack towards Anafarta Sair. The 6th RDF are in support of the centre, and the 6th Royal Irish Fusiliers in reserve. […]

At 05.00 we moved off to the neighbourhood of the well called ALI BEY CHESME and fixed our Battalion HQ there as it was an easy place for messengers to find and there were several tracks running to it.

The fighting had hardly started when we got an urgent message from the 6th Lincolns to send up reinforcements. B Company had hardly started moving when another message came asking for more help, so Colonel Cox sent B and C companies together in charge of our 2nd in Command MAJOR JG JENNINGS.

I tried to signal messages of what we had done to the 33rd Brigade but could get no response, so had to send a runner instead. There must be a lot more Turks here than there were yesterday as the rifle fire was very intense.

By 06.00 the firing line was taken over by us with C Company (Captain J LUKE) on the left and B Company (Captain WH WHYTE) on the right. Casualties began coming down at once, among the first that I saw was Lieutenant Charlie Martin of C Company who had his arm smashed by a bullet near the elbow. He was without coat, helmet or equipment. Captain John Luke of C Company came down soon afterwards with all the fingers of his left hand cut off by a piece of shell which smashed his rifle in pieces. He said there were several snipers up in the trees we had passed, and several of his men had been shot from behind. He was in fearful pain and was damning the Turks and their snipers in awful language. He turned up again in half an hour without having gone to the dressing station at all, and carrying a lot of water bottles of wounded men, to get them some water from the well. I could see the white bones of his hand sticking out of the flesh. Paddy Cox cursed him and ordered him off.

The well became a death trap as the bullets were banging into it like hailstones and Couper's dressing station in the slight hollow near it had to be moved as several bearers were hit and wounded men hit again.

The firing was worse than I imagined it would be and I felt very scared, but I saw our good old Regimental Sergeant-Major, Jock Campbell, going about his job of looking after the ammunition supplies with the greatest coolness, and I profited by his good example. We had no messages from the front line and could not hear what was happening, nor could we get any messages from 33rd Brigade, so I went over myself to Chocolate Hill. I could not find anybody at the place they showed me, and I found they had moved round to the sea side of the hill facing LALA BABA where they got down into a Turkish trench, and from which they could not see us or HILL 70 at all. General Maxwell in the devil of a funk and incapable of giving proper orders.

About 09.00 we had to send the reserve (D) Company under Captain PTL Thompson to help the 6th Border Regiment on the right in response to their urgent messages. These orders to reinforce the front line should of course come from the Brigadier General but he seems useless and doesn't know what is going on and doesn't try to find out.

09.30

By this time the Irish Fusiliers seemed to have gone up into the line as I didn't see any of them about. Colonel Cox decided that as his whole battalion was now involved he would move up nearer the front line, leaving the Regimental Sergeant-Major and a couple of orderlies at the well headquarters in case of messages being sent there. We moved up to a point about 500 yards near the line [...].

10.00

We met Bill Whyte coming to explain the position personally as all the messages had been knocked out, and he had had no acknowledgement of his messages. He was so cool and collected as if on a Field Day at home, and said that instead of our supporting the Lincolns, that we were doing the attacking and trying to keep the Lincolns from running away. Major Jennings reported killed, also several junior officers. I went barging about through the scrub trying to find where people were and I found parties of Lincolns and Borderers all over the place lying up in funk holes. Finally when I got to D Company, who were on the right in touch with A Company, a whole lot of these two regiments started running away like mad, shouting out that they were 'cuts to ribbons' etc. Thompson, Billy Richards, & I had a job to prevent them clearing out altogether and even had to threaten to use our revolvers, even to the officers. I found that there were no troops on D Company's left to the south of HILL 70 for several hundred yards so I managed to persuade a party of Borders about twenty strong with two officers and a Company Sergeant-Major to follow me up the track leading towards ABRIKJA and I got them lining a bank, as far as I could judge, about 105-N-5, with a good field of fire in front (east) and also towards HILL 70. I couldn't succeed, however, in making any of them put their heads up and fire although I showed them good targets. The worst of them was a fat Company Sergeant-Major who would only lie down in the ditch and announce 'we are all cut to bits'. Then an extraordinary thing happened. A big hare got up behind us and raced out past us through a gap in the bank and on towards the Turk. The brave Company Sergeant-Major and one or two others lifted their rifles and started blazing away after the hare although they were too much afraid to shoot at the Turks. I noticed on looking back over the bare ground behind us where the hare had come from, the strike of the Turk bullets all over the place knocking up little spurts of dust as if a hail shower were falling. I don't remember noticing the bullets before that, and I wonder I weren't hit as I was strolling about it all morning.

There were some bad fires raging about us in the scrub mostly behind and to each flank, but they did not seem any fires in front where there seemed to be a ravine with very precipitous sides on the opposite bank.

The position of the troops at 10.00 seemed to be, from right to left:–

| | |
|---|---|
| on Green Hill (50) | 5th Royal Irish Fusiliers |
| at <u>G</u> in TORGUT CHESME | A Company 6th RDF |
| at 105-N-1 | D Company 6th RDF |
| on their left | a party of Border Regiment. |
| on South side Scimitar Hill (70) | 6th Royal Irish Fusiliers. |
| near 105-J-A | B Company 6th RDF |
| on their left | C Company 6th RDF |
| further left | 1 Coy? 7th South Staffords |
| at 105-J-1 | mixed party 6th RDF, Lincolns and Borderers facing N[orth] E[ast] |

Small parties of Borderers, Lincolns and South Staffordshires scattered about the west slopes in 105-A and 105 G lying doggo!

The bulk of the Lincolns had apparently gone off for a bathe at A Beach!

About 10.30 very heavy shelling of Hill 70 started again and some of our men were pushed back a short distance although two platoons (5 and 8 of B Company) were still holding out on the forward slope.

About 11.00 Paddy Cox got information (I don't know where) that he would get some reinforcements, and shortly afterwards two companies

2/4th Queen's Royal West Surreys (160 Brigade 53rd Division) arrived and were sent up to Captain Whyte, who was organising another attack on the hill.

At 11.30 Paddy decided he must go up into the front line and take charge himself as he could get no orders nor advice from the 33rd Brigade. So, leaving Lieutenant WR Richards to deal with anything [which] might arise, he and I went off. We found men of the Lincolns and Borderers lying about everywhere there was cover, and many more making their way out of the line on one pretext or another. We had wordy warfare with some of the these, especially with some officers one of whom Paddy Cox hit over the head with his telescope. When we got the top of Hill 70 there was a very heavy bombardment, and it seemed to me as if some of it was the medium sized Naval shells from <u>our</u> ships. The scrub was also burning fiercely in many places and smoke and dust hid everything further than 30 or 40 yards away. The Queen's West Surreys bolted the minute the heavy shelling started, leaving Bill Whyte with a mere handful of men. Casualties have been very heavy and owing to the smoke and high scrub it is impossible to see how many we have left. At about 13.00 Colonel Cox having failed to get any help for the left flank which appeared likely to be turned, and seeing that it was impossible to push on, decided to withdraw the front line to a partly dug Turk trench about 300 yards from the crest of Hill 70 and which we had passed in the morning. This trench ran along the 40 contour approximately, astride the track leading west, to the ALI BEY CHESME [...]. I believe this trench saved the line today as we would never have held the scattered units together without having this rallying point. As soon as we got back to it, all the attached units went off to look for their own people, and we held it for the remainder of the day with A and D companies having B and C companies in support 70 or 80 yards behind. On our <u>right</u> were the 6th Royal Irish Fusiliers, and then the 5th Royal Irish Fusiliers on GREEN HILL. On our <u>left</u> were the Queen's West Surreys, and on the left I believe there was a mixed mob of 33rd Brigade, and then the 1/4th Royal West Sussex Regiment.

It is evident now (13.00) that not only has the attack on HILL 112 failed, but we have failed to capture even HILL 70. This is entirely due to two things. 1st the failure by the staff to work out any proper scheme at the beginning while there was a chance of our getting there without much opposition, and 2ndly the extraordinarily bad behaviour of the 11th Division troops and some of the 53rd. Our day was divided between trying to keep the 33rd Brigade <u>on</u>, and the Turks <u>off</u> HILL

70. The bulk of the 33rd Brigade cleared off early and went the whole way to the beach. I am perfectly sure that if we had our own 10th (Irish) Division here complete, we would have smashed the Turk defence and got to our objectives.

We spent the evening digging in and joining up with Green Hill without any interference from the Turk. I couldn't see any of them at all but am sure they are digging hard too. They can't very well counter-attack in this sector as the naval guns would knock them endways as soon as they came over the crest, although the flat trajectory of these guns prevents then putting shells behind the crests. I don't think we had any field guns supporting us today as I suppose very few have been landed yet, although I saw one battery at least at Lala Baba yesterday.

Our men were wonderful today under fire for the first time. They were shooting steadily and carefully whenever Turks showed themselves, and never showed the least sign of shakiness when the other units ran off. The Battalion messengers have done really fine work taking messages about under fire quickly and not stopping for shelter. Private CAHILL of B Company I noticed specially for his coolness. I am afraid several runners have been killed or wounded, and most of the casualties were caused by the failure of the 33rd Brigade to keep in touch with us, and moving their HQ far away. If we had known the sort they were, we could have saved these men, as we got no help at all and were just as well off working on our own.

I felt absolutely wearied out this evening, but about 18.00 I had some food and discovered it was hunger that was the matter, as I soon bucked up after the feed. Very busy trying to ascertain what casualties we had today and eventually got these figures. Eleven Officers and 259 other ranks in three companies, B, C & D.


## Tuesday, 10 August 1915. Hill 70/Ali Bey Chesme

The casualties among the officers yesterday were

| Major JG JENNINGS | 2nd in Comm[an]d 6th RDF | wounded and missing* |
| Captain J LUKE | C Company | wounded |
| Captain JJ Carroll | B Company | wounded |
| Lieutenant DR CLERY | D Company | missing* |
| Lieutenant JJ DOYLE | D Company | killed* |

| Second Lieutenant WLG MORTIMER | A Company | wounded (v. bad) died later same day |
|---|---|---|
| Second Lieutenant W MCGARRY | B Company | killed* |
| Second Lieutenant R STANTON | B Company | killed* |
| Second Lieutenant CR MARTIN | C Company | wounded |
| Second Lieutenant FB O'CARROLL | C Company | killed* |
| Second Lieutenant RW CARTER | C Company | wounded[19] |

*never seen again

I am afraid that the bodies of most of those who were killed must have been burned as we could hardly find any of them.

We stood to arms at 03.00 after having very little sleep. I and Fritz Cullen spent a good while at our outpost line and beyond it but saw no Turks, although we could hear digging just over the crest of HILL 70 just where the trees are. The fleet started a tremendous bombardment about 05.00 and kept it up for three hours. We had to withdraw our outposts who were near the top of Hill 70 on account of the huge splinters flying about. Here is a sample of the kind of orders we got from this wonderful 33rd Brigade:–

"[…] The 53 Div will attack enemy's lines today. If attack successful all units attached to the 33rd Bde will take part in the advance. Until such opportunity offers, units will remain in the positions at present held by them. 33rd Brigade 05.00"

This is a useful order to get for an important battle! No information about what positions are to be attacked, nor at what time, nor even what part we are to take in the advance. Apparently only attached units to move, the 33rd Brigade to sit still like yesterday and leave us to do the work. Many of them did not even sit still but cleared off to the beach and some got into the lines of the 31st Field Ambulance near A Beach and were found by Colonel Shanahan who drove them out with his fists. Father Murphy tells us it was the only time he was ever in a rage – 'God forgive me, I hit some of them.'

We had a view of a Brigade of the 53rd Division coming up to the line. They marched out from behind LALA BABA about 06.00 in column of route (!) and then deployed in the plain and advanced in lines

---

19  Drury noted after 'wounded' that Carter had 'died later at sea', but it has not been possible to verify that.

of Battalions about 100 yards apart. They came along in the bright sun across the plain on a frontage of about 1,000 yards, without a particle of cover, with bayonets and brass work glinting in the sun. They were simply plastered with shrapnel and long-range rifle and machine gun fire all the way and suffered heavy casualties. It was a wonderful sight, and would have looked well at a Field Day at Aldershot, but whoever ordered it here should be shot. They landed yesterday and I know of nothing to prevent their leaving long before dawn and get under cover before daylight. (I notice the Turks have more guns firing today than yesterday.) The attack was a fiasco. Most of them stopped when they were about level with us, but some charged right up to within 200 yards off point 70 only to retire immediately at the double. A lot of Turks followed them over the crest, but we opened fire and drove them back at once. It was a rotten show with no method and devoid of any show of determination. A lot of sniping all day, with a good many casualties. It is impossible to find where the snipers are firing from, but sometimes it seems as if they are somewhere in the trees behind us. The ALI BEY CHESME is almost unapproachable as they have the range of it to a yard. The Turk gunners often spray it with shrapnel if men are seen at the well. I had a bit of interesting shooting during this afternoon at a sniper I spotted with my glasses, away on our left front. I had Sergeant Fuller spotting for me and I got him after four or five rounds. Range 850x. I took Fuller with me on a tour behind our lines to search the trees for snipers, but did not catch any. We found one 'nest' in the bushy top of an oak tree. There was a dark brown blanket, several bananas, some raisins, an empty water bottle and a big leather strap which I suppose was to keep him from falling out of the tree if he went asleep. Some of the men say that a woman sniper was found but I don't believe it.

Meals are rather amusing, but no one seems to have much appetite owing to the great heat and the flies. Menu:– Breakfast. Tea with muddy water, hard biscuit soaked in it. Dinner. Same plus greasy bully beef. Supper. Same minus bully beef. Making tea is a frightful extravagance as some of the precious water is wasted in steam, but it is mightily refreshing all the same.

[…]

At 18.00 a bombardment of Scimitar Hill (70) started with Naval 9″ & 6″ guns and 18lb field guns on LALA BABA, but when the guns switched off, the Middlesex & others of the 53rd Division on our left for some reason did not attack and made no move at all although we were told they were going to do so. These Terriers are a perfect nuisance at night, keeping on passing messages along the line such as 'are your magazines loaded' [and] 'keep a look out on the right'. Bill Whyte told one of their officers that if he passed any more of his idiotic messages along to us, he would go along and shoot him! Peace after that. They also keep on blazing away thousands of rounds from MGs[20] & rifles into the dark. I can't see what is going to happen here. Every hour we lose is making it harder, and every day it is evident the Turks have got up more reinforcements and more guns.

At 18.30 we got sudden orders to relieve the 5th Royal Irish Fusiliers on GREEN HILL (50). We had to fall in the men without having been able to get them any tea. We were relieved by the 10th Middlesex Regiment 53rd Division and we pushed off in file through the scrub to the base of Chocolate Hill near the supply dump, where we had to wait for several hours: why, I don't know. I got most of the men a further supply of water at the well. With better management the men could have had a meal before they moved. I went with Paddy Cox to see Colonel G Downing of the 7th RDF near the top of Chocolate Hill. Horrible place, with a lot of unburied Turks lying about. One was lying in the bottom of the trench and I blundered on him in the dark. Uck! There was some desultory shooting down behind the hill but we couldn't find out what it was about, although someone told us that a party of Turks had been found hiding in the scrub about 104-P-4.

At last the guides turned up and we filed through the Chocolate Hill trenches and through the long communicating trench to the back of GREEN HILL. Relief complete about 24.00.[21]

## Wednesday, 11 August 1915. At Green Hill (50)

Had no rest and stood to arms at 03.00. Very busy ever since relief, connecting up companies with HQ by phone and making cover in the line for the operators.

I had a scare about 02.00 when laying a line in the scrub behind the front line. I bumped suddenly into a Turk behind D Company's bit who

---

20  Machine guns.
21  Drury noted that from a landing strength on 7 Aug 1915 of 27 officers and 782 other ranks, the strength at 22.00 on 11 Aug was 16 officers and 507 other ranks. D1, p. 96.

jabbed at me with his bayonet but missed me as I did a world's record standing jump sideways. I loosed a couple of rounds at him with my Colt automatic (.45 calibre) but didn't hit him. Thompson and I chased him but we lost him as soon as he got off the skyline. Hard at work trying to improve trenches, but it was very hard as we are down the rock in many places and have only entrenching tools to dig with. A lot of casualties from snipers whom we can't find. Kennedy tried searching all the trees in front with bursts of MG fire, and finally got one fellow who had constructed a shelter from some coarse straw which was lying about.

Water is still very hard to get and the men are really suffering very much from thirst. I don't think any of us knew what thirst really is. Most of the men are probably accustomed to drink, regularly, a good deal more than we are, at home, and they feel it more here not getting a good supply. A nominal pint per man per day is not much for washing, cooking and drinking. However, they are sticking it well, but are awfully tired and sleepy. Rations take a long time to get up and the ration parties have to carry the boxes and tins of water right through the Chocolate Hill trenches up to us. Our headquarters, as near as can make out are now at 105-M-7. The men are getting very careless and are exposing themselves too much. Had to lecture my fellows and tell them it wasn't brave. I think we could advance from here by keeping the machine guns back on the hill behind to give overhead fire. The country just in front is not nearly so thick with scrub and by this time there should be some artillery available.

## Thursday, 12 August 1915. At Green Hill

Stood to arms 03.30 – day much the same as yesterday but less water. Someone in the 7th RDF left a bottle with some whiskey in it beside Colonel Cox while he was asleep – a good soul. Great news arrived during the day – that we are to be relieved this evening by the 8th Duke of Wellington's West Riding Regiment 11th Division and are to rejoin the rest of the 30th Brigade. It bucked everybody up. The men were always great pals with the 6th Royal Munster Fusiliers, and were delighted at rejoining them. The relieving battalion did not turn up till about 23.00. They seemed in an awful state of nerves. Just about the time of the relief some Turks crept up quite close in the scrub, and started loosing off at us at close range. Our fellows held their fire till the Turks were only ten or fifteen yards away and then let them have it in the neck. The affair only lasted ten minutes & we had no casualties.

It took over two hours to get the West Ridings in and settled in. Our men had to get out of their trenches and lie down in the scrub behind and then let the others file into their places. Our orders were to march across the plain and up to KARAKOL DAGH to a spot about ½ a mile above A beach which they called for some reason, not obvious, a REST CAMP! [...]

## Friday, 13 August 1915. The Rest Camp

[...] During the morning we arrived at the 'Rest Camp' about 117-H-5. I suspect the Division of having a subtle wit. Anything less like a Rest Camp you couldn't imagine. It was a bare slope, cleared in the scrub and having tracks of a 'hay' crop of hard wiry burnt grass. The sun was beating down with a heat such I have never felt before. There was no shade. After having been so long without food (15 hours) everyone lay around limp and sweating and unable to sleep for the flies. [...]

[...] We were all looking forward to the cool evening and a long night's sleep when an order came from the 30th Brigade HQ to go up to the line at once. Everyone felt about done in for want of sleep, and I think the men have not been eating enough food. I don't blame them as the 'bully' was simply <u>awful</u>. It pours out of the tin in a greasy mess and has no taste whatever. A lot of the small round biscuits are weevilly, but the big ones are all right but very hard. When we had climbed up onto the ridge and felt the sea breeze and saw the magnificent view we bucked up wonderfully and were like different men. 'Stuffer' Byrne (Quartermaster) managed to get us up some more food, and we had the first fine meal for over a week. They were using small mules led by Indians to carry up rations and PACKHALS[22] of water. Thompson delighted some of them by stopping and chatting in their own lingo.

The KIRETCH TEPE SIRT, or KTS Ridge for short, is very steep-to along the sea, the highest point being 210 metres or 685 feet. It is covered with thick prickly scrub, in some places shoulder high, and it is heavily scored with little rivulets which run down in wet weather. The top of the range is very rocky and all along the backbone there is a peculiar outcrop of rock sloping seawards which affords a certain amount of shelter. There is a most striking view of the European coast and the islands of SAMOTHRAKI and THASOS, and the sunset was most beautiful. [...]

---

22  A leather water-carrier.

## Saturday, 14 August 1915. KTS Ridge

Fighting strength today fifteen officers 463 OR

Had a grand sleep from 20.30 last night till 03.00 this morning – the first real sleep since landing. It was astonishing to find the night actually chilly up here. We stood to arms at 03.00 but everything was quiet except for occasional shots. There was a most beautiful sunrise. What a lot one misses at home. I had an early breakfast of some cocoa and a biscuit, and then 08.00 a regular feed consisting of sardines, bully beef, biscuits and marmalade all of which one fellow mixed together. We had one of our men bayoneted during the night by a sentry through not answering the challenge. I noticed this extraordinary reluctance to answer when we were at home, and always warned the men of what would happen. I think it must be an Irish failing as I never noticed it anywhere else. We received during the morning from Major General Hammersley a gratifying message thanking us for 'the invaluable help rendered to him by the 6th R. Dub. Fus. while attached to the 11th Division.' We were busy during the day strengthening the position which appears to me to be rather peculiar. The line runs across the foothills fronting the Suvla plain, and then mounts up to the top of the KTS Ridge about halfway along. It then runs forward along the top for a few hundred yards, and at a point marked on the ANAFARTA SAGIR 1:20.000 map with a bench mark, it turns at right angles and runs down steeply to the sea. Therefore the centre part of the line is enfiladed by fire from the high ground near EJELMER BAY, where the Turks have some small guns. The rocks on the top of the ridge, however, give a fair amount of cover.

There was great excitement during the afternoon as some letters arrived up – the first we have had since leaving home on the 10th July. I got several [...]. I got a badly needed jacket from my tailors. I am in rags already from the thorny scrub. [...]

## Sunday, 15 August 1915. KTS Ridge

Had another grand sleep last night until 03.30 and feel as fit as anything after it. Some Australian bushmen have arrived for special sniping stunts, and one of them arrived in our lines having been right behind the Turks. He was a hardy looking case with skin burned the colour of chocolate. We heard today that the submarine E7 often goes up to the sea of Marmara in spite of the defences, and bombards supply trains and ships. What nerves those chaps must have. I wonder if the Turks are short of gun ammunition, as they often get the range of a jolly good target and only fire a couple of rounds of shrapnel over it and then stop. I climbed down to the beach […] and had a ripping bathe. Clothes off for the first time since August 5th. Had a good scrub all over and a change of socks. I got a long drink of water from an angel in the guise of a naval officer in charge of a picquet boat. He offered me some cigarettes but I didn't take any as I have some left. The climb back to the top of the ridge was terrible with the heat and flies and for a while completely took away feeling of freshness of the bathe. We were sniped at a good deal on the way back. About 12.00 orders came to prepare for an attack to the end of the ridge from Jephson's Post, so called after Major JN JEPHSON of the 6th RMF who captured it and held it against all counter attacks.

[…]

We deployed on the left of the RMF in a line from the Post down to the sea. The plan was to do a right wheel sweeping up our left so as to capture the whole crest of the ridge. The 54th Division (Major General FS INGLEFIELD) was on our right and they were to move forward simultaneously to the high ground between KAYAK TEPE and ASHAGI KAPANJA […].

14.00. We were good deal held up by snipers who potted at anyone showing their heads, but we soon established superiority of fire. We had a good many hit in the early stage of the attack. Captain Lennon A Company was hit in the arm. Second Lieutenant Healy had a bullet in the thigh. Second Lieutenant Moloney[23] […] had a scarified scalp. It seemed to me a pretty tough proposition to take the ridge including the climb up. The advance was naturally slow owing to the dense scrub and precipitous hill side seamed with gullies, but the men were magnificent, and they walked up the hill through the scrub with fixed bayonets and in open order.

17.55. When about 50 yards from the top we charged and reaching the top drove out the Turks with the bayonet sending them rushing down the other side. WR Richards killed here, and Captain Preston badly wounded. Tremendous cheers from all the troops whose blood

---

23  Michael Moloney, born in 1893 in Derrygareen, Co. Cork, volunteered in Oct 1914 and applied for a commission, his initial service being with the 6th RDF. He was taken prisoner on 8 Dec 1915 and served the rest of the war as a prisoner of the Bulgarians, until being repatriated in Feb 1919. He ended the war as a Lieutenant. See WO 339/901.

was up, and from the destroyer HMS FOXHOUND which gave great help with her guns all joining in shouting 'well done the "old Toughs"'. It was really a marvellous bit of work by men who were very, very tired and who had been short of sleep, food, and water for the past ten days. A lot of Turks were done in by machine gun fire from the right flank at Jephson's Post where our guns and four belonging to the Naval division were stationed. Ronnie Kennedy was looking really happy and his gun members were all enjoying themselves. There was a trench running round the S[outh] W[est] side of the spur we call KIDNEY HILL in 136-Q and the Turks kept running out of the end it in the open and were downed one after another. I saw three men in white who may have been German officers or Turk Naval men as they appeared to be carrying telescopes. Two of them legged it as hard as they could, hareing [sic] it away down the hillside over boulders and bushes with the bullets kicking up the dust in spurts round their legs; they didn't get far till they were downed and rolled like rabbits. The 3rd chap took things quite coolly and stopped to take a look through his glass. Kennedy himself took one gun over and with his first burst of five did in this chap. The Turks were fairly routed, throwing away rifles and equipment and fairly hooking it. There was such a heavy rifle fire and MG fire that I don't think many got away. About 18.30 when enemy opposition had ceased, the RDF and RMF combined, rushed right to the end of the Ridge [...] where the ground drops steeply about 250 ft. No opposition. Arranged line thus, 7th RMF from the sea to halfway up – 6th RMF from there to near the top. 6th RDF holding the end and back a little along the top of ridge.

19.00. It was getting dark by this time and we were very busy consolidating against counter-attacks. I am sure we will be, as the 54th Division never moved at all. These Terrier divisions seem hopeless; first the 53rd and now the 54th let us down. We sent them messages, and we flagged to them saying we have driven the Turks from their front and Kidney Hill trenches were now empty and now was their chance. I watched them through my glasses and could see individual platoons here and there showing some signs of moving, but in the end nothing was done. We are now facing along the front of the 54th Division with our left sticking out towards the Turks. About 23.00 we were relieved at the end (136-M-4) of the ridge by the 7th RDF, and we moved back 600 yards into support near Jephson's Post [...]. Felt awfully hungry as I had nothing to eat since about 06.00 so I melted a couple of soup squares and had some soup and a biscuit. I think we should not have stopped when we had the Turks on the run; the RMF should have been pushed out past us to the high ground east of us. Very busy night getting up rations, water and ammunition.

[…]

## Monday, 16 August 1915. KTS Ridge

Early in the morning the Turks counterattacked using bombs and I think some kind of trench mortar. Major Harrison 7th RDF killed in a bayonet charge. We have practically no bombs to reply with. I only saw one box sent in reply to requests for some. We went back into the line, but it is a rotten spot as there is no room at the end of the ridge to use many men, and they are shelled at close range as they come up. Poor Billy Richards who was killed instantly yesterday being hit by a piece of shell in the forehead, and Johnny Preston who was hit in the chest and died as he was being carried to the dressing station, were buried to lay side by side on the BROWN PATCH (our 'Rest Camp'), and we put a board over with their names burned into the wood. Bill Whyte was hit in the neck but not very seriously I think. I saw him looking very game but very pale. There were many heavy casualties from the Turk bombs which they lobbed up over the rocks. We couldn't get at them as we had no bombs and if one stretched up to shoot down behind the rocks, they got potted by MGs further back. I saw Fritz Cullen doing great work today; – was actually fielding Turk bombs and hurling them back before they could burst. The Turk seemed to be using about an 8-second fuse. I met Paddy Beard of the 5th Royal Irish Regiment, our Pioneers, who seemed in good form, also George Kidd of the 6th Royal Irish Fusiliers and Captain Scott of the Royal Irish Regiment.

Had terrible trouble with the Company telephone line getting cut. We lost several signallers too and I couldn't get a place for them with proper shelter. D Company bit was the worst. The Turks were enfilading us from the direction of KIDNEY HILL which had not been captured and it was a bullet fired from this direction that wounded Captain Whyte in the back of the shoulder. It became obvious in the evening that we could not go on losing men at the rate we were, to hold the end of the ridge. The rotters in the plain have not advanced at all and we are attacked from both sides. Colonel Cox sent several appreciations of the position to the 30th Brigade and also made suggestions to attack over towards KIDNEY HILL, but got no reply. Finally, he sent me to see General NICOL and explain the position to. I found him (the General) in an awful temper at our previous messages and practically accused us of having the wind up, and for no reason! Afraid I was a bit insubordinate and I invited him to accompany me up to the KNOB to see for himself. He did not go, but questioned me closely, and then held a consultation with the Brigade Major. Finally, about dusk orders were issued that we were to move back to the line we have made, down from JEPHSON'S post. A timetable was arranged with the supporting HMS FOXHOUND to shell the end of the ridge to keep the Turks down while we moved. I had a rotten job going round the companies with the orders and synchronising watches. I thought I would have been blown to bits before I got back. The move was carried out in excellent order, the men carrying back wounded, and all ammunition and spare rifles. I saw Regimental Sergeant-Major Campbell standing on a high rock and shouting out as a guide to the men as they filed back. The destroyer kept belting away at the Knob and we had very little trouble except shrapnel. We had a good many casualties but we got all the wounded safely back. Some of the dead had to be left. Poor old Nesbitt of C Company, one of the best of fellows, was badly hit in the side and while a man was helping him with a field dressing he was hit again and killed and the man wounded.[24] We could not find his body. Corporal E Bryan[25] of the stretcher bearers (our big drummer) remained behind when we withdrew and spent the whole night between the lines searching for Nesbitt's body, but he could not find it. It was a jolly fine attempt. He was promoted Sergeant shortly after. When I was with the General this afternoon, his cook, one of our men called McManus, got a maconachie ration to cook. He had never seen one before, but faithfully followed the notice stuck on the tin 'heat on the fire before serving'. He never thought of putting a hole in it, so presently when there was a good head of steam up it blew to pieces and shot hot meat and vegetables over the Brigade staff who were in the next hole in the ground.

Casualties. seven officers and 62 other ranks today.

## Tuesday, 17 August 1915. KTS Ridge

We are in support of our old HQ on the ridge. Nothing of note occurred, felt very tired. I have been made Adjutant vice Billy Richards, and am

---

24  https://www.cwgc.org/find-war-dead/casualty/689221/nesbitt,-william-charles/ [accessed 19 April 2021].
25  13197 Edward Bryan (WO 372/3/143681).

now like the funny man we used to see when we were children who played all the band instruments at the same time. I am Adjutant, Scout officer, Intelligence officer & signal officer. [...] Several men carrying up water from the beach were sniped at, and the beach is still being shelled. The Navy fellows got a big canvas tank rigged up under the cliffs on the beach below us, and this improved the supply enormously and was not so far away as A Beach. The men are detailed for this fatigue in threes and are allowed a free drink on the beach for their job. DM FRAZER of the MGs of the 7th RDF lost his way last night and was arrested as a Turk by one of our sentries. He was like us all, very dirty, very burned, and very unshaven, and the sentry kept him prisoner ever so long and sat with a bayonet within an inch of his chest! Frazer insisted that I knew him, and at last I was sent for and released him to the great disgust of the sentry who was very proud of his first catch. Yesterday one of our stretcher bearers got a Turk prisoner somewhere, and caused great merriment by marching him along, alternately kicking him behind and shouting 'G'along ower that' and then when the Turk tried to run on, hauling him back by the coat, with 'Hike ower that'. Poor old Johnny Turk looked as if he expected an immediate and unpleasant departure for Gehemma! Our MO[26] Couper had a narrow shave today when a shrapnel bullet hit the stem of his pipe breaking it off and leaving an inch in his teeth, and scorching his lips. He was at some pains to tell all within hearing, what he thought of the Turks, what time he collected the pieces, and repaired them after a fashion with sticky plaster, making the pipe quite serviceable.

---

26 Medical Officer.

# 4

# Gallipoli: Digging In,
# 18 August–October 1915

Late evening on 17 August the 6th Royal Dublin Fusiliers were sent to 'A' Beach for rest. This was a welcome move for Drury who was beginning to suffer from dysentery, and it also provided an opportunity for reinforcements to settle in the battalion, whose strength was now 487 men and just four officers.[1] On 21 August the 10th (Irish) Division was once again sent to the front, at Lala Baba, but only in reserve as the 29th Division and 11th (Northern) Division attacked Scimitar Hill and W Hill. They came under fire but saw no major action.[2] The next six weeks saw them rotating in and out of trenches and attempts to advance in the area ground to a halt. Trench warfare ensued. During this time, Drury was again ill and left the battalion for treatment on 27 August, returning three days later.[3]

As September began, nights were colder, but during the day flies were still a persistent problem.[4] Daytime work was primarily focused on improving the line, but there was also burying of the dead with efforts made to retrieve bodies from No Man's Land.[5] Drury was promoted to Captain and given command of 'B' and 'C' Companies in mid-September.[6] He noted, 'These are very quiet days, and except for the morning and evening "hate" there is hardly any shooting.'[7] Shell

---

1    Diary entries, 18–20 Aug 1915.
2    Diary entry, 21 Aug 1915.
3    Diary entries, 22–30 Aug 1915.
4    Diary entries, 1–2 Sept 1915.
5    Diary entries, 1, 4, 9 and 12 Sept 1915.
6    Diary entry, 14 Sept 1915.
7    Diary entry, 8 Sept 1915.

fire and unexpected encounters with individual Turks provided shocks.[8] Religious services became important as a coping mechanism, along with material comforts from home.[9] Drury noted that sermons were 'but just the simple truths one hears from the cradle, which now seem invested with a new meaning'.[10] Drury noticed how the Anglican and Roman Catholic chaplains got on well and that many Catholic soldiers went to hear the former, just as he had himself visited the latter. He reflected, 'If the two creeds could come together at home as they do here, what a different story there would be.'[11]

The most dangerous situation faced by the 6th Royal Dublin Fusiliers was the result of a misunderstanding. On 27 September, great cheering was heard from British lines and that led to heavy machine gun and rifle fire in response from the Turks. Drury learned later that the cheering had been caused by men hearing news of what was said to be progress at the Battle of Loos and 'When Johnny Turk heard this he thought it meant an attack by us, as he is in the habit of blowing bugles and shouting to ALLAH to help him when he attacks. So the Turk started blazing off as hard as he could.' Drury noted that the result of the 'misunderstanding' was that his battalion lost one officer and fifteen men.[12] That was the 6th Royal Dublin Fusiliers' last action at Gallipoli. News came on 30 September that they were to be withdrawn, initially, it was thought, for another part of the peninsula, but it turned out to be a complete withdrawal.[13] Drury wrote that as the battalion left the shore on lighters, 'Everyone seemed to have a strange feeling almost of regret at leaving Suvla. It's hard to say why, as I didn't love the place at all.'[14]

Allied operations at Gallipoli ultimately came to nothing. In early December, the British cabinet decided to give up on the campaign entirely. This was driven by the entry of Bulgaria into the war alongside the Central Powers, which had two consequences. First, there was now a direct rail route from Germany to Turkey, and so any deficiencies in Ottoman forces in arms and ammunition could more easily be met. Allied forces already bogged down faced the prospect of much

---

8    Diary entries, 14 and 18 Sept 1915.
9    Diary entries, 20–21 Sept 1915.
10   Diary entries, 12 and 19 Sept 1915.
11   Diary entry, 26 Sept 1915.
12   Diary entry, 27 Sept 1915.
13   Diary entry, 30 Sept 1915.
14   Diary entry, 1 Oct 1915.

heavier artillery than before an there was no prospect of any kind of advance. Second, Bulgaria joining the war threatened the position of Britain and France's allies in the Balkans, which meant that it made more sense to move the Gallipoli force to Salonika to take part in action from there.[15]

---

15   Macleod, *Gallipoli*, 64.

# Wednesday 18 August 1915. A Beach

During the evening we got word that we were to go down to A Beach for a rest. The relief was arranged for 16.00 but as the ridge was under shell fire, it was postponed to 20.00. We have now with us our 1st Reinforcement who left us at Mytilene, and have been waiting at Mudros. They consisted of CAPTAIN JM TITTLE,[16] LIEUTENANT CORBET-SINGLETON[17] and 157 N.C.O.s & men. Corbet-Singleton called "Corbo" is a grandson of old Admiral Singleton of Ardee, Co. Louth. [...]

[...] Our Quartermaster Lieutenant R.C. Byrne is magnificent, and not merely efficient, but so thoughtful for everyone's comfort. When we arrived down at A Beach under guidance of one of Byrne's men whom he had sent up for the purpose, we found he had a grand meal and hot tea ready for the troops, and a place arranged for them to sleep. He raised a piece of cold roast beef for the officers, but nothing would induce him to say where he got it. He had all our valises already laid out for us to turn in and have a pyjama sleep.

# Thursday 19 August 1915. A Beach/Karakol Dagh

Had a touch of dysentery the last few days and felt a bit groggy about the knees, but the grand sleep I had from 00.30 to 09.00 this morning mended this. I and Arnold[18] had a bathe in a little cove down near SUVLA POINT, and then a good rub of a rough towel and a change of underclothes, and felt A1 after it. After running up and down the little cove to dry ourselves we found a little notice board facing inland which was a warning from the RE the beach was mined, and it must not be approached! What an escape!

The beaches are a wonderful sight – what gigantic quantities of stuff have been landed since we came ashore. Tons of rations, iron and biscuit; water jars and tanks; next to this, great quantities of oats and flour; in another spot hundreds of cycles, motor cycles and some cars! I don't know what they expect to do with these! There are lots of troops about,

---

16  John Moore Tittle (WO 372/20/42345).
17  Morice Grant Corbet-Singleton (WO 372/18/87194).
18  William John Arnold, Lieutenant in 6th RDF, later transferred to 4th King's African Rifles and ended war as Captain in the regiment's 3rd Battalion. See WO 372/1/120867.

all dug in well, as the beach is shelled every day. During the forenoon we moved up to a safer camp over the lower part of KARAKOL DAGH [...]. There is a grand view of Tenedos, Lemnos and Imbros and the European coast near DEDEAGATCH. We have a good shelter from the sun under some large rocks, and are well up in the breeze. [...] We received very strict orders today about the use and storage of water. [...] The absolute maximum supply possible is now four pints per 24 hours per man on the Ration Strength. No wandering by parties nor by individuals to the beach in search of water is permitted as this would deprive others of their proper ration. Anyone doing so will be arrested and courtmartialled. This ½ gallon is the theoretical allowance as measured at the beaches, but we don't get that amount owing to spilling, leakage and evaporation, and the mules and water bags getting hit by shrapnel. There was rather a high wind blowing at night and there was a heavy shower, but I slept very comfortably as there were no shells nor rifle fire reaching us. I was lucky in having my valise up here to sleep in. Stuffer Byrne makes a joke about the weight of my valise saying that it would take a GS Waggon to carry it. I pacified him by giving him the little ribbed capok fibre mattress out of it.

## Friday 20 August 1915. Karakol Dagh

I slacked in bed till 08.00 and was very busy afterwards with Orderly Room work. Canon MCCLEAN CF held a voluntary C[hurch] of E[ngland] Communion Service on the side of the hill. Colonel Cox, Arnold and self went. It was very impressive and seems to pick everyone up out of the worry of things here, and make them feel at peace for a while. The Canon is a dear fellow, and he and Father Murphy are loved by everyone. There may be other Padres who come up to the line, but I never saw nor heard of any except these two good men. A good many shells screamed over during the service, but everyone was well sheltered. At 16.00 orders came for us to move to a new post [Lala Baba] after dusk. Lieutenants AA Cullen, MG Corbet-Singleton, and DB Gilmore went to hospital sick, also Captain Tittle. Our strength has now dwindled down to four officers and 487 men. When we left the "Alaunia" the strength of the Battalion amounted to 30 officers and 952 men, so that we are now short of our establishment by 26 officers and 485 men.

# Saturday 21 August 1915. Lala Baba

<u>Fighting strength four officers and 469 other ranks</u>

[…]

We marched off after supper last night and had a fine march across the plain by HILL 10 to LALA BABA. Someone I don't know shouted at me from a tent and gave me some apples. Didn't think of asking the good Samaritan his name. When we were resting near Hill 10 very early in the morning, a very heavy Rifle and MG fire broke out among several miles of front. It made a tremendous din, and there seems something menacing and awful about really heavy rifle fire heard from some distance. I don't consider it nearly as bad to be up in it. We arrived at LALA BABA about 06.00 after a long march, and settled down in a gully on the west side […] and beside the sea. There are two batteries of 18lbrs near us firing indirect over the hill. Fine looking lot of men, and don't seem tired. I suppose it's because they don't carry equipment and have horses and mules to carry everything they want. I watched a Colonel of a battalion of yeomanry catching fish by throwing into the sea bombs made out of old milk tins, and then swimming out and catching the fish stunned by the explosion under water. There was great dashing back to the shore when one failed to explode to time. The sea was a wonderful sight as there were thousands of men having a swim, and shells dropping in the water here and there only roused roars of laughter at those who were nearly choked with the spray they threw up. I got a couple of letters this morning and a tin of State Express cigarettes. […]

There is to be a big attack made, so far as I can learn, on a front from SCIMITAR HILL (Hill 70) to the left of ANZAC with three Divisions 11th, 29th and 2nd Mounted Division, including the 29th from Helles. The 10th (Irish) Division is in reserve to the other three and the 30th Brigade in reserve to the 10th (Irish) Division. I don't know where the 31st Brigade is but I think they must be on our left. We met our 1st Battalion during the morning. They have only one of the original officers left and they have got through over 3,000 men since they landed at Helles. […] The Navy commenced a tremendous bombardment about 13.00. There were big monitors with 14.2″ guns also the Swiftsure, Chatham, Canopus and Triumph (fitted with big derricks for some purpose) all firing hard with 6″ and 9″ guns and occasionally 12″ guns. The noise was perfectly ear-splitting as the ships were close in shore, and were firing just over our heads. There was a queer mist or fog over the ground and

I don't know how they can see where they are shooting. I suppose they had observation posts ashore and some way of signalling hits or misses. Some of the guns make magnificent smoke rings when they are fired, which circle up in the still air for hundreds of feet. We did not move off till about 17.00 and then we went with Battalions in artillery formation and moving in Echelon. It was very hard to keep direction with the fog and dust of shells falling. We got a heavy shelling most of the way up, but we did not get it as badly as the RMF who were more in the open away from the trees. Major Aplin[19] was wounded in the foot but is carrying on. General Nicol was walking along at the head of the 7th RDF when a big shell exploded beside them, and hid the General in a cloud of smoke and dust. Some hard case in the 7th sang out 'Thank God there's the ould divil gone at last'. 'Not yet my boy' said the General emerging from the stour without a scratch, and quite amused at the incident. We lost touch with A Company under Lieutenant Arnold who had the Regimental Sergeant-Major with him, and the whole Battalion got a good deal scattered. There seems to be heavy fighting in front, but we have no news of what is going on or how far they have got. A lot of casualties are passing down. Heavy fighting all night with a lot of bombing. [...]

## Sunday 22 August 1915. Kazlak Chair

Stood to arms 03.30. Got no rest. Went searching for A Company and at last found that Arnold had got the men into fairly good trenches, and I told him to stay there till the heavy shelling had stopped. I took one of his men back with me as a guide. A Company reported in (with Regimental Sergeant-Major Campbell) about 05.00. He has lost about 25 men. We had a good many casualties during the morning although we are 700 yards from the line. My Orderly Room clerk Private CORDIAL was killed this morning beside me while making up returns of casualties for Brigade HQ. Strength today: Ration six officers 458 ORs. Fighting four officers – 429 ORs. The officers now are Colonel Cox, Lieutenant Drury, Lieutenant Kennedy, Lieutenant Arnold and Lieutenant Quartermaster Byrne, Lieutenant Couper RAMC. We seem to have made some progress during the night, but not much, as we obviously have not got onto the hills, and the casualties have been fearfully heavy. I don't know where the naval shells were going to, for the trenches around here show no

---

19  Henry Aplin (WO 372/1/102665).

signs of being shelled at all. The country about here is very flat and too close to see through. It seems to have been cultivated and there are a good many footpaths here & there. At 18.30 we received orders to move up to the front line [...].

[...]

We started relieving units of the 11th DIVISION 34th Brigade at 19.30 along the AZMAK DERE between KAZLAR CHAIR and KAVAKLAR with SUSAK KUYU about 1,000 yards in front of us. There was a fearful muddle when we came up to relieve. There seemed seven or eight battalions represented, all jumbled together. They had no system and didn't have any information for us nor any guides, and their whole object seemed to get out somehow as quickly as they could. There didn't seem to be any Turks about although we pushed out sentries well in front. The relief was not completed till nearly midnight, and we were heartily glad to see the last of the blighters.

## Monday 23 August 1915. Azmak Dere

Stood to arms 3.30. No sleep. Very busy since the relief was completed posting sentries & listening posts etc. and arranging improvements. It is difficult to understand the position we are in, as we don't seem nearly enough forward to join with the ANZAC left. It seems that in general terms the big attack was a failure as it did not secure the high ground. There seems a big gap in the line where we are, and I could see what I believe to be a company of the Gurkhas digging in quite close to SUSAK KUYU. If so, they are right in the air. During the morning we got a few shells from a 4.5″ Howitzer battery on the ANZAC front who don't know where we are I suppose. During the day I went along to our right past a lot of people who seemed to be in support and doing nothing in particular. The Herts Yeomanry, Middlesex Yeomanry and some MG sections. I then struck the 5th Brigade Australians, New Zealanders, and Gurkhas. I had a long chat with General HV COX who was very kind and gave me a drink and some cigarettes, and a candle. There were no arrangements made by the 11th DIVISION for cross communication and he was very glad to get definite information on the 1:20.000 map of our positions. His left is held by the 5th Gurkhas and is practically in the air [...]. Our nearest position to his left is [...] at KAZLAR CHAIR. Our Headquarters are at the three poplar trees. The gap is going to be filled by establishing two Australian posts of 100 men each [...]. Each would dig to their right and join up with the Gurkhas. Did some Orderly Room work during the afternoon and had a rest for a couple of hours, having had no sleep for three nights. Part of our line runs through the AZMAK DERE riverbed and we get some shelter under the banks. Some parts of the line are so badly sited that there is no field of fire and there is a footpath sunk below the level of the rest of the ground, and bordered on each side by a low bank with bushes growing on the top. We have to keep this patrolled as it would be a useful collecting point for the Turks. The ground about here is only a few feet above sea level, less than ten metres, and looks very dry, but we dug into water at four feet down when making trenches. Couper condemned it for drinking, but we are able to have a good wash in fresh water for a change. However, owing to the high wind and the awful dust from the Azmake Dere, I was nearly as dirty as before. The flies round here are even worse than before. It is impossible to keep them off food, and one never gets a moment's peace throughout the day. It is impossible to rest as they crawl all over your face, neck, hands & knees and sting and bite till one is driven frantic. We got one or two letters today, older than those we got at LALA BABA on the 21st. I had a good sleep at night, as there was no attack, only going round about 01.00 for an hour or so, and I did not wake the Colonel [Cox] but let him sleep on till "stand-to".

## Tuesday 24 August 1915. Azmak Dere

Still very high wind and very dusty, thick clouds of dust blowing over us continually. We are still digging hard at a communicating trench from the AZMAK DERE to the line made by the 7th South Staffords (33rd Brigade 11th DIVISION). Signallers very busy mending telephone wires. I met a Gurkha signaller today heading down over some brigade wires, and noticed some queer looking thing hanging from his neck which looked like a lot of figs on a string. I made signs to know what they were and he astounded me by grinning broadly and exclaiming excitedly "Turk! Turk!" and at the same time making a sign of cutting off an ear. It seems that every time he killed a Turk he cut off one of his ears, and dried it in a fire and hung it round his neck to show his prowess. He showed me his KUKRI and it had an edge like a razor. During the afternoon the following order [...] arrived.

[...]

You are directed to take over the trenches dug by [8th] NORTH-UMBERLAND FUS[ILIERS] [...] connecting KAZLAR CHAIR with the Australian Post No 2 West of SUSAK KUYU after dusk tonight. The trenches must be improved and connected up.

[...]

When we moved up we found practically no trenches at all. Just a few holes here and there [...]. We had to re-site a lot and work out the ground, the idea being to get every man under cover the first night, and then connect up throughout. The Colonel [Cox] & I and Kennedy got nearly done in by MG fire while we were working out of the line of the trenches. Two guns spotted us and dust was flying from under our feet and bullets whizzing past our ears. We had holes in our clothes, and Colonel Cox had his glasses hit. Kennedy had one heel knocked off his boot and I had a hole through my helmet and in my water bottle. There was a full moon at night but we were not troubled much, as the Turks were hard at work too. We have no wire so we tried a scheme of stakes driven into the ground and pointed at the top, to prevent our being rushed. We got down fairly well during the night but are not connected with the Australians. Of course, we have sentry groups in the gap between us and No 2 Post near the three poplars. Tonight I had a man hit beside me. He was Private Fairclough of the Pioneers, and I was standing beside him pointing out a place to make for HQ when he suddenly sank down at my feet. He was hit through the body from side to side, and as I was standing shoulder to shoulder with him I can't imagine how I was not hit. He died almost at once. I could hardly see the bullet marks, only two little blue spots.

We had a visit tonight from General PA KENNA VC, DSO[20] and I showed him all over our positions. He agreed with our layout of the line and made some useful suggestions. He doesn't seem afraid of the front line like many of the other Generals. [...]

---

20  Brigadier General Paul Aloysius Kenna, 1862–1915, killed in action at Gallipoli on 30 Aug aged 53. He had won the VC at Omdurman in 1898. See https://www.cwgc.org/find-war-dead/casualty/606875/kenna,-paul-aloysius/ and https://livesofthefirstworldwar.iwm.org.uk/lifestory/4134962 [accessed 9 July 2020].

# Wednesday 25 August 1915. Susak Kuyu

Men all very weary, but have to keep digging. They won't call a spade a spade after this, but a damned torture instrument. I feel fit to drop for want of sleep and my inside has gone wrong again, confound it. We had a very heavy dose of shrapnel over during the morning and had a good many casualties. Canon McClean and Father Murphy came round about 13.00 and insisted on going round and chatting to the men in spite of the risk. I don't know what we would do if anything happened [to] either of them. They are the only two Padres we ever see near the line and the men are delighted to see them. General NICOL 30th Brigade was round twice today with Villiers-Stuart[21] (Brigade Major). He is very anxious about the gap in the line in case of a Turk attack, but congratulated all on the amount of work done. He's a great old chap, and his energy is amazing considering that he must be nearly 60 years old. He is always nosing about and won't be satisfied until he sees every inch of the line himself. We let the men rest for a few hours during the hottest part of the day as there was no dust cloud to cover their movements. [...] The Base people are the limit! I got a chit today asking how many Presbyterians we have in the Battalion! I could tell them how many B[lood]y fools there are at the base who have nothing else to do but ask silly questions.

# Thursday 26 August 1915. Susak Kuyu

There was heavy bombing and rifle fire at 02.20 near No 2 Post. Got everyone standing to, and presently went along to the Australians and found that a few of their men without knowledge or permission of their officers or NCOs had raided the bomb store, and had gone out on the quiet to have a little sport with the Turk. Of course, Johnny thought an attack in force was coming and started loosing off. The only result of the stunt is that we have had several casualties among men working in the open, who could have been under cover if notice had been given. Stood to arms again at 03.45 and stood down at 05.30 and everything quiet. We have now joined up with the Australian No 2 Post [...] and they are up to No 1 Post on their right and on to SUSAK KUYU. These Australians struck me as rather indifferent soldiers, and the officer I spoke

---

21  Probably Patrick Villiers-Stuart, formerly Royal Fusiliers. *Monthly Army List*, Nov 1915, col. 53.

to didn't know anything about his front or where the line ran or who was on his right! His trenches were far too deep and almost impossible to get out of. They would be regular death traps if the Turk got on with the bayonet. Paddy Cox gave them a lecture! I see today by IX Corps orders that Lieutenant General The Hon. Julian H. Byng[22] has taken over command of the Corps vice Sir F. Stopford – and a good job too!

## Friday 27 August 1915. Susak Kuyu/B Beach

Still feeling beastly rotten. Hope to goodness I'm not going to crook up. There's nobody to do anything, even the Colonel [Cox] sleeps with his head on the fire step like everyone else. We had a good deal of shrapnel and high explosive over during the morning, and it looks as if the Turk had got some fresh supplies, he is using so much. […]

[…]

[…] I had been feeling very ill all day and finally Couper insisted I must go down to the 31st Ambulance for a day or two to rest, or else I might crook up altogether. The Colonel agreed too and said there wouldn't be much to do as we would soon be relieved. So I went down with the ration party at night, feeling very sticky. When I arrived I found the ambulance […] not more than 25 yards from the sea and ¼ mile from C Beach where we landed. Lay down on a stretcher – most uncomfortable, and found the sand better. Was fed on arrowroot! Doesn't seem much use for a growing lad, but I really didn't want anything at all. The air was lovely and fresh and everything nice and quiet. […] Slept very soundly as I was very tired.

## Saturday 28 August 1915. B Beach

Feeling very rotten and constantly having to get up. The fleet are doing a heavy shoot at neighbourhood of Hill 60.

---

22  General Julian Byng, later Field Marshal and 1st Viscount, 1862–1935 (*The Times*, 7 June 1935, p. 9).

## Sunday 29 August 1915. B Beach

Feeling a bit better today. I seem to have slept most of the time since I arrived here. Canon McClean and Father Murphy held services during the morning. About dinner time a Taube flew over and dropped two bombs. One landed in the water on the beach and the other fell in the middle of a group of orderlies at the cook house, killing two and wounding 8. I was lying only about twenty feet away and a lot of burning hot particles of sand fell on me making little blisters all over my arms and knees. During the night Brigadier General Kenna VC 21st Lancers was brought in very badly wounded, and he died about 02.30.

## Monday 30 August 1915. B Beach

Decided to get back to the Battalion this evening, as I heard they had gone into line again. I had a long chat with Canon McClean. He & Father Murphy live in an old horse ambulance with their beds on the seat along each side. They have the entrance decorated with trophies like shell cases, old rifles & bayonets. I heard from one of our men who came down sick that the battalion had shifted up to the left of the 6th Royal Munster Fusiliers towards Hill 50. Had a very long tiring walk up from the beach and arrived about 22.00 to find the relief still going on. Lay down about 02.45 feeling dead beat.

During the day General Kenna VC was buried out in the open. It seems as if the Turks noticed what was going on as they never fired a single round in that direction, although there were a great many people present, and most of the Generals in this sector were there. A very enticing target which Johnny Turk was too decent to take advantage of. Brigadier General Longford KP[23] was also killed near Scimitar Hill.

## Wednesday 1 September 1915. Green Hill

All was quiet again at stand to at 04.00. They sent us up from somewhere an acetylene searchlight which we have mounted up at the highest point

---

23  Thomas Pakenham, 5th Earl of Longford, born 1864 in Dublin, killed in action on 21 Aug 1915, aged 50. See https://www.cwgc.org/find-war-dead/casualty/602354/pakenham,-thomas/ [accessed 19 April 2021].

of our line near Hill 50. We also got an issue of one periscope per platoon – a fairly heavy zinc affair. Another weight for Tommy's back! The flies are worse, if possible, than ever before and are enough to drive one out of one's senses. They have got so vicious that no amount of waving handkerchiefs will keep them off. They look like ordinary house flies but instead of a sucker they are armed with a long probe which they stick down 1/8 inch through the pores of the skin. Busy all day improving the parapet and removing the useless loopholed arrangement made by the other crowd. In many places it had been made so high that a man would want to be 6'6" high to be able to shoot over it. Some of these people don't use common sense. […]

[…]

[…] We have been having a good many men hit when out burying at night, but thank goodness we have the job nearly done – it's not pleasant. There has been one persistent sniper the last few days that we can't find. He has hit several men including a stretcher bearer whose leg was hit and both bones badly smashed up. We have sprayed with MG fire all the trees within range and every spot we can think of and we can't spot the brute.

## Thursday 2 September 1915. Green Hill

The nights are getting very chilly although the heat of the sun is as great as ever. Byrne got us up some blankets and they are very welcome at night. Some of the men off duty during the day wrap themselves up completely to keep off the flies, with the result that they are streaming with perspiration as if in a Turkish bath. […]

## Saturday 4 September 1915. Green Hill

Usual sort of day, trying to strengthen and improve the line. There was not much gun fire, but a lot of sniping from positions we can't locate. The Turks keep themselves very close, and we don't often get a shot at them. We got word that we were to be ready at 17.30 for relief by the Bucks Yeomanry 2nd Mounted Division but later the hour was changed to 21.30 as they had to cross the open and must do so in the dark. We tried to get into touch with them to tell them the order to arrive in, but we couldn't get them. These terriers are a shocking lot and don't seem like soldiers at all. They arrived all mixed up anyway and the only idea they had was to get into the line, without any regard for the need for having companies and platoons together. These fellows arrived straggling along in any order, and our company and platoon guides were no use to them. Every man was barging along with a big bundle of sticks or branches of trees for firewood slung across his back. These were often so long that they stuck across the trench and block[ed] everyone behind. Instead of keeping silent they were shouting to their pals to keep places for them, and some even sat down in groups between the traverses and began to feed. We couldn't get them to space out properly and had to leave them so. Their officers seemed as bad and didn't seem to take any particular interest when we gave them all the information we could about the front and work in hand. We did not get away till after midnight. I can't imagine why the officers of these terrier battalions are so bad. They must have had plenty of training, but they don't show the most elementary knowledge.

## Wednesday 8 September 1915. Ali Bey Chesme

These are very quiet days, and except for the morning and evening 'hate' there is hardly any shooting. We hardly fire 100 rounds of SAA per day I think. Once or twice we heard the Turks commence shouting Allah! Allah! Allah! and making a rhythmic noise as if thumping the butts of their rifles on the ground. A few got leisurely out of their trenches as if to attack but a few cunningly laid bursts of MG fire sent them scuttling back some of them screaming with pain. We indented on the Royal Engineers the other day for a few thousand sandbags & today were informed that 500 was the most we could have. They won't go far. They have all been used to make comfortable houses for the beach wallahs.

## Thursday 9 September 1915 and
## Friday 10 September 1915. Ali Bey Chesme

Busy improving the line, and making MG emplacements. At last we have got a decent supply of wire up including French 'crinoline' wire. We have done a lot of work and the line here is getting quite strong. The men are benefiting enormously by the change to the higher and drier ground, and they are getting more sleep. The food is A1 too, but we get far too much rice and have not enough water or firing to cook it properly. The Colonel

[Cox] made representations about it to the base and asking for it to be reduced and some extra tea issued in lieu, but it could not be done. We have so much rice that we could not use, that some of the bags were used for No 2 MG emplacement on the left near SULAJIK. The place looked as if a dozen weddings had taken place after a few HE shells had hit the place. Had to send an escort for 12098 Private [Charles] Cooney who was arrested on the beach by the Assistant Provost Marshal 10th (Irish) Division. He has been there for three weeks. We have been having great difficulties since the landing in carrying on the signal office and Orderly Room for want of light. We are supposed to get candles but have had hardly any. Also stationery for writing orders and returns practically ran out. […]

I have a little baby tortoise which is only about the size of a penny. He feeds on bits of grass and green leaves. He is a funny little chap with most deliberate movements, and is about the only young thing I have seen which has no inclination to run and fling itself about. […]

## Saturday 11 September 1915. Ali Bey Chesme

[…]

Canon McClean and Father Murphy arrived up in the evening to arrange services for tomorrow. They brought up several loaves of bread which they had begged from a hospital ship in the bay. They are great sports and keep telling yarns against one another, each one saying he hates coming up to the line, but does so to keep the other from getting into mischief. I have recently been kept awake when I lay down, by pains in my back and Couper astonished me by telling me it was lumbago! Fancy that now! I tore a strip off my blanket and use it as a body belt with a great improvement. I have a fig tree just over my shelter and I have been able to get some figs off it after dark, but they are too sweet to eat many of them.

## Sunday 12 September 1915. Ali Bey Chesme

Canon McClean had a C[hurch] of E[ngland] Service at 09.00. It is very hard to shelter him from view on account of his white surplice. There is nothing much doing except improvement of the line, and getting up more wire. We have heard nothing yet of any move forward.

These last few nights I have been going out and creeping around in no man's land to see if I can find any trace of any of our fellows who are reported missing on the 9th August. I haven't found any up to the present, and I'm afraid the scrub fires got some of them. But I think most of them were too far on, probably behind the present Turk line, as I could find practically no rifles nor equipment. I had several amusing encounters with Turks out on patrol, who always seem to go out singly. I was close up to the Turk front trench and saw one between me and our line. He was slinking slowly along with bent back and I only spotted him by the glint of his bayonet. If I fired at him I would have got done in myself by fire from the Turk line, so I threw a pebble at him and I nearly burst out laughing to see him jump and then sprint away cursing. The Turk trenches are here between 400 and 500 yards from ours. They are very cleverly hidden, and some of them are much nearer than we thought they were, so I have marked in most of them on a map to send to the gunners. I got up into a big tree opposite D Company before dawn this morning and had a good look around before it was fully daylight. Noticed two of our MG posts looking far too conspicuous. [...]

[...]

## Tuesday 14 September 1915. Ali Bey Chesme

Had a great sleep till 10.00 when I was waked by the heat of the sun. Was appointed Adjutant from 15th August vice Captain WR Richards killed, also promoted Captain and put in command of B and C companies. [...] I had a narrow shave today at Brigade HQ. Webb,[24] Goodland[25] and I were leaning over a map on a small table when the fuse of an AA shell buzzed down through the canvas shelter, right through the map on the table and buried itself in the ground between our feet, without touching anyone. [...]

---

24  Webb was a Lieutenant in the Royal Engineers. See WO 95/4836: 30th Brigade HQ, 5 Oct 1915. He was possibly ME Webb (WO 372/24/64625), but his personal record has not survived in WO 339 or WO 374.

25  Captain Herbert Thomas Goodland (1874–1956), of the Royal Munster Fusiliers, serving on the Staff of 30th Brigade, later Lieutenant Colonel. He was Deputy Controller of the Imperial War Graves Commission in 1919–28. See WO 339/10632.

## Saturday 18 September 1915. Ali Bey Chesme

Strength today eight officers 368 other ranks.

Today I took a walk with Ronnie Kennedy starting at ALI BEY CHESME and going over all the ground of our advance on the 9th August. The place looks so different now from what it did on that never to be forgotten morning. Then it was all thick scrub and wiry grass and no tracks anywhere, but now it is as bare as your hand, and the scrub all burned off, and there are reserve and rest trenches dug all over the place. One of our men got a rare fright this morning. He was scrounging round for some dry sticks for a fire, and when leaning over a bank it gave way and he landed down right on the top of a Turk who was hiding underneath. Our fellow recovered from his astonishment first and secured the blighter who must have been secreted behind our lines since 9th August. Whether he has been responsible for any of our casualties it's impossible to say.

[…]

About 17.00 the Turks commenced a heavy bombardment of the whole line from SULAJIK to JEPHSON'S POST on the KTS Ridge. There seemed to be many more batteries than we have noticed before. This shell fire lasted for exactly five minutes and then it stopped suddenly and heavy MG fire and rifle fire broke out along the line. No attack was made so far as I could see with the telescope and in half an hour all was quiet again. We heard later that in some places the Turks had left their trenches in a half-hearted way and then went back again. They had a lot of casualties.

## Sunday 19 September 1915. Ali Bey Chesme

Canon McClean held a C[hurch] of E[ngland] service. Had three hymns and a short but very effective Address. None of those deep discourses one hears in Sermons at home, but just the simple truths one hears from the cradle, which now seem invested with a new meaning. 'Stuffer' Byrne often comes up at night with the ration party and stays and chats for a while. His visits do us an amazing lot of good. He has an unlimited number of yarns which he tells in a way peculiarly his own, and which seem to bear repetition as often as he likes. He keeps us in roars of laughter and it is like a play to see the expressions on his face and the movement of his hands. He managed to get the navy to undertake the washing of all the underclothes of the Battalion which is a great boon.

## Monday 20 September 1915. Ali Bey Chesme

[...]

I received a note via the 5th Royal Inniskilling Fusiliers from William Lethem of Ferry Road, Edinburgh, saying he had arrived in Gallipoli and been attached to the 31st Ambulance. I got to leave to walk down C Beach in the afternoon and was very glad to stretch my legs. I felt quite tired when I got down. Very glad to see him again and hear all the news. We had a good tea and a bathe. He brought me a parcel from Mrs Lethem with biscuits, Edinburgh rock and chocolate. So kind of her to think of it. Surprising how one craves for sweet things. [...]

## Tuesday 21 September 1915. Ali Bey Chesme

Strength today eight officers and 362 ORs. We moved up into the line again to the same place and relieved the 7th RDF at 17.00. We found the 9th Worcestershire Regiment on the left and the 6th Royal Munster Fusiliers on the right. We drew two watercarts from Chocolate Hill today, so will be able to have a more regular and a cleaner water supply. I think it would be quite possible to have cookers up here and keep them down behind the thick scrub below COLLEGE GREEN. We started work by marking out a new fire trench in a better position and a good deal further out. It starts from the point where D Company's fire trench and support trench join and runs across the front in a slight bow to the forward end of the sap near A Company's right. The 6th Royal Munster Fusiliers will carry it on from here. Captain WH Whyte turned up in the afternoon from Lemnos looking fit and none the worse of his wound. While in hospital somebody stole both object lenses out of his field glasses, making them useless, and he did not discover it till he got back to us. I suppose some RAMC orderly was short of matches. When we left Basingstoke we had ordered and paid for a small box of supplies to be sent to the mess each week, and some whiskey. The first consignment arrived tonight. Screwdrivers never seemed to work so slowly! At last the case was opened and a cork whipped out of one of the bottles and some of the contents poured into a mug. The smell seemed queer and when we examined it we found the stuff was salt water! Every one of the bottles had been emptied and filled with sea water. We then examined the box of provisions and found it cleared and filled with tins of bully beef. I wish I could catch the culprit. I think we could almost have forgiven him if he had put stones into the box, but, bully beef ...!!

## Sunday 26 September 1915. Ali Bey Chesme

A quiet night and no interruption to the work. Took another prowl round in front and found that the Turks had commenced a new trench 50 yards in advance of their old one. It is very well hidden and they must have carried away all the earth out of it as none is to be seen. The extra men we now have available make it much easier to arrange a rest for the men and things are going much more regularly now with proper trench routine. Canon McClean held a service at 10.30 in the little gully behind our HQ. I notice that many R[oman] C[atholic]s go to hear him as well as the C[hurch] of E[ngland] men, and I have been often to hear Father Murphy. If the two creeds could come together at home as they do here, what a different story there would be. These two padres are quite different yet when they come together they seem complementary to one another. Of course, Father Murphy (Captain CF No 2) is a Regular and it is his job to be up here, but the dear old Canon just does it because he thinks he ought to. He is really too old for this climate and rough life, and we notice a considerable change in him since he came out, but he is as cheery as ever, and loves going along the line and chatting to the men. I hear he goes off to the hospital ships and spins such terrible yarns about the hardships of the men that he seldom, if ever, goes away empty handed! [...]

[...]

## Monday 27 September 1915. Ali Bey Chesme

[...]

The day was quite quiet until about 19.00 when just as we were going to have something to eat, a great burst of cheering started away on our right somewhere about GREEN HILL (Hill 53). It was immediately followed by tremendous rifle and MG fire which opened rapidly all along the line past us and away to the left. We rushed up into the front trench and found everyone blazing away like mad, and the Turks doing the same. The artillery then commenced on both sides and our Naval guns started plastering HILL 70 with heavy stuff, the shells passing just over our heads. The din was terrific and the star shells and VERY lights lit up the whole place. I had to rush back to the phone as the Brigade kept ringing me up to know what was happening. I could get no news from the Company HQ as the phone wires were all 'dis.' [disconnected] in spite of laddering and duplicate lines. I replied that I didn't think any attack had been made yet. Messages came from 19.15 from D Company for more ammunition. By 19.40 all the Regimental reserve had been sent into the line and more asked for from Brigade who said they would not send any. At 19.50 reported to Brigade that the Turks were not attacking us although they were keeping up a tremendous fire, and again asking for more ammunition. They replied, 'am sending one company from the 7th RDF to you'. These came up and waited in reserve under cover in DUBLIN ROAD, ready to support if required. However, we did not want them. I informed Colonel Cox that the Brigade would not send up any ammunition, and he ordered me to send Jock Campbell (Regimental Sergeant-Major) and a party to Brigade with orders to bring up 50 boxes SAA and this eventually arrived. In the meantime the firing gradually died down and by 21.00 all was as quiet as usual. Poor Ronnie Kennedy came down wounded in the lower part of the neck between the shoulders. He was unable to move and seemed paralysed. He seemed quite cheery and chatted with me for a while. He was just in time to see Mediterranean Expeditionary Force list No 29 confirming his promotion to Captain. We had fifteen men hit one being killed, and it seems extraordinary that so few were hit considering the heavy firing and shelling. We got through about 35,000 rounds of SAA altogether!

We heard later that the cause of the trouble was the following wire from 'K[itchener] of K[hartoum]' copies of which were sent round during the evening. 'Things are going well in France. 23,000 prisoners, more than 40 guns up to the present and I hope more to come. This ought to have a good effect in the East.' This was the Battle of LOOS. This message was received by the Lovat's Scouts and was read out to the men in the front line. They had a bagpipe up in the trenches with them and when they heard the news they started cheering and playing the pipes up and down the front trenches. When Johnny Turk heard this he thought it meant an attack by us, as he is in the habit of blowing bugles and shouting to

ALLAH to help him when he attacks. So the Turk started blazing off as hard as he could. The Scouts hearing this thought the Turk was attacking them, and they dropped the pipes and commenced issue back. This sort of thing is most infectious and it spread rapidly along the line, and the absence of decent officers and NCOs made it difficult to stop it. Our wiring parties and covering patrols were all out while this was going on and so were the Worcester men. They all managed to get cover in holes and folds in the ground and none of them was hit. One man got the wind up and came belting back in A Company's line, and was then lucky he wasn't either shot or bayoneted as he came in. They recognised him in time however. So the nett result of a misunderstanding was that we lost one officer and fifteen men.

## Thursday 30 September 1915. Ali Bey Chesme

Message came in early that we were to be relieved tonight. The Colonel [Cox] was over at Brigade HQ early and when he returned he told me privately and I was not to repeat it, that we were going to be relieved tonight by the 5th Wiltshires 13th Division 40th Brigade and were going to leave SUVLA and go to MUDROS. He believed we were going to make a landing somewhere else, but was not sure. What Ho! […]

[…]

We were to have been relieved by the Wilts at 19.30 and we had all the Company and platoon guides ready but we waited for hours and there was no sign of them. I had previously sent them a chit showing the order in which they should arrive and where they would meet our guides to show them the beginning of our in-going communication trenches. Bill Whyte and I walked up and down College Green for hours, and Brigade could tell us nothing about the cause of delay.

## Friday 1 October 1915. Lala Baba

The Wiltshires did not arrive till nearly 04.00. They came from a bit of the line away on the left, and could not leave until they were relieved, and then they lost their way in the fog. General Nicol was in a ferment, because we couldn't leave till properly relieved, and if we did not get away in time to reach LALA BABA before daylight we would have to wait till the next night or else be shelled to blazes going down by daylight. We warned all the men that there would be no halts once we moved off until under cover at the beach and that a fast pace would be set. We finally got the companies out one by one and assembled in the open space near Brigade HQ and we moved off at 04.45. There was a heavy mist on the ground but we knew that the sun would melt it away but we chanced it lasting long enough. Such a march! The men were staggering about all over the place not having done any walking for so long. I was trying to urge on wretched fellows with every argument I could think of, when all the time I was feeling as bad myself. The sun began to show before we were halfway to LALA BABA but the mist still remained thick although we could see it slowly getting thinner. We had our MGs in the rear and one of the men carrying the gun was so exhausted that he dropped down unable to go on. The old brick of a General [Nicol], who was following behind with the Brigade Major [Villiers-Stuart], himself shouldered the gun, and Villiers-Stuart helped the man by carrying his equipment, and they carried them the whole way. Shortly after this, when the mist showed signs of departing altogether we decided not to march in fours any further, but to let everyone go as fast as ever he could. We were all bedecked with rifles and packs and even the Colonel [Cox] was carrying two rifles of men who were done up. He looked very tired and was in great anxiety, but kept as cheery as ever urging on stragglers. We got the last man over the crest of LALA BABA at 06.00 and only just in time, as the breeze rolled away the mist just as we got to cover, and I could distinctly see our old spot we had just left. Stuffer Byrne as usual rose to the occasion and had a good meal for everyone, & then we just lay down where we were and rested. There was a cruiser, the *Thetis* I think, shelling the Turk communication trenches at ANZAC and was making wonderful shooting. Six guns on a broadside going slap into the trench at evenly spaced intervals. Then she would turn round and let fly another six guns a little higher up the trough. She was combing out the trench properly.

[…]

The Colonel and four companies embarked at 19.30 on 'B' lighter and I followed on 'C' lighter with the Regimental baggage and 70 details, at 20.30. There was a good deal of delay in sailing away from the pier, and we did not move off till 22.30. Stuffer Byrne most amusing, and pretending to be scared out of his wits when he found he was sitting on a box of bombs. We were on one of the 'beetles' which were used for the landing, and we puffed about for ages in the dark before we could find the steamer we were to sail on. Finally we came alongside the 'OSMANIEH' and got the baggage on board. The beaches were a marvellous sight when seen from the sea by night. From up in the line, absolutely nothing was to be seen, but from the sea the whole place was a blaze of lights like a town, shining out from dug-outs and shelters and the openings of tents facing seawards. Everyone seemed to have a strange feeling almost of regret at leaving Suvla. It's hard to say why, as I didn't love the place at all.

And so we sailed away from Gallipoli on a Friday which has always been our day for moving, and ended our first spasm.

5

# The Serbian Front and the Battle of Kosturino, October–December 1915

The 6th Royal Dublin Fusiliers arrived in Mudros Bay on 2 October 1915 and spent a few days there until it became clear that they would be deployed to Salonika[1] to fight the Bulgarian forces who were attacking Serbian territory. After being courted by both the Allies and the Central Powers through 1915, it became apparent in September 1915 that Bulgaria would soon join the war on the side of the latter. Serbia had repelled Austro-Hungarian attacks in the early months of war, but by the autumn of 1915 they were facing a stronger combination of forces. Germany and Austria-Hungary launched an assault against Serbia on 7 October 1915, and it looked likely that Bulgaria would soon join the offensive, which it did on 14 October. Serbia's army retreated through Montenegro and Albania to Greece, as Serbia was occupied by its enemies. A request from both Serbia and from neutral Greece, which had treaty obligations to Serbia, for allied troops in early October 1915 was met with the dispatch of British and French soldiers from Gallipoli. Initially composed of 13,000 British and 18,000 French, the Salonika force would rise to 300,000 with the allies there until the end of the war. The territory in which they fought was then widely referred to as 'Macedonia' but strictly contained two areas: the territories of northern Greece which used that label and the country now internationally recognised as the 'Republic of North Macedonia'. The latter was ruled as part of Serbia prior to the First World War, and it was there – in what was known as the

---

1   Now Thessaloniki.

'Macedonian Front' – that fighting took place between British/French and Bulgarian forces as the latter continued to pursue the Serbian army in the final months of 1915.[2]

Parts of the 10th (Irish) Division were among the first British forces to arrive in Salonika on 5 October.[3] The 6th Royal Dublin Fusiliers boarded their transport at Mudros that day and were due to leave on 6 October, but their ship became entangled with anti-submarine nets and they did not depart until the evening of the 9 October, arriving at Salonika the next day.[4] Drury reflected, 'I think we will probably get it in the neck, as they [the Bulgarians] are all fresh and ready, while our fellows are worn out and tired. But still I am looking forward to the change, as I want to see a bit more of the map'.[5] On the voyage, Drury had seen Mount Olympus and noted, 'The top was covered with snow which was tinted salmon colour with the morning sun. No wonder the old Greeks thought and wrote such a lot about it.'[6] Landing at Salonika Quay at 10am on 11 October, the battalion marched to their camp at Lembet where they would be under canvas.[7]

On his first visit to Salonika town Drury encountered Greek soldiers whom he said 'seem effeminate and out of condition and are sneaky looking. I wouldn't trust them an inch.'[8] The next day, shopping was possible, and Drury purchased 'some red bunting to make a "fusee" for our famous green flag'.[9] As the battalion began marches to improve fitness, rain started and this would be a major problem around Salonika, turning the ground to wet mud.[10] At least the battalion was brought up to strength (nearly 1,000)[11] with the addition of nearly 400 from the Norfolk Regiment, although there would initially be tensions between these men and the Irish soldiers. The Norfolk Regiment were apparently

---

2   Kristian Coates Ulrichsen, *The First World War in the Middle East* (London: Hurst, 2014), 93–4; Rob Johnson, *The Great War & the Middle East* (Oxford: Oxford University Press, 2016), 105–6; Alan Wakefield and Simon Moody, *Under the Devil's Eye: The British Military Experience in Macedonia 1915–18* (Stroud: Sutton, 2011; Barnsley: Pen & Sword, 2017 edition), 3.

3   Stanley, *Ireland's Forgotten 10th*, 55–6.

4   D2, pp. 4–10.

5   Diary entry, 5 Oct 1915.

6   Diary entry, 10 Oct 1915.

7   Diary entry, 11 Oct 1915.

8   Diary entry, 12 Oct 1915.

9   Diary entry, 13 Oct 1915.

10  Diary entries, 15–16, 18, 23–26 Oct 1915.

11  Diary entry, 21 Oct 1915.

unhappy about being in an Irish regiment and although Drury found them 'well educated and pretty smart' he also felt them to be 'uppish'.[12] Eventually, at the end of October, with the men much fitter than they had been 'and getting more flesh on their bones than they had a month ago', it was time to head for the front in Serbia. Drury later added a marginal note to his diary, noting with some pride, 'The 30th Brigade were the first British troops to go up to Serbia.'[13]

The 6th Royal Dublin Fusiliers moved to the front nearly 60 miles north from Salonika at Bogdanci on 29 October encountering 'unfortunate natives [...] streaming along the road southwards all eager to get away from the invading Bulgar'.[14] With the 7th Royal Dublin Fusiliers, the 6th were the first British units into the front line on 31 October, taking over French positions.[15] They held a range of places in early November[16] and part of the battalion supported a French attack on Memisli[17] on 3 November,[18] but most of the battalion spent that month rotating in and out of the front line, often under shell fire, often at Crête Simonet[19] and Memisli.[20] Food and water were difficult to obtain and the temperature became steadily colder.[21] By late November, it was so cold that 'Our overcoats are frozen hard, and when some of the men tried to beat theirs to make them pliable to lie down in, they split like matchwood.'[22]

It is likely the 10th (Irish) Division had not fully recovered from their time at Gallipoli because they seemed more susceptible to physical breakdown than men in some other units.[23] Drury wondered what was being achieved, writing, 'I don't know what we are hanging about here for. It doesn't seem possible to help the Serbs any longer by staying in the country and it looks to me as if we might easily get into a bad mess considering there are large numbers of Bulgars away behind us'.[24] While at the front at Kosturino, much time was spent working on defences,

---

12  Diary entries, 17 and 19 Oct 1915.
13  Diary entry, 28 Oct 1915.
14  Diary entry, 29 Oct 1915.
15  Wakefield and Moody, *Under the Devil's Eye*, 17.
16  Diary entries, 30 Oct–3 Nov 1915.
17  Now Memesli.
18  Diary entry, 3 Nov 1915.
19  Diary entries, 5–8 Nov 1915.
20  Diary entries, 13–14 Nov 1915.
21  Diary entries, 9, 15–18 Nov 1915.
22  Diary entry, 27 Nov 1915.
23  Wakefield and Moody, *Under the Devil's Eye*, 19–20.
24  Diary entry, 19 Nov 1915.

trying to make them less visible to the enemy in contrast to what Drury believed were rather obvious targets in the form of stone sangars[25] created by the French.[26]

By late November, while the 6th Royal Dublin Fusiliers were resting at Tatarli[27] it became clear that the Bulgarians were about to attack, although the British and French were already preparing to withdraw believing they could not hold their positions.[28] When the Bulgarians did attack on 6 December,[29] beginning what would become known as the Battle of Kosturino, the battalion was in reserve and sections of it were called up to the front on that day and the next to plug holes in the line.[30] However, they did not see heavy fighting until 8 December when they were covering a general retreat. While doing that, 'I didn't feel a bit easy, and in fact I felt sure this afternoon we were to be scuppered to let the rest get safely away.' Although Drury and his men could not see the enemy due to fog, he noted, 'We must have got a lot of Bulgars as we could hear their shouts and groans.'[31]

However, the battalion was not sacrificed and instead was required to retreat in as quickly and orderly a manner as it could, aided by the fog which obscured the battalion's movements.[32] They eventually reached Doiran[33] on 11 December[34] and then headed by train for a camp outside Salonika which they reached a day later.[35] Even though it had become clear that the Bulgarian forces would not cross the Serbo–Greek frontier, the British and French commanders did not want to leave their troops in exposed positions on Greek hills. Thus the withdrawal took place not simply to the border but to Salonika itself which could be more easily defended.[36]

25  Sentry posts.
26  Diary entries, 20–29 Nov 1915.
27  Diary entries, 30 Nov and 4 Dec 1915.
28  Wakefield and Moody, *Under the Devil's Eye*, 19–23.
29  Diary entry, 6 Dec 1915.
30  Diary entry, 7 Dec 1915.
31  Diary entry, 8 Dec 1915.
32  Diary entries, 9–10 Dec 1915.
33  Now Dojran.
34  Diary entry, 11 Dec 1915.
35  Diary entries, 10–11 Dec 1915.
36  Wakefield and Moody, *Under the Devil's Eye*, 30.

# Tuesday 5 October 1915. Mudros

[...]

[...] This begins the 2nd Phase of our 'Cook's Tour'.[37] If we have to fight the Bulgar, as some say we will, I think we will probably get it in the neck, as they are all fresh and ready, while our fellows are worn out and tired. But still I am looking forward to the change, as I want to see a bit more of the map and possibly get nearer winning that bet that the RDF will go home via Buda-Pest–Vienna & Berlin! [...]

# Sunday 10 October 1915. Salonika

I woke up early and saw the most magnificent morning with Mount Olympus on our Port hand. The top was covered with snow which was tinted salmon colour with the morning sun. No wonder the old Greeks thought and wrote such a lot about it. [...] We came to an anchor off Salonika about 09.00. It is a most fascinating place stretching round in a big curve for two or three miles on either hand and climbing up the hills behind to the culminating feature which looked like a big fortress of the mediaeval type. Beautiful slender minarets, pure white in colour, spring up here and there from the general level of the houses. [...]

I had a good look at the town through a good telescope from the bridge. The fort on the hill is surrounded by several loopholed walls with bastions and turrets, and the main part of the town is surrounded by walls which seem broken down in several places. The hills round look very bare, without any trees, but seem to have a lot of scrub like the hills of Gallipoli. At night the town looked very pretty with the streets lit up and some theatres and Café gardens brilliantly illuminated. It reminded me very much of the town of Douglas, Isle of Man, as you approach it from the sea at night. [...]

# Monday 11 October 1915. Lembet

We landed on Salonika Quay at 10.00 and fell in in column of route and marched out through the western part of the town for about five miles.

---

37  A reference to the travel agent, Thomas Cook.

There was no demonstration of any kind and the people seemed quite pleased to see us on the quay. The town seems a most interesting old place with queer mysterious courtyards and shuttered windows with faces peeking through the slats. The population in the streets were obviously impressed with the smartness and discipline of the men who were very smartly turned out and marched excellently, but I thought that the 'men in the street' did not seem so pleased to see us as the loafers on the quay. The climate was delightful with a cool fresh air. We marched out along a fairly good main road of good width bearing due North which the maps show running to SERES[38] about 50 miles away. After a little over an hour's march from the city we came to a peculiar conical mound at the right hand side of the road and turning in behind it to a small valley, we camped on the N[orth] slope facing South. This area is known as LEMBET.[39] During the day we got a few tents – about fifteen – but a good many had to sleep in their greatcoats. Food also was a bit short and it seems as if water will be a bit of difficulty. [...]

## Tuesday 12 October 1915. Lembet

We had a Battalion parade for the CO at 10.00 and he gave them a little fatherly advice as to their behaviour in the town and towards the inhabitants. I spent the remainder of the morning marking out our lines with stones and cleaning up the place generally. In the afternoon I went into Salonika with 'Doc' Paine[40] and 'Tiny' Arnold getting a lift in an empty ration lorry. It is an extraordinary old town with ancient and modern sitting cheek by jowl. The paving stones are slabs about two feet square and it is no unusual thing for one of them to be six or seven inches below the level of the others. The place seems stuffed with Greek troops who are a most sloppy-looking lot of cut-throats. The officers are generally very smartly dressed and look fearfully pleased with themselves. However, I don't much like the look of those I have seen as they seem effeminate

---

38  Now Serres.
39  This was about 2¾ miles north from the centre of Salonika, in the area now broadly called Stravroupoli. See WO 95/4836: 6th RDF.
40  It seems likely that 'Doc' Paine was Lieutenant (later Captain) Frederick Paine, who appears to be the only F. Paine in the RAMC with the right ranks. If that is correct, then he first served in France from March 1915. See WO 372/15/93047. His personal record has not survived in WO 339 or WO 374.

and out of condition and are sneaky looking. I wouldn't trust them an inch. [...]

[...]

# Wednesday 13 October 1915. Lembet

[...]

We went to a big store owned by the Turk firm of Orosdi-Back, and bought some red bunting to make a "fusee" for our famous green flag, and also to make corner flags for the lines. We made arrangements with the manager to run a canteen for our Brigade and fixed a schedule of prices to be charged. He promised to send out a wooden shed in sections and visit it next day. We had tea at Flocca's café sitting at one of the small tables out in the roadway, and watching the astonishing variety of people passing by. Many of the women are very pretty and are magnificently dressed, but most of them are too fat.

The manager of Orosdi-Back or "Rustyback" as we call it, is a wonderful fellow. I thought he was an Englishman as he not only spoke English perfectly, but used the ordinary colloquialisms correctly. A French officer who was with me declared he was French bred and born. However, he told us he was an Armenian and could talk perfectly, English, French, German, Spanish, Italian and Russian, and had a useful knowledge of Greek, Turkish, Bulgarian, Czech, Serbian and Arabic. A very useful collection! He is said to have married the daughter of the British Consul at Constantinople, but she lives in Paris.

# Friday 15 October 1915. Lembet

Took the company out early for a long crosscountry march doing about ten miles out, and coming back by the walls of Salonika; about 25 miles altogether. The men marched well, and are getting into good condition. We came across many old trenches made during the Greek v Turk war of 1913. [...]

[...]

## Saturday 16 October 1915. Lembet

The 'early' rain has started and it has been pouring steadily since midnight. The camp is in the most awful mess. Paine, the Doc, made me stay in bed all day, and, to tell the truth, I didn't feel much inclined to get up.

A draft of eight officers and 388 other ranks from the NORFOLK Regiment arrived. They were intended for Mespot,[41] but were switched off at Malta to us.

## Sunday 17 October 1915. Lembet

I felt a bit better and got up this morning, as I had to see about the new draft. I had a bit of a row with Colonel Cox about their disposition. He told me he wanted them all put together in one platoon, and any over to be kept together in another. He said he was doing the same with the companies, D Company being commanded by Horner[42] and having all Norfolk men. I strongly disagree and cited the 7th RDF and their D Coy I told him I was responsible to the CO for the work done by my company, but that I should have a free hand in the organisation of it, and that he ought not interfere. The Colonel said he was determined on it and I must do as ordered. Of course I have to give in, but I don't believe it will be for the good of the company or the Regiment. [...]

## Monday 18 October 1915. Lembet

Still raining heavily and stayed in bed all morning. Don't know what is wrong with me. I feel awfully crocky about the knees. The CO inspected the draft this morning and addressed them before sending them off to their companies. The camp is in awful state and we still have not enough tents for so many men, some of them housing twenty men and their kit. Bill Whyte told me today he believed we were going up country to Serbia to help them against the Bulgars, but didn't know for certain.

---

41  Mesopotamia.
42  Eric T. Horner, originally 1st Norfolk Regiment (WO 372/10/42786).

It certainly doesn't look as if we would be in time to do any good as the papers say the Serbs are almost scuppered already.

## Tuesday 19 October 1915. Lembet

[…] The Norfolk Regiment are a well-educated and pretty smart lot but seem a bit 'uppish' and I have overheard a few remarks about their "hard luck" in being attached to an Irish Regiment. By the Lord, I'll make them have sense. It isn't everyone has the honour to be in the oldest Regiment in the Army, making Empire history ever since 1641. I have a little booklet which I must read them extracts from on parade, and make them learn our Battle Honours.

[…]

## Thursday 21 October 1915. Lembet

The Battalion paraded at 09.00 for a route march. They looked fine, being nearly 1,000 strong. On Paine's advice I did not go as I still do not feel fit. I don't know what has been wrong with me lately. I feel weak and shaky and have a touch of dysentery. I can't understand why I kept so fit at Gallipoli when others and mostly younger fellows went sick, and now with plenty of water and food including A1 bread, I feel rotten. They tell me both Sir Bryan Mahon, & General Nicol are laid up; but they are old men. Paine says it is the after-effects of the strain and want of sleep on the Peninsula and that a few days taking it easy will make it all right. I hope he is correct, as I wouldn't for the world go sick now that we are up to strength and going to have a new start and see some more country. […]

## Saturday 23 October 1915. Lembet

The Battalion paraded this morning at 08.15 for a route march. The morning was fine and bright and it looks as if we have finished with the rain. Thank God for that. It's enough to break everyone's tempers when the camp is in such an awful state; it's impossible to go four paces without getting covered in mud to the thighs. You can't tell off men for

being dirty on parade when you are in the same state yourself, and yet I
must buck everyone up and get more smartness on parade. [...]

[...]

## Sunday 24 October 1915. Lembet

The Church parade for this morning was postponed at the last minute
owing to the pours of rain. However, it cleared up in the afternoon and at
17.00 we had a very fine Service under Canon McClean CF. The General
was there and about 2500 men. It was a very large parade and the singing
was something to remember. The dear old Canon was greatly pleased,
as all his services up to now had to be small ones of less than a company
at a time. Everyone loves him. He doesn't spout a lot of rhetoric, but
just plain helpful words on the rewards a man will get just by doing
his damnedest at whatever job he has to do and cheerfully sticking out
discomfort and fear. Everyone could realise how sincere he was, as he
was exactly carrying out his own precepts. All the time we were on the
peninsula he was casually bearing the greatest dangers day and night that
he might help the men's bodily and spiritual welfare. I know it was not
a case of ignorance of the dangers he ran day after day in the front line,
for he was acutely conscious of them, but this kindly elderly man who
might have remained at home in his quiet parish preferred to come and
help us, caring nothing for his own comfort or safety. I think he knows
that all the men know that, and it makes him happy.

[...]

## Tuesday 26 October 1915. Lembet

The weather is better and no rain today but the mud is awful. I sucked
off a pair of gum boots today which sank in the mud until the slick came
in over the tops. It has been forbidden to ride horses into camp as they
get stuck. [...]

I wrote to the Army and Navy Stores, Alexandria, for a small box of
stores for B Company officers mess, to be sent weekly, containing soap,
candles, laces, paper, tinned fruit, potted meat & matches. Each officer
subscribed £3.

# Thursday 28 October 1915. Lembet

I have been feeling much fitter the last couple of days and I notice that all the men are looking much better and getting more flesh on their bones than they had a month ago. My company at any rate have been well fed and their food has been well cooked. The company cooks Mannion[43] and Morrissey[44] are ex-Regulars and jolly good men, and I always see the food myself. [...]
I had a chat with Sir Bryan Mahon at the paymaster's office. He said he was quite fit again and asked how we all were and whether we felt fit to fight a bit more. I reassured him! The 'old Toughs' and 'Blue Caps' are always ready and our motto is 'spectemur agendo'.[45] Mahon was wearing one of the older type tunics with the close fitting collar like a Tommy's jacket. He looked thin but well.

Just afterwards I met Paddy Cox in the street who gave me the joyful news that we were off first thing in the morning. So I hurried back to camp and found we were to parade at 06.15 tomorrow. The 6th RDF to be leading battalion, leaving the military station by 1st train at 10.00. The distance across the plain from our Camp to the station is about 4½ miles, but a party of officers who went out to look for a track, returned reporting no passage. The whole place under water and so boggy that nothing could get through, so we have to march right into Salonika and then turn out along the Monastir road to the station – about twelve miles or more.

[...]

[Marginal note from Drury:] The 30th Brigade were the first British troops to go up to Serbia. The 29th & 31st Brigades did not arrive in Serbia till later. The 29th Brigade arrived between the 13th and 15th November and the 31st between the 7th and 10th Nov.

---

43  Likely to be either private 12614 Martin Mannion who was first deployed in the Balkans, or Private 25883 James Mannion whose first theatre of deployment is not recorded (WO 372/13/107943 & 107390).
44  Too many Morrisseys served in the RDF to establish exactly who this was.
45  Latin, translates as 'Let us be judged by our acts'.

# Friday 29 October 1915. Bogdanci

Friday has always been our day for shifting; we left the Curragh, Basing-stoke, Alexandria, Mitylene [*sic*], and Suvla Bay all on a Friday, and now here we are starting off for a new adventure from Salonika on a Friday all merry and bright. I was up at 03.00 and had all the transport packed and away by 05.15 in spite of the dark and no candles. We had rather a sketchy breakfast in our mess but got some sandwiches. We paraded at 06.15 32 officers and about 980 men and had the greatest difficulty in getting out of camp owing to the mud. Several times my horse stumbled so badly in it, that I thought I was going to be fired headfirst into the slime. It would have been like Dante's Inferno. We were to entrain at the 'military station', the first station out from Salonika on the Uskub[46] line, and we had to march into Salonika [...] and then out along the western or Monastir road. The train did not get away until 11.00, and then bumped along at a leisurely pace on an incredibly bad 'permanent' way. The engine was made in Germany and had the usual continental unsightly excrescences. All the bearings badly wanted renewal and it went off the boil a couple of times and stopped. Nearly left several men behind by starting off without any warning, but they picked us up by running! We crossed the VARDAR river at KARASULI[47] (about ten miles south of the Greco-Serb frontier) at 13.30 and reached GJEVGJELI[48] in SERBIA at 14.30. Between Karasuli and Gjevgjeli the railway runs through a magnificent gorge on a shelf cut out of the rock, overhanging the river about 50 or 60 feet below, and following the bends of the river. It was a very fine bit of work and must have cost a lot of money. There are some fine mountains away to the west of us, marked on the map as over 2,000 metres (7,000 feet).

GJEVGJELI (pronounced Gevgelly) is a fairly big town with some big buildings, most of them having Red Cross flags flying over them. The station which has several sidings was filled with people, apparently refugees from up country, and there were also a lot of Serbian troops there. I have never seen any of these before, and I was surprised to see such fine-looking men, smartly dressed and in such good form. There were several smart looking Serbian officers in the station wearing their serious angular looking service dress caps with the little glazed khaki

---

46  Now Skopje.
47  Now Polykastro.
48  Now Gevgelija.

peaks. We had a good deal of delay and trouble unloading the GS waggons and limbers and cookers as there was no proper loading bank. We had to haul them off the trucks sideways onto the low platform and then wheel them along to the end, and bump them down onto the rail level. There were some men selling Serbian coins of various values, and several of the men bought them, only to find later that they were fakes! As soon as we had all the luggage de-trained we marched off under the guidance of a Serbian officer who spoke perfect English. We turned east from the town and in a few hundred yards crossed the VARDAR to the left bank by a very fine steel girder bridge. The river was greatly swollen from the recent rains, and was about as wide as the Shannon at Athlone. In about a mile and a half we turned almost North, crossing a stream [...]. The road was little better than a new track and was badly flooded in places, some of it being partly washed away. I preferred to lead my horse and feel my way in the water with a stick, and risk having a fall and a ducking. One transport waggon fell down into a hole about ten feet deep where the road should have been, and the mules were nearly drowned, but we managed to release the snap catches on the harness and get them safely out. We had a cold and a wet job retrieving the ammunition out of the waggon and then hauling it up. After marching seven or eight miles we arrived near a village called BOGDANCI about 19.30 in the dark and bivouacked for the night ½ mile S[outh] W[est] of the village. Everyone was very tired after a long day during which we had marched over twenty miles altogether, through mud and flood. We had some supper of native bread which we got in the village, a box of sardines, and water to drink. The unfortunate natives were streaming along the road southwards all eager to get away from the invading Bulgar, and trying to carry away as much of their goods as possible, usually the least useful, I'm afraid.

## Saturday 30 October 1915. Cerniste[49]

Saw the first day-break over the mountains on the Serbo–Bulgar frontier, the BELAŠ DAGH or BELASHITZA mountains.[50] In the village of Bogdanci near which we bivouacked last night, and which had been evacuated by its inhabitants, we found some chickens and big marrows

---

49  Now Crnicani.
50  Now Belasica.

or pumpkins which seemed very plentiful, and took a supply with us. The Battalion paraded at 09.00 and marched off North East through a most beautiful valley with magnificent beech and plane trees, and lots of pretty wild flowers: in fact the whole scene could easily have been matched in Ireland. The leaves were getting their autumn tints and looked delightful in the bright fresh morning. The road had all been surveyed and well-engineered, but only completed in parts, and instead of bridges, had paved hollow causeways for streams to cross. The air is beautifully fresh and cool after the heat of Salonika and the sun shone brilliantly. The men felt in great form and went swinging along in great style. We passed the villages of VOLOVAN and HODZA-OBASI,[51] and after marching seven or eight miles we were met by Villiers-Stuart the Brigade Major and told us that the French Battalion we were to relieve were not ready to move. So, about 13.30 we turned off into a nice level field and bivouacked immediately under the C in CERNISTE (VODENA, 1:200,000). It was rather amusing to see the troops 'pile arms'. It was so long since they had done such a thing that they had almost forgotten the detail. We had a fine view of the mountains in front of us; and away to the westward we could see the French camp complete with tents. There are large numbers of mulberry trees growing here, and there are fields of Indian corn and patches of pumpkins. We had our lunch of roasted mealies, stewed pumpkin and a dish of magnificent blackberries with condensed milk over them. They were the biggest blackberries I have ever seen, and being so far away from civilisation were clean & free of dust. There was a heavy dew at night but I kept dry under a waterproof coat. I slept under a fine walnut tree, but the only nuts on it were dry and shrivelled. It was dark about 17.30. [...]

## Sunday 31 October 1915. Dedeli

The sunrise on the mountains this morning was a wonderful sight. We moved off in the order HQ, C, D, A & B companies. We had to scramble down anyhow to a river bed and reform on the other bank. Had a bit of a job with the transport, but Loveband[52] and Byrne are

---

51  These villages no longer appear on modern maps.
52  Guy Yerburgh Loveband.

old hands now at the game, and so is Sergeant Chapman,[53] Transport Sergeant. We soon passed one of the French camps and marched to attention, saluting the French Colonel who was standing there with some of his officers. He returned our salute himself but didn't turn out his guard as he should have done. Here we joined a main road running N[orth] W[est] from Lake DOIRAN to STRUMITZA,[54] and marched along it for several miles along the level plain, and then down a magnificent pass (the DEDELI Ravine), several times crossing the river on well-made cut-stone bridges. We soon came in sight of a fine valley below us and running at right angles to the pass, having a fine range of mountains (part of the BELASHITZA range) four or five miles away on the other side. At the top of these runs the Serbo-Bulgar frontier. Near the end of the pass we turned up to the right or EAST to a village called DEDELI on the hillside, where a battalion of the 175th French Regiment of the 156th Division was quartered and whom we were to relieve. We saw their CO and arranged about taking over from him, but we found the village so filthy that we preferred the open, and bivouacked on a fine level piece of grass like a village green. About 16.00 a heavy thunderstorm came on with very heavy rain, which drenched everyone and put out the fires when we were getting the tea ready for the troops. It cleared up about 19.00 but the night remained cold. I found that a blanket rigged up like a French bivouac kept the rain off well, the rain running down the nap like it does off the West of Ireland cloaks, as long as it was not touched.

## Monday 1 November 1915. Dedeli

There was another magnificent sunrise this morning with the colours striking the tops of the mountains and gradually spreading downwards, while we remained yet in the dark. We remained here all day. I took the company for a climb up the hillside during the morning to warm them up after their wetting last night. In the afternoon we had to go out road-mending to help the transport, and found the day very hot in spite of working without jackets. I have a rotten cold today and feel good for nothing, so I hunted around for something to make a shelter for the

---

53  Possibly, but not conclusively, 13183 Richard G. Chapman or 15924 Cecil Sutton Chapman (WO 372/4/84289 & 80219).
54  Now Strumica.

night, and found a sort of tarpaulin with which we made a comfortable bivouac for B Company officers. There are no signs of actual fighting yet although I thought I heard gunfire away on our left so perhaps the French have got into touch with the Bulgars. It was quite dark this evening at 17.30 but the night was fine.

## Tuesday 2 November 1915. Tatarli

We paraded at 10.00 and marched down the remainder of the DEDELI pass and out into the valley below and turned East along by the DIOALU DERE also called KOZLI DERE or BAJIMIA DERE[55] and going about two or three miles, halted in a field behind a battery of French 75 m/m field guns in a tobacco field, while the Colonel went off to interview the French. Shortly afterwards we moved off again up a steep boreen about 300 yards long, and bivouacked on the N[orth] slope of a small hill which arose between the river and the village of TATARLI which was occupied by the French. A Company being first for duty today had to turn out and make a road to the transport to get up by. General Sir Bryan Mahon, Brigadier General Nicol, and the French General Bailleux spent over an hour with Colonel Cox during the afternoon discussing plans. There have been persistent rumours that the Turks have chucked their hands in, but I don't believe it. What is there to make them, when they are holding us easily at Gallipoli[?] There are several batteries of French artillery near here including some very old looking guns of about 105 m/m bore, mounted on high caterpillar wheels, and apparently without any recoil gear. There are also Zouave and Senegalese troops here. I rigged up quite a comfortable bivouac with some timber which I found in the village, and found it kept the wind off quite well. About 18.00 a battery of 75s moved up the track past us towards the village of CALKALI[56] which practically touches TATARLI, and I hear they are going to attack N[orth] up the hills in the morning. So far, we have seen the Bulgars – and there are no natives left in the villages – but they have been reported holding a line up in the hills a couple of miles away somewhere on a line PRSTAN[57] (on

---

55  Approximately halfway between Tatarli and what is now Sobri (then Sobre-zir and Sobre-bala).
56  Now Chalakli.
57  Now Prsten.

the right) – MEMISLI – KAJALI[58] and so on NW. I had a chat in the evening with Colonel Cox on the general situation and so far as we can understand it, the Bulgars have pushed the Serbs away west, clean out of Serbia, into the wild mountainous country bordering the Adriatic; and we and the French are to make attacks on the Bulgar lines of communication running across our front, to try to ease the pressure on the Serbs. From the latest news of them, it looks as if we have come too light, and we may find that the Bulgars have plenty of troops to squash us, especially as they have no other enemies hammering at their back door. There are rumours of a large Bulgar force 80 or 100 miles S[outh] W[est] of us on our left rear near Monastir.[59] This fact coupled with the very doubtful attitude of the Greeks makes the outlook a bit blue – anyway, I would rather be humping my pack about here, and leading the open-air life in a strange and interesting country, than floundering in the bogs of Flanders, [at] what time the Bosch chips you with MG fire.

## Wednesday 3 November 1915. Tatarli

We had Reveille at 05.00 and the Battalion moved back a few hundred yards over to the south side of the hill we were on, so as to have some cover in case of shelling. We had breakfasts after we moved. The French attack began about 06.40 by two batteries of 75s opening rapid fire. They were firing at a considerable elevation up the hill, and as the shells were dropping over the crests we couldn't see the bursts. There was not much Bulgar fire in reply until 08.00 when they gave the N[orth] slope of the hill behind which we were, a great plastering with shrapnel. We could see part of the attack on the near ridges, which seemed to be well carried out in sectional rushes. The rifle fire which was fairly heavy, gradually got further off and then died down. We returned to our camp at noon, and got news that the French had captured two villages KAJALI and MEMISLI and were pushing on to the next ridge. They lost a good many men from shrapnel and bullet wounds, and some bayonet wounds. They say they got in at the Bulgar twice with the bayonet. The French are very fond of their thin, 3-cornered, long bayonet which they call 'Rosalie'. It looks to me too frail and thin, but I suppose the temper is very good, and it certainly gives them a longer reach. While we were down behind

---

58  Now Vrahia.
59  Now Bitola.

the hill this morning, my men all had a bathe and washed their clothes in the nice clear running stream; and the sun was quite hot. I was detailed to prosecute at a FGCM[60] on Sergeant Johnson,[61] signal sergeant 6th RDF for being drunk the day we left Salonika. It was to have taken place at Dedeli at the HQ of the 7th Royal Munster Fusiliers at 15.00 but was postponed. This has been Sergeant Johnson's great failing. He was in trouble in the 1st Battalion, and only for me he would have been up both at the Curragh and at Basingstoke. He was a first class signaller and a good teacher, and I did my utmost to keep him running straight. At Salonika there was no signal officer and therefore Johnson was more or less on his own. I had to turn out two Platoons (No 5 McKenna[62] and No 8 Pearce)[63] at 15.30 to carry ammunition up to the French near KAJALI; and at 17.30 had to send the other two up to the ridge above TATARLI on outpost duty. This has been called Signal Ridge as we have a signal station there; the next ridge beyond and above it is called CRÊTE SIMONET after Colonel Simonet of the 2nd Regiment de Marche d'Afrique Zouaves who captured it this morning. I had dinner on stewed mutton and pumpkin also a small bit of brown bread which I got from the French in exchange for some jam which they are always keen to get. Poor old 'Corber' (Lieutenant MG Corbet-Singleton grandson of Admiral Singleton of Ardee Manor, Ardee, County Louth) went off sick to hospital tonight. He has been looking rotten lately, and is full of nerves. He is suffering from rheumatism.

## Friday 5 November 1915. Crête Simonet

I paraded the Company at 09.00 and started off for the Simonet ridge. The truck started off up the steep slope behind the villages of TATARLI and CALKALI through the trees and undergrowth over the W[est]

---

60  Field General Court-Martial.
61  13904 Albert E. Johnson (WO 372/11/4773).
62  James O'Neill McKenna, born in 1895. Undergraduate at University College Dublin medical school on applying for a commission in Aug 1914, and from Carrickmacross, Co. Monaghan. Later served in the 5th Connaught Rangers and the Machine Gun Corps. Ended the war as a Lieutenant. See WO 339/910.
63  This is likely to be Reginald John Finch Pearce of the Norfolk Regiment (WO 372/15/171711), as the only Pearce to serve as an officer in the RDF (William Hugh Pearce) was not commissioned in the regiment until Aug 1917, serving with the 8th Battalion (WO 339/103070).

shoulder of the 'signal' ridge, and then steeply up the rough and boulder-strewn side of the higher or 'Simonet' ridge. It was an awful climb, taking 2½ hours. The sun was very hot and there was no wind, and the men were heavily laden carrying 150 rounds SAA, one greatcoat, one blanket, one ground sheet, and one day's rations. The line consisted of a series of detached trenches or rifle pits along the forward slope of the hill 50 or 80 yards down from the top, and extending about a mile in a slight arc. There was a fine field of fire and no dead ground for the enemy to collect in except on the right flank where I made a detached post on a separate knoll, held by one platoon and one MG (Vickers). The French had done their old silly trick of building big stone sangars along the sky line which made a beautiful target for enemy guns. We left these standing when we made the forward, but inconspicuous, trenches. [...] Our side (on the near side) of the ridge faces due South, and the heat in the middle of the day is like a very hot midsummer day at home. It is very hard to get water or food up, as the mules can only get up part of the way, and the men have to hump it the remaining part, bringing the water in empty ammunition boxes which of course are lined with tin. I spent part of the day correcting up to date, the Company Roll and making out a new copy. [...]

## Saturday 6 November 1915. Crête Simonet

Everything was quiet during the night, and we stood to arms at 04.45, and at 05.30 I withdrew most of the men behind the crest, leaving two main posts and various sentries along the front, but keeping the 1 Platoon complete on the right. This post overlooks the slope down to the ravine which runs down from in front of MEMISLI to PRSTAN, and is a very important one, as it prevents the enemy working into the valley behind us between Simonet Ridge and Signal Ridge. The sunrise was the most magnificent sight I ever saw, beating even the view of Imbros and Samothraki from Gallipoli. Soon after dawn I noticed a peculiar pink light far away to the southward, which gradually became more pronounced and brilliant in colour, and looked rather cone shaped. After setting the map carefully and taking compass bearings it was obvious that this was the sun shining on the snow on Mount Olympus in the north of Greece. The distance must be well over 100 miles. The colouring was magnificent, but it gradually faded as the light got stronger, and soon I lost sight of it altogether. The tumbled mass of mountains and hills in the new distance across the Vardar was a fine sight with the changing lights and shade in the valleys as the sun rose. I will never forget it. The French Regimental Commander, Colonel Forey has his HQ fairly close to mine, and he has three cows and some goats to keep him supplied with milk! [...]

[...]

## Sunday 7 November 1915. Crête Simonet

Sundays are just the same as week days in wartime except when troops are in Camp or Barracks. Strafing started very early by our 18lbrs and French 75s on the right, and by several '75' batteries on the left, but no infantry attack was made. We can see a good many Bulgar troops in the distance in the mountains to the N[orth] E[ast] of DOROL OBA[64] and BOLUNTILI,[65] but so far they don't seem to have made any attempt to attack us or drive south again. The French seem to think they are to be here for years to judge by the amount of stores of all kinds which they are rushing up. Water is a difficulty up here, and our supply did not arrive up till 11.30, so that I couldn't get any tea made for most of the men's breakfasts. We were lucky to receive a half bread issue (6ozs per man) of excellent bread, and I secured some bread for my own breakfast from the French in exchange for some jam. They get no jam in their rations, but they get a small quantity of wine which is dark, rusty looking stuff tasting like vinegar. [...] The French made an attack on the slight hill which stands on the east of the road up to KOSTURINO on our left between 19.00 and 20.00 using hand grenades. I believe they got in two bayonet charges, and found the Bulgar a very handy fighter. The French have just shot six spies from a village near, who had been previously warned. They rounded up the whole of the villagers – men, women and children [–] to see the job done. The six men were made to dig their graves first and then five of them were shot, the remaining man being made to bury the others, and then came his turn. It must have been a brutal job but I suppose it will have the desired effect on the others. [...]

---

64  Now Dorlombos.
65  Now Buluntili.

# Monday 8 November 1915. Crête Simonet

The morning broke very dark and cloudy and cold. It was quite dark at 05.00 when we stood to arms. I had to keep on the move the whole night along the line to keep warm. I took two platoons out of the line at 06.00, one from the right and one from the left. I got a full ammunition box of water for each of the remaining platoons, and must try to get them some hot tea during the day. The trouble here is that there is nothing to burn to make a fire; it is just a bare stony mountain. We have made big improvements of the line since we have been here, and I find the trenches are almost invisible from the front, in great contrast to the French stone sangars which can be seen from miles around. They give no protection from shell fire and the flying stones only increase the casualties. We moved 50 yards or so down the forward slope and dug trenches as deep as the ground would let us, building up low breast works of stone and sods, and covered thickly with earth and scrub on the front and also up behind, so that from the front no break appeared. They are not deep but give good protection to men kneeling or lying and they are well traversed to localise the effect of shells. I believe that if the Bulgar attacks here, he will waste his shell fire on the sangars above. [...]

Captain French[66] of the 6th Royal Munster Fusiliers arrived up about 18.00 with orders from Brigade to relieve his other Company in reserve, and to send them up to relieve me. I showed him all the work in hand, and projected, and he approved and arranged to carry it on. We started off down about 19.00 in the pitch dark and got down OK as far as the top line of the trees but coming through the woods we completely lost the track in spite of the trail being blazed. We had an awful time scrambling down and many a good fall, but I managed to get the company into camp at TATARLI by 23.00 and only one man missing. He will probably find his way all right.

# Tuesday 9 November 1915. Tatarli

The missing man turned up during the night OK but tired and hungry. [...]

[...]

---

66  Bernard Russell French (WO 372/7/160428).

We got a mail today with some letters, also a parcel from Jack[67] of some under clothing and a pair of Norwegian ski boots. Prices at home must be getting very high judging by the bill. [...] I wish I could hear who is gone out from Dublin and who the slackers are. [...]

[...]

Some of the houses in the village of TATARLI have been cleared out, and may be used by the companies on wet nights at the company commanders' discretion.

## Saturday 13 November 1915. Memisli

[...]

The Battalion paraded at 14.00 and moved N[orth] E[ast] up the river (BOJIMIO DERE) towards PRSTAN intending to pick up D Company on the way. There was a good track shown from PRSTAN to MEMISLI, but we found no sign of one at all, although we rode all over the place through the scrub and trees. We had to come back to TATARLI where we found a French soldier who knew the best way up having been there several times before. The route led up over the E[ast] shoulder of Crête Simonet and finally by a fairly good track to KAJALI [...]. When we arrived at the French HQ to take over from them they said they knew nothing about us – they were quite comfortable where they were and weren't going to move! We put one company bivouacked at KAJALI and another on a beautiful piece of green at MEMISLI, and the HQ and two companies further back at the head of the steep gully with the five fountains. We sent messages back to Brigade HQ about the position, and were expecting orders but we did not get any. Loveband and Byrne arrived up with the rations about 21.00. Byrne was most amusing about the big Bulgars he saw lying about saying they were bigger than DMP men. One the fellows lying at the junction of the tracks to KAJALI and to MEMISLI would make a fine signpost for him in the dark in future!

---

67   His youngest brother.

## Sunday 14 November 1915. Memisli

[...]

[...] We saw a lot of dead Bulgars lying about most of them being elderly men of big size and well clothed. They wore a kind of rough tanned sandals instead of boots, which are very silent moving about at night, and give them a great grip on the rock. They all had the older type Mannlicher rifle, but I saw some of the new .275 high velocity ones lying about, which is said to be the best rifle in Europe. We also came across some of the Bulgar pack saddles and the special steel boxes lined with felt for carrying MG ammunition. It is much better made than ours and quicker and easier to fix. One can easily see the influence of the mountainous country on their equipment and also the experiences gained in the recent Balkan Wars (read the 'Cockpit of the Balkans' by Crawfurd Price).[68] The weather is still nice and warm by day, but the nights are a bit chilly.

[...]

## Monday 15 November 1915. Kajali

Yesterday was the first day that the rations were short. Byrne got no groceries at all, but managed to send us up a half ration of tea and sugar from his reserve. We moved the Battalion to KAJALI at 10.00 but met Colonel Cox and Major Villiers-Stuart coming up and I walked around the position with them. We decided to make a series of sangars and posts on the ridge N[orth] E[ast] of the village well down on the forward slope and carefully camouflaged. We put up quite a lot of Chikori or hill partridges while walking round. There is a magnificent view over the mountains N[orth] and W[est] of us from the plateau in front of the village. It is like looking out over an expanse of the open sea on a stormy day – all hollows and hills in confusion as far as the eye can see. There are a lot of dead Bulgars about, and it looks as if they had to leave the village in a hurry as they left a great deal of their 75 mm ammunition behind and also a lot of SAA. The gun ammunition looks exactly the same as the French, and I believe they have French guns which they bought during

---

68  W.H. Crawfurd Price, *The Balkan Cockpit: The Political and Military Story of the Balkan Wars in Macedonia* (London: T. Werner Laurie, 1914).

the 1911 & 1913 Balkan wars. The Bulgars all wore heavy underclothing. Some have sheepskin shirts, but most have a sort of quilted cotton shirt stuffed with cotton wool. Many of these Bulgars had well made knee boots of excellent leather, and some had leather sandals or moccasins strapped over the boots. The Bulgar bayonet is short and strong and in shape very like the one we use with the long territorial pattern Lee Enfield rifle. They like bayonet fighting and stand up well to it. Rations are short again today – no tea nor sugar. ½lb bread & ½lb biscuit & ½lb bully per man. However, there is plenty of good water here which is something to be thankful for after our past experiences.

## Wednesday 17 November 1915. Kajali

[…]

It has become bitterly cold and I was going about with gloves, woolly waistcoat and muffler. I hear rumours of strong Bulgar reinforcements arriving on our front and a heavy attack is expected. One of our fellows, Jackman,[69] has been away on some intelligence stunt and I hear has been in Strumitza for two or three days making notes of troop movement. Everything is quiet at present, however, and the night was passed without incident, our patrols found no enemy posts and we heard no movements. There is great delay here in the telephone working and important messages are taking hours to get through. The trouble is that the distances are so great and our wire […] is in bad condition and frequently going 'dis' [disconnected] through short-circuits. The cable has to be laid across the bare mountains, and as there are no roads, the ration convoys take their own course and often the mules break the wire in the dark. There are no trees to pole it up and the ground is too rocky to bury it. The result is that we have the linesmen out the whole time. […]

Late at night we got this message from […] OC 6th RDF.

'The French Brigade staff have asked me to get you to send in writing to them a copy of the order as to the move of the battalion to the line MEMISLI–PRSTAN today. […]'

---

69  Cecil Davis Jackman of the Norfolk Regiment, born 1893 and living in Dorchester at the outbreak of the war. Later served in the RAF (see WO 339/45707 and AIR 76/251/29).

This is infernal cheek of the French. I referred them to the 10th (Irish) Division and refused to send any copy. The 10th (Irish) Division is now holding its own portion of line and is not responsible to the French for support, or reserves. It's a good job we are clear of them for such filthy troops I never saw. They haven't the rudiments of sanitation or cleanliness in camps nor billets. They are typical of the French nation for selfishness, thinking their convenience alone is to be considered.

## Thursday 18 November 1915. Memisli

Did not have breakfast till 08.30 and washed in hot water! There was hard frost last night and a bucket of water outside my tent was frozen up. Later in the day the sun came out very warmly, and the air was delightfully fresh and makes one feel full of 'buck and beans'. I had a chat during the morning with Colonel Forey of the 175th French Regiment who was very pleased with the fine shooting at extreme range of Major Reeves'[70] battery, which did in many Bulgars at ORMANLI. There was an impressive funeral of a French officer who was buried just outside the village (MEMISLI). I attended officially on behalf of the Regiment and several others were also present, which the French appreciated. I have no cigarettes left and we have heard that the boat with our mails has been sunk. We sent Parish[71] today to Salonika to get new glasses as he could not see with the broken ones. He had commissions from everyone to buy cigarettes and warm clothing, and he says he will never be able to bring back all the things as he would want a waggon to carry them. [...]

During last night the French sent us a message that there was a night attack by the Bulgar, but it was nothing more than a wandering goat which a volley from C Company managed to bring down! By the kindness of a French MG officer named Demogeot I had a good look at a new French mitrailleuse. It is much heavier than our Vickers gun but in some respects more convenient. There is a very clever timing system which, by varying the tension of the fuse spring, enables a gun to fire at any rate from 200 to 500 rounds a minute – the leisurely tap-tap-tap of the

---

70  Major Robert Clanmalier Reeves, the only Major Reeves serving in the Royal Field Artillery at that time (*Monthly Army List*, Dec 1915, col. 526; WO 372/16/185318), with R.C. Reeves confirmed by the 67th Brigade RFA as serving in it (see WO 95/4831). He ended the war a Lieutenant Colonel. His personal record has not survived in WO 339 or WO 374.

71  W.O. Parish, formerly Norfolk Regiment (WO 372/15/108166).

French gun being quite remarkable. The tripod seemed to me unnecessarily heavy and it carries a metal seat for the gunner shaped like a B10 Brooks cycle saddle. There is an ingenious arrangement of spring clips for the elevating screw instead of the pins in the Vickers. The barrel is very thick and is air cooled. I don't know anything of the accuracy of the gun in action but obviously it would have to be sparingly used in action or it would overheat and jamb. The new French uniform which the troops have here is a sort of steel blue and seems well made. It is extraordinarily difficult to see when the troops are scattered about through the boulders in an attack. The trousers are worn like ours turned down over putties of blue colour to match, and they are a little looser in the leg than ours, a waistcoat with sleeves is worn and forms their fatigue dress. Instead of a tunic they wear a greatcoat, and when marching the front corners are buttoned back behind the hips leaving the legs free. Their pack is made in waterproof grey canvas lined with plywood to keep it in shape (rather useless I thought) and is not very big, as the greatcoat is never carried in it. Every man carries a waterproof sheet and stick to make a bivouac, the edges of the sheets having press buttons to join them. The blanket is folded inside the sheet and carried across the top of the pack and strapped down each side, lying quite neatly. Sometimes a pair of boots is mounted on top of this and finally the mess tin crowns all, being on a level with the top of the man's head. The new steel helmet seems a good idea to keep off shrapnel, but I think it should be wider in the brim to protect the neck and shoulders. Their rifles and bayonets are rotten.

[…]

## Friday 19 November 1915. Memisli

Nothing special doing; indeed I don't know what we are hanging about here for. It doesn't seem possible to help the Serbs any longer by staying in the country and it looks to me as if we might easily get into a bad mess considering there are large numbers of Bulgars away behind us near MONASTIR. The weather is still very cold but fine. […]

# Saturday 20 November 1915. Kosturino

[...] We made all the usual arrangements for our relief by the 5th Royal Inniskilling Fusiliers. They arrived about 16.30 and took over at once. We waited till our rations arrived and were distributed and then moved up through KAJALI to the KOSTURINO ridge running S[outh] E[ast] from the village. We relieved a Battalion of Zouaves and found one of the senior officers (French) so drunk that we had the greatest difficulty in getting him out of his funk hole and safely away in charge of his servants. The relief was completed at 21.30. We are now the left Battalion of the 10th (Irish) Division, and our left is in touch with the French right, on the road over the pass to STRUMITZA. The night was bright moonlight and we were very lucky to have some light to see how to place our men. The French had, as usual, built huge sangars of stone all along the skyline forming a grand target. They told us to take care, as they were always being shelled and had had many casualties! We decided on a line further down the forward slope of the ridge, and laid out a series of rifle pits to be carefully hidden in the scrub between the trees.

# Sunday 21 November 1915. Kosturino

[...]

There is a bitter wind blowing up here and it is hard for the men to keep warm. We can't light fires near the line or we draw shell fire at once. This morning I took a raiding party into the village of KOSTURINO. The place is full of derelict dogs – big brutes like partly trained wolves – which set up such a din when we appeared that I thought we would get shelled. This village is the usual deceptive one. From a distance it looks clean enough and picturesque, but a closer acquaintance is not pleasant. Some of the houses were quite big and airy, with two storeys and good sized windows. They don't seem to know the use of paint to protect woodwork, as I saw no painted doors or windows or even inside doors or staircases. Most of the houses had piles of quilted underclothing and old skin rugs and rubbish of all sorts. There were no beds and few tables or chairs and I believe the family sleep on the piles of skins. Everywhere I saw silk worms and very crude silk spinning machines. There was also a lot of tobacco tied up in the leaf in bundles and left to dry. They use little churns like those in use in Ireland in which a shaft with a piston on the end is pumped up and down by hand. [...] I went into the Mosque or

Church, I am not sure which, but I think it was Greek Orthodox. There were funny little pews sat facing each other. The pulpit was very high up on the wall with a long, rickety stair leading up to it. Some portly divines I know at home would get a bad drop if they tried it. There was also a small gallery with a queer wavy front also rickety and unsafe. On the walls were hung a few very dirty and blackened pictures, so dirty in fact that I couldn't even make out what they were about. Several shells have come through the roof and had somewhat deranged the furniture. There were several large Bibles I suppose they were, written in some language that looks like Russian. It wasn't Greek nor Turkish – possibly it was Serbian or Bulgarian. [...]

[...]

# Monday 22 and Tuesday 23 November 1915.
# Kosturino ridge

Things much as usual. Very hard work day and night making trenches and MG emplacements. There is an exceedingly bitter North wind – 'rude Boreas'[72] – nasty fellow! But it is dry which is a matter to be thankful for. We have a very strong line here now and I think we will give the Bulgar a run for his money if he attacks us here. [...]

[...]

# Friday 26 November 1915. Kosturino

There was a heavy fall of snow during the night more than six inches deep out in the open and blown into deep drifts by the high wind. It turned to rain during the morning, and back again to snow later on. The poor troops are soaked through; the movement of working sopping the wet through everything – even their greatcoats are soaked. The whole place is in a morass and nobody can get warm. [...] This would be a bad time for the Bulgar to attack us, but indeed he is probably as bad as we are or worse perhaps. Battalion strength today 25 officers 904 other ranks.

---

72  Boreas was the personification of the north wind in Greek mythology.

# Saturday 27 November 1915. Kosturino

Very bad night – no shelter from the cold and wet. I had a rotten passage around the line, falling and stumbling about in snowdrifts up to my shoulders in some places. The snow kept on falling yesterday evening and part of the night, and then changed to the most intense frost. This morning everything is frozen hard and every track is too slippery to walk on. There are now about two feet of snow everywhere and much more in the places where drifts have formed. Our overcoats are frozen hard, and when some of the men tried to beat theirs to make them pliable to lie down in, they split like matchwood. The men can hardly hold their rifles as their hands froze to the cold metal. Everyone is falling and tumbling about in the most ludicrous way.

# Sunday 28 November 1915. Kosturino

It's impossible to get warm, everything is frozen solid. There were 42 degrees of frost last night – ten degrees below zero. We had an enormous sick parade this morning nearly 150 men reporting. There were many bad cases of frostbite in hands and feet and ears. The poor men are suffering badly but sticking it out well. After the heat of Gallipoli and Salonika this cold is very trying. […] At last we have got the men some hot food! We lit big fires down in the ravine and heated up the fantassies we got yesterday (steel water tanks covered with thick felt and holding seven or eight gallons) with boiling water. We then poured boiling cocoa or bovril into them and hurried them up to the line on mules, having previously cut special tracks through the snow and ice. It was an awful struggle getting the mules up, and we could only get them part of the way, and had to manhandle the fantassies the remainder of the distance. In spite of the delay we got the stuff up really hot, and followed it up with hot stew later in the day. We heard that the cocoa was a present from some naval officers who had been up on leave to see the line – God bless them. The bovril was 'medical comfort' from the ambulance. […]

We managed to get some biscuit tins and punched holes in them to make braziers to put in the bottom of the trenches. We also risked getting shelled and lit several fires down the rear slopes and sent men in batches to thaw their clothes. This and the hot cocoa is doing a lot of good for the men. Courage seems to exist in direct ratio with physical comfort. We have 61 men to hospital with frostbite and the stretcher bearers are having a hard time. I find it impossible to wash properly as the water freezes as fast as you can use it after boiling. The hot milk at breakfast was frozen solid in the jug before we are ready for a second cup of tea. We are a comical sight at meals. Imagine a hollow three feet deep and eight feet circumference dug in the hillside, leaving a round block of earth in the centre for a table. Huddled round this sit four or five figures like esquimaux[73] wearing balaclava woollen helmets, woollen gloves, mufflers and as many coats as one possesses, legs wrapped in muddy and torn blankets. In fact nothing to be seen of the individuals except eyes, noses and lips. Yet the jokes & laughter might surprise a visitor. Stuffer Byrne's story of how he got us all two cardigans each by bluffing Sewell the Quartermaster of the RMF kept us in roars of laughter; only Byrne could describe Sewell, standing on the outskirts of Calkali as the mules with the bales passed along, in his rich Cork brogue saying, 'Goodbye to me car-r-digans'. How it was done I don't know and the wise ones never ask Byrne how he does these things, but all we are interested in is that he landed up here today with an issue of cardigan jackets plus the issue intended for the 6th RMF (who are in billets in Calkali). […] We got a small mail up with the rations, but no cigarettes came. It's surprising how one puts up easily with anything except having no smokes. I got a present of a grand big box of biscuits from Harold Jacob[74] and David Baird[75] and they note that they were going to send on some more too. Jolly kind of them to think of me.

## Monday 29 November 1915. Kosturino

The cold is as bad as ever. I never thought I could feel as cold. Even hard climbing up the ridge only puffs one but doesn't make one feel warm. It's almost impossible to do any Orderly Room work although Sergeant Peake has burrowed far into the hillside and has got up such a fug that he manages to keep warm enough to write out returns. The Bulgars are still very quiet and only poofed a few shells at the French on our left, and one at us. The men were a little better off last night, but still the doctor had a lot of bad cases this morning. Bill Whyte and I were up all night trying to get the men to march up and down after coming off sentry, to get them warm. It was almost cruel but it saved a lot from

---

73 French for 'Eskimo'.
74 Of W & R Jacob, the biscuit producers.
75 Presumably an associate or friend of Harold Jacob.

getting frostbite. We also made them take off their boots & socks and rub each other's feet till they got a good circulation. I don't know how I would have fared without my big Norwegian ski boots. I am sure they save me getting frostbitten feet and also saved me a broken leg when I got falls among the rocks. During the morning this message came over the wire: '[…] The 7th RMF will relieve the 6th RDF in front line, relief to commence 17.00. […]'

[…] The 7th RMF under Lt Col DRAGE was a little late in arriving owing to the ice, and the relief did not start till 18.30. The frost was so hard that the men could hardly stand on the paths and were tumbling about all over the place. The companies went off separately as they were relieved. After we had handed over and explained everything Bill Whyte and I who were the last away called in to see Paddy Cox and report, at Brigade HQ at KAJALI. He was awfully kind, and had hot coffee made for us and made toast for us himself while we lay and thawed and rested near the fire. I didn't want to go away at all – I felt as if I could have lain there for ever. After we had got well warmed and our clothes dry and warm we went off down to TATARLI and caught up with the tail of the last company before they got into the village. It was a terrible walk for we were sliding and falling about like imbeciles and were black and blue all over. When we got down into the trees above TATARLI we picked up the good old Stuffer, and passed the Connaught Rangers' bivouacs where we were to have gone. When we got down to the village a grand sight met us. There were huge fires burning outside each billet and the field kitchens were steaming merrily with a hot supper for everyone. Byrne is really a grand fellow in an emergency. He got extra rations from somewhere by some means of his own. He had got houses cleaned out, and great stacks of logs cut for the fires and everything ready for the weary men, even getting straw from somewhere for them to sleep on in the houses. I was so tired and sleepy that I could hardly keep awake long enough to see the men comfortably settled. I turned in […] without eating anything more than I had had at Brigade Headquarters.

## Tuesday 30 November 1915. Tatarli

Everyone stayed asleep till about midday resting, and thawing the frost out of themselves and their clothes. I did very little except doze near the fire and wash my underclothes, and generally clean up a bit. I sent word round to Company Commanders to see that the first thing done was to clean rifles and check and clean ammunition, as there is no knowing when we may be wanted up again.

## Saturday 4 December 1915. Tatarli

[…] Today practically the whole Battalion is out road making in various places principally the KAJALI–DEDELI road North of the river […]. I don't at all like this scattering about of the Battalion over miles of country. It would be the very devil to collect them if we had to push off into the line in a hurry. However, I suppose the Division know what they are doing. We had Bertie the Turkey for dinner, and he tasted jolly well in spite of his freezings and journeyings.[76]

## Monday 6 December 1915. Tatarli

[…]

It was a cold night but the sun today was very bright and warm. The constant drain of men to hospital is very annoying, but fortunately a lot of them will come back soon. There was very heavy artillery fire, starting early this morning and lasting nearly all day, and it is evidence that the Bulgar has brought up a lot more guns. The effect of the firing in these hills is rather strange. In many cases you don't hear the sharp snap of the discharge followed by an echo, but usually only a gradually increasing boom that seems to linger around the valleys as if reluctant to die away, so that, today there is an almost continuous roll of sound waxing and waning, but without definite beginning or end, and not unpleasantly loud. There was a good deal of rifle and MG fire up KAJALI way and we heard that the 7th Royal Munster Fusiliers and 5th Connaught Rangers have had some fighting. If the old RMF handle things properly they should do good work in the line we made on KOSTURINO ridge. Second Lieutenant Jackman rejoined this morning from the Dump at HASANLI,[77] and says he saw a lot of troops there.

---

76 D2, p. 58: Drury had found a turkey at Kosturino on 25 Nov and had resolved 'I must try and feed him up for Xmas', but he obviously decided on an earlier meal.
77 There no longer appears to be a settlement at this place as there is nothing in this name or any other indicated at this location on modern maps.

I wonder they don't move up some of them. Anyway they ought to make the right flank secure if they move N[orth] E[ast] round the lake a bit. [...]

During the afternoon we heard that the 5th Royal Irish Fusiliers had been pushed off Pitou Rocheaux but had retaken it with the bayonet. About 16.00 Colonel Leman 'Q'-Branch 10th (Irish) Divisional Staff came round and gave us verbal orders to move up Butler's Road (TATARLI–KAJALI) to the hairpin corner, usually called Butler's Corner ((A Battery 67th Field Artillery Brigade), he made the track to get his guns up). We paraded about 18.00, nineteen officers 556 OR, 170 rounds per man, 4,000 rounds per company, in reserve, and 46,000 rounds for M[achine] Guns, and proceeded up to the corner on the KAJALI road where the valley S[outh] of CRÊTE RIVET turns off to the West. Here we were to remain in Divisional reserve, and to return to TATARLI at daybreak if not required. The 6th Royal Irish Fusiliers are holding the line near MEMISLI and we sent them two orderlies to stay at their HQ for the night in case they wanted messages sent to us. We spent a miserably cold night in a thick wet mist. The 31st Brigade gave us practically no news of the position and if we had to push into the line in a hurry we would have been at a great disadvantage as we didn't know precisely where the various units were. Several scouts were out during the night trying to get in touch with the units of the 31st Brigade on the right but they had the greatest difficulty in finding their way, and we got almost no ammunition. I know what a desperate job it is finding one's way over these bare hills at night even without a fog; there are no landmarks and one boulder looks like every other.

## Tuesday 7 December 1915.
## Butler's Corner/Crête Simonet

We moved back down to TATARLI in conformity with orders. The fog is still dense, and we heard that the Bulgar again rushed the 5th Royal Irish Fusiliers off the Rocky Peak. On arrival at TATARLI we found a large parcel mail waiting for us, including a couple of mess boxes from Fortnum & Mason of Piccadilly. It seems ever thus with these damned P[ost] O[ffice] people. They leave us without anything when we want it, and wait till we are in the middle of a battle and have no way of carrying anything, and then they bunk off and empty the whole car on top of us. We divided up a few things as quickly as possible, and had a perfectly gigantic breakfast of tinned ham and bangers, and lashings of Oxford marmalade. We gave the remainder to the transport people to carry if they could manage it. […]

At the same time we sent a chit to the company commanders telling them to be ready to march off at a moment's notice, as we felt sure the Division would want us back at once at Butler's Corner. The Division were not long in replying and my own orderly who was waiting there brought this from 31st Brigade […] 'Get the Battalion up again to position you were in last night. […]'

We paraded at once and moved off by 09.00 still in thick white fog. We left our horses behind and sent them away with the transport as they would be a hindrance instead of a help. We left some signallers at TATARLI to keep on the Brigade line until we arrived up and could tap in somewhere near. The Division sent a message to TATARLI which was sent after us by runner saying: 'Report when your Battalion has arrived in position of last night – 09.51' (received by us 10.00). We were in position by 10.45 and reported so to Division via 31st Brigade.

At 11.00 I got a note from Pearce (Sig[nal] Off[icer]) saying:– 'Am now in touch with 30th and 31st Brigades. Any orders received will send them to MARTIN'S POST. Am in same place as last night. […]'

Martin's Post which we made our HQrs and report centre, was a strong point on a sort of subsidiary spur on the East side of Crête Simonet, and Butler's Road ran along the East foot of it. It was called after Lieutenant CA Martin of our C Company who made it early in November.

It is evident that a heavy attack is being made by the Bulgar near MEMISLI and on towards the left of Rocky Peak. Just as we arrived at Butler's Corner we saw three men struggling down the track, two of them slightly wounded and helping between them a very badly wounded man. They were Connaught Rangers, one being a very intelligent NCO. He told me that the 7th Royal Munster Fusiliers have got pushed off KOSTURINO ridge by their flanks being turned (just what I feared). The badly wounded man had several bayonet wounds and in spite of it all was in great spirits. We asked him what was going on and he said, 'Begor Sir, them Bulgars kept coming at us, all during the night and we couldn't get them to keep out o' that till we took the bayonet at them. We had three fine charges at them this last couple of hours!'

This waiting about without knowing what is going on is rotten – one can think out no plans or make any disposition of troops or MGs. The fog makes it very difficult to hear anything. Sometimes we can hear heavy MG and rifle fire, and then it fades away. Once we distinctly heard cheering that I would bet any money was coming from the 'Common Dangers'.[78] I had only a few biscuits to eat all day, but didn't want much after our big breakfast. I had a box of biscuits sent me by Harold Jacob which arrived in new condition as they were soldered up in the tin. Fortunately, it is not thirsty weather as there is no water up here, but we have got accustomed to doing without water. However, we sent a special warning round the men to go easy with their rations and water as we didn't know when they would get any more. Early in the afternoon a lot of stragglers from the 10th Hampshire Regiment and 7th RDF began coming down, and we collected a good lot of them and kept them with us. They seemed under the impression that the Hampshire Regiment had broken and that the whole line was being pushed back, but no definite news could be got from anyone what line was being held. About 15.00 a Divisional message came in ordering us to take up and hold a position on Simonet ridge, which we at once did, holding our old line there with B and D companies and having A and C companies holding an outpost line on the two small spurs between us and Crête Rivet. The Simonet ridge was to be the main line of resistance, and we held this as follows from the left: two companies 7th RDF – B Company 6th RDF – one officer & 60 other ranks of 10th Hampshire Regiment (all we could find) – one company of Royal Irish Fusiliers – D Company 6th RDF. About this time the fog got a bit lighter and we were able to report back to Division that Bulgars appeared to have taken KAJALI and MEMISLI and to be holding the line of sangars along Crête Rivet. We received a message from Martin of C Company by runner, timed 15.30 'Two Coys of 7th R Dub Fus have come back and have joined up with our left.' This message from 31st Brigade confirmed the verbal phone order from Division: '[…] Take up positions – 6th RMF are coming up to help you to cover rallying of 30th Brigade. Try to get in touch with 31st Brigade left. [...]'

The GOC 31st Brigade[79] seems perfectly useless, and when I saw him he was mooning about as if he didn't know nor care what was going on. He doesn't seem to realise that we are fighting about ten times our numbers of Bulgars, and that only by keeping wide awake will he get his troops safely away. His Brigade Major [W.J.N.] Cooke-Collis is running the show and doing all the work. Later in the evening Paddy Cox (OC 30th Brigade) came along and told us that the Bulgars were in great force (10th (Irish)

---

78  The 5th Connaught Rangers.
79  Brigadier General James Gerwood King-King (WO 372/11/171659).

Division staff estimates them as twelve to one, 80 Battalions) and had over run the whole line and that things looked rather black. He had nearly been captured in the Brigade HQ at KAJALI – the bullets were coming in at point-blank range while he and the staff were bundling up the last of the Brigade papers. The Hampshire Regiment were worrying him; the right was held by 31st Brigade near PRSTAN, and they were very shaky (like their General!) and he couldn't find out anything about the French on the left who seem to have cleared out away to VALANDOVA[80] and beyond. There is an 18lbr battery C/67 Field Artillery Brigade (Butler's) out on a spur S[outh] E[ast] of MEMISLI and it appears to be captured. It was put there by order of the CRA against Butler's wishes. The spur is surrounded by a huge ravine on the North, East and South, and the only exit from it is through MEMISLI and the sunk road leading S[outh] from it. Now that MEMISLI is captured, the guns can't possibly be got away. We sent a message to Loveband and Byrne at TATARLI to pack up at once and clear out as quickly as they could. They must not get stuck as I have given them all the Orderly Room papers, orders, maps & War Diary, to carry. About 18.00 or so I had a verbal message over the phone from Division via 31st Brigade to retire on DEDELI as soon as the 6th Royal Inniskilling Fusiliers on our right (31st Brigade) had moved out. I had just commenced issuing orders to that effect when I had another phone message cancelling the orders to move and saying we must hold on to Crête Simonet. All this time the Bulgars seemed very quiet and we could hear no firing anywhere and our outpost line and nothing to report.

Colonel Cox came over and made his HQ with us for the night as his phone had gone 'dis' [disconnected] and we had a good line via 31st Brigade to Division. We then reverted to 30th Brigade from Divisional Reserve. Things were very quiet during the evening and night on our front, but we could hear heavy fighting away on the left in the French line in the direction of TERZELI. […]

Close on midnight three companies (weak) of French arrived up from VALANDOVA. They had lost their way a bit but were to take up position covering their right flank, which appears to be somewhere between the 7th RDF left and the STRUMITZA road.

The position tonight so far as I can discover is that the French line runs from somewhere near MIROVČA[81] station on the Vardar river – along the ridge N[orth] of VALANDOVO and RABROVO – joining our

---

80  Now Valondovo.
81  Now Miravci.

left near the stream which runs down from near KAJALI to just west of TATARLI. There our line begins, held by two companies of 7th RDF – then we hold the Simonet Ridge with B Company on the left and D on the right as far as Butler's Road. We have two companies, A & C, out ½ mile in front. On our right the 6th Royal Inniskilling Fusiliers, and I suppose the 5th, too, hold a retracted flank down towards CALKALI. What comes then I don't know. Let's hope there's someone there!

## Wednesday 8 December 1915.
## Crête Simonet/Yellow House/Dedeli Pass

It was a very cold night and we got no sleep. Bill Whyte & I lived on the tin of biscuits that Harold Jacob sent me. We had nothing else except water. There was no fighting going on during the night and the Bulgar was very quiet; probably moving up more troops and guns. I think the Bulgar imagines there are more troops here than is the case, and is therefore moving cautiously. At 03.50 we were ordered by the 30th Brigade to send A & C companies to hold Crête Rivet as a reconnaissance showed that there were no Bulgars there. They were told to keep all but the necessary observation posts under cover on the rear slopes and particularly to avoid all unnecessary movements. I don't understand this move, as our companies are supposed to be part of Divisional reserve, and part of the 31st Brigade should have been on Crête Rivet. It seems as if they must have moved to their right during the night after making the reconnaissance and our companies in the valley between Rivet and Simonet are really in the front line.

We got a report from Lieutenant Martin C Company who was on the left of the outpost line, timed 08.10, that he had taken up his position without loss. He reported very heavy fighting on his left on Hill 350 which the French are holding. He also said that enemy snipers were very active. The secret is out at last! The whole British and French forces are leaving Serbia, as they cannot help the unfortunate Serbs any more. At 09.30 we got a message from the 30th Brigade that 1st line transport would be parked near YELLOW HOUSE and supplies for the 9th instant would be handed to the troops there when they arrived. We had never heard of Yellow House and had to send to Brigade to enquire. They replied that it was at the top (or South end) of DEDELI Pass.

Soon after daylight the Bulgar started shelling a good deal and there was also a lot of rifle and MG fire somewhere in front, but the fog was too thick to see anything of the other two companies. I went up to the centre of Simonet ridge on B Company's right, but could not see nor find out anything. I received a message at 11.10 saying that the Bulgars were holding KAJALI and MEMISLI in force and were trying to work around the right flank of A Company. This message was sent off by runner at 09.10 and was signed 'M Moloney[82] 2/Lt OC A Coy'. This must mean that Lieutenant Gilliland[83] was either killed or wounded. The orderly didn't know what had happened. I sent this message on to Brigade asking for some artillery support, and got a reply from Colonel Cox 'Will ask Division to help, but do not think we have any guns. [...]' The next information we got was from C Company timed 11.35 and sent by runner. This said that the Bulgars were massing in large numbers on the left flank of C Company and that they would have to retire if seriously attacked. This was quite in accordance with orders making Simonet ridge the line of resistance. The message was signed 'R Turner[84] 2/Lt OC C Coy' and a footnote added 'Mr Martin is wounded'. The orderly who brought the note said Martin was wounded in the arm, and had gone down the ravine between us and the French to get to an ambulance on the TATARLI–DEDELI road. He said their Company were having a very heavy rifle and MG fire from the front and flanks, the MG fire coming from the Mosque tower in KAJALI. I have not been able to get any information about the right flank. Patrols sent out by D Company's right platoon have not got into touch with anyone. About midday the fog showed signs of lifting a bit and I could distinctly see a large number of Bulgars, 700 or 800 I estimated, making their way into the ravine South of DOROL OBA, and are probably trying to make their way round behind us at CALKALI via PRSTAN.

At 13.30 we got this message which further complicates the outlook. 'No 4 platoon A Co[mpan]y are now in valley on side of Crête Simonet (near 7th RDF). We had to withdraw from the position owing to being enfiladed and caught in rear by three machine guns from KAJALI village. I then moved the platoon round to face a threatened attack by Bulgars on our right flank which we beat off – awaiting orders. CD Jackman

82  Moloney was captured by the Bulgarians on this day and remained a prisoner until the end of the war. See WO 339/901.

83  Lieutenant William Edward Gilliland, formerly Norfolk Regiment, who does not appear to have been killed (WO 372/8/22597).

84  Richard Turner was born in 1892 in Londonderry and enlisted as a private in the South Irish Horse in Sept 1914, by which time he was living at Ranelagh, Co. Dublin, but was commissioned two months later and transferred to the RDF. He ended the war as a Captain. See WO 339/744.

2/Lieutenant [...].' We told Jackman to remain where he was on the left of B Company. The fact of Jackman having to face his right flank and being driven diagonally across behind C Company looks as if the right flank generally was in serious danger. The trouble is that our lines of supply and retreat lead off to the right flank and the Bulgars have therefore a fine chance to cut us off. However, if the 31st Brigade & the 29th (wherever they are) do their job for a bit longer, the Division should be OK. We haven't much spare ammunition, but we can give the old Bulgar a pretty good knock yet before we go. At the same time as the above message we got one from 30th Brigade as follows. '[...] Strong Bulgar forces are reported to be concentrating against CRÊTE RIVET. Your companies there must take precautions to guard their right flank and hold the path KAJALI–TATARLI. They must only retreat if very hard pressed, and then in conjunction with the French. Am sending 4 MGs and 2 Coys 6 RMF to support right of Crête Simonet. You will be in charge of firing line on Crête Simonet and must hold it at all costs. The French have reinforced their left with 2 Maxims. [...]'

The two companies of RMF were under Captain French, a jolly fine soldier. His orders were to attack with the bayonet if the Bulgars try to turn out right flank. I think the Brigade are wrong about the position in front, as I don't think our companies there have the French on their left. I believe the French are about level with the left of the 7th RDF 800 yards back. At any rate we sent a message at 13.05 to B and D companies telling them that the other companies might have to retire, and to cooperate with and help them, and telling them about the RMF coming on the right flank. The trouble here is with communications. We have no phone wire to run out to the companies and the fog prevents visual signalling. Two orderlies I sent out have been hit or killed as they haven't returned with answers. The situation in front is not at all clear, and I'm afraid the two companies have been split up into platoons and are fighting it out independently of each other. Captain ET Horner Norfolk Regiment made some feeble excuses to the Brigade about the Brigade transport needing an experienced officer to look after things, and they allowed him to slope off! He had the wind up properly and the dirty blighter went off at a most critical time, when he was most wanted as second in command of the battalion. If I have anything to say to it I would have him courtmartialled for cowardice – and I told him so. What must the men think of him!

We heard this afternoon from the intelligence people that the Bulgars have seven divisions and eighteen guns on our front, and as their Divisions are normally twice the strength of ours, it looks a happy state of things.

During the day we were continually shelled with HE and shrapnel, and not a single gun of ours replied. The most important message so far was received about 15.45, saying, 'Enemy are reported getting round 31st Brigade right flank. If true you must find your way back to DEDELI. We will let you know on the phone – 30th Inf Bde. 15.30.' A phone message came soon afterwards and said the position was still obscure, but critical as the 31st Brigade had given way. We had no news from A or C companies for some time until now, when small parties began falling back on our line on Crête Simonet. They said they had been very heavily fired on by guns and rifle fire from both flanks and in front, and had been rushed in the fog by large numbers of Bulgars. The accounts were very conflicting, but it seems certain that many platoons found themselves surrounded a good many of the men being wounded and captured, and others fought their way out. B Company also sent in a message at 16.00 that the Bulgars appeared to have captured Crête Rivet and could be seen in great numbers moving about behind the sangars. They also had mounted two small guns which were shooting straight into B Company's MG positions. I think we may prepare to stay here and fight it out. Most likely the Bulgars are already behind us in TATARLI. Anyway they ought to be, but they have been most unaccountably 'sticky' and instead of exploiting their successes and pushing hard on, they have dawdled along as if afraid to meet us.

Bill Whyte was over at 30th Brigade HQ for a good while in the afternoon and when he returned he said it had been decided to retire the whole line in the evening from the ridges on the North of the TATARLI–RABROVO valley, instead of waiting till Saturday 11th as at first arranged. The French have been so confident staying here indefinitely that they brought up enormous supplies of all kinds right up to their most forward positions. When it was seen that we must clear out, the French kept putting off our move from day to day to let them get their gear safely away – although the Bulgars were steadily piling up their forces against us. It seems that Sir Bryan Mahon had agreed to several postponements to cover the French withdrawal, but had now decided that he would not risk getting his force scuppered to save some French baggage.

A timetable was arranged for this evening, and the Battalions of the 30th & 31st Brigades were to move out in echelon from the left. […] The 29th Brigade were said to have gone already leaving our right flank and rear open. I personally went round the line and explained to everyone what the move was, and compared watches. All the 6th RDF were to concentrate at the old transport lines at TATARLI. As it would be dark when we moved, the men were told that they must make their own way to TATARLI even if split up into small parties.

When I got over to D Company on the right and asked for Lieutenant Cullen who was in command, his Sergeant-Major told me that, not being satisfied with the reports of his scouts, he had gone out himself to try to get some information of the Bulgars' movements. It was by this time practically dark and the fog was very dense and wet – just the conditions for the Bulgar if he was enterprising. I got the company dressed and standing to arms, and just then Cullen came dashing in lugging his orderly, who had been wounded, with him, and told us that a large mass of Bulgars was creeping up in the fog and were only about 50 yards away. We hastily formed up the men and fired five rounds rapid along the ground into the fog. Almost at the same time we heard B Company on our left firing too. We must have got a lot of Bulgars as we could hear their shouts and groans. The Bulgar then charged and we gave them another five rounds rapid as they loomed up in the fog. Some of our fellows even got at them with the bayonet. The old Bulgar was so shaken up that he retired into the fog to pull himself together a bit. As it was now almost exactly 18.00, this part of the line withdrew and moved diagonally across the South face of the ridge towards the western end of it where the ravine down to TATARLI runs down through the woods.

Having got these people away OK we withdrew the left half of the line at 18.15 and moved down after the other party. They made a terrible noise stumbling over rocks and falling about in the dark. Just as we had got everyone away behind the left flank and some 400 yards down, the Bulgar charged along the whole crest and arrived at the top, making the devil of a row, cheering and shouting and blowing bugles and I suppose wondering where we have got to. They also burned coloured flares to show their artillery where they had got to. They didn't come any further than the crest but kept shooting down the slope of the ridge and onto the face of the next one (the 'Signal' ridge), evidently thinking we had retreated the whole line straight to our rear. Instead of that we were away to the flank going down the ravine and had nobody hit. We had very few casualties in the line holding Simonet ridge. One was Lieutenant DB Gilmore who was rather badly wounded in both legs during the afternoon – as he came down past our HQ he apologised most humbly and said he couldn't help it! He is a jolly good lad and so is Arthur Cullen who took over command of D Company Corporal Crosbie (signaller) was hit through the neck but not badly. We had a lot of shrapnel and HE over our HQ but no one else was hit. Young Pearce (Signal Officer) was in a considerable funk during the day and I tried to make out everything was all right. All the same I didn't feel a bit easy, and in fact I felt sure this afternoon we were to be scuppered to let the rest get safely away. We had an awful peramble in the dark down the ravine and through the woods above TATARLI. There was only the trace of a track and we missed it several times. One of the MG section carrying the gun fell down into the ravine and lost the gun. We searched all over the place among boulders and undergrowth but owing to the darkness we could get no trace of it. Finally, we all arrived in TATARLI and sorted out the men of other Battalions. Here we broke open some cases of biscuits and bully beef which Stuffer Byrne had placed there for us, and gave each man as much as he could carry. I was delighted to get something to eat as I felt perfectly ravenous. Shells were plugging down into the village and a lot of overshy rifle bullets but we had nobody hit. The men were A1 performing a most difficult job of retiring under such circumstances, without the least show of excitement or nervousness. Having fed we marched off in column of route along the new road leading over the ford to DEDELI. The Bulgars were still shooting away ammunition at the air from the top of Crête Simonet and shelling TATARLI and the valley, but they did not reach us.

When we got to the DEDELI Pass we found a frightful crush of French troops, guns, baggage waggons etc, all tracking south as hard as they could go, without any formation. They had set fire to their stores at VALANDOVA and RABROVO and the whole valley behind us was lit up with the huge blaze.

We managed to squeeze along up the pass in single file sloshing along in deep mud and soaked with a wet mist. It is a shame the way the French are thieving everything they can lay hands on belonging to civilian Serbs. Every vehicle and animal is piled high with tables, chairs, carpets & copper cooking utensils; and besides this they have cattle, sheep and goats being driven along – but it's possible this may be part of their rations, although I doubt it.

Just as we came up the steep incline into the village of DEDELI four guns just over our heads started firing. The sudden crash and brilliant flash only a dozen yards away and facing us fairly made us jump. They were the first of our guns that we have heard for two days or more.

We found Stuffer Byrne apparently in command at the top of the Pass. He had made arrangements for each Battalion's bivouacs and had guides ready. He had big fires lit and hot food ready for everyone. Then he was ordering French batteries and Irish regiments, Zouave pioneers and English gunners, creating order out of chaos as if he were Quartermaster General. That man ought to get the DSO. He rises to the occasion and no job is too big for him to run when the need arises. We arrived here (Yellow House) about midnight and bivouacked on the N[orth] side of the road. We had a fine hot meal which everyone badly needed. Byrne had a limber cover as a bivouac for me.

## Thursday 9 December 1915. Yellow House

A very cold damp night but I had a good sleep. We were covered by the 5th Royal Irish Regiment and the 10th Div Cyclist Company (the blighters we had known at KOSTURINO), and two batteries of the 68th Field Artillery Brigade. The 3rd battery (Butler's) was captured yesterday near MEMISLI, the gunners continuing to fire point blank until the Bulgars were on them. They then blew up the guns and scrambled away down the ravine in fog and I hear that all the personnel of the battery escaped. So far as I can make out at present, our casualties have been five officers & ten other ranks wounded and three officers & 150 other ranks missing – total eight officers & 160 other ranks. [...]

We fell in the Battalion about 08.00 and had a roll call and made enquiries about casualties, and, as usual, had most contradictory statements – the men usually have extraordinarily little idea of what is going on, and an orderly going off with a message is sometimes reported as a whole platoon being driven from their positions! A good many men who have lost their way got attached to other Battalions are coming in, but most that we collect belong to other regiments. It is a most miserable day and everyone is soaking wet and we have no news of the Bulgar. We have only ¾ rations but are really not badly off. I was kept very busy trying to reconcile company strength returns with reports of casualties. It would never do to make a mistake and give unnecessary gyp to people at home. [...]

[...]

About 18.00 we sent out D Company under Lieutenant AA Cullen to our right flank to do escort to Major Anstruther's[85] battery of the 68th Field Artillery Brigade.

---

85  Robert Abercrombie Anstruther, born in Carnbee, Fife, in 1879 and educated at
     Wellington College. Served from 1896 and in the South African War in 1900 with

Everything was still very quiet, but the guns occasionally shoot off into the fog on previously registered points.

## Friday 10 December 1915. Yellow House

The mist is still as thick as ever and everybody and everything is wringing wet. Major Reeves' battery (67th Field Artillery Brigade) in the Dedeli Pass was banging away all night firing at known tracks and places they have registered, and a French 75 mm battery is doing the same. I suppose this is keeping the Bulgar back a bit, and the fog is helping as it makes him uncertain of our movements. All the same, the Bulgar must be pushing along our right flank unless he is a fool. [...] At 10.00 we sent out B Company with Second Lieutenant AC Corbetta[86] in command to relieve D as escort to the guns, taking their day's rations with them. D Company reported that everything was 'extremely quiet' during the night: they had not been unable to find any Bulgar patrols and had heard nothing. They had patrolled the ravine at SOBRE ZIR and over as far as SOBRE BALA.[87]

[...]

Sir Bryan Mahon came along during the day and had a talk with Colonel Jourdain[88] 5th Connaught Rangers, Bill Whyte and self. The position is very obscure and he hadn't much to tell us, but it seems the Bulgars are pushing the French hard, down the Vardar Valley. [...]

We have been attached some pack mules today – three per company and three for HQ. One is for water pack hauls and two for ammunition. This evening there was heavy firing away on our left rear and we heard that the French had taken a bad knock at FURKA halfway between us and GJEVGJELI on the Vardar river. It was said practically the whole of their 67th Brigade had been scuppered with General, staff and guns.

---

the RFA. In Salonika with the 68th Brigade RFA from Oct 1915 to Aug 1917, being awarded the DSO in June 1917. Went on to hospital with neurasthenia and eventually left the army on retired pay in 1921 'on account of ill-health contracted on active service'. See WO 374/1936.

86  Algernon Charles Corbetta, formerly Norfolk Regiment (WO 372/5/23497).

87  Now both covered by the area called Sobri.

88  Lieutenant Colonel Henry Jourdain, 1872–1968, see: https://ww1.nam.ac.uk/ stories/lieutenant-colonel-henry-jourdain/#.XwdVSChKiUk [accessed 9 July 2020].

If it's true it's not a nice position for us or our guns in DEDELI Pass. If the Bulgar are as far round our left flank as FURKA and also come round our right near DOIRAN, we will have to put up a useful scrap to get back. The Greek–Serb frontier is at DOIRAN and there seems a doubt if the Bulgar will cross this, as he has not declared war on Greece. In fact I think he expects the Greeks to join with him. In that case we may have to mishandle the Greeks somewhat to get back to Salonique [Salonika]. [...]

No orders of any kind yet nor have we had information from Brigade today. The men are resting or sleeping – the officers prowling about soaked to the skin and afraid to lie down in case of sudden orders for a move. Captain Horner who rejoined yesterday after practically deserting us on Crête Simonet went sick today with a sore toe! I'd like to give him the weight of mine for a rotten scrimshanker. Parish also went off sick. Most of the people who have gone sick have been [from the] Norfolk Regiment and soon we will be shot of the whole crowd. There has been no sign of any enemy attack on our front and our patrols saw none of his. About 21.00 I lay down to try to have a sleep for a while, but it was too wet and cold, so I tramped up and down instead, to try to get warm.

## Saturday 11 December 1915. Doiran

At 00.20 the following message arrived from the Brigade. '[...] Retirement begins at once. The 6 RMF – 7 RMF – 6th RDF – 7 RDF – 5 Connaught Rangers – 10 Hampshire Regiment will concentrate immediately at Brigade HQrs at SCOTCH HOUSE. [...] Scout officers and twenty men per Battalion to remain behind to deceive enemy if possible till noon tomorrow and then retire to DOIRAN. [...]'

Second Lieutenant RA Clay[89] our Scout Officer, and twenty men of his platoon were accordingly sent off for this duty. They travelled light only taking rifle and bayonet, 170 rounds ammunition and their rations. Their orders were to light fires behind various crests which would shine on the fog overhead and make the Bulgars think that troops were camping there in large numbers. They were also to patrol widely and fire shots

---

89  This is probably a temporary attachment to the battalion, Robert Angus Clay, of the 3rd Princess Louise's (Argyll and Sutherland Highlanders), born in 1887 in Peru and living in Liverpool when he volunteered in Dec 1914, applying for a commission in March 1915. Ended the war as a lieutenant. See WO 339/40044.

here and there. I sent a message to B Company by orderly telling them to march independently with all speed to DOIRAN and join us there, keeping the orderly with them. However, the orderly came back to report the Company moving off now as the guns had gone some time and Major Anstruther had told Corbetta to expect orders to move at any minute. We did not move off from Brigade HQ until 04.00 after a long delay getting the other Battalions collected and closed up. [...]

The whole column marched very well indeed, and at a fine swinging pace. The road was quite a well made main road and is not nearly as muddy as I expected. Save after we moved off we heard a series of big explosions which turned out to be the Royal Engineers blowing up the bridges in the DEDELI Pass behind us. As this is the only decent road in this part of the country the Bulgar will not be able to bring up his big guns after us. We had a ten minutes stop about halfway, and then went right through the town of DOIRAN (where the road was awful) to within ¼ mile of the station on the Constantinople railway. We crossed the Greek frontier at 08.00 at a point about halfway between the town and the station. Near DOIRAN we passed the 64th Brigade of the 22nd Division[90] camped on the N[orth] side of the road in tents. They made our men perfectly furious by jeering at our fellows marching by, and shouting 'Hi, the Balkan runners, look at the Balkan runners'. I really thought the men would break ranks and go for them. Our fellows had stood all sorts of hardship and trouble and were still a fine fighting unit, and here were these pampered blighters calling them cowards. These people had tents to sleep in and huge fur coats with the fur outside and heavy gloves and mufflers, and everything to make them warm and comfortable. All their wheeled transport was there and their cookers were going full blast with their breakfast. These fellows had never seen a Bulgar nor probably any other enemy and that's the way they behave to our veterans. We heard later that a company from this Brigade (I think they were East Yorks)[91] had been sent out during the night to see what the Bulgar was doing and not a single one of them came back, the whole batch being scuppered.

The whole 10th (Irish) Division bivouacked together inside Greek territory, on a flat place near the station. We had all the transport loaded

---

90  Drury was mistaken about the Brigade because the 64th Brigade was part of the 21st Division who were not in this theatre. The 22nd Division included the 65th, 66th and 67th Brigades.

91  There were no units of the East Yorkshire Regiment in the 22nd Division, although the 9th East Lancashire Regiment were in the Division as part of 65th Brigade.

up and everything ready for an immediate march. The dawn was breaking as we came in sight of DOIRAN lake and the fog had largely disappeared. The lake looked very pretty with water like glass. Not a ripple anywhere except close to the edges where the reeds grow in the water. There are a lot of duck here, and a French officer lunatic created alarm and despondency by going duck shooting with a carbine!

We found the road from DEDELI was quite good as far as where it joins the lake at KARA OGLULAR,[92] but alongside the lake under the high cliffs and through the town it was atrocious, with deep ruts and holes and mud over the top of one's boots. Everyone was very tired and sleepy, and soon there was not a sound in the camp. Stanley Cochran[93] produced a tent from somewhere and took me and Bill Whyte into it and made us comfy. He produced breakfast and ground sheets to lie on, and finally got an oil drum with holes punched in it to make a brazier with some charcoal he got in the village. We soon had a fine fug going and I don't know how we all escaped being gassed, as the brazier was going full blast in the middle of the tent with six or seven of us lying round. Stanley was in an awful state from wearing a suit of armour! He had got one of those bullet proof waistcoats and when the sudden orders came to clear out of Tatarli as fast as possible he put it on; but the constant movement of his body while riding have made the edges of the little plates forming the shield pinch his clothes and skin until he was almost bleeding and his shirt was in flitters.

[…] Clay and his warriors came in during the afternoon not having seen many Bulgars. They only met a few patrols, and did in several of them, the remainder clearing out double quick. A lot of French troops poured past us during the day and it is scandalous the way they have stolen tables and chairs and fittings out of the houses of the natives, and are driving away flocks of goats and sheep. Private Cusack[94] pinched one of the sheep while the French weren't looking, and rushed it into the lines and killed it. He put his head into our tent and announced to our surprise that we would have liver for breakfast in the morning. At 17.30 we heard that the 6th & 7th RMF had gone off by train to Salonika and that we were to march back and do right flank guard to the guns and waggons. Seeing that the Bulgars are in Monastir, 100 miles behind us, what are the odds on our getting back? The trek would take four or

92  Now Nov Dojran.
93  Private 15234 (WO 372/4/179617).
94  Probably 16454 Bernard Cusack (WO 372/5/138625).

five days even if not molested, with the country as wet as it is now. At 21.30 a message, timed 21.15, came in from 30th Brigade 'get ready to march at once' but in half an hour this was cancelled, and we lay down again. However, shortly before midnight we got orders to march off to the station and entrain for Salonika – what a relief – nobody relished the flank guard stunt. I believe it is to be done by the 22nd Division dogs of war!

## Sunday 12 December 1915.
## Doiran Station/Salonika

We reached the station of Doiran about 01.00 but there was no train there. There was a fearful crush of troops there and the place a quagmire owing to the transport waggons and animals having been parked there. We lay down the platform about three deep in the wet fog and tried to get warm but it was no go. The sleepers which formed the platform did not touch each other, and a bitter wind whistled through and chilled everyone to the bone. I'll never forget the sight of the place under the one small acetylene lamp on a post, shedding a pale glare over a steaming mass of tired and weary humanity. At last a train came in at 07.30 and we crammed ourselves in. We had twelve in our compartment and we closed up every chink and shut the ventilators and tried to go asleep. The engine made a feeble attempt to pull the train up the hill [...]. The rotten old machine went off the boil & the man on the safety valve wasn't heavy enough, so they had to take half the train up first and send the engine back for the other part. By this time we were all sound asleep, and I only waked up when we had arrived at the military station on the Monastir Road at Salonika at 16.30. We were the funniest sight on the platform as everyone was staggering about only half awake and almost too stiff to move. Here Gerry Watt had a meal ready for us of hot cocoa and a new kind of biscuit made by Jacobs, called No 4, which were the nicest we have ever had. There were lashings of cocoa, biscuit and cheese for everyone and we soon felt a bit warmer, but still very clammy. Then the rain came down as soon as we began to eat. After about an hour a base wallah came along with orders to march off to a camp that was prepared for us near SHAMLI[95] [...] North West about five miles across the

---

95 Now subsumed by Thessaloniki.

Constantinople railway and the GALIKO river.[96] It was a rotten march in pouring rain and bad roads and everyone tired. We went on and on and saw no signs of a camp until presently we came on a few tents in bags lying at the roadside. We were too fed up to bother about them so we dossed down for the night as we were. Owing to some scandalous neglect the camp had never been got ready.

## Monday 13 December 1915. Shamli/Dudular[97]

Sir Bryan Mahon was round early in his car to see us and was furious about the camp not being ready for us. He had given special instructions to have everything done for the men's comfort and food ready, and all that had been done was to dump half a dozen tents on the side of the road two miles further than the place arranged. He said he would send home whoever was responsible. He got Stuffer Byrne into his car and rushed him off to the ordnance stores and got more tents, blankets and clothing, and turned out another Regiment to pitch the tents, and get our cooker going to give our men a hot meal.

Our strength today is twelve officers, 480 other ranks. [...]

Here endeth the 2nd Spasm and for the second time the Battalion has been saved by the fog.

About 11.00 we got word that we were to shift our Camp to place about two miles N[orth] E[ast] of where we are now where the whole Brigade would concentrate, but at 12.00 orders came in cancelling the move for today. Some of us wanted to get leave to go into Salonika to buy some things we badly wanted, but could not go, for after all, we moved to our new camp North of DUDULAR overlooking both the railway and the Galiko river. We are very comfortable with plenty of tents, and we have had three blankets and one cardigan jacket issued to each officer and man.

---

96  Now the Gallikos River.
97  Shamli is now an unnamed industrial area between the railway line and the main road running west from Thessaloniki. Dudular is now Diavata.

# 6

# The Salonika Front and Hospital, December 1915–September 1917

Having withdrawn to Salonika, the British and French soon began to extend their defensive positions beyond the city. They created an area which became known as 'The Birdcage', extending about 15 miles west, 10 miles north and around 40 miles east to the coast of the Gulf of Rendina.[1] This meant that after arriving at Salonika in mid-December 1915, the next six months saw the 6th Royal Dublin Fusiliers located in a number of places just outside the city. Initially, they recovered from their time at Gallipoli and took stock of their equipment.[2] Little more than a week after their arrival they began to work on digging and building the Birdcage.[3]

By mid-January Drury believed that 'The defence works are getting immensely strong and I don't think any Balkan army, as usually equipped, could get through.' He described how the placing of wire would force attacking troops to bunch together in gaps covered by machine gun crossfire.[4] Work was hard, but there were opportunities for tourism and Drury wrote many accounts of his outings. In one, he described the Turkish bazaar in old Salonika.[5] The amount of material gathered by officers and men suggested that many had patronised local traders.[6] There were also battalion exercises and sports competitions.[7] In late April, 'We got the most astounding news [...] that a rebellion had broken out in

---

1 Wakefield and Moody, *Under the Devil's Eye*, 34–6.
2 Diary entries, 14–22 Dec 1915.
3 Diary entries, 23 Dec 1915–5 Feb 1916.
4 Diary entry, 14 Jan 1916.
5 Diary entry, 26 Feb 1916.
6 Diary entry, 25 March 1916.
7 Diary entries, 11 March, 15 and 22 April, 26 May 1916.

Ireland.' Drury feared, 'I don't know how we will be able to hold our heads up here as we are sure to be looked upon with suspicion.'[8] However, such fears appear to have been ill-founded as there were no signs in later diary entries of them being realised. Drury's duties within the battalion changed in early May as he lost his Adjutant responsibility and became Assistant Adjutant with, again, a role in signals.[9] All of this time around Salonika was calm, with the nearest sighting of enemy forces being a Zeppelin which was shot down,[10] although martial law was imposed on the town in early June[11] after the Greeks had withdrawn their garrison at the entrance to the Struma[12] Valley. This raised fears that Greece might capitulate to the Bulgarians and a standoff ensued between British/French and Greek forces, after which Greece eventually agreed to demobilise its forces.[13]

By that point, the weather was hot which took its toll on the men, not least because British/French lines were steadily being extended northwards from the Birdcage, due north towards Lake Doiran and north-east towards the Struma Valley, as a prelude to a possible allied offensive.[14] The timing of work parties was altered so as to avoid the worst heat.[15] Drury contracted malaria and, after a week of illness, had to leave his battalion for a fortnight first at a Casualty Clearing Station and then 29th General Hospital before he was sent by hospital ship to Malta in late July.[16]

Drury had hoped to be recuperating for only a few weeks, but he was in fact away from his battalion for a year. On 24 October 1916 he was invalided from Malta to Mudros on the Hospital Ship *Valdivia* for transfer to the UK on the Hospital Ship *Britannic*, arriving there on 6 November. By this time the 6th Royal Dublin Fusiliers had taken part in their last major action of the Salonika campaign, in the Struma Valley, part of the wider Allied Monastir offensive which ran from 12 September to 11 December. On 3 October they were ordered to take the village of Jenikoj.[17] The battalion moved from the Karadzakoj[18] area at 1.45am and

---

8   Diary entry, 29 April 1916.
9   Diary entry, 6 May 1916.
10  Diary entry, 6 May 1916.
11  Diary entries, 3 and 10 June 1916.
12  Now Strimon.
13  Wakefield and Moody, *Under the Devil's Eye*, 50.
14  Wakefield and Moody, *Under the Devil's Eye*, 50–2.
15  Diary entries, 17 and 30 June, 5 July 1916.
16  Diary entries, 10–27 July 1916.
17  Now Provatas.
18  Now Variko.

crossed the River Struma by the Jungle Island Bridge at 2.30am alongside the 7th Royal Munster Fusiliers. An artillery bombardment preceded their attack for about an hour, with the village captured by 6.20am. The 7th Royal Dublin Fusiliers and 6th Royal Munster Fusiliers followed to consolidate defensive positions. The wider offensive did see the capture of Monastir, though it did not ultimately succeed in relieving pressure on Romania nor force Bulgaria out the war.[19]

There was no repeat of such fighting at Salonika for the 10th (Irish) Division, though they remained there for nearly a year in and around the Struma Valley. Although periodically in frontline positions, days were mostly filled with similar activities to those carried out in much of 1916, with danger coming in the occasional patrol or enemy shellfire.[20] The Salonika front gained a reputation for inactivity, with the British force labelled the 'Gardeners of Salonika' (as they did cultivate the land).[21]

Meanwhile, Drury was treated for malaria and corneal ulcers at the 2nd Western General Hospital in Manchester's Whitworth Street, and by mid-March 1917 he was back in Dublin.[22] He eventually finished his medical treatment in May 1917 and was sent to Victoria Barracks, Cork, for a month's light duty. Leaving there on 24 June, he travelled to Salonika by boat from Southampton to Cherbourg and then across France and Italy by train, meeting a ship bound for Salonika from Taranto.[23] After a four-day sail Drury arrived off Salonika on 14 July and disembarked the next day.[24] On arrival, Drury sought to find a friend from home, Bunty, who was working as a nurse and appears to have been connected in some way to Drury's brother Kenneth, and they did manage to meet on a number of occasions.[25] By the time they met though, Drury had once again succumbed to malaria and also to eye problems that kept him in hospital again until late August.[26] When he returned to the 6th Royal Dublin Fusiliers he learnt of their operations in the Struma Valley, and the battalion was soon preparing to leave Salonika for Egypt. It did so on 9 September.[27]

---

19  Wakefield and Moody, *Under the Devil's Eye*, 60–5.
20  Grayson, *Dublin's Great Wars*, 216.
21  Ulrichsen, *The First World War in the Middle East*, 94.
22  WO 339/32747.
23  Drury 3, pp. 1–4.
24  Diary entry, 15 July 1915.
25  Diary entries, 17 and 20 July, 13 Aug 1917.
26  Diary entries, 18 July–28 Aug 1917.
27  Diary entries, 29 Aug–9 Sept 1917.

# Tuesday 14 December 1915. Outside Salonika

Had a grand sleep last night having over twelve hours without a move! We tried again to get leave to go to Salonika, but this is the answer we got from Brigade HQ.

'[…] Several substantial reports having been received of rowdy, disgraceful behaviour on the part of British officers in Salonika town, the GOC regrets that he has no alternative but to place the town out of bounds for all officers as well as other ranks, excepting those actually on duty. Officers entering the town on duty must be provided with a pass signed by an officer of not lower rank than Lt Colonel. The Olympos Hotel Restaurant is placed out of bounds for all ranks other than those possessing a special pass to be obtained only from the Base Commandant. Above orders will be made known to every officer under your command. […]'

I suppose some of the new people arriving while we were up country have been making fools of themselves, and we have to suffer for it.

Today we have been busy making up lists of deficiencies in kit and sending in notes of arms, equipment and clothing required to complete everyone to scale. They are kicking up the devil's own row about the machine gun we lost when it fell down the ravine at TATARLI. They seem to think we threw it away on purpose. As a matter of fact we found another gun the same night lost by some other unit so that we are now complete.

We are all having a good rest and making up arrears of sleep. Personally I feel very fit, but some of the men are not too perky. We are spending the time cleaning rifles & MGs, ammunition and kit, greasing boots etc. I am having a very busy time with Orderly Room work, specially in connection with casualties and those posted as missing. […] The Bulgars seem to have stopped short at the Greek frontier, and did not cross it anywhere.

# Monday 20 December 1915.
## Hortackoj/[28] Langavuk[29]

Today we have had bivouac sheets issued to us, like those the French have, and we will now be independent of wheel transport for carrying tents, and every man will have a shelter where ever he is. […]

---

28 Now Chortiatis.
29 Now Langadikia.

## Wednesday 22 December 1915. Langavuk

We had a good night's sleep and found the new 'bivvies' very useful. The Colonel went off early to look for a more sheltered spot for our camp and a bit further from the village, and later I marched the Battalion 500 or 600 yards up the Zagliveri ravine, and into a smaller ravine, opening on the right or East bank, where there was a fine snug spot for a camp and there was shelter among some trees and bushes for the horses and mules. The soil is all sand and it should keep in good order in the rainy weather. No work done today – only getting camp fixed up, as we are to stay here for a couple of weeks I hear. [...]

## Thursday 23 December 1915. Langavuk

[...]

We have now started digging in a new defence line. It is very different work from what it was in Gallipoli. There we had to dig in anywhere we happened to be whether it was well-sited or not, but here we can site our trenches and redoubts so as to give the best field of fire, and we can walk along out in front and see how they look from the approach. There is no enemy in front of us, as they have not crossed the Greek frontier, and we have cavalry patrols out keeping watch on them and to give a good warning if they do commence coming south.

## Friday 24 December 1915. Langavuk

[...]

It seems that while we were up in Serbia, some of the MLOs at Salonika got the wind up and started all sorts of yarns among the newly arriving troops about our all being scuppered, and the rest driven out of the country. A lot of the newer troops not knowing what was happening thought they had come in for another Gallipoli show.

Sir Bryan Mahon therefore sent around the following message which should make them sit up:–

'[...] It has come to the knowledge of the Army Commander that certain of the military landing officers are spreading a misleading and pessimistic summary of the situation here among troops being newly landed. The Army Commander wishes intimation to be clearly conveyed to all officers that he will not tolerate cowardly, mischievous, and unsoldierly gossip of this nature. So far from sharing the pessimism of these officers, and their exaggerated notions of the dangers and discomforts to which they think themselves exposed, the Army Commander is wholly satisfied with the military situation; has full confidence in his troops and those of our allies; and is filled with only one anxiety – that the enemy may fail to attack, and receive the very warm reception which is now being prepared for him. Disciplinary action will be taken against any officers or others who, by their attitude or conduct, do not maintain the spirit of cheerful confidence, which all traditions of the British Army entitle the Army Commander to expect. By disciplinary action is meant trial by General Court Martial under section 5 "spreading reports calculated to create unnecessary alarm or despondency", with liability to penal servitude if convicted. [...]'

[...]

## Saturday 25 December 1915. Langavuk

Happy Xmas everyone! Loveband arrived early after a trek over the mountains, bring[ing] us a letter and a parcel mail, and sausages, hams, fruit etc. for the men which he bought with PRI funds. I got cigarettes and sweets from the ladies of Rathgar Church, a plum pudding from Winifred,[30] and a big box of biscuits from Harold Jacob. We have a committee to arrange about the grub for the men [...] and their greatest exploit was getting up some barrels of beer from the Olympos Brewery Company Salonika. The men have quite got over their experiences in Gallipoli and Serbia, and are now looking very fit. The rations here are good and plentiful and there is lovely water, and we now have bread instead of biscuit on most days. The hard work digging and a long sleep at nights are making everyone fine and hard. We could do with a draft or two from home as our strength is only fourteen officers and 433 other ranks.

[...]

---

30  It is not clear who this was.

## Week ending Saturday 8 January 1916.
## Langavuk/Salonika

The work on the trenches, MG emplacements, and redoubts still goes on fast. We have done an enormous amount of revetting trenches with brushwood so that they won't fall in when not in use. The wire entanglements are wonderful and I hear that we have used no less than 1,000 miles of wire per mile of front. I have had a lot more riding about, generally with Bill Whyte and sometimes Arthur Cullen and have visited a lot of the villages out in front […]. The natives seem quite friendly and pleased to see us. They have had so many wars round here, and so many changes of masters that they don't seem to have much heart for improving anything and only want to be left alone. There are a lot of storks nesting in LANGAVUK where they have a nest on the roof of nearly every house as well as in many of the trees. They look most ungainly on their nests with their long legs sticking out, and they seem forever clapping their beaks at each other. The people don't seem to mind them on their roofs although the nests must be very heavy.

[…]

## Friday 14 January 1916. Verenos[31]

The defence works are getting immensely strong and I don't think any Balkan army, as usually equipped, could get through. There is a magnificent field of fire everywhere, and every range is carefully checked and noted down on boards in every platoon sector. The wire entanglements are designed to make troops bunched together in spots covered by the crossfire of many machine guns. […]

## Week ending Saturday 22 January 1916. Verenos

During the week we have been working away on the usual things, and the line is getting quite formidable. Captain Horner and Second Lieutenant Pearce went off sick on the 17th and Second Lieutenant Parish rejoined from hospital today. It's a good riddance getting quit of Horner. It is

---

31 Now Nikomidino.

amazing how nasty a whole bunch of officers from one district, can be. Most of the Norfolk Regiment are lazy, and many of them don't seem to have much training and they are not instinctive soldiers. Horner, who is a Regular, belonging to the 1st Norfolk Regiment, is the laziest of the lot, and I can't understand how Paddy Cox puts up with him. When Paddy returned from the Brigade and Horner had to revert from 2nd in command to commander of A Company, he continued to hang about HQ and did practically nothing with the Company, and I only got hard words when I spoke to Colonel Cox about it. I wanted him sent to C Company which badly wants pulling together.

We had a visit from the 12th Corps Commander General HF Wilson[32] (known as 'Scatters') during the week and he had a hearty laugh at our HQ. We had some petty malefactors out on fatigue doing up the fronts of some HQ dugouts, and they had traced out the pattern of our Regimental Crest with white pebbles stuck into the clay, and had the motto 'Spectamur [sic] Agendo' underneath. Wilson stopped and admired the work and turning to the man who did it, asked him if he knew what it meant. The man saluted smartly saying 'yezir'. Well, what does it mean, said the General. So the man hummed and hawed and said he 'didn't rightly know'. The General then told him to give the meaning of it in his own words if he knew it. So he began:– 'If ye were in a village on a Saturday night and ye seen a lot of fellows coming out of a public house drunk and singing, ye might say Them's Dublin Fusiliers!' This immensely pleased General Wilson who roared with laughter.

## Week ending Saturday 29 January 1916. Jerakaru[33]

[…] There has been a bit of a rush this week to get all the draining of trenches done, as we must soon expect the 'latter' rain, which is usually heavy although not as bad as the 'former' rain we experienced when we first came to Salonika. Here is some of the work we have already completed here.

400 yards of fire trenches complete.

1,000 yards of communication trenches.

---

32  Lieutenant General Henry Fuller Maitland Wilson, 1859–1941, GOC of XII Corps from Sept 1915 to Feb 1919 (*The Times*, 17 Nov 1941, p. 6).
33  Now Gerakarou.

180 yards of wire entanglements, using about 100 miles of wire.

3 redoubts guarding JERAKARU ravine and approaches.

2 miles of mule bridle paths made and signposted.

In addition we have cut an enormous amount of wood and made entanglements stake, dugout roofing, firewood etc.

## Week ending Saturday 5 February 1916.
## Jerakaru/move from Verenos/Kapudzilar[34]

On Sunday the 30th we got orders from the Brigade that work on redoubts was to be stopped and every available man concentrated on the front line, and asking how long the men actually worked, and how long they had for dinner. We replied they worked according to Brigade orders 7½ hours actual digging – ¾ hour for dinner and ¾ hour for marching to and from work – total nine hours. Parade 08.00, return 17.30. […]
Preliminary orders came in on the 31st that the 10th (Irish) Division is to move back from the line and have a refit and put in some intensive training. Half of the 30th Brigade is to go to KAPUDZILAR near Kalamaria, a suburb of Salonika, and quite close to the sea. […]
When we arrived at Kapudzilar we found a beautiful camp, which had been left spotless for us by the 1st Leinsters. The tents had all been fumigated, the ground carefully drained, refuse buried and the whole place was spotless, latrines & cookhouses all ready and even a fresh supply of water had been drawn ready for us. That's the right way to do things, but we have been otherwise treated before now. […] There is a deep ravine on the North and East side of the camp. On a plateau to the North of us is the 30th Brigade HQrs and on another piece of ground like ours, to the Eastward the 7th Royal Munster Fusiliers are camped. We are quite close to Salonika and the tram lines at Kalamaria are only about two miles away. We got word that a lot of mails and parcels for the Salonika army were lost when the steamers KAJOLA, LA PROVENCE, and HUNSGROVE, were torpedoed. Curious coincidence that the Hun U boats should torpedo the last named!

---

34  Now Pylaia.

# Week ending 26 February 1916. Kapudzilar

[…]

I had a most interesting time on Sunday. I started off about 10.00 from Kapudzilar and rode across the foothills above Kalamaria and passed above the Greek Infantry Barracks, and entered the upper part of the old town of Salonika through the breach in the wall near the Turkish Cemetery. This part of the town is altogether Turkish and we were always warned that it was dangerous to go in there. However, I was received with open arms by everyone. I left my horse in charge of a café keeper, and went for a walk through the bazaars and watched the craftsmen sitting at work at the open fronts of their shops. I saw most exquisite work in silk weaving, brass and copper work, shoe making etc. Copper seems to be dirt cheap in this country and even in the poorest villages there seems to be nothing but heavy copper cooking pots etc. I bought one or two things at some of the shops – a Tarbush or fez with a long black silk tassle – a silver enamel riding whip handle – a pair of miniature Greek shoes with a big ball of wool on the toes, like the people here wear on swell occasions. I had lunch at the café where I left my horse, consisting of coffee and native biscuits and sweet cakes made like a quoit – fruit – 'Turkish delight' – and a sort of sweet made of nuts – and some native cigarettes. They turned out the local band in my honour while I sat in the street at lunch. There was a bass drum about 3'6" diam[eter] and only 1'0" wide – a bagpipe made of a goatskin with three droves stuck in the places of three legs and a chanter in the fourth – and a couple of large crude instruments looking and played like flutes. The music was in a sort of minor key but not true to scale, and it wandered on in a queer unending fashion. In a way I liked it but it was hard to say what was expressed by it. The natives seemed to enjoy it thoroughly to judge by the applause, in which I joined to their evident gratification. In the afternoon I went on up to the extreme top of the town and came out at the citadel or fortress called JEDIKULE. This is separate from the town and has its own walls which are very high and have the usual devices for protection from attack. The whole place looks very old but is in good repair and is at present used as a prison for the use of local malefactors. There was a nice grove of trees between the city wall and the citadel with a good café under them which was going full blast when I arrived. I had another cup of excellent coffee here, and at once became the centre of attraction, as a big crowd of people kept passing me, and examining me very thoroughly, likewise my horse and harness. It was all quite friendly however, and they saluted and smiled at me, and when I gave a few lepta as baksheesh to some small πεδια³⁵ [children] they all seemed very bucked about it. They all seemed very impressed and interested in the good quality and workmanship of my saddle and bridle, and they kept handling them and pointing out to one another details of the sewing etc. I had a delightful ride back in the gloaming to camp after a most enjoyable day. Salonika is a wonderful old place, and the view from the upper part of the town is magnificent. I was very surprised at the cleanliness of the Turkish quarter, although I could see no signs of any proper drainage system. Of course the smell of any Eastern town is quite unlike anything at home and therefore we probably notice it more, but they would probably say the same if they chanced to visit Dublin. They told me that their water is brought down from the hills by several conduits built in the time of the Romans and kept in use ever since. I must have a look at these some time.

[...]

## Week ending Saturday 11 March 1916. Kapudzilar

We had a great time this week with MG and other competitions. 'Fritz' Cullen who is our MG Officer, is an absolutely first rate young fellow, as keen as he can be, and A1 at organisation, with the result that our team were far the best in the Division. We have pack equipment now for carrying the guns and ammunition on mules, and the competition consisted of one gun team from each Battalion loading up gun and ammunition, dashing off about one mile over rough broken country, bringing the guns into action against targets at unknown ranges. Having knocked out the targets, the guns had to be repacked and the sections hurry back to the start. The times for all this were taken and marks allotted, and marks were also given for accuracy of fire and minimum of ammunition expended on the job. There were also marks for smartness of turnout and full condition of packing on return. Heavy loss of marks would be incurred by any loss of equipment or ammunition due to hasty packing or hurrying over their country. We won this competition easily, scoring full marks. There was also a cross country race between teams of one officer, one sergeant and five men of five miles in full marching order, which we won, but I wouldn't give much for their clothes at the end of

35   This is the form used by Drury, but he presumably meant παιδιά.

it. We finished with a marching competition for old men over 40, when marks were given for smartness of turnout etc. This was won by Sergeant Burke our Regimental Cook Sergeant, who has now had 43 years' service with the Regiment! He has been known for years by the nick-name of 'General' Burke. When he won and went up to receive his prize from Sir Bryan Mahon, there were tremendous shouts of 'Well done General' 'Good old General' etc. Mahon seemed a good deal mystified, thinking the men were making some remarks on his adjudication, but we explained the reason to him, and he called up Burke, and shook his hand calling him 'General' Burke and congratulated him on his prowess and his long service. Sir Bryan Mahon is immensely popular in the Division and the cheers given him when he was leaving must have pleased him. Although he is now commanding the whole Salonika army of five divisions, I think his heart is in the old 10th.

## Week ending 25 March 1916. Azrameri[36]

On Monday the 20th we moved away from KAPUDZILAR, as we had finished the Kalamaria to Hortackoj road, to a place on the north slope of the hills near the village of AZRAMERI. [...]
We had Reveille at 05.30 – Breakfasts 06.15 Waggons packed 07.15, all tents struck and packed by 07.30. Battalion Parade 08.30. Haversack lunch taken on Hortackoj plateau. This move of ours will surely be historic. We have been so long in a comfortable camp and near Salonika that we had accumulated an enormous quantity of rugs, mats, lamps, tables & chairs for the messes etc. and were naturally loathe to dump them if by any means we could carry them to our next camp. [...]
Thus the 6th Royal Dublin Fusiliers left Kapudzilar, with an enormous baggage train stretching so many miles of road that when the head of the column marched into the Hortackoj plateau, the last of the transport waggons had only just cleared the old campsite 5½ miles away! The whole countryside was out to see us pass, as if we were the Lord Mayor's show, and many's the joke shouted at us as we passed. The Brigade Major rode down a bit of the way from Hortackoj to meet us and he nearly had a fit when he saw the procession. Fortunately, General Nicol was away at a conference at 16 Corps HQ, or there would have been trouble.

---

36  Now Ardameri.

We had a very beautiful day for our trek, and we arrived in our new place about 15.00 and at once set about putting up tents. We found ourselves quite near the 5th Royal Inniskilling Fusiliers, and the 5th Royal Irish Regiment who are our Pioneer Battalion. The country is beginning to look lovely, and there are any amount of primroses and violets and miniature hyacinths growing about here. We are doing a good deal of training here too, as well as road making, and have started classes in MG-Bombing-Signalling and scouting, and we have started making a rifle range up to 350 yards. There is a fine road being made here which will run down from Hortackoj plateau through Azrameri to Jerakaru, and there is a branch turning east through SARAKINA towards ZAGLIVERI and down the ravine to Langavuk. We have a beautiful camp here, although it is a little cramped being on the top of a subsidiary spur jutting out North and overlooking Azrameri down below about ½ a mile. We have planted beds of wild flowers round each tent between the fly and the pegs, and each company vies with the others to display their company Orderly Room tent with a great colour scheme. Even after the men have finished a hard day's work they are doing something to beautify the camp until it is black dark in the evening. Byrne has managed to raise a small marquee from somewhere which we use for all sorts of purposes, such as lectures in the evening – canteen for the men – writing and reading room. We have now withdrawn all the jerkins, sheepskins, mufflers etc. issued in the cold weather, as it is now too warm to use them.

[…]

## Week ending Saturday 15 April 1916.
## Langavuk relief stunt/Hortackoj

Battalion strength on 10th April 31 officers 866 other ranks.

This week we had a great stunt, when the 30th Brigade practised trench relieving and other routine[s] with the 82nd Brigade of the 28th Division. We were to change with the 2nd Royal Irish Fusiliers, and we marched down in the afternoon of the 11th via Azrameri and across the spur to the Langavuk ravine. Here we were met by guides for each platoon and for company and Battalion HQ. Everything was beautifully done, and even water and firewood were provided in each company cookhouse. They had direction posts everywhere and range tables in platoon HQ and MG emplacements. The Colonel, Orpen-Palmer,[37] and his officers entertained our HQ royally in their mess in a marquee, and even had tents pitched for us and servants detailed to look after us. Of course, it was not a regular relief as the Irish Fusiliers only withdrew their men from the trenches to the usual bivouacs behind. However, it was good practice for all concerned specially for them (we had done its scores of times before under real conditions). There was a skeleton enemy out in front and we had to find them out by patrols and send back reports as to the position. The signalling arrangements were very well done, with laddering and alternative lines. We purposely broke several connections during the night to test our linesmen for rapidity in locating faults, and they did this very well. The line held was JERAKARU–LANGAVUK–VERENOS both inclusive, with the 6th Royal Munster Fusiliers on the left – 7th RDF – 6th RDF & 7th Royal Munster Fusiliers on the right. General Nicol 30th Brigade & General Macpherson 84th came round to the line between 23.30 and 02.00 and inspected everything, and asking questions of the men. Some of our officers seem to have little imagination as their reports came in with monotonous regularity 'nothing to report' – 'all clear' etc. instead of making up something to test message writing and transmission. Cullen (MGO) was the only one who correctly gave me his HQ position, and Captain McCreery[38] concocted a great message giving casualty lists – noting blue flares burned by the 'enemy' at 23.00 in a certain place, and giving enemy gun positions by cross bearings on their flanks, and the calibre of the shells dropping in his sector. The whole practice was very good, and the 2nd Royal Irish Fusiliers, who although Regulars, have had no fighting so far this war owing to being in India, were impressed with the quick way our men got the hang of the defence scheme and the lie of the trenches. We were greatly helped, however, by the forethought of the Irish Fusiliers and the way they arranged everything for our convenience. I couldn't help contrasting then with some of the blighters in the Terrier battalions at Gallipoli, and the hectic night we spent near SUSUK KUYU trying to relieve a jumble of idiots who were as bad as a lot of hens in front of a motor car.

[…]

---

37  Lieutenant Colonel Harold Bland Herbert Orpen-Palmer, 1876–1941, later
    Brigadier General (*The Times*, 21 Oct 1941, p. 9).
38  Mona James Nathaniel McCreery, died of influenza in Grimsby in Oct 1918. His
    mother lived in Kilkenny. See WO 339/19084.

# Week ending Saturday 22 April 1916. Hortackoj

We have a nice camp here on well-drained ground, and we get lovely water from the old aqueduct which supplies Salonika. We are duty Battalion this week and have all sorts of guards and parties to find, amounting to one officer and 75 men, some of them going as far as the ORENDZIK[39] ammunition dump [...]. Major Whyte is conducting classes for senior NCOs and subaltern officers in tactics etc, and every spare man is training all morning. We have football in the afternoon and then lectures. Otherwise nothing special. There are a great number of tortoises of all sizes here which have been hibernating under rocks and in holes. The warm sun and spring feeling in the air is bringing them out, and the men are having great fun with them by chalking their numbers on the backs of the animals, and then lining them up ten yards from their holes and seeing which wins. [...]

# Week ending Saturday 29 April 1916.
## Leave to Salonika/Hortackoj

[...]

We got the most astounding news on the 27th that a rebellion had broken out in Ireland. Isn't it awful. Goodness knows what they think they are going to gain by it. It's a regular stab in the back for our fellows out here, who don't know how the people at home are. The only news we have is a wire we received on the 27th through Signals, as follows.

'Mr Asquith stated in Commons martial law proclaimed in Dublin. 11 insurgents have been killed and drastic action is being taken by us to suppress the movement and arrest those concerned. Outside Dublin the country is quiet. Troops from Belfast and England have arrived, and the building called Liberty Hall is already occupied by soldiers.'

I don't know how we will be able to hold our heads up here as we are sure to be looked upon with suspicion. The men are mad about it all, but don't understand who is mixed up in the affair. I am sure Germany is at the bottom of this somehow.

---

39  Now Pefka.

# Week ending Saturday 6 May 1916. Hortackoj

The only other news so far of the rebellion in Ireland is a wire from London to the 'Balkan News' dated 30th and appearing 1st May saying that the rebels are confined to a few localities, the principal one being Sackville Street with their HQ in the G[eneral] P[ost] O[ffice]. Considerable sniping is going on from various houses in the city and considerable damage has been caused by fires, a large one still burning in Sackville Street. Other places affected are County Galway, Enniscorthy, Killarney, Clonmel and Gorey. Other parts of Ireland appear normal. Another wire appearing beside this says that there was heavy fighting near Loos, most of it being done by Irish troops who used the bayonet with effect. 'The gallantry of Irish troops is an answer to the German plots and attempts to rouse sedition in Ireland.' We also got news that General Townshend had been forced to surrender at Kut-al-Amara, by exhaustion of his supplies of food. The troops consisted of 2,970 British troops and 6,000 Indians and followers. This is damned bad luck on him. He put up a stout show, but it's not easy to see why he had to stand at Kut at all.

On Wednesday Colonel Cox told me he was going to make Second Lieutenant Esmonde Adjutant and make me Signal Officer and Assistant Adjutant. I asked if he were not satisfied with me as adjutant, and he said it was not that at all, but that GHQ were coming on very strong about communications during moving battles, and said I must take the thing in hand. I have my own view about the matter – the Colonel seems to be greatly struck with Esmonde and only because he is the old Regular Drill Sergeant, and he thinks that is all that is wanted in an Adjutant. I pressed the Colonel to let me go back to my company, from which I had been taken when Shadforth got ill, but he would not agree to do this. I don't think he is fair about it, but we must do as we are told I suppose. I therefore took over the signallers and all equipment. I found there were altogether 31 signallers including those with the companies, but not all these have passed the tests as signallers. The equipment was nearly complete the exceptions being items already on indent but not yet in possession.

[…]

We had great excitement in the early morning of the 5th. About 03.15 we heard aero engines over us, and found there was a Zeppelin heading to Salonika passing directly over us and seeming to be only 500 or 600 feet up. We had a signal station working with Mikra Karaburnum fort on the Bay of Salonika, and we sent the usual Zeppelin message – a series of 'Zs' in Morse (– – . . – – . . – – . .) (this always reminds me of the cooing of a wood pigeon!). We saw all the searchlights stabbing the sky and waving about searching for the gasbag. I had no idea there were so many available – they seemed to form an almost complete ring round the town. Soon they picked the Zep up and never lost her till she was downed. The Zep was heading S[outh] W[est] when over us making towards the big wireless mast at Kalamaria, and when the searchlights first got her she was almost on a level with our eyes (i.e. about 2,000 feet over sea level). Many guns started shooting from all over the place, dozens & dozens of them, and we could see the bursts going up far too high. Then the Zep turned at right angles and pointed N[orth] W[est] and tilted the bow sharply up and started climbing. The shells then seemed to be bursting all round her. After a few minutes she seemed to slow down and shudder as if hit, and then began rapidly sinking down but keeping an even keel. Then the firing stopped and she was hidden from our view by the hills round Salonika. In a few minutes more we saw a tremendous flare up that lit the whole sky, so we knew she was done in all right. This was confirmed by distant cheering and frantic blowing of ships' sirens and whistles. Soon afterwards we got this message. '[…] Zeppelin brought down early this morning. No trace of its crew. [...]'[40] [...] Later we heard that the shot which brought her down was fired by a 6″ gun on HMS *Agamemnon* out in the Bay, which had gone right through the gasbag from end to end. The Zep came down in the marshes at the mouth of the Vardar river due W[est] from Salonika. The crew landed safely and collected their papers, charts etc. and set fire to the envelope.[41] They were finally rounded up wandering in the marshes.

[…]

We had a most amusing footer match on Saturday between the 6th Royal Irish Rifles and the 32nd Field Ambulance in one of the rounds of the Divisional Cup. The Rifles are reported to have the whole of the crack team of soccer players in Belfast – Glentoran or Distillery or something. However, they made it three goals all, but the Rifles refused to play on. The 30th Brigade were on the touch line almost to a man, and the witticisms shouted at the teams during the game were most amusing

---

40  See Figure 2.
41  The 'envelope' was the skin of the Zeppelin.

to listen to. Shouts of 'Lower your sights Bill' greeted a high kick and the ambulance men were encouraged to further efforts by cries of 'Up the No 9s', 'go it the poultice wallahs'. The Rifles mostly had the title 'sticky backs'. I don't know why, but one of our fellows brought down the house when he shrieked out at then 'Go it, the Coniacks', the point of this was that three of the Rifles' team had been run in the previous night for being tight on Coniac[42] as the men call the local poison properly termed Mastika. It is something like absinthe or vodka. The reason the Rifles wouldn't play on was that they were afraid of getting beaten, so they wanted to wait for their three malefactors to be released.

## Week ending Saturday 3 June 1916. Hortackoj

In the evening [3 June] we had a message that Salonika was out of bounds to everybody and martial law had been proclaimed. I wonder what is up. I had a look at some of the trenches we are to take over, and found that an enormous amount of work had been done. The place is very strong and full of every sort of trap. A fine battle HQ is deeply dug into a spur jutting out in the middle of the sector, and duplicate phone lines run everywhere.

## Week ending Saturday 10 June 1916. Hortackoj

[...]

During the afternoon the 79th Brigade Signal Officer [...] brought an official message of a naval battle in the North Sea,[43] a good many of our boats being sunk, and more of the Germans who raced back to their harbours. He also told us about martial law having been proclaimed inside the fortified area, and the seizure of enemy consuls in Salonika.

In the evening McCreery of ours arrived with an advance party of twenty men. He said the Battalion had been ordered out at 16.00 yesterday to march to Salonika in case any trouble started. They had not returned at 10.30 this morning when he left and their rations have been sent on

---

42  From cognac.
43  The Battle of Jutland.

to them. The Hampshire Regiment marched off at 04.00 on Monday to [...] make roads.

During the day I made a map of the position and plans of trenches and communications and on Tuesday about noon the Battalion arrived. They had had nothing to do at Salonika, having remained all the time at the control post on the Kalamaria–Kapudzilar road, at the tramway to the brick fields.

## Week ending Saturday 17 June 1916.
## Guvezne[44] area, Kilo 35[45]

On Monday the 12th we got orders to move out of the line here and go north, on Tuesday evening. [...] On Tuesday the 30th Brigade moved to GUVEZNE which is on the main road to SERES at kilo 23. [...]

[...] We remained here during the day on Wednesday, and in the afternoon Colonel Cox got a wire from the 10th (Irish) Division that he had been granted home leave. This gives him a clear fortnight in England. He got his things together, handed over the Battalion to Major Whyte, and said goodbye on parade and went off in a great state of excitement, but trying not to show it. I hope I'll get a chance soon as I haven't been home for sixteen months.

This was a scorching day and easily the hottest we have had yet, but it was a little cooler when we paraded at 17.45 and marched up to Kilo 35 where we arrived very hot at 21.30. [...]

[...] The scheme of work here is that the men arrive for work at 04.30 and start on their section at 05.00 and carry on till 09.30 reaching camp by 10.00. In theory they rest and sleep till 16.00 when they go off crossing-sweeping again until 20.00. Actually nobody could possibly sleep either in a bivouac or out of it in this heat with a black swarm of flies buzzing and crawling over everything. I think the flies are almost as bad as Gallipoli, and being younger are more active! [...]

---

44  Now Assiros.
45  The various 'kilo' locations refer to places on the road north and then north-east from Guvezne. A detailed map of this area including hospital locations is available online through the McMaster University Digital Archive at http://digitalarchive.mcmaster.ca/islandora/object/macrepo:4141 [accessed 6 April 2020].

## Friday 30 June 1916. Kilo 46

We have got to know the country around here pretty well, so Bill Whyte, Cullen, Loveband and I go out nearly every morning spying out the land and trying to correct the maps which are very inaccurate. The weather is hotter than ever and the midday heat is absolutely scorching. The flies are the limit and remind me of the old story told of some manoeuvres in the West of Ireland under different conditions. A small party had lost themselves and were soaked to the skin and mighty miserable, and they were examining a map to see if they could locate their position. One suggested one place, and another a different one, and then their officer said he was sure they were at the 'S' of Castlebar. One of the men who had ventured no opinion so far then said 'Begob, I know where we are – we are at the Y of Bloody'. Everywhere you go are flies in myriads, everything you eat is covered with them and even sleep is almost impossible as they are crawling all over you and biting you. A huge joke was played on us by GHQ – they announced that an issue of fly netting was available for men to sleep under and units were to indent on ordnance for it. When it arrived we found that each man was allotted one square foot of gauze!

We have been having a lot of sickness and malaria and sunstroke, and Paine's sick parade the last few days has been nearly 100. Officers seem to be sticking it all right but Esmonde has been a bit seedy. Captain Clark[46] got word today to report for temporary duty as General Staff Officer 3 at 10th (Irish) Division HQ. I suppose they think because he is a Regular that he is better than any of our fellows. What about Shadforth, Luke or others?

[…]

## Wednesday 5 July 1916. Kilo 46

Absolutely the hottest day I ever felt. The full heat of the sun is absolutely stunning and the air is so hot that it seems hard to breathe. I don't know how the horses or mules stand it. We have tried to make sun shelters with branches, but they are not much good. However, they are sticking it out all right. […]

---

46 Captain R. Clark, 2nd Norfolk Regiment, who had briefly become as second-in-command of the 6th Royal Dublin Fusiliers on 20 June (see WO 95/4836: 6th RDF).

## Monday 10 July 1916. Ill at Kilo 47

Had an awful night with nightmares and bad headache. Paine came along in the morning & said I had a very high temperature, and thought it might be a touch of the sun. He wanted to send me off to hospital but I begged him not to do it, & said I would be all right in camp. Finally he agreed I might stay provided the Battalion didn't get orders to move. The heat & flies are terrible.

## Saturday 15 July 1916. Ill at Kilo 47

I don't remember much about this week. [I] seem to recollect intervals of violent shivering and then sweating until my blanket was soaking. I seem to have spent most of the time dreaming most awful dreams and vague sensations of some terrible doom impending. Some strange fellow that I think was one of Paine's orderlies seemed to be looking after me, and hinted that my servant was in jug[47] for something or other. I remember some time during the week Paine sponging my face & hands & chest and sticking up some more branches to make a bit of shade. Today someone produced a bottle of soda water which was delicious. It is remarkable how rotten food seems when one is not up to the mark, and I don't think I ate anything this week as the thought of rations made me sick.

## Sunday 16 July 1916. Ill at Kilo 47

[…] Paine seems alarmed at my temperature & says I must go down. There was a shower and thunder this morning that made a delightful change in the air. I can hardly move and am as stiff and sore all over as if sjamboked.[48] […]

## Monday 17 July 1916. Ill at Kilo 47

My fate is sealed – Paine announced he had arranged for an ambulance waggon to be sent up tomorrow morning at 8 o'clock. Expostulated, but

---

47  Prison.
48  Whipped.

could do no good with him. In fact, I don't seem to have the will or the power to think clearly of anything. It's amazing how I shiver with the sun at 120° or 130°. Sometimes I feel as if I were going mad.

## Tuesday 18 July 1916.
## 40th Casualty Clearing Station

Went off to the 31st Field Ambulance about 08.00. I am really not very clear about the whole proceeding, as the first thing I recollect clearly is being jolted and bumped about until I felt as if the top of my head was coming off. Dear old Paine! I have a vague idea of having cursed him when he saw me off the premises! About noon I left the 31st Field Ambulance in a motor convoy and went to the 40th Casualty Clearing Station at kilo 22 near GUVEZNE.[49] [...] This is a nice place, & the beds are awfully comfy. A nurse washed me all over with something like Eau de Cologne in the water and [I] felt fresher, but the shivering came on again until even the bed rattled. Wonder why they serve tea in such large bowls instead of cups?

Doctors came round and poked about and looked grave and then announced I was to be sent off tomorrow to the 4th Canadian General Hospital at Kapudzilar.

## Wednesday 19 July 1916. 29th General Hospital[50]

More sweating and dreams last night and [I] feel worn out this morning. About 09.00 the motor convoy arrived and I was shoved on a stretcher and put on the top tier with my face about one foot from the roof which felt like a furnace. It was a terrible journey over awful tracks and I had to keep my hands jambed against the roof of the waggon to prevent my head from being battered. What on earth happens to wounded men is hard to imagine. Here was I with nothing wrong with me and I could hardly stick out a few hours of it. At Lembet the convoy was stopped and switched off to the 29th General Hospital on the Monastir Road. We had to cut across country and bump about over new railway lines. What a relief to lie in bed again. The sister who came round seemed alarmed at

49  Now Assiros.
50  Located just south of Kalamaria.

my temperature and rushed off for the MO (Dr Maxwell). He hinted at some enormous figure like 106° and proceeded to take a sample of blood out of my ear. If he took a gallon of it, it might improve the sweating and shivering and headache. A marquee beside the one I was in caught fire during the evening and was totally burned in an incredibly short time. There were no patients in it I hear.

## Friday 21 July 1916. 29th General Hospital

Not very clear about anything until a thunderstorm and rain came on about 16.00, and then a lot of anti-aircraft guns started shooting which made my head ache again. I feel awfully weak and can hardly move in bed and they are constantly changing the sheets which get soaked with perspiration. […] I have a violent singing in my ears & feel very deaf as a result of taking doses of quinine. I believe I am taking 35 grains a day. […]

## Saturday 22 July 1916. 29th General Hospital

Slept better last night and feel better this morning. A great gale got up in the night and sent everything blowing all over the ward, and threatening to blow down the marquee. The gale blew till noon when it died down. Major Darnley & Second Lieutenant Bush were told this morning that they were to start at 17.00 tomorrow for Malta. Lucky chaps!

## Sunday 23 July 1916. 29th General Hospital

Nothing special – sleeping and feeling a bit better. The MO asked if I would like to go to Malta so I said no, unless I could stay on the boat and come straight back. I would like the sea trip very much but don't want to chance not getting back to the Regiment before they move up to the Struma. He said he thought it could be arranged.

## Monday 24 July 1916. 29th General Hospital

Feel better today as I had the first solid night's sleep for weeks. Temperature is now much below normal which makes one feel lazy. A great many aeroplanes passed over towards Salonika about 08.00 but I did not hear any shooting. In the afternoon the MO told me to get up for a bit, and when I tried to get out of bed I fell down and hit my head on the next bed. I was groggy about the knees and couldn't stand. They helped me into a chair in the porch of the marquee where I sat in the shade and had the first cigarette for a long time. The CO of the hospital came and chatted to me & said it was a 'double' one and had 1500 beds. He is a TCD man.

## Wednesday 26 July 1916. 29th General Hospital

[...]

I got dressed today for the first time, and had a shock when I saw how my clothes hung on me. My legs looked grotesque. My riding breeches which fitted well now look like 'slacks'. Feel rather dicky trying to walk, but I must be OK as they have put me on full diet.

Was told to be ready to start at 15.30. Feel quite elated at getting out again and going off for a trip. The convoy did not turn up at the right time, so the six of us who were going away were given a special tea in the surgical ward which was empty. We had tea, cucumber sandwiches, bread & butter, and tinned peaches. Convoy came along at 17.00 & I managed to get into the leading car to avoid the dust. Made rather a fool of myself trying to walk over to the ambulance – couldn't manage it & had to be 'manhandled' – most ignominious. Said goodbye to the kind people here and was awarded with a big envelope tied with string to a button hole and told not to look at it.

When we arrived at the Quay we were brought on a tug 71 which is used to convey patients to the hospital ships which are too deep draft to come into the quay. There were two old ladies (English) established on the tug with a coffee stall and they went around with the tea and lime juice and biscuits and gave each man a packet of Woodbines and some matches. One of the hands told me they ran this themselves at their own expense and had been on this boat for months, and were always ready day or night. It's astounding – and they look 60 years of age.

We got to the ship at 18.30 and found it was the Royal Mail Steam Packet Company's ESSEQUIBO which runs usually to South American ports. The MO in charge is Major Ellis RAMC. I was sent to ward 'C' & bed no 16. Feel very done up as the heat of the sun seemed worse than ever and my eyes started paining in the glare. The mysterious envelope was duly opened and seemed to create some alarm or despondency and

I was told to turn in. This ship is magnificent and there is not a fly to be seen.

## Thursday 27 July 1916. Hospital Ship *Essequibo*

Slept soundly for over twelve hours and feel very fit this morning. It is very hot but there is an electric fan near my bed which is a great boon. The great event was a bath of salt water which is worth all the medicine going. Breakfast at 08.00 beautifully served. What a treat is nice linen and silver and a menu to choose from. We had to remain by our cots at 09.00 while the MO came round. He showed me a temperature chart out of the secret envelope. It was written up by Paine and added to by others. It looked like a map of the Himalayas and no wonder I feel groggy. He said I must rest as much as possible as my heart was not good! What rot – my heart is as solid as a stone.

We sailed away from Salonika at 10.40 and I took a couple of photos of the town and one of a French submarine, and one of HMS *Agamemnon*. There was a most invigorating sea breeze blowing outside the bay and the view was magnificent. Turned in and slept till lunch time. Still feel shaky on the pins, and I had to sit down every few minutes, so I hope it isn't rough in the Mediterranean as I will have to lie down all the time. Have a bit of a headache again and my eyes feel uncomfortable with the glare off the sea. Am rather worried this evening as the MO says I must land at Malta & go to hospital for a while as I couldn't possibly be let back to the Battalion for some weeks. Damn!

[Drury returned to Salonika a year later].

## Sunday, 15 July 1917. Salonika

We were turned off the ship on to lighters at 07.30 and kept sitting in the heat alongside until 14.00 with nothing to do or eat or drink. We got pushed on ashore at the pier of the 'White Tower' where I got a lift on a lorry up to No 3 Base Depot at Summerhill near Lembet. I felt rather beastly all day and in a bad temper which wasn't improved by the accommodation in Camp. Rotten mess with no arrangement for feeding so many – hardly any water to be had – cheeky Mess Corporal and waiters. Sent wires home announcing safe arrival and one to Bunty asking her to meet me for tea at Flocca's on Tuesday at 15.00. Put in for an all-day pass to Salonika and got it, as I heard we were to wait for the arrival of another ship before a convoy for the front line was made up. Wrote to Colonel Cox telling him of my arrival.

## Tuesday 17 July 1917. Summerhill

Left Summerhill Camp, 10.00 and got a lift in an empty Sunbeam ambulance into Salonika. Had my hair cut and bought a few things and lunched with Aylward, Hartopp and Williams[51] in the new restaurant of the Hotel Splendide Palace, which did us very well indeed. Waited for Bunty at Flocca's but she had not appeared at 15.30, so went to the Army Signal Office which was just round the corner and rang up the 42nd General Hospital, where she is attached. They told me she had been sent sick to the Nurses Wing at the 43rd General Hospital, so I tried to get on there but couldn't get through, so, after a long time, I gave it up and decided to go out to see her. Took a tram out to Kalamaria and witnessed a frightful altercation between the conductor and a priest about the fare (10th of a penny) – thought they were coming to blows. Walked out to No 4 Canadian Hospital and asked the way and found the 43rd General was beyond it, up at the top of the hill. I asked for the Matron and was told she was in her quarters, so wrote a note explaining my visit. Was kept waiting nearly ¾ of an hour until the Matron came in. Very young and flighty-looking person. She told me Bunty had malaria and had been sent up that morning to the Nurses Convalescent Hospital, which I believe is somewhere up the hills behind the Italian Hospital. I couldn't go up to find the place as it was already 18.00 and I had to be back at Salonika at 18.30, so thanked the Matron, who looked as if she expected an invitation out to dinner, and left. I wrote a letter in the Orderly Room to Bunty telling her what had happened and saying I would do my best to see her soon and hoped she was better. It's too bad she is ill, and Kenneth will be very worried.

[…]

---

51  It is not clear who any of these are, but they do not appear to have been RDF officers.

## Wednesday 18 July 1917. Summerhill

When I got up, I felt as if I had malaria and my left eye was very sore. The MO, who was the only decent fellow in the place, gave me a lotion to use and said to take it easy. Later, I was put on an anti-gas course, in spite of having passed as First Class Instructor a few weeks ago! However, it keeps me off other worse parades.

## Thursday 19 July 1917. Summerhill

Feeling rotten, both eyes feeling very painful and somewhat out of focus. It's the limit if they are to go wrong again. The MO sent me in a Ford van to the 30th Stationary Hospital near Orendzik to see the eye-man, who said I had corneal ulcers, conjunctivitis and iritis, a nice jumble of things. Said I was to come in four or five times a day for treatment, but, when I said I couldn't do the distance that often, he arranged for me to stay there for a few days. I went back to camp for my baggage and returned at 16.30. The eye-doctor, named Brewer,[52] says I will only be in for a few days.

## Friday 20 July 1917. 30th Stationary Hospital

Eyes simply rotten, can't stand the least bit of light, finally the doctor bandaged them both up.

[...]

Had a delightful surprise when Bunty walked in on Tuesday, 24th.[53] She had not had malaria, but a touch of dysentery and was now recuperating in a convalescent camp near Hortackoj plateau. She said Kenneth was in good form and was Deputy Director Medical Services 6th Division, 1st Corps, in France.[54]

---

52 Captain Alexander Hampton Brewer, born in Hackney in 1875 and educated at Epsom College. Joined the Territorial Force in 1913, while living in Woking, describing himself as a 'Physician & Surgeon'. Served on the Western Front in 1914–15 with 83rd Field Ambulance in 27th Division. Was at Salonika from May 1916 to Nov 1917 and left the army in 1920. See WO 374/8842.
53 See Figure 3.
54 See Figure 4.

## Wednesday 1 August 1917.
## 30th Stationary Hospital

Relieved from bondage at last, after what seemed years. Would have gone mad, I think, only for the very nice fellows in the Marquee. One was a naval fellow, very bad malaria, had been through the Dardanelles, several times, with a submarine, as 2nd in command, and afterwards commanded a monitor. Tremendously able fellow and could talk most delightfully on a great range of subjects, he used to keep me company with yarns of all the different boats and stations he had been on. Two others in the ward were in the 7th Wiltshires that I had visited last year. They seem to have got it in the neck up near Gjevgjeli on the Vardar river.

The Sister who looks after us is named Martin and one of the fellows saw the name of a Miss Martin in the papers as being given a new title of 'Dame' so we call this sister 'Dame' Martin (gradually changed into Dam[n] Martin!). I had a row with her today but I think we will be good friends. A couple of times I have thought I heard crying but didn't know what it was, but, today, I saw the little VAD in tears and asked her what was wrong. After some trouble, I ascertained that this was the VAD's afternoon off and she had made arrangements with some others from another hospital to go for a picnic. Half an hour before she went off duty, 'Dame' Martin calmly told her she couldn't go till next day. There is nothing in the way of recreation here for these girls and tomorrow she couldn't have arranged any little fun. Sister Martin was just showing her authority for no particular reason and has done so before. I told her what I thought of her spiteful action. I notice women are frequently the same way when put in authority over other women, and they often show a petty spite and unreasonable interference that is disgraceful and unkind.

## Friday 3 August 1917. 30th Stationary Hospital

[…]

My eyes are feeling ever so much better, but the MO won't let me get up except when the sun goes down. I'm feeling a bit groggy in the knees but otherwise OK.

## Wednesday 8 August 1917.
## 30th Stationary Hospital

Thought I would be able to get away from here, but got a rotten bad 'go' of malaria. Not so bad as last year, but violent shiverings and a lot of sweating – eyes feeling bad again.

## Monday 13 August 1917. 30th Stationary Hospital

Temperature gone down again below par. Bunty came along again, looking very well and had tea. She's awfully kind, bringing me fruit and some home papers. She is to be at the Convalescent Camp on Hortackoj plateau till the 18th, when she expects to be sent to the 36th General Hospital attached to the Serbs, near Monastir.

## Friday 17 August 1917. 30th Stationary Hospital

Feeling much better and eyes seem nearly OK except that the glare of the sun hurts a bit. The MO says he won't let me go for a bit as I might do permanent injury to my eyes.

## Saturday 18 August 1917. 30th Stationary Hospital

A great fire broke out in Salonika during the afternoon and we could see the huge clouds of smoke rising above the hills. There is the hot 'Vardar' wind blowing strongly which will make matters difficult. At night, the site was wonderful as the flames were reflected in the enormous cloud of smoke which piled up in the air thousands of feet high.

## Sunday 19 August 1917. 30th Stationary Hospital

The fire is still raging even worse than before. We can't see the city from here but reports keep coming in which say that two-thirds of the town is destroyed. All Venezelos Street gone – Crosdi-Back, Stein, and Flocca's gone too, and all the front along to the 'Tour Blanche', all telegraph communication has been destroyed and crowds of refugees pouring out into the country. It is terrible to think of this historic old place being destroyed, but I don't wonder, as the only light in the covered bazaars is supplied by big paraffin flares, hung on the fronts of the booths.

## Tuesday 21 August 1917. 30th Stationary Hospital

The fire in Salonika has been a dreadful disaster. Two-thirds of the city is wiped out including all the best part of it with the Hotels and business houses. Nobody knows how it started, but, of course, everyone says 'Enemy agents'. I think it was one of the old paraffin flares that are used to light the small shops and work-rooms, as I often thought that some such disaster would follow the bursting of one of these.

Some of our doctors have been down to see what help they could give and they say there are 100,000 people homeless and destitute. The people themselves don't seem to mind much, and one man I asked, who was passing with a swarm of refugees up the Orendzik road and lugging along a feather bed, how he was going to get any dinner for his family, smiled and said 'Johnnie bring' meaning that our Tommies would get him something. What a faith these sort of people have in the British. It seems that our troops and sailors did all the work of saving people and getting them safely away. They say the French and Italians looted everything they could, and got drunk on stolen wine, leaving the people to look after themselves, and the fire to spread itself as it liked, and now the town is out of bounds to the British and not to any others. It has been an arduous work providing food and drink and accommodation for all these people, who include infants and children and sick people. It has been done somehow and I'm sure the people here won't forget it.

## Week ending Saturday 25 August 1917.
## 30th Stationary Hospital

Had a surprise visit from Bill Whyte who told me the battalion were encamped near Lembet and that, although kept secret so far, were going off to Egypt. I saw the MO at once and told him I wanted to get discharged at once and said if I didn't get back to the battalion now, I probably would never see them again. He said I must wait a few days yet, so Bill Whyte said he would give me good notice of any orders to move and I determined to desert the hospital if necessary. Bill was looking very fit and the colour of chocolate. He said I looked rotten but I feel OK now again, and my eyes seem quite well.

## Tuesday 28 August 1917.
## 30th Stationary Hospital/Summerhill

Yesterday I had a note from Bill Whyte that the battalion had moved to DUDULAR and were on six hours' notice to move to the quay, so I went to the Colonel (Ryan, I think, his name was, and an old Trinity man) and explained to him that I wanted to go straight back to the battalion at once, without going to that awful Summerhill reinforcement camp. He said the MO reported me fit for light duty and therefore he could discharge me, but that he must send me by the usual channels. However, he was a TCD man and a great sport, so he said I might depart in the morning in one of the hospital Ford vans and could do as I liked when I was clear of his lines, and he promised not to let me down if enquiry was made.

So I said 'Good-bye' to all the good people and left at 07.45 for the base depot at Summerhill. The van had to leave me here and I managed to slip in by a back way to the Regimental Dump and I saw Sergeant Carolin and collected any of my belongings that he had, and put them and my valise which I had brought from the hospital, in his charge, arranging to send for them later. Nobody seemed to know exactly where the battalion was except that it was 'towards DUDULAR' and I started to trek away across the hills and walked for miles and miles. I was awfully slack after being in bed so long and I don't know how I stuck it out. At last, however, I saw some camps and found the whole 10th (Irish) Division there, with the 6th RDF, of course, the furtherest away unit. At last, I arrived and was received with acclamation. I was dead beat and had to spend the rest of the afternoon on Bill Whyte's bed.

## Wednesday 29 August 1917. Dudular

Paddy Cox is in hospital at the 43rd General with a slight fever or a touch of the sun and Bill Whyte is in command. There is a new organisation of battalion now in use and all the headquarters and special people are arranged in a 'Headquarter Company'. I am now appointed signalling officer and to command the HQ Company. There are a good many new officers, but Stuffer Byrne, Whyte, Paine, Esmonde, Shadforth and others are still here, and all in the best of form. Heard a lot of the doings of the battalion in the Struma valley where they distinguished themselves at Jenikoj and many other places. It's really magnificent to be back in the bosom of the family again – I didn't think one could get so fond of a lot of good men and true. Had to slack during the hot part of the day as I felt awfully tired, so wrote a few letters [...]. Byrne is up to his ears in work refitting the battalion according to a new scale, and in the cool of the evening I rode over to the Ordnance Depot with him. Felt very queer on the horse as I had got awfully thin and soft.

## Saturday 1 September 1917. Dudular

Sudden orders arrived from 30th Brigade at 04.30 to pack up and be ready to push off on two hours' notice, but after a hectic morning, it turned out to be the same dear old chestnut of 'False Alarm'.

Got a letter by hand from Bunty saying she had been to the 30th Stationary Hospital to see me and found I had gone, and asking could I see her before I left Salonika. I have already written her this morning so didn't reply further; her move to Vertikop is off.

Sad news this morning – Colonel Cox has been ordered home 'for other employment'. This means he will get the Brigade he has twice been promised, but we are all sad at losing him. I persuaded him, with some trouble, to let me get a photo of him, which I did outside his tent in shirt sleeves and breeches, and the old stick he carries everywhere.[55] He is not to go away with us but will wait here for a passage home. I wonder who will get Command – I'm afraid Bill Whyte won't, as his deafness was a bar in the past. Some think 'Charlie Chaplin' otherwise Major H Aplin of the RMF, but I hope to goodness this won't be our fate. Some people say he is a good soldier, but all admit he is an unpleasant one.

[...]

We had a cricket match today with the 6th RMF using a strip of coconut matting as a crease[56] – quite good.

---

55  See Figure 5. Various other photos of officers and local scenes were taken at a similar time, see Figures 6–10.

56  Drury must have meant 'wicket' not 'crease' as the latter is simply a line on the ground, whereas coconut matting was and is commonly used as a playing surface.

There are fine sun shelters here for the men to feed under, with tables and benches, and they can have their food decently served, being beside the Base. Stuffer Byrne manages to get even more than full rations for them and they always have a full bread ration and no biscuits. Fresh meat comes nearly every day and a certain amount of vegetables which we buy locally.

I am rapidly putting on flesh again and feel very fit, and thanks be to goodness, my eyes feel nearly OK but I wear dark glasses when out in the glare of the midday sun.

## Monday 3 September 1917. Dudular

At breakfast this morning, we decided to try and get up a concert this evening to celebrate the departure of the 6th RDF and we divided ourselves into Committees to deal with the various arrangements. The main difficulty was that we had no money to buy things and even if we had, Salonika was out of bounds. Stuffer Byrne undertook to get from somewhere, a piano, two marquees, floor matting, timber for platform and chairs or seats. I and Loveband were to issue invitations and arrange transport and escort for nurses. Others looked after performers and food. We got a piano from Major Chevens (Army Ordnance Department)[57] who delivered it in camp. Byrne secured the marquees, etc. and a fair number of chairs. Invitations were issued to the staffs and nurses and VADs in the 41st, 29th, 61st, 62nd, and 63rd General Hospitals, and Loveband and I spent a warm few hours galloping round with the invitations.

The concert started at 20.00 and we had over 50 nurses and VADs, as well as several MOs. The show was very good and Stuffer Byrne's songs 'McCluskey's White Vest' and 'The Conversazione' fairly brought the house down. On arrival, the ladies were given a couple of spare tents to titivate in and halfway through the concert there was an interval during which we brought the guests into the second marquee where supper was served. We had no tables, so we dispensed with chairs and sat about on the ground with all the grub arranged down the middle. We had coffee, lemonade and soup, tinned fruit, sandwiches and biscuits and also a small quantity of champagne which Byrne said he got as a present from some admirer (probably a fair one). Then resumed and had step dancing and other turns by the men, for whom we had secured a barrel of beer. We

---

57   Herbert Glyn Chevens (WO 372/4/102122).

did not break up till 23.30 when we all saw the dear girls back to their hospitals by the light of the silvery moon. It was a great show altogether.

## Sunday 9 September 1917. At sea

Away at last. We left camp near Dudular at 03.00 and arrived on the English Quay at 05.45 and were shipped straight on board HMT[58] ARAGON. This is the notorious HQ ship which was at Mudros for so long while we were at Gallipoli, laden with brass hats. The story goes that, when at last she was ordered to sail, she wouldn't move, so divers were sent down and found her hard aground on a mountain of whiskey and champagne bottles!

We left the quay at Salonika at 10.15 with an escort of two destroyers, and we had a good look at the town. What a miserable sight. Three-quarters of the place is destroyed, including such gems as the Church of Demetrius and others where the mosaics and coloured tiles are said to be even finer than in the famous Church of Saint Sophia in Constantinople. One curious thing was very noticeable, the delicate thin, pure white, spires of the mosques seemed quite undamaged except for the loss of the long thin copper-coloured points. These had been melted or burned off but not a trace of blackening or damage could be seen on any of the numerous shafts which were dotted all about the city. I tried to photo the scene, but there was a great glare off the water and a haze over everything so I don't suppose it will come out well.

[…]

58  His Majesty's Transport.

# 7

# Egypt and Palestine, September–December 1917

The UK's central strategic concern in the Middle East was the defence of the Suez Canal. Since it opened in 1869 the canal had been an artery for imperial communications, not only but especially on the routes to India and Australia. During the war, it was also vital for supplies first to Gallipoli and then to the Salonika front. More widely, Egypt was an important supplier of cotton and food, while Alexandria and Port Said were crucial staging posts for keeping the Salonika campaign resourced.[1]

Threats to the canal, and the reasons for a strong British presence in Egypt, came from two sources: Turkey and pan-Islamism. Prior to the First World War a British strategic aim in the Middle East had been to preserve the Ottoman Empire in the name of stability and to prevent Russian expansion, partly by urging internal reforms to strengthen it against critics. However, when the Ottomans attacked Russia at the end of October 1914 and joined the war on the side of the Central Powers, British war aims shifted. They now became to transform the Ottoman Empire into a federated state, containing provinces which would be autonomous, although the French and the Russians aimed to break it up entirely. The place at which such aims would be fought over was in Palestine, bordering Egypt and which the Ottomans had controlled for almost 500 years. The complexity of the situation can be seen in Egypt's legal status. Sovereignty was notionally Ottoman, but it had been under British military occupation since 1882. When war broke out, the Egyptian figurehead, the Khedive Abbas Hilmi II, declared for Turkey. He was deposed and replaced with a pro-British nephew, Hussein, and

---

1  Johnson, *The Great War & the Middle East*, 60, 112.

Egypt was declared to be a British Protectorate. This meant an end to any illusion that the British were merely in Egypt in a supervisory role, and that from now on, they would control the defence of Egypt as they wished.[2] Meanwhile, the British feared 'pan-Islamism' on the basis that the Muslim population of Egypt (and elsewhere) might side with their co-religionists in the Ottoman Empire and threaten Britain's control of the areas it occupied. One method for dealing with this in Egypt was that the declaration of the British Protectorate included an assurance that no Egyptian would be required to fight to defend the country.[3] These measures enabled the British to mount a successful defence of the Suez Canal against Turkish forces in early February 1915. They had crossed the Sinai Desert (formally part of Egypt but effectively unoccupied) to attack the canal but were held off.[4]

From 1915, the war in the Middle East expanded. British troops had fought in Mesopotamia (now Iraq) in late 1914 and endured a siege at Kut al Amara in 1915–16, and there would be fighting in the region until the end of the war.[5] The British and French supported the Arab Revolt in the Hejaz, Transjordan (now Jordan) and Syria, in 1916–18.[6] However, the 10th (Irish) Division's war in the Middle East as part of XX Corps under Lieutenant General Philip Chetwode[7] would be focused on the border between Egypt and Palestine, and the push towards Jerusalem. Following the successful defence of the canal in early 1915, there were no major operations in the area until British forces entered the Sinai in late 1916 taking the Egyptian coastal town of El Arish and then the border town of Rafah early in 1917. From March 1917, the British sought to capture Gaza in southern Palestine. This was part of a strategy of applying pressure on the Central Powers on a range of fronts. The British government hoped that conquering Palestine would boost British strength in the Middle East after humiliation at Kut, while supporting the Arab Revolt and drawing Ottoman forces away from their fight against British in Mesopotamia and Russia in Armenia. By the time the 10th (Irish)

---

2   Johnson, *The Great War & the Middle East*, 26–9, 54–5, 62; Ulrichsen, *The First World War in the Middle East*, 102.

3   Johnson, *The Great War & the Middle East*, 65; Ulrichsen, *The First World War in the Middle East*, 28, 102–3.

4   Ulrichsen, *The First World War in the Middle East*, 103–4.

5   Johnson, *The Great War & the Middle East*, 132–53, 204–25.

6   Johnson, *The Great War & the Middle East*, 174–203, 244–5.

7   General Philip Chetwode, later Field Marshal and 1st Baron, 1869–1950 (*The Times*, 7 July 1950, p. 6).

Division arrived in the region, two attempts to take Gaza, in March and April, had failed.[8] Renewed efforts would soon be made after the appointment of General Edmund Allenby[9] as Commander-in-Chief of the Egyptian Expeditionary Force in June 1917.[10] For most of their first four months in Egypt and then Palestine, the 6th Royal Dublin Fusiliers saw little action. Drury's diary was principally concerned with descriptions of the geography and people,[11] and the ways in which British forces adapted to alien conditions. Simply walking on dry sand was something which had to be learnt,[12] but there were opportunities to trade with local people which helped boost rations.[13] W.H. 'Bill' Whyte took command of the battalion in mid-September, a popular choice with Drury.[14] Drury took the opportunity to visit Cairo[15] and noted, 'One of the ambitions of my life has been achieved and I have seen and climbed the Pyramids of Giza.'[16]

In late September the battalion was briefly based at Ismailia and then Kantara,[17] before spending October in Rafah.[18] That was a prelude to being in reserve during the Battle of Beersheba[19] (a prelude to the third Battle of Gaza) at the end of the month and then holding positions around Gaza in early November.[20] It had, eventually, been secured on

---

8 Ulrichsen, *The First World War in the Middle East*, 106–10.
9 On Allenby in the Middle East and related issues, see Matthew Hughes, *Allenby and British Strategy in the Middle East, 1917–19* (London: Routledge, 1999); Matthew Hughes, ed., *Allenby in Palestine: The Middle East Correspondence of Field Marshal Viscount Allenby* (Stroud: The History Press, 2004); James E. Kitchen, *The British Imperial Army in the Middle East: Morale and Military Identity in the Sinai and Palestine Campaigns, 1916–18* (London: Bloomsbury Academic, 2014); Kristian Coates Ulrichsen, *The Logistics and Politics of the British Campaigns in the Middle East, 1914–22* (Basingstoke: Palgrave Macmillan, 2011).
10 Cyril Falls and A.F. Becke, *History of the Great War: Military Operations Egypt & Palestine From June 1917 to the End of the War, Part I* (London: HMSO, 1930), 1–12.
11 Diary entries, 12, 13 and 16 Sept 1917.
12 Diary entry, 14 Sept 1917.
13 Diary entry, 17 Sept 1917.
14 Diary entries, 17 and 18 Sept 1917.
15 Diary entries, 19, 20 and 22 Sept 1917.
16 Diary entry, 20 Sept 1917.
17 Diary entries, 25 and 28 Sept 1917.
18 Diary entries, 29 Sept and 6 Oct 1917.
19 Tom Johnstone, *Orange, Green & Khaki: The Story of the Irish Regiments in the Great War, 1914–18* (Dublin: Gill and Macmillan, 1992), 321–3.
20 Diary entries, 29 Oct–8 Nov 1917.

7 November.[21] Mid- to late November saw the 6th Royal Dublin Fusiliers training and doing the best they could to survive sandstorms.[22] They took no part in the capture of Jerusalem in early December[23] but did send two representatives to take part in Allenby's entry into the city.[24] Drury noted 'I hear it was most impressive, although quite unlike the warlike bombastic entry the Turks would have made. He just walked in on the 11th at noon, unarmed and carrying a cane.'[25]

As Rob Johnson has argued, 'The capture of Jerusalem marked a significant turning point in the Middle East. [...] From this point on, the Ottoman Empire could only fight a rearguard action.'[26] However, that was not yet apparent and Jerusalem still needed to be defended. Based at Beit Anan and then a location known as 'L10', the 6th Royal Dublin Fusiliers prepared for any possible Turkish counter-attack[27] spending 'a miserable Xmas day with chattering teeth and aching bodies. Everyone soaked to the skin and no firewood to make a fire big enough to dry clothes, everyone hoping and praying that Xmas might never be like this again.'[28]

---

21 Ulrichsen, *The First World War in the Middle East*, 111–12.
22 Diary entries, 10–30 Nov 1917.
23 Diary entries, 1–11 Dec 1917.
24 WO 95/4583: 6th RDF.
25 Diary entry, 14 Dec 1917.
26 Johnson, *The Great War & the Middle East*, 202.
27 Diary entries, 18, 19 and 24 Dec 1917.
28 Diary entry, 24 Dec 1917.

## Wednesday 12 September 1917.
## Alexandria/Ismailia

I got leave from the General to go ashore for a bit this morning so I went off about 08.30 with Esmonde and Jowett and bought a few things I wanted at Davies, Bryan & Company, also got some cigarettes and a patent cigarette lighter.

We paraded on the Quay at 11.00 and the first train pushed off at 11.30. We had a very comfortable carriage, and there was a nice cool breeze blowing through.

This is a most wonderful looking country in the Delta, as every inch of the place seems cultivated, principally with cotton, but with a good deal of various vegetables, mealies, etc. The system of water supply through various sized canals and water-courses is amazing, and they have enough water even in the roasting summer, to flood some of the fields a foot deep. The villages look poor, and, in the distance, look rather like a gigantic manure heap into which rabbits have driven some burrows.

Father WJ O'Carroll,[29] the RC chaplain, seemed surprised that the Egyptians wore any clothes, as he said he thought '"Natives" never wore clothes'. He is a perfect specimen of the Maynooth-trained young priest – bigoted, narrow-minded and (from a worldly point of view) absolutely uneducated. We had a most delightful trip, stopping for a short time at Zagazig junction and passing Tel-el-Kebir, arrived at Ismailia junction on the Suez canal at 18.30 or one hour in advance of our schedule. We detrained at Moascar station which is about 1½ miles from Ismailia and had only a short way to go to our camp which is pitched in the dry sand. It will be a terrible place when the wind blows as the sand is loose and soft, and one's feet sink in it several inches when walking.

[...]

## Thursday 13 September 1917. Ismailia

We had no special parades today but spent the time settling up camp and checking stores and cleaning arms and equipment. We have a mess

---

29  There does not appear to have been a Chaplain in the British Army by the name of W.J. O'Carroll, but there was a William Joseph Carroll who was probably in the Middle East at this time (WO 372/4/29900).

hut made of wood framing and covered with reed mats which keep out the sun yet allow a certain amount of breeze to get through.

The air here is extraordinary, because it is hotter even than upcountry in Salonika, 1,000 miles North of here, and yet it is dry and bracing and everyone feels fit for work. The arrangement is that we stay here to acclimatise for a short while and get the men accustomed to marching in the sand and then we move up across the canal.

The Front now is a few miles short of Gaza on the left, and the right end's "in the air" out in the desert in the Beersheba neighbourhood. It seems that they had a go at Gaza in March and practically had the place, but someone high up got cold feet and retired back to the starting line again, suffering heavy casualties in doing so. The same thing occurred at the second battle in the middle of April, and, as a result Sir Archibald Murray[30] was recalled and General Sir E Allenby was sent out from France to command at the end of June. No serious attack has yet been made but great preparations are going on, and a big show is expected shortly. That is why they have brought over the 10th (Irish) Division from Salonika, as they all say it is the best Division in the East. The story we were told was that General Milne[31] was asked which was his best Division and he replied the "10th (Irish)", and was then told to send them to Egypt. The others are gnashing their teeth.

All the supply work here is done with camels and the men are very interested in them but also a bit afraid of the supercilious brutes. However, they were not long in making friends of the Gippy camel men who seem very hard-working fellows and look after their animals very well.

We received an invitation to make use of the French Club at Ismailia, called the 'Cercle du Canal' and, in the evening, Bill Whyte, Tony Shadforth and I went down there for dinner.

The town has been laid out by the Canal staff and purports to be a copy of the Place de l'Etoile in Paris with all the radiating avenues. The Club occupies the place of the Arc de Triomphe and the Club grounds are circular with the narrow club buildings stretching across the diameter, leaving open spaces at each side. One of them is beautifully shaded with tall trees and is used for serving tea in the afternoon, while the other

---

30  General Archibald Murray, 1860–1945, commanded the Egyptian Expeditionary Force from Jan 1916 to June 1917 (*The Times*, 25 Jan 1945, p. 7).

31  George Milne, 1866–1948, 1st Baron, commanded the British Salonika Force from May 1916 to Sept 1918, and Chief of the Imperial General Staff in 1926–33 (*The Times*, 24 March 1948, p. 6).

side, which has only a few trees, is used for dinner, at which time no shade is required.

They gave us a very good dinner indeed and we enjoyed the evening very much, as we met various friends from other units which are here. Flies very bad and most pugnacious.

## Friday 14 September 1917. Ismailia

We arranged parades here just as we did in Salonika, working in the mornings and evenings and slacking during the heat of the day. The heat from 10.30 onwards is tremendous, with a trying glare off the dry sand, but I love it as it is so invigorating that you feel up to anything. They camp is most comfortable with plenty of room and the water supply is not at all bad. Each Company has a dining shelter with a roof made of rush mats to keep the sun off, and long tables and benches. 50 men per company are given leave into Ismailia in the evenings and they are very well turned out and behave very well.

I have now started the HQ Company on a Lewis gun class so that they may be able to do the needful in a scrap.

We are also practising marching in the soft sand, which everyone finds very tiring at first. I think the secret of comfortable marching is to lean slightly forward and not to straighten the leg when taking a pace. Thus one rather trots along than marches. There was some talk of giving the men Canadian snow shoes, but I have not seen any of them, nor heard any more of the project.

[…]

## Sunday 16 September 1917. Ismailia

[…]

This town is a most lovely spot, situated on the edge of Lake Timsah, which is one of the chain of lakes joined up to form the Suez canal. Ismailia is about halfway between Suez in the South and Port Said on the Mediterranean Sea and these are the junction of the railway lines from these two places and on to Cairo or Alexandria.

There is a small promontory jutting into the lake, on which is the Signal Station which transmits orders to ships whether to stop or allow other ships to pass, or to proceed. There is a boat club and a swimming club and we had a sail in the afternoon in a fresh breeze.

The whole town is thickly planted with trees, many of them being the 'flame' trees with their wonderful bright red blossom. The houses are well-built on the bungalow style with verandahs and sun blinds. The delightful effect of the whole is increased by the fresh feeling in the air owing to the fresh water canal which passes through. We have had to read out to the men on parade a warning on no account to bathe or even wash in the fresh water canals, as they will get a disease known as Bilharziosis,[32] or, as the troops call it 'Bill Harris'. It seems to be a bug which burrows through the skin and lays an egg which gets as big as a football. If you get more than six of these inside you, it is probably fatal!

[…]

## Monday 17 September 1917. Ismailia

Great news. Major WH Whyte was in Orders today as Lieutenant Colonel and to command the Battalion. I am so glad as he is a damn fine fellow and a white man.[33] He breathes the spirit of the Regiment and loves it better than anything. He knows the whole history of it and is always instilling it into the men. One malefactor when brought up at Orderly Room found himself sentenced to learn all the Battle Honours and their dates by heart.

[…]

Some very enterprising people called Choueri & Mouchbahani of Port Said with branches at Ismailia, Kantara[34] and El Ferdan, sent a representative to sell us mess groceries. They have excellent stuff and very cheap. We buy eggs, butter, fruit, cake and soda water. They have also sold us a kind of springy crate of wicker which we use as beds. They are very comfortable.

---

32  Now known as schistosomiasis.
33  To 'play the white man' was, in Drury's time, a phrase used to denote behaving in a decent manner (based on a racist belief among colonists that 'white men' could be trusted but that 'natives' could not).
34  Now El Qantara.

## Tuesday 18 September 1917. Ismailia

Bill Whyte turned up at Orderly Room today with his crown and star on, amid hearty congratulations from everyone. It's a huge relief that we haven't had a dago sent to command. We have a new second in command, though, which is a great shame with men like John Luke, Tony Shadforth and others available. He is one William Vance,[35] Lieutenant, Temporary Major, from the Royal Irish Fusiliers, and is a Regular. He was a ranker but seems a good fellow, knows his job and is most energetic. Looks a bit of a sketch on a horse, as his legs are very short and fat.

[…]

## Wednesday 19 September 1917. Ismailia/Cairo

[…]

Arrived Cairo 17.00 and put up at Shepheard's Hotel, the famous pub where 104 generals were living in luxury in General Sir A Murray's time. This is a great place and I luxuriated in a fine bath and then toyed with dinner, which was served in the open air, in the gardens at the back of the Hotel. Had a walk round afterwards and arranged for a guide to tomorrow, fixing up with Mohamed Ahmed, who was recommended to me. Seems a good fellow and has done a lot of European travelling with parties. Dressed in a long linen night-shirt with small buttons all down the front as close as they could go, from his neck to his boots.

## Thursday 20 September 1917. Cairo

One of the ambitions of my life has been achieved and I have seen and climbed the Pyramids of Giza.

---

35 Born in 1876 in Augher, Co. Tyrone, enlisted as a Private in the Royal Irish Fusiliers in 1894. Served in South Africa in 1899–1902. Was a Sergeant-Major at the outbreak of the war, with home service only until his commission in May 1915. Awarded the MC. Retired from the army in 1921 then briefly served as a District Inspector with the Special Constabulary in Belfast. Died in 1922 of heart failure. See WO 339/29007.

In the morning went off to the Citadel which seems to overlook the Mokattam quarries, whence the stone for the pyramids was quarried. Saw the alabaster Mosque built about 120 years ago by the notorious Mohamed Ali. He built it of slabs of alabaster which covered the pyramids, entirely stripping the big one and all but a small cap on the top of the middle one. Visited a couple of other Mosques too and found them very big but beautifully proportioned and with exquisite workmanship. I got some photos which I hope will turn out well. Visited also the tomb of Mohamed Ali.

In the afternoon I drove out to the Pyramids. It's no use trying to describe the one's feelings on looking at these marvellous monuments. It is all too wonderful to grasp at first and one can hardly realise the incredible trouble and labour expended in such work when none of the modern mechanical appliances are available. I kept thinking of Herodotus' account where he speaks of the Pyramids when he visited them being incredibly old even then, and he seems very ancient to us. He says two possible methods of building were explained to him but, being unable to decide which was the more probable, like a faithful scribe, he gives both accounts.

Saw also the Sphinx and the Temple of the Sun at its base – a perfect gem. Fancy the Sphinx as it was in the old times before 'Nap' damaged it when fighting the Mamelukes,[36] covered with alabaster and showing a perfect human face – the worshippers down in the Temple at its base in the early hours of the morning waiting silently for the first rays of the morning sun to light up the face, while they yet remained in the gloom. The magnificent polished red granite pillars in this Temple came all the way from Aswan nearly 1,000 miles up country and must weigh twenty or thirty tons each.

Climbed up the big pyramid over 6,000 years old; magnificent view. One side, the Nile with its emerald strip of verdure, on the other, the light brown desert as far as the eye can reach.

I had tea at Mena House and felt mightily replenished. Got back to Cairo at 18.30 and left films to be developed at the Kodak place. [...]

---

36 There was a popular myth that Napoleon Bonaparte's forces had damaged the Sphinx, but this probably happened many years before that time: https://www.napoleon-series.org/faq/c_sphinx.html [accessed 6 April 2020].

## Saturday 22 September 1917. Cairo

Spent the morning in the Egyptian Museum. It would take weeks to see it properly, but even in a few hours, you can see enough to marvel at the civilisation and craftsmanship of the ancient people. Everything is beautifully arranged with plenty of light and space round each exhibit. The old papyrus writings were so clear that they would be remarkable if only done ten years ago. The gold work on beds and chairs and the entirely modern-looking cane seats of the latter seem incredibly new. The statues are most remarkable for the wonderful facial expressions. There were some little statues of Chephren (or Khafra)[37] which were little gems. They were found thrown into a deep shaft sunk in the floor of the Temple of the Sphinx at Memphis. The air here is so dry that they can exhibit things that would be soon destroyed anywhere else. I never saw mummies anywhere that looked so perfect and 'new'.

[…] I left Cairo by the 18.15 train and had a jolly good dinner on the way and arrived at Ismailia at 21.30. Before I left Cairo I went to Nicholas Soussa's factory and arranged for a supply of 'Khedevial' cigarettes to be sent to me each week, depositing with them 500 piastres, the price working out at 4/6d. per 100.

## Sunday 23 September 1917. Ismailia

Nothing special – rumours of an early move. A lot of our officers have applied for transfer to the Royal Flying Corps among them Shadforth, who, I think, is sick at not getting second in command. John Luke and Shadforth are both senior to Vance, who is only Lieutenant, Temporary Captain, Acting Major; and I hear Bill Whyte is trying to get Vance sent back again and Luke made second in command.

## Tuesday 25 September 1917. Leaving Ismailia

Nothing special yesterday, except orders to march out today.

The battalion paraded in the evening and marched out at 18.00 being played through the town by the 10th (Irish) Divisional brass band. All the other units turned out and cheered us. We had a very hot, tiring

---

37   A 4th Dynasty Pharaoh (*c.* 2570 BC).

march and arrived at EL FERDAN[38] about 23.30, where we found the remains of shelters which had been used when the canal was the front line. Several men fell out, who had had malaria, but they all joined in later after taking it easy. Everyone is very pleased we are off up the line, although we enjoyed being at Ismailia. The conduct of the men there has been exemplary and the subject of favourable comment in Army Orders. The last day in camp the Aussies opposite made a set on some of our fellows to try to make them drunk, and a few weaklings succumbed. It was a rotten trick as our canteen was practically dry and they seemed to have unlimited quantities of spirits and beer.

## Friday 28 September 1917. Leaving Kantara

[...] We left camp at 15.30 and were entrained at 16.00 – smart work. [...]

We had dirty open goods waggons with high creels round the sides like the cattle trucks used at home. There were four waggons behind the engine with small coal and slack, then a waggon for the officers and men in the rear. Most uncomfortable journey, as we were enveloped in clouds of coal dust as well as sound from the track, and gales of wind blew up through the chinks in the floor. All the same, it was a most interesting trip through the night, across the lonely desert, meeting at intervals, so-called stations such as KATIYEH and ROMANI, which are really only crossing places, protected by a guard. The night was bitter and we were sore from sitting on the hard floor.

## Saturday 29 September 1917. Rafa

We arrived late at El Arish[39] and found we were only to have a quarter of an hour's stop instead of one hour, but we got a hustle on and got the men some tea which was very grateful and comforting.

I shall never forget the enchanting appearance of El Arish as we saw it under the moon-light and bright stars, with the reflection from the dancing waters of the Mediterranean. The platform was 50 feet or so over the sea level and 200 yards back from the beach, and all-around

---

38  Now Al Firdan.
39  Now Al Arish.

grew palm trees who[se] feathery tops were closely discernible. There were tents all about but no lights to be seen, and the only people awake were the Railway Operating Division personnel. There appears to be a sizeable wadi running out here which turns it into a sort of oasis. We arrived at RAFAH at 07.00, looking like coal heavers, and with all our clothing ruined, and feeling very hungry and tired. We marched up over a rise in the ground and found our camping site about half a mile away, on very loose sand. We also found that water is very scarce indeed and a long way off. These Brigade wallahs are always trying to be funny and their latest exhibition is to mark out the Brigade camp so as to pack us up together until we have hardly room to move, as if the whole desert were not available free of rent and taxes.

[…]

## Week ending Saturday 6 October 1917. Rafa

We have had a pretty hard week's work doing some intensive training, marching, etc. We parade about 05.30 and each unit must do a minimum of six miles march before breakfast. The early morning is hot but nice and fresh as the wind is always blowing in from the sea, but about 09.30 it always changes and blows from the South or S[outh] E[ast] and becomes baking hot. At sundown again, it changes back to North. Therefore, we always do our heavy marching, if possible, before breakfast, while it is comparatively cool, and then do shooting, MG, signalling etc. later and in the evening. One day, I arranged the march for the HQ Company after the morning work and took them down to the sea almost due North from camp. It was a very heavy trek through very loose, powdery sand, but everyone enjoyed the swim. […]

We have here the first example of the wire netting roads we have heard of. A track ten feet or so wide is roughly levelled in the sand and two rolls of one-inch rabbit meshing are laid down side by side and then just rolled along the ground, and then two more joined to the ends, and so on. At intervals, of about a yard or so, wooden spikes are driven in at the edges to keep the netting in place. One would imagine the wire would sink into the sand, but it does not do so to any appreciable extent, and it makes an almost perfect road for cars and ambulances. It has the advantage of being quicker and cheaper than making any ordinary road, and, when we move on, the wire can be rolled up and used anywhere else it is required. They don't allow marching on it as the nails and tackets in the men's boots catch in it and break it. There was one piece, however, about ¾-mile long towards the sea which we could use, and it was delightful to walk on, and was springy like a ball-room floor. Heavy guns or baggage waggons are moved about over the sand by Holt tractors, which have powerful petrol engines, and a continuous flexible steel band 15″ wide running over special wheels. This reduces the pressure per square inch so much that these heavy machines do not sink at all in the soft sand.

I had my first ride on a trotting camel this week and enjoyed the ride very much after I got accustomed to the extraordinary movement. In speed, I found that it could travel on the soft sand faster than a horse at full gallop on good ground. Leaning over taking corners was like motor cycle racing. These good trotting camels are very valuable and I was told they cost about £130 each. One is used by the commander of each camel company for getting round his commands. They are no use for carrying loads, and the ordinary pack camel could not be used for trotting. Another thing I heard was rather interesting and that was that the camels have to be carefully trained to do without water and if plenty of water be available, they drink as often as other animals. They are very particular about their water, and take a long time to drink, splashing their noses about in the water, and taking little sips. About an hour is usually allotted for drinking the camels, and they have it every three days here. The Gippy Labour Corps camel men seem to take great care of their animals and I have often seen them come in from a long march, picketing their camel, laying out a cloth on the sand and giving it its food on cloth, and, as the pile gets smaller, patting it with their hands into a cone so that the camel can pick it up easily. The drivers will never start their own food until the beast has finished. My horse, hates the smell or sight of a camel, and if the wind happens to be blowing from the direction of the camel lines, our horses are never easy.

## Monday 29 October 1917.
## Leaving Rafah/Wadi Ghuzze[40]

This day two years ago we were also on the move but up to Serbia. I think this show should turn out very differently from that one. Who knows if

---

40  Now Besor.

this rotten old war will be over in another two years. We didn't think on 29th October, 1915 that we would still be at it in two years.

We saw a wonderful fight today between a Bristol fighter and a Bosch plane over our bivouac. This was the first Bosch we had seen over and it was important he should not get back with information of the numbers and directions of troops moving up. The planes were so high up that they looked like tiny specks of mother-of-pearl in the brilliant blue of the sky. They circled around each other giving occasional burst[s] of MG fire and it was hard to understand what the tactics were. However, our man seemed to get above the Bosch who then put his nose down and fell like a stone for thousands of feet, but he could not shake the Bristol fighter off. The Bosch then tried various turns and twists and suddenly one wing of his machine seemed to be shot away and the machine fell thousands of feet, spinning round and round, nose first on to the desert. Our fellow landed a short distance away and went over to the wreckage, and recovered some maps and orders. Another unit supplied a guard over the remains of the pilot and his machine. I hear that the pilot was AA Cullen, till recently our Machine Gun Officer.

We have now got a fair outline of the show which starts at Zero or dawn on the 31st. The idea is that the army is to strike at Beersheba[41] from the south and east with a bigger force than the Turk could imagine we have available, and push them north, that is, diagonally behind their line, gradually bending back the Turk's left, hingeing about Hareira[42] and Sheria.[43] He will then probably rush his reserves (which are mainly in the Gaza area) over to this flank to prevent us getting up the Hebron road towards Jerusalem, and when his reserves are well on their way, a heavy attack is to be made on the sector from Gaza to the sea at Sheikh Hasan. Then, when the two ends of the line are bent back to form a wide V, the apex at Hareira and Samarra[44] on the railway is to be bitten off and cavalry pushed through to seize Huj and El Hesi[45] where water is available. If possible, they will cut off Turks' right wing retiring from Gaza, but this seems to me a tall order for both forces and men in this heat without water or rations. The 20th Corps (Chetwode) are taking

---

41  Now Be'er Sheva.
42  Roughly halfway on the road from Be'er Sheva to Gaz, approximately where Tidhar is now located.
43  About 5 miles north of Be'er Sheva, just south of modern Rahat.
44  3 to 4 miles south-east of Hareira.
45  7 miles north of Gaza.

the right wing, and the 21st Corps (Bulfin)[46] the left. The 60th Division are to attack Bir Es Shaba [Beersheba], the 74th Division come next on their left, and then we (10th (Irish) Division), now left more or less in the air, but some mounted people, I don't know who, are to look after the gap between us and the right Division of the 21st Corps. Cavalry are to make a wide sweep from about Khalassa[47] towards Zanna[48] and sway in from the east towards the hill Tel Es Saba[49] and across the Hebron (El Khulil) road. The Turk is said to have a very strong second line some miles behind but we may prevent a lot of them getting back to it.

We paraded at sundown and marched off at 17.30 on a compass bearing to bring us to the passway down into the Wadi Ghuzze. Everybody in a great state of delight at getting a move on at last and, specially, as we know beforehand the general outline of the scheme. Why does no other commander realise that the men are capable of taking an intelligent interest in things, and that if they know what is going on, are much more likely to hit on the right solution when things don't go exactly according to plan? Thank goodness, Allenby has some common sense and understands his Tommy Atkins.

We arrived at Shellal at 22.30 exactly right for time and direction. We marched straight for the passway and arrived just on the heels of another crowd in front, so we had no delay but marched straight down into the wadi, picking up our guide on the way and bivouacked for the night in the bottom of the wadi.

## Tuesday 30 October 1917.
## Wadi Ghuzze/Wadi Imleih[50]

This Wadi Ghuzze is the most amazing place you could imagine. The flat desert originally had a perennial stream running over it towards the sea and this cut down deeper and deeper into the soft soil until at present it is about 100 feet deep with vertical edges, and half a mile wide on the average. In places there were hard spots which did not wear down so that now there are irregular blocks and pillars standing up here and there,

---

46   General Sir Edward Bulfin, 1862–1939 (*The Times*, 22 Aug 1939, p. 12).
47   Now al-Khalasa.
48   Now Khashem Zaneh.
49   Now Tel Sheva.
50   This area is about 5 miles north-west of Be'er Sheva.

the tops of which are level with the surrounding country. The place is, in fact, a miniature Grand Can[y]on of Colorado, except that there is none of the brilliant coloured strata, but only a desolate light grey. There is no visible water at present, but, by making shallow cuttings in the sandy bottom, running water is found, and a bit higher up than where we were, the Royal Engineers have made a dam and formed a reservoir, which I expect will be washed away in the winter rains, when, however, the water problem will have been solved. We have been for some time on two pints today which is hardly enough. I would like more.

At 06.00 I started off with Bill Whyte and a few others to visit the front line about eight miles or so away. On the way, we saw several of the 'pits' into one of the sort Joseph was thrown. They are about twelve feet deep and are about twelve feet wide at the bottom, tapering steeply to a mouth about two feet diameter. They are used for storing grain and water and are lined with a hard cement-like finish, and, when full, are covered with a round stone slab. Anyone falling in could not possibly get out without help.

We arrived at the bivouac of the 1/4th Welch Regiment 159th Brigade 53rd Division our old Gallipoli crowd, and found a most extraordinary crowd. Officers unshaved and dirty, dressed in 'grey backs'[51] and 'pigging' it in the same holes in the ground as the men. They were most disinclined to help pass or give us any information, so we left our horses and went on foot to the top of the low hill or ridge overlooking the Wadi Imleih. When their CO heard we were going up, he emerged from his funk hole and roared out after us 'Come off my sky-line, damn you' and sundry other remarks about our manners. Bill Whyte dealt suitably with him and we had a good decko round, having a good view of the Rushdi system of trenches[52] and those at Kauwukah[53] near the railway bridge. We could also see Hareira in the distance. No enemy movement of any kind could be seen but a good deal of activity was obvious behind us as we could see the clouds of dust rising from the Wadi Ghuzze and beyond it, showing troops and convoys on the march. Having had a good look at the ground we were to hold we said farewell to our 'hosts' who regaled us, not with refreshments which we did not expect, but with blood-curdling accounts of a scrap which took place here a few days ago (morning of the 27th October) when the Turks came over to see what was happening, and

---

51  A grey flannel shirt.
52  About 1 mile south-east of Hareira.
53  Later Kawfakha but now depopulated.

making out the old Turk to be a more fearsome fellow to meddle with. We knew him of old, however, and still retained our appetites when we got back to the Wadi at 13.30.

We found the enemy on the North side of the Wadi very heavily wired in case of attack, and we had to make sure of the way out for tonight in the dark.

The Battalion paraded at 17.15 and marched to the Brigade starting point outside of the wire. Arrived at our new position about 21.00 and took over from the 1/4th Welch, reporting the relief completed, at 21.35. They are a dirty-looking crowd and it was almost impossible to distinguish their CO from the battalion runner.

The day has been fearfully hot but the night was a little cooler, and the full moon and brilliant stars lit up the whole landscape. All the same, it made everything look artificial and it was very difficult finding one's way about. It is not expected we will have much to do here during the first few days of the battle, unless the Turk tries to counter-attack or get round the left flank of the 60th Division. If he does this, we are to jump on him good and strong. Our turn will come when the Rushdi and Hareira redoubts are to be attacked. The cavalry should now be working out east of Bir Es Saba [Tel Es Saba], ready for tomorrow's show.

## Wednesday 31 October 1917. Wadi Imleih.
## The 3rd Battle of Gaza begins

The great show has begun, but nothing doing here yet. Most peaceful night and we met no Turks when patrolling, and this morning at daylight, there is practically no movement to be seen. [...] About midday we could watch the fight open on the 60th Divisional front, but soon everything became obscured by huge clouds of smoke and dust which shut out the whole countryside, but the sound of the guns and the gradual lifting of the range showed that they were pushing on. The Turk gun-fire in reply seemed to us feeble, but there was very heavy MG and rifle fire. At 14.43 a wire came from the 20th Corps via 30th Infantry Brigade, '[...] Parties of enemy reported by airmen leaving SABA [Tel Es Saba] by Khalassa road [...]'. This was followed by another wire timed 14.45 and received by us at 15.20, '60th and 74[th] Divisions have captured all objectives.' Great work. It must have been the limit keeping direction in the dust. During the day, we could see an enormous loss of our troops away behind us moving S[outh] E[ast] and we pitied them in the heat and dust, and short of water too. Our water is very short and is stored in a canvas waterproof sheet like a waggon cover, held up at the sides by heavy stakes driven into the ground. There is a certain amount of leakage, but a good deal more is lost by evaporation in the heat of the day. At 15.00, we heard a heavy shoot to the eastward of us for an hour, but didn't hear what was doing. At 13.00 several of us went off on a reconnaissance on the right of the Brigade line, to [...] relieve a battalion of the Queen's Regiment (4th Royal West Surreys) 53rd Division (160th Brigade) tonight, but, after our return, we found that the move was cancelled. However, we are pushing out strong patrols tonight along the Wadi Hanafish [...] up past the junction with the Wadi Imleih,[54] as far as the lone tree [...]. There was another outburst of gun-fire on our right about 19.00 but there was nothing doing on our front. The heat was tremendous and the flies almost as bad as at Gallipoli. At 22.25 we received a wire from the Division, '[...] Beersheba occupied at 19.40 by the Light Horse Brigade [...]'. This is great news and the men are all delighted. We sent the wires round the line as soon as received and let everyone read them. [...]

[...]

## Thursday 1 November 1917. Wadi Imleih

We had a very quiet night and hardly a shot [was] fired on our front. There is some sort of water supply being developed behind our line about a mile away and have [we] just sent off one NCO and three men as a guard over it. It is only to be used by 10th (Irish) Division troops and for washing water only. The drinking water is very scarce and is very dirty and tastes horribly salty. Still, it might be worse.

We are evidently not wanted to move just yet as we got orders that all the Brigade camels were to proceed at 06.00 tomorrow under Loveband to Wadi Ghuzze to water. In the evening a sort of temporary pumping plant was started [...] and we have about 100 men down there working at it.

During the day we saw a lot of enemy reinforcements marching across our front through Sheria and Abu Irgeig[55] moving S[outh] E[ast] to try to stop the rot at Beersheba, I suppose. This is just what Allenby is

---

54   This area is about 5 miles north of Be'er Sheva.
55   About 5 miles east of Be'er Sheva.

playing for. I could see the huge columns of men, and guns, and baggage waggons moving along in clouds of dust. They were not shot at by us, I suppose to keep them in ignorance of our strength here and to get them well-away from Gaza when the blow falls there. We hear that the number of prisoners taken at Beersheba is now 3,000, with nineteen guns, 60 MGs and 85 officers. This number, together with killed and wounded and deserters, should account for most of the garrison.

[...]

## Friday 2 November 1917. Abu Irgeig

There has been a lot of heavy gun fire going on at Gaza for several days but, last night, it seemed specially severe, as we expected that the push there was commencing. We patrolled further out during the night and didn't meet much. One of my fellows fell in to one of the cisterns that had no cover on it and we had a job to get him out by tying rifle slings together. During the morning, the Brigade line was pushed out and Abu Irgeig railway station was occupied. We found a petrol engine and water pump in working order, and the Turk had shoved a bomb into the pump so that it would go off if moved. We expected it, however, and now the pump is going and giving a fair supply.

[...]

The 7th RDF have relieved us in the front line but we are getting up a lot of wire for some strong posts we are going to dig tonight. [...]

## Saturday 3 November 1917. Abu Irgeig

We are cursing the dust raised by the Khamsin wind which blows from the east with steady, persistent force. You can hardly see twenty yards, and everything I possess is full of sand. It finds its way into the very centre of a tightly rolled valise, and as to food, well, you must just eat it dust and all.

[...]

## Sunday 4 November 1917. Wadi Hanafish

Battalion moved at 08.00 eastwards across the Wadi Hanafish [...]. It is absolutely the hottest day I have ever felt and, although we had only a mile or so to go, several men fell out exhausted. I thought I would never get over without having to stop. The air was hot and heavy and seemed to sap all the energy and strength out of the men. [...]

[...]

## Monday 5 November 1917.
## Wadi Hanafish/Samarra bridge

Remained in the Wadi Hanfish for the day. We got a few parcels and letters for the battalion including some cigarettes for the men. During the day, we dumped all blankets and kits so as to be able to move fast. Hope we will get them all right again. Had a complete change before dumping my valise.

[...]

We paraded at 17.15 and moved up to the Wadi close by Samarra bridge. When we were moving up in the dark with the strictest orders against showing a light or making any noise, we were quite startled by a light suddenly rushing overhead like a Very light. It proved to be a wonderfully brilliant shooting star which shot across the sky directly overhead from horizon to horizon. It lit up everything and I could plainly see other columns of troops to our right and left which I didn't know were there. We arrived in position about 22.00 and waited for the night.

[...]

## Tuesday 6 November 1917.
## Samarra bridge/Rushdi

Had a great view of the battle. It was the most magnificent sight and I will never bother to look at a military review again. The 60th were the limit of stickiness and wouldn't push on although I was positive there was nobody in the trenches opposite to them. In fact, I was strolling about on top of a wave or undulation in the ground and not a shot was fired at me and only a few shells dropped about. Later in the forenoon we had to go and take the place for them and we swept up the whole of the Kauwukah redoubt and reached our arranged line in the Rushdi system […]. I could see the 53rd Division through my glasses having a heavy fight away on our right in the hills. There were several heavy counter attacks which they seemed to drive off but the dust and smoke of the shells hid a good deal of what was going on. I had a great view of two batteries of 18-pounders galloping up under heavy shrapnel. They tore along at top speed over the desert and, when they got to 50 yards of where I was, they wheeled round and got the guns into action like a flash. I had the pleasure of getting them on to a Turk battery which nobody was able to spot and which was doing a good deal of damage. I found them by the puff of dust from the crest of a rise every time one of the guns was fired. The battery was dug in behind the rise in the trench system […] and when we reached there later, we found the battery absolutely flattened. The horses had just been hooked in to get the guns away when our shells got them. What a mess. Gunners, horses, broken guns and limbers scattered around mixed up with bivouacs, empty and full rounds. I patted my own back as nobody else seemed to think of it. […]

Tonight we knew the Turk was beaten for certain as he blew up an enormous ammunition dump near Sheria and set fire to his stores. The whole countryside was brilliantly lit up with a bright rose-coloured tint.

## Wednesday 7 November 1917. Hareira/Rushdi

Last night was bitterly cold and I got no sleep. Had no coat or blanket. The men were cold too but had a fair amount of digging to do reversing trenches in case of counter attack.

Today was the 'grand finale' of the Turks' great Gaza–Beersheba line. We finished clearing up the Rushdi system with very little opposition and then attacked the Hareira system. Hareira is a hollow hill like a volcano about 200 feet high, round the south-eastern side of which runs the Wadi-Es-Sheria in a deep gulley. This gulley has on its southern side a lower hill or spur of the main hill. The Turk[s] seem to have expected the attack from the south and west and also up the wadi bed, as most of the defences were facing that way, and they had large mortars aligned on the wadi as the most likely assembly place for attack. However, Allenby's scheme of rolling up the Turks' left allowed us to attack this redoubt from the eastward and although the Division were allotted most of the day to take the place, it was ours in a couple of hours, with a lot of prisoners and supplies, but, better still, a water supply and a clear road for the cavalry.[56] The 60th Division were as usual behind their timetable taking Tel-El-Sheria. We were to move to Sheria after the 60th Division, but this was countermanded and we had nothing special to do except stroll about and see all that was going on, and to prevent any Turks doubling back into their trench systems. The Desert Mounted Corps were waiting behind us for the word to push off and presently away they went. It was a thrilling sight, and the whole battle area was just perfect for using cavalry. They swept up the rising ground towards Sheria in a big left-handed sweep, moving in lines of sections at about 250 yards interval between the lines. The frontage was about two miles, and the thunder of the hoofs and the glitter of arms was a sight never to be forgotten. [...]

We heard that one of the big explosions which occurred in the night was the blowing up of the railway bridge at Sheria, when the local commander heard that Gaza was gone. Got a wire message from Allenby 'Congratulations on your brilliant victory' and another from Chetwode, commanding 20th Corps 'Cannot sufficiently express my admiration for the dash and gallantry displayed – Heartily congratulate all ranks.' That was rather nice of them, as the men did clear the Kauwukah–Rushdi–Hareira systems in real 'blue cap' style. Clive, Coote and Neill still live![57]

## Thursday 8 November 1917. Rushdi

Our job is finished for the present. The Turks are away with the cavalry after them as hard as they can go. It would be impossible for us to keep up even if it were possible to water and feed us.

Last night, we moved back into the Rushdi system and held a local defence line, as there was no room for us at Sheria. I found a Bosch armourer's tool chest, almost new and complete with tools which I handed to our Armourer-Staff-Sergeant Hill.[58] He admired it very much and

---

56  See Figure 11.
57  References to key figures in the history of the Indian-based units seen as the predecessors of the RDF: Robert Clive, Major General and 1st Baron, 'Clive of India', 1725–1774; Sir Eyre Coote, 1726–1783; and James George Neill, 1810–1857. The latter's death in the Indian Mutiny bestowed on the RDFs the nickname of 'Neill's Blue Caps'.
58  It has not been possible to identify a Sergeant Hill in the RDF.

said it was much more complete than our pattern. Also found a Turk 'draught' board and men laid out. Some fellows were rumoured to have found a company pay chest full of cash but I didn't get any of it. At 08.00, we got orders to march back to Karm[59] but almost at once this was cancelled and we were told to stay where we were and concentrate in Brigade group [...] ready to move at one hour's notice. We got a few letters by the ration party and also managed a small quantity of water. I washed my feet and had a shave. Feet a bit sore, as I have not had my boots off for 75 hours and only have slept about six hours in that time. [...] Tried to sleep in afternoon but only managed half an hour as the sun was too hot and the flies awful.

## Saturday 10 November 1917. Karm

Orders came in during the night for the Division to concentrate at Karm as we were not to go forward yet owing to the difficulty of feeding and watering the cavalry while they were moving forward so fast. The Brigade marched off at 08.00. It's a damned shame marching men at such an hour through the heat when it is not necessary. We could just as easily have moved off at 04.30 and got in before the full heat of the day. 31 men dropped out of the line of march and of these seven were kept in the Field Ambulance as unable to rejoin. The Khamsin is blowing again and the dust is so bad that you cannot see people fifteen yards away.

We have some tents here and no reasonable amount of water but, of course, all the supplies for up the line go off first. There is also a YMCA canteen beside the railway where a few things can be bought. Pencils are badly wanted, also candles and matches, toilet paper and soap.

[...]

## Friday 16 November 1917. Karm

Here we are still at KARM – at least, we believe we are, for we have not seen anything for several days. The Khamsin has been blowing hard and the dust is terrible. It seemed even worse than the dust storm described

---

59  About 5 miles west of Be'er Sheva.

by Kinglake in 'Eothen'.[60] One can hardly breathe and, in addition, the flies are the very devil for no reason I can see except the presence of so many camels.

[…]

Tonight, orders came in for a move tomorrow which were received with acclamation by all ranks.

## Saturday 17 November 1917. Belah[61]

The battalion marched off at 06.00 en route to BELAH. Colonel very wroth with me for being late on parade with HQ Company. It was really the fault of the poor old Gippy camel people who turned up late, but no excuses are taken although I have nothing whatever to do with their orders or movements. We bivouacked for the day at a spot known as the 'Grange' […]. Some rain fell which was pleasant and the sky remains overcast and cloudy. I saw a lot of storks which seemed to be on the trek somewhere. Perhaps they came from the 'storkeries' we saw in the Balkans.[62]

[…]

## Thursday 22 November 1917. Gaza

We have been hard at work training – MG, signalling, shooting, etc. Today we had a Brigade signalling competition between teams consisting of one officer, one NCO and twelve privates from each battalion. We had to open visual communication between two stations some two miles apart, with helio and flag, then lay a phone cable to another point and then communicate back to start by runner. Several messages had to be sent round, one point being lost for every minute or part of a minute behind first arrival, and five points off for every mistake. Maximum marks, 100. My fellows some way made a mess of it, principally because the man

---

60  Alexander William Kinglake, *Eothen: or traces of travel, brought home from the East* (London: Ollivier, 1844).
61  Now Deir al-Balah.
62  See diary entry, 8 Jan 1916.

reading helio at the out station (Fox)[63] suddenly developed a fearful stutter and couldn't call out the words to the men writing. He was no good at reading but was A1 at other work. Fox never showed this failing before, even in a scrap. The wire laying and re-reeling, and buzzer work was very good. [...] The weather here has been very nice and not too hot and our bivouac is very comfortable. At night, the jackals prowling about and barking or howling are unpleasant. We have been having some sport tent pegging with some lances we found lying about where cavalry casualties had occurred. Loveband's pony is A1 at it, some of the others, specially mine, being a bit heavy on the hand. I won a quid off Gaffney[64] yesterday revolver shooting at bottles. Also had some sport chasing jackals on horseback and shooting at them with revolvers. My pony expostulated the first time I loosed off about a foot from his ear, but we are good friends again.

A lot of natives are gradually returning to Gaza and the villages near. They seem a very un-warlike, mercantile lot, who just want to be left alone, to rob and cheat the troops. The railway is being pushed on hard day and night.

## Tuesday 27 November 1917.
## Gaza/march from Gaza

The whole 10th (Irish) Division moved off this morning at 09.00 to BEIT HANUN[65] marching in three columns of Brigade, half a mile apart on parallel courses, having artillery, divisional train, ambulances, etc. in rear of each Brigade. [...]

The march today was very pleasant as the sun was not too hot and the going was wonderfully good and everyone was feeling at last we were getting a move in the right direction. We reached our bivouac area on the foothills half a mile east of Beit Hanun at 16.45. A warning was circulated to all troops warning them not to touch nor interfere with Turkish bombs or ammunition lying about. Some of the bombs have been set to explode instantaneously and one of the native camel leaders

---

63  Too many men named Fox served in the RDF to identify this individual.
64  Captain James Gaffney, born in 1887 and living at Ballinagh, Co. Cavan, when he volunteered in May 1915. Prior to serving with the 6th RDF he had served in France with the 16th (Irish) Division. Awarded the MC. Killed in action in Oct 1918. See WO 339/2380.
65  Now Beit Hanoun.

was blown to bits this afternoon by one which he picked up. Water <u>very</u> scarce, at one time we thought we would get none at all. We had quite a long halt at mid-day and had quite a picnic, several friends coming over from other columns to see us. No more news. The sleepers used on the railways here are made of steel. They make a very noisy track but last well, and are proof against ants etc.

## Wednesday 28 November 1917. Beit Duras[66]

We moved off this morning at 08.00 in the same formation, our destination being Beit Duras, or as the men call it 'bate your ass'. We moved parallel with the Gaza–Latron[67] track, passing Simsin[68] and Beit Tima[69] on the right, and Beit Jerjah[70] and Esseh[71] on the left. We stopped a mile or so […] for lunch from 12.30 to 14.00 and then crossed both the road and railway and moved up the west side of them to our bivouac area close to Beit Duras, and dossed down for the night […]. Felt very tired after an 18-mile march, day very hot and there was a lot of dust.

This coastal plain is a magnificent place for growing crops, with deep, rich soil and well-watered in the rainy season. It seems to be all cultivated and those of the natives who left the villages are returning in large numbers and commencing work. There are any amount of natives along the route offering oranges for five piastres for three oranges, which we wouldn't pay as being exorbitant.

During the march we passed a lot of Turkish dumps, and abandoned waggons and gear of every kind. There were also a lot of dead horses and camels which were offensive. At Julis I saw a lot of women going off to draw water at some cisterns. They carry enormous earthen jars on their heads and walk with a most stately and magnificent gait. They have to keep their heads up straight and steady, and this causes a queer expression in their eyes, through trying to look downwards at the track. I estimated the total load of jar and water at probably 56 lbs at least and possibly up to 70 lbs. It is fairly common for women to die of a broken neck through stumbling when carrying these weights on their heads.

---

66  Later Bayt Daras, but no longer populated.
67  Now Latrun.
68  No longer standing, but close to the modern kibbutz of Or HaNer.
69  Now Bayt Tima.
70  Now Bayt Jirja.
71  Probably now Ezer.

Already some Gippy police are controlling the villages under Military Foot Police NCOs and the people are settling down, apparently quite satisfied that the Turks can never get back here. What touching confidence in Tommy Atkins.

[...]

## Thursday 29 November 1917. Junction Station[72]

Resumed our march at 08.00 as before, recrossing to the eastward of the railway and road close to El Kustineh,[73] and halting for lunch at El Mesmiyeh.[74] Near here, we recrossed the Gaza railway which swung away eastward to join the Beersheba line at Et Tineh.[75] We finally reached the neighbourhood of Junction Station where the Beersheba and Jerusalem lines join and runaway north through Ramleh[76] and Ludd,[77] and, crossing the road and the Wadi El Merubbah, took up our bivouac area on the hill north-west of the station half a mile. Here our box respirators were re-issued, so they must be expecting some gas in the hills.

[...]

## Friday 30 November 1917.
## Junction Station/Latron

Moved off at 08.00 for Latron at the junction of the Gaza–Jerusalem and Jaffa–Jerusalem road. The country here is getting very hilly and rocky, not unlike parts of Serbia. [...]

We arrived close to Latron at 13.00 and bivouacked for the night. We bought several camel loads of oranges for the men with PRI funds. [...]

Latron is quite a fine-looking place with a good metalled road. There is a handsome monastery on the hill-side built of stone with a lot of

---

72  About 7 miles south of what is now Ramla, close to the modern Yatzitz. See Figure 12.
73  Later Qastina, but no longer populated.
74  Later Al-Masmiyya al-Kabira, but no longer populated.
75  Later Al-Tina, but no longer populated.
76  Now Ramla.
77  Now Lod.

other houses and gardens round and having some very handsome trees growing in the grounds. There must be plenty of water here.

[…]

## Saturday 1 December 1917.
## Beit Sira/Valley of Ajalon[78]

[…]

We paraded at 10.00 and marched to BEIT SIRA up a very rough, stony track. We are now temporarily attached to the 31st Brigade, as they had to leave two battalions behind at Junction Station, to make an aerodrome. We heard a good deal of shooting going on in the hills in front of us, and we were stopped at a spot known as 'Jerusalem-085-L-10' and told not to move on until dark. […]

[…]

We stayed here until dark, and then moved up through Beit Sira to a point on the 'ancient road' 2,000 yards due west of Beit Ur El Tahta.[79] This place and its sister Beit Ur El Foka[80] were the old-time 'Beth-Horon the lower' and 'Beth-Horon the upper', which were the scene of the victory of Joshua over the five Amorite kings when the sun stood still to give him extra hours of daylight. It's extraordinary how history is repeating itself here, where we are fighting the Turks in the Valley of Ajalon and chasing him up the same track.

As soon as we got up to our position we took over the sector from the 5th Argyll & Sutherland Highlanders, 157th Brigade, 52nd Division. Their HQ were in a cave in the battalion lines and we took it as our HQ, but I preferred to stay in the open for the night, as the cave was damp and smelly.

The 5th and 6th Inniskillings are holding the right and left hand sectors respectively of the Brigade front. There is a fair amount of shooting going on with occasional bombing but no gun fire. I'm afraid we will not be in the actual capture of Jerusalem as we are much too far to the westward. Allenby is determined he will have no fighting in

---

78  Now Ayalon.
79  Now Beit Ur al-Tahta.
80  Now Beit Ur al-Fauqa.

Jerusalem and has issued orders to that effect. He is trying to force the Turks to abandon the city by threatening or attacking his flank and lines of communications running north by the Nablous[81] road through Ram Allah[82] and Beirah[83] (the ancient Beeroth). [...]

## Sunday 2 December 1917. El Burj[84]

Very hot day with Khamsin wind blowing. Went up among the rocks as far as I could and found a good spy-hole and had a good look round with the glasses, and spent a good while with map and compass, identifying places. Found the map decidedly poor. It's a most difficult country to get the hang of and it will be hard to keep any sort of formation when attacking. Any decent troops should be able to hold three times their number. It is not clear yet what our role is to be, as there seems to be a shuffling of troops going on. I suppose units have got a bit mixed during the fast work on the plains, but now we are in the mountains the pace can't be too fast, and we must work methodically.

[...]

## Thursday 6 December 1917. Et Tireh[85]

They give us very little news of what is going on, but we believe that heavy fighting is going on over at Nebi Samwil[86] and El Jib[87] and to the south-west of Jerusalem. The line on our right gradually bends southward until it runs parallel to the main road through Hebron and Jerusalem and on to Ram Allah. This part of the line, hinging about the point we are at, is gradually being left wheeled with the intention of sweeping past each side of Jerusalem, until the whole line from the sea runs approximately west to east. The 10th (Irish) Divisional line has the 1st Royal Irish [Regiment], 30th Brigade, on the left near Tahta, then

---

81  Now Nablus.
82  Now Ramallah.
83  Now Al-Bireh.
84  Later Al-Burj, but no longer populated.
85  Now Tira.
86  Now An-Nabi Samwil.
87  Now Al-Jib.

the 6th RMF and 6th RDF hold along to Et Tireh with the 7th RDF in Brigade reserve […]. The 29th Brigade are on our right in the order – 6th Leinsters – 1st Leinsters, 5th Connaught Rangers, and the 5th Royal Irish Rifles in reserve […].

We now have the Turks in front of us showing proper respect, or rather showing not at all. The smallest sign of movement gives them a dose of lead. We did in a few more last night when out raiding. They seemed to belong to the 19th Turk Division, 61st Regiment.

[…]

The weather looks like breaking and there is a very cold wind indeed except in the middle of the day. At night, it is bitter when going round the line, and not much sleep can be got. We now have some firewood up in the line and the men get their regular hot meals. The Somersets told us they had been afraid to light any fires and their men had not had anything hot for several days. They must be a very useless, unenterprising lot, as we got the Turk completely to heel in twelve hours.

[…]

## Saturday 8 December 1917. Et Tireh

Nothing special – believe our troops are nearly into Jerusalem, and Bethlehem has been captured. Some of us went out and stalked the deer I saw on the mountain behind us, but we never saw a sign of them. We have the Turks in front of us in a regular fizz of nerves. We are always hammering them, and, on the slightest excuse, they put barrages down in front of their line. We had to clear all the people out of Et Tireh and send them back as we suspect them of firing on our men. We found several rifles when searching houses.

## Monday 10 December 1917. Et Tireh

Great news at last. Jerusalem has been captured and the Turks have been driven out without any fighting in the city and no damage of any kind has been done.

It is hard to imagine the Holy City in Christian hands again after so many hundreds of years. I hope the politicians won't botch up matters after the war and let the Turks come back to it again. That's the sort of thing we are all afraid of, as history shows that the troops win the wars but the politicians nearly always lose the peace. These dammed Welch Fusiliers didn't turn up till 07.00 this morning. They were 'done to the wide' when they got here and absolutely unable to get into the line and take over. I never saw such a sloppy lot and the officers were the limit of dirt and inefficiency. I have seen some other of these Welsh people out here and they are all the same – no esprit de corps – no smartness – no initiative. Our fellows would have died rather than appear before a strange battalion in such a state of dirt, confusion and exhaustion. Anyway, we took pity on them and filled as many dixies with water as we could and gave them all a cup of hot tea. After an hour's rest, they started up to the line with our guides and the relief was reported complete about 11.00. I stayed behind with them to explain everything to their CO and signal officers.

[…]

We are to make an attack tomorrow to drive the Turks off the ridges at Tahta and Foka, but no general advance seems to be decided on yet. They will have to shove on near Jerusalem, I should think, so that the Turks can't shell the place, for that is just what their Bosch gunners would like to do. […]

## Tuesday 11 December 1917. Beit Anan

The night was warmer than usual, and dry, and we had a well-earned sleep. In the morning, we heard that the Turks have cleared out of Foka and Tahta and therefore the stunt would not come off, but that we were wanted up to support the 74th Division who are holding a position near Beit Dukku[88] and Beit Izza.[89] […]

We could only move in the dark as the road is exposed to view and is always being shelled, so the camels and mules were sent down to Latron to water. They were rather late getting back and it was 18.30 when we moved off. The road is the old Roman road and in use ever since then for getting from Jaffa to Jerusalem. It was reported to us as fit for wheels, but we found the hill so precipitous and the road so bad that twelve mules had to be hitched to each limbered waggon and the transport were all

88   Now Beit Duqqu.
89   Now Beit Ijza.

night on the road. We had a very heavy march in the dark and the clay was like glue. The HQ Company stuck it well, singing and joking all the time. The men are really wonderful – when there is nothing except 'ENNUI' to grumble about, they grouse like hell, but when they are up against something really stiff, such as recent long climbs in the rain and wind, and several nights running without sleep, they sing. It's marvellous. We don't find those Welshmen singing, but only bemoaning their fate in finding themselves in a country only second to their own for misery and inhospitable climate.

[…]

## Friday 14 December 1917. Beit Anan

[…]

Allenby has made his official entry into Jerusalem. I hear it was most impressive, although quite unlike the warlike bombastic entry the Turks would have made. He just walked in on the 11th at noon, unarmed and carrying a cane. He was followed at a considerable interval by the Staff and Corps Commander. There were two guards of 50 each made up of representatives of all units in the Corps. Proclamations were read aloud in Arabic, Hebrew, English, French, Italian, Greek, and Russian telling the people that they were under martial law, but to carry on their lawful business without fear, and that sacred spots, shrines, etc. would be maintained and protected by guards. Everyone weeping for joy.

We had a nice message from General Chetwode thanking the Corps for the 'soldierly' 'qualities displayed', and referring to the cold and wet and shortness of food and water.

Various operations are being planned, but we don't know what they are. However, all we can find out is that nothing they will take place for some days yet, and only small 'rectifications of the line' north of Jerusalem are taking place.

I think the difficulty is the getting up of supplies, which at present have to be brought by wheels across the coastal plain which is now an appalling quagmire. I suppose they are rushing the broad gauge railway forward so that supplies need not be trans-shipped till they get up to the hills.

# Tuesday 18 December 1917. Beit Anan

A long message arrived from the GOC in C[hief][90] 'thanking all ranks for the magnificent work accomplished'. In 40 days, the army has advanced 60 miles on a 30-mile front. Troops have 'carried out very long marches in great heat without water, made attacks on stubborn rearguards without time for reconnaissance, and suffered cold and privation in the mountains' but 'plans were carried out with boldness and determination, and devotion and gallantry beyond praise'. The 'C in C's thanks and appreciation to be conveyed to every officer and man of the force which he has the honour to command'.

[…]

Had a letter from Kenneth on leave in London saying he was very well and Bunty the same when he heard from her. Messages of congratulations on the capture of Jerusalem pouring in from every sort of person from the King downwards. I applied for, and got to leave, to go to Jerusalem tomorrow with John Luke and Tony Shadforth, and we are taking a pack mule with us in case we can get some vegetables. […]

# Wednesday 19 December 1917. Beit Anan/Jerusalem/L10

[…]

John Luke, Tony Shadforth and I started off at 08.45 for Jerusalem, taking Luke's servant, Collins,[91] on a pack mule. We intended making a line through Biddu – Beit Iksa – Lifta[92] and the Jaffa road into Jerusalem or 'El Kuds' as the Turks call it. The morning was nice and mild at first but later on the wind was very cold on the mountains but the rain kept off fortunately and we were able to get a good view of the country. The track we followed has been a recognised road since the Roman occupation and it still has the flat stone slabs in places, with which they made the surface of the road. Our maps show the track running down into the Wadi Hannina 1,000 yards north of Lifta and then up the hill on the east side of the Wadi, but all traces of a 'road' seemed to disappear

---

90  Allenby.
91  Too many men named Collins served in the RDF to identify this individual.
92  Now Mei Neftoach national nature reserve.

and we had to make our way as best we could. There was a good deal of water in the Wadi Hannina but we crossed without getting very wet and, making our way through the trees which fringed the wadi bed, we found ourselves faced with a perfectly precipitous ascent through a small village or suburb of Jerusalem which was not marked on the map. We had an awful job getting the horses up, and had to unbuckle one end of the reins and scramble up the rocks on hands and knees, and lug the animals up without hurting them, after us. The horses were very game and scrambled up in great style, sending sparks flying from their shoes. The natives seemed rather surprised at the exhibition but didn't offer to help, although they were quite friendly. This climb saved us a lot of time over the usual track through Lifta and round the western suburbs and time was important as we had to be outside Jerusalem by 16.00. We got to the Jaffa gate at 11.45 taking only three hours from Beit Anan, which was very fast going in such a country.

We left our horses and mule outside the Jaffa gate in charge of Collins, and, giving him some money, made our way to the Military Governor's office for passes into the city walls. I think Jerusalem is the dirtiest place I have ever been in, and the whole atmosphere stinks with rotting matter thrown into the streets and alleys.

We didn't know how to see all we wanted to see in the time available, so we enquired for a guide and got a Jew who was a native of Jaffa and had been a sort of sub-agent for the P&O steamship people there before the war. Luke was disgusted with the dirt and smell and said he would not come round with us, as all he wanted was a bath and a drink, so we arranged to meet him for lunch at the Hotel Fast.

It is impossible to put down all the things we saw, but the most wonderful of all was the Dome of the Rock on Mount Moriah which stands in the centre of 'Haram es Sherif' or 'temple area'.[93] We approached the site of the Temple by David Street which is dark and narrow, and suddenly emerged on the great plateau which must be nearly a quarter of a mile long north to south by 300 yards wide. Almost in the centre of it stands the magnificent Kubbet Es Sakhran or 'dome of the rock' with its perfectly wonderful blue dome of glazed tiles. Just as we got our first glimpse of it, a ray of wintry sun lit up the dome and the effect was enough to take one's breath away. We could only stand and wonder with crowded thoughts running through our minds.

93 See Figure 13.

This shrine is not a mosque although some people call it the Mosque of Omar. The real Mosque of Omar is a very much smaller, but equally beautiful, building standing to the south of the Dome of the Rock.

We found that Allenby has arranged guards over all the sacred spots in Jerusalem, and only those belonging to the religion concerned were allowed in. A magnificent Sikh sentry was mounted at the 'Dome' which is Mahomedan and we could not get in.

None of King Solomon's Temple is said to remain except the site, but we saw the remains of many fine pillars and arches. The Dome of the Rock stands on the site of the Holy of Holies, which was on the extreme top of Mount Moriah where Abraham made offering of Isaac.

We went out through St Stephen's Gate and crossed the valley of Jehoshaphat to the Mount of Olives and the Garden of Gethsemane. The squalor and dreariness caused many mixed feelings, as one's mental picture of the place took no account of that. But the thing that annoyed me was the modern 'showman' way of pointing out marks of our Lord's feet, etc. on stones and in the ground, and expecting that rubbish of that kind could impress people who were already sufficiently impressed with the feeling of being on the site of incidents which stir most of the world's inhabitants.

We retraced our steps and went up the Via Dolorosa which has brand new buildings of a French convent on one side of it, containing the reputed place of Christ's trial. Here a rival guide came up and told us not to mind what our fellow said, as he himself would show us the real spot where these things took place. We found the same thing all through. There are several reputed sites for every happening, each boosted and pushed by the various religious bodies who have appropriated the spot. I, myself, don't believe in any of them except the Mount of Olives. It stands to reason that a city which has been completely ruined and destroyed three times and has lain several hundred years each time, before the next city was built on the remains of the old one, cannot preserve particular spots and stones thousands of years old. Why, some places are proved to be built on 50 or 60 feet of piled up rubbish.

We visited the Church of the Sepulchre and other places which we would never have seen but for the guide. Also saw the Jews' wailing places, which is along part of the main wall, here about 50 feet high and built of enormous blocks of soft stone. The Jews wail for the loss of Jerusalem by Christendom, and yet, now that it has been restored to them from the hands of the infidel, they still weep. They must be like the Irish. (Turk and German officers have carved their names on many of the stones of the wall along the wailing place, greatly annoying the Jews who count the place sacred.) 

We came out of the city past David's Tower and the Tower of Hippicus, and we saw the bit of the wall that Kaiser Bill had pulled down for his entry into the city. Our guide had seen that show and had been one of those appointed to arrange for food and water for the Kaiser's party, and he said the people were not impressed as was intended.

We then went along and found John Luke striding about and swearing horribly because Fast's hotel had lived up to its name and we would have to fast there as they had absolutely nothing in the place. He had not been able to get even a bath or drink there, so the guide showed us a little native cafe where everything was filthy and smelly, but we were too hungry to mind. We had some "lamb" and cabbage and some not bad 'vin rouge' and felt much better after it. Then we went into the city again and bought a few mementoes, and also bought matches, candles, post cards, vegetables, and a few bottles of wine for the mess, and a couple of loaves of bread, and loaded up the mule and started off about 15.45 for Beit Anan. We had quite a good run home and did not lose our way, having carefully blazed the trail on the way out.

When we reached our camp site, all was still and not a fire or light to be seen, and we found the battalion gone. What's to be done? Soon we discovered an orderly snoozing over the remains of a fire, who had been left to tell us to follow on to Beit Sira where the battalion was camped for the night. [...]

[...]

## Monday 24 December 1917. L10

This is the anniversary of the day this miserable child came into this world and it's the worst one I ever spent. No smokes, no fire, and rain torrenting down without ceasing. It's like the time we spent in Salonika in October 1915, only more 'demned, demnition damp'. Then, we had tents to sleep in and mess in, but now, no such luxury. I wish they would let loose on the Turk and we'll flay him for this.

[...]

# Tuesday 25 December 1917. L10

Was absolutely washed out early this morning. The rain got even worse, and a huge torrent swept down the hill-side through the boulders, sweeping everything before it. My valise was flooded, and boots, clothes and papers swept down the hill-side. Some of the things I never saw again. We spent a miserable Xmas day with chattering teeth and aching bodies. Everyone soaked to the skin and no firewood to make a fire big enough to dry clothes, everyone hoping and praying that Xmas might never be like this again. If only Zero day were announced. Fighting in the hills would be far preferable to this sitting down in seas of mud waiting for something to turn up.

Great scare and straf because Paine has found three cases of trench foot. No wonder, I think, when we have been on half rations for a week and have been soaked through the day and night for three or four days.

[…]

8

# Defending Jerusalem and the Battle of Tell 'Asur, December 1917–July 1918

In late December 1917 the 6th Royal Dublin Fusiliers were peripherally involved in the defence of Jerusalem against a Turkish counter-attack, advancing around Deir Ibzia[1] west of Ramallah.[2] However, the enemy often retreated rapidly, so in the months to come there was little direct engagement as the battalion strengthened positions and provided work parties for tasks such as road building.[3] Meanwhile, in late January and early February, Drury took part in a 'contact patrol' signalling course with members of the Royal Flying Corps and flew over both Jerusalem and Bethlehem in a Bristol fighter.[4] His battalion's only major action of their remaining time in Palestine came in the Action of Tell 'Asur[5] in early March which followed the capture of Jericho by British forces.[6] The purpose of the attack was to lengthen the British front along the Jordan valley to allow later operations east of it, in part to support the Arab Revolt.[7] The battalion had targets which meant climbing high ground and Drury described how 'It was impossible to see over any terrace to the one above, and every moment we expected a shower of stick grenades on

---

1   Now Deir Ibzi.
2   Diary entries, 26 and 29 Dec 1917.
3   Diary entries, 5 and 19 Jan, 23 Feb and 2 March 1918.
4   Diary entries, 26 Jan and 2 Feb 1918.
5   Now Tall Asur.
6   Diary entries, 9 and 16 March 1918.
7   Falls and Becke, *History of the Great War*, 310; Ulrichsen, *The First World War in the Middle East*, 155.

our heads. We pushed up in as uneven formation as possible, every man either pushing up his pal first or pulling him up from above.' Following a furious charge by units of the 10th (Irish) Division, 'old Johnny Turk broke and ran as hard as ever he could leg it, throwing away his rifles and equipment and bombs, and just clearing out – vamoosing – for all he was worth.'[8]

A period of strengthening the line followed[9] and Drury again visited Cairo in late April,[10] but in mid-May he once again succumbed to eye problems. These put him in hospital[11] until early July. By this time it had become clear that the 6th Royal Dublin Fusiliers would be moved to France. In the face of the German Spring Offensive of March 1918, Allenby had been told that he must send British units to the Western Front, replacing most with Indian ones. Twenty-three British battalions in the Middle East were sent, with another ten broken up as reinforcements. Just one British battalion remained in each brigade as part of this process of 'Indianisation', so the departure for France marked the end of the 10th (Irish) Division as an 'Irish' formation. None of the three battalions which remained in the Division's three brigades was original 10th (Irish) Division.[12]

As news of the transfer to the Western Front emerged, Drury, still in hospital, was concerned that he would not travel with his battalion. Medical officers refused to allow him to travel but he managed to persuade some with the necessary authority to at least allow him to go to Alexandria, with a friend surreptitiously taking his luggage there. From Alexandria, in his own words, and with the connivance of his battalion Commanding Officer, Drury 'deserted'. Meeting his battalion at the docks, they left on 3 July on HMT *Malwa*.[13]

8   Diary entry, 16 March 1918.
9   Diary entries, 23 March–20 April, 11 May 1918.
10  Diary entry, 27 April 1918.
11  Diary entries, 18 May–6 July 1918.
12  Johnstone, *Orange, Green & Khaki*, 337, 401–2; H.E.D. Harris, *The Irish Regiments in the First World War* (Cork: Mercier Press, 1968), 146.
13  Diary entry, 6 July 1918.

## Wednesday 26 December 1917. L10

Zero day at last. The news came in about 15.00 and at the same time, a short gleam of watery sunshine seemed to be a good omen. I was lucky enough to get up my Norwegian boots through the exertions of Stuffer Byrne and have at last got to my feet dry. [...]

## Week ending Saturday 29 December 1917. Shamrock Hill/Wadi Kelb[14]

The strength of the Headquarter Company is now three officers and 75 other ranks, including the Regimental Sergeant-Major Ferguson,[15] but excluding Regimental Quartermaster-Sergeant Grant.[16]

On the night 26/27th, the Turk made his expected counter-attack to recapture Jerusalem and needless to say, he didn't do anything but lose a lot of his men and get driven further away than the line from which he started, in most places seven or eight miles and, in others, even more.

We moved up in the evening of the 26th to the junction of the wadis Ain Arik[17] and Sunt,[18] where we established phone communications with the Division and made an ammunition dump. The mud and dirt were perfectly appalling but everyone was in great delight at moving at last. We passed some troops in the dark and found they had not had any smokes for a week so a lot of our fellows very decently collected some Woodbines from their meagre store and handed them over.

Next morning, we attacked the high ground [...] including the village of Deir Ibzia – a pretty little place right on the summit of a steep hill and having three very prominent tall palm trees growing in the courtyard of a mosque. It struck me that this would be a nice name for a yacht – 'Deir Ibzia'.

The country here is very difficult, the assent of the wadi sides is precipitous and the wadis wind about forming overlapping spurs which hide any lengthy view of the wadi. The Turks had many well-concealed

---

14   This area was north of Jerusalem.
15   6128 Samuel Ferguson (WO 372/7/47346).
16   13535 George Grant (WO 372/8/98607).
17   Now Ein 'Arik.
18   South-east of and running through Tahta to the north-west. See Figure 14.

machine guns – all of them firing to a flank, and impossible to see or locate from the front so that we were constantly finding ourselves under a cross fire, and the roar of the guns echoed around the hills in such a confusing way that you never could be sure even from what direction the fire was coming. However, by telling everyone most carefully what their objectives were and keeping moving in small parties of three and 4, we had very few casualties. Our principal concern was that we hardly ever saw a sign of the Turk and it was perfectly hopeless to capture either prisoners or MGs. Whenever they found that we had turned the flank of a position or even got unpleasantly close frontally, they just packed up and slunk back quietly, [by] what time we were toiling and sweating up in the sticky mud, or on hands and knees through the rocks and boulders.

I don't recall anything special about the weather beyond the fact that the hill-tops were clear of clouds.

By the night of 27th December, we had reached all the high ground north of the Wadi Ain Arik […] and on our right the 74th Division had taken Ram Allah and Beirah (both considerable towns as they go out here), an advance of 4,000 yards on a six mile front.

I don't think we had any guns with us at all – I didn't notice any of ours shelling any of our objectives – as there is no way of getting them up. It is not possible to get them direct over the ridges, so they have to make tracks up the wadis and subsidiary streams and make gradual grades over the cols between the heights.

Our general direction during these days was north-east but a lot of the hills had to be tackled almost north and when the top was taken and cleared, the general direction was resumed. The only places the Turks put up any sort of hand-to-hands show was at Ainein[19] and Khurbet Rubin[20] where we killed a few and shot others.

A lot of the hills and places here have no names on the map so one enlightened individual on our Brigade Staff (probably recently out) taking his cue from the Variety stage, adopted a saying of George Robey,[21] 'Archibald, Certainly not', and we suddenly found ourselves in the middle of the country abounding in such names as 'George' Hill – 'Robey' corner, 'Archi Hill', 'Knot Hill', 'Wadi Certainly'.

---

19    The hill Abu el 'Ainein, about 1 mile north of Ain Arik.
20    West of modern-day Ramallah, roughly halfway to Deir Ibzia.
21    George Edward Wade, who, using 'Robey' as a stage name, was one of the most prominent music hall performers of the era, born in 1869 and knighted in the year of his death, 1954 (*The Times*, 30 Nov 1954, p. 11).

By Saturday 29th, the Turk attack had collapsed and Jerusalem was safe. The attack on the 53rd and 60th divisions had been very heavy, I hear, but our push had made the Turk transfer some of his troops to our front and ease the situation on the right. They didn't make much difference to us, as we had an almost bloodless victory.

## Week ending Saturday 5 January 1918.
## Wadi Kelb/Kelb Corner

This week we pushed out our line still further and without much opposition. We had only to go out in some force when the Turks, after a few rounds from their MGs at long range, packed up and departed. I don't think there was anything in front of us except a light screen of outposts as I saw no indication of there having been any inconsiderable number of men in the villages, nor were any prepared positions to be seen, only a few hastily dug rifle pits and MG emplacements built up with rocks and stones.

On 30th and 31st December we were holding a line on the south of and overlooking the Wadi Kelb, with Battalion HQ in the hollow between Shamrock and Diamond Hills [...]. The weather was bad and on the last night of the year it poured all night with a steady downpour.

We got orders to leave early on January 1st, 1918 and seize the high ground north of the Wadi Kelb. We had a terrible day, and I don't think I was ever so near the end of my endurance. Packing up in the early morning was a sore trial, as our blankets and valises got soaked with rain as well as covered with mud and the bundles weighed twice the usual amount. I had to turn out a squad of men soon after daylight to reel in all the phone wire we had in use and overhaul it. These we found on the hillside and were calmly informed by the Brigade Signal Officer (CA Murray[22] of Dundrum, County Dublin) that we must lay our line from Brigade HQ to wherever our HQ were to be. This was a shameful demand as every unit is supposed to lay 'forward', i.e. Brigade lay lines up to battalions and battalion men lay up to their companies in the line. Of course, everyone's duty is to keep in touch at all costs so that I couldn't refuse to lay his line. The Colonel couldn't say where his HQ were going to be until he went up and selected a spot – he couldn't even say on which side of the valley he would be on. The Brigade HQ were

---

22  Possibly of the 5th Royal Irish Fusiliers (WO 372/14/157373).

located [...] on the north side of the Wadi Kelb and I decided to lay along the north side of the wadi as this would help us to advance quicker and might protect the wire somewhat, as the mule convoys seemed to find better going on the south side. It was a terrible day with a heavy persistent downpour which made the soft clay on the hillsides into a quagmire nearly knee deep. My men had to carry all their equipment and rifles plus signalling stores and heavy drums of D3 cable. The battalion did not seem to be having any fighting today and I saw no sign of a Turk all day. We struggled along slowly constantly finding the line 'dis' [disconnected] through bad insulation and sometimes being broken. Soon we came to a small wadi [...]. This was too wide for an air line and as it looked a good route for the next advance, we didn't like to lay the groundline as it would soon get chewed up with traffic, so I decided to fix up an air line across the Wadi Kelb to the south side and trust to luck. We gradually pushed on hour by hour feeling fit to drop until we had a breathing space while we sent to Brigade HQ for more cable. On past the north of the Wadi Certainly on the south side opposite to Ain Kanieh[23] which stands halfway up the west slope of a curious shaped hill we named Tower Island as it looked like an island, with wadis all round it, and it had a tower on it.

About 18.00, I got a message from the Colonel asking why the devil he wasn't in touch with Brigade HQ and more in the same strain. I thought silence was golden on this occasion, as I knew if I said anything, it would certainly be pretty strong. It was after midnight when we had the Brigade and the companies connected up to Battalion HQ. The men were done in completely and we had had neither dinner nor tea and were soaked to the skin. To make matters worse – when the first jar of rum was opened to give the men their ration – it was found that some 'Base wallah' had extracted the contents and refilled the jar with linseed oil! This wasn't seen in the darkness and several men swallowed it down before they noticed the stuff. [...]

The Colonel's HQ were on the north side of the Wadi after all, and we had to carry the line across overhead. There was one of the stone watch-towers here which gave us some shelter and warmth. These towers, which are often mentioned in the Bible, are built in the olive groves so that the owners can keep an eye on the fruit. They are square blocks about fifteen feet along the sides by about twenty feet high and are one-storeyed, having a stone roof sunk down three feet below the top of the walls which form

---

23   Now Ein Qaniya.

a breastwork round the flat top. A small stone stair rises from the floor to the roof where the owners live in the hot weather under an awning of branches. The entrance is about four feet high by two feet wide, so it is rather hard to get in with kit on, without going down on the knees in the mud. We pulled the branches off the roof and lit a fire, using the stair opening in the wall as a fire-place. Colonel most unreasonable, with, apparently, no thought of the men's endurance. I badly burned one of the legs of my field boots trying to get warm and dry.

[…]

## Week ending Saturday 19 January 1918.
## Kelb corner/'Byrne's Bridge'

We finished up our signalling week […] on Thursday and handed over to the 31st Brigade. The men worked very well and not a single hitch occurred. During this week, the 66th Company Royal Engineers made a wooden bridge over the Wadi El Kelb […] quite close to our camp. Stuffer Byrne made a dugout for himself in the bank on the north side of the bridge and almost facing it, and formed his dump of stores there, as it was a drier place than where he had been under the trees on the south side of the wadi. In conformity with the rule, a notice was put up on the ends of the bridge showing the kind of traffic it was intended to carry. To everyone's amusement it read 'Not for wheels, laden camels singly, laden mules led in pairs, or Stuffer Byrne by himself.' […]. Byrne, who weigh[s] about sixteen stone, was as much amused as the others, and the notice remained there long after we moved out of the area.

[…]

## Week ending Saturday 26 January 1918.
## 14th Squadron Royal Flying Corps/Junction Station

I got word that I was to go down to the 14th Squadron Royal Flying Corps near Junction Station for a course in 'contact patrol' work (in which planes are allotted to the infantry in attack and receive messages from them and note their positions and carry the information back to Brigade or Division HQ. No accommodation would be available at the

Squadron HQ so I took my servant, (Faithfull),[24] and my bivouac and valise on a second horse. [...]

[...]

The course started with a lecture on the theory of contact patrols and the various methods of communication between infantry and aeroplanes. Here I first saw the Lucas electric daylight signalling lamp which is about the size of a motor-cycle headlamp, with a Mangin lens mirror hinged on its horizontal axis and capable of slight tilting movement. Fixed to the back of the lamp is a pistol grip and trigger, the latter being connected to the mirror and having a light return spring. There is a sighting tube fixed along the top of the lamp, about 8″ long and ¾″ diam., with cross wires for sighting. This is accurately aligned with the beam of the mirror in free position. A battery box is either hung on the belt or placed on the ground and flex-connected to the lamp. When signalling, the object, either aeroplane or other signal station is kept focused in the tube and the Morse alphabet can be spelled out with the trigger, whereby the light is flashed on or off the target without moving the lamp. With a little practice, we found it quite easy to keep the lamp aligned on a plane flying overhead or circling around. We sent messages which the observer read and wrote down, then dropping them in a message bag for checking and correction. Later, we were taken up and shown ground strips, flares, etc. in the most suitable positions for the plane to see them, and also ones badly placed as regards light, slope of ground, etc. as examples of how not to do them. We also got a lot of useful information about the best way to camouflage troops, bivvys, and stores. We went up in 'R.E.8', 'B.E.2.c', and some other machines whose types I forget.

I had two most interesting (unofficial) flights in a Bristol fighter and saw Bethlehem, Jerusalem and the Nablous road, and also part of the front we will be attacking. I also got a few very interesting photos, one of them from quite low down of the Church of the Nativity in Bethlehem.[25] I saw the photo people at work making photos of sections of the front, taken at different positions of the sun and then printed on top of each other, which made trenches, sangars and strong points and redoubts stand out in high relief where they could hardly be seen in a single photo.

---

24  Private 18441 Nicholas A. Faithfull of Ballinrobe, Co. Mayo (WO 372/7/11506, and see photo in D3, p. 86).
25  See Figures 15 and 16.

## Week ending Saturday 2 February 1918.
## Deir Sineid/²⁶ Janiah²⁷

[…]

I started back for the line on Tuesday morning, 29th, after a most delightful experience. It was more like a holiday than a course, and we were mutually impressed and interested by the remarks of infantry and airmen anent²⁸ various battles and manoeuvres, and the subject generally of aerial help and guidance for infantry. Most of the Royal Flying Corps officers here had been in line regiments and therefore could appreciate our point of view.

[…]

I arrived at Janiah on Wednesday evening and found the battalion settled into the new sector and busy improving the defences. A lot of the houses were being cleaned out so that if the weather got extra bad, we could get the men into shelter. I liked Janiah very much as it was high up and a fine fresh breeze blew. There was a very good field of view in front and, in fact, all-round. […]

The houses in Janiah are quite numerous and well-built, most of them having sort of cellars where olive crushing is carried on, in fact, all the villages reek of crude olive oil, as the staple industry is the crushing of olives. The presses in use all seemed extremely old and were excessively crude, the screw of the press being the bole of a tree with a rough thread cut into it with an axe and finished off roughly with a hand knife. The remains of the olives seemed to be used for firing, and the crude oil was stored in large earthen chatties containing about ten gallons each. In one house on the eastern outskirts I found a modern metal press with the name of a German firm in Mannheim cast on the framing.

There seemed to be very few Turks near us and we used to patrol out in front as far as a mile or more, and only met small parties that we had no difficulty in dealing with. We kept in touch with the parties by flag or helio and we gave names to wadis after the officers who explored them. Altogether it was a most pleasing sort of warfare at Janiah as, on the whole, the weather was good, with fine air and good view[s].

---

26  Now Dayr Sunaid.
27  Now Al-Janiyah.
28  About.

# Week ending Saturday 23 February 1918. Ain Arik

Last Sunday, we got orders to move on relief by 31st Brigade to Ain Arik to work on an important new road. We moved off on Monday in torrents of rain, the companies going independently, HQ leading. [...] There was considerable doubt where we were to bivouac, so I picked up the best spot I could find [...] where we spent a miserable night with no firing and everyone soaking wet. Next morning, we moved up past Kefr Shiyan [...] where we pitched a good camp. Fortunately, the morning was dry and the sun shone brightly and everyone dried up. We are to complete the road from Ain Arik to Ram Allah and on to Beirah where it joins the main Jerusalem–Nablous road. There is a lot of heavy digging and grading, and boulders have to be rolled down the hills to make the foundations. The Duke of Connaught is expected to pay a visit to Palestine and this road will be used to reach parts of the front.

[...]

# Week ending Saturday 2 March 1918.
# Ain Arik/Ram Allah/Wadi Dougal/Abu Shukheidim[29]

[...]

The battalion moved off on Friday, 1st March, via Wadi Certainly, Wadi Kelb, Ain Kanieh and Wadi Hamis to a position in the Wadi Dougal. The track from our camp on Irish Road [...] ran steeply down the side of Wadi Certainly to Robey Corner. It was not fit for the transport which had to go round by Deir Ibzia to Kelb corner and thence to Wadi Hamis. [...] Our orders were to move with every precaution to conceal movement, and A Company to provide local protection for the new bivouac. We had a lovely day with warm, bright sun and the terebinth and olive trees were coming into leaf. We saw nothing of Johnny Turk and there was no shelling. In the evening, we got the orders for another move to take place during the night 2nd/3rd March, exact hours to be notified later. [...]

---

29  Now Abu Shukhaydam.

## Week ending Saturday 9 March 1918.
## Abu Shukheidim/Sheikh Kalrawany[30]

No Turks were seen until close to the village when a small garrison started shooting but they soon cleared out and A Company's platoon seized the place about three o'clock. It was rather better built than most of the villages, principally, I think, because it was built on the flat instead of the top or side of a hill, and therefore the houses and enclosed gardens were more orderly. C and D companies' scouts pushed out to the ridge which was their objective [...] and had a bit of scrapping with Turk outposts but nothing to speak of.

[...]

On Friday, 8th March, we received our orders for the next show [...]. The 20th Corps (Chetwode) is attacking north with three divisions. The 53rd Division (SF Mott)[31] on the right – the 74th (Eric Girdwood)[32] in the centre on the Nablous road, and the 10th (Irish) Division (JR Longley)[33] on the left. The right Division of the 21st Corps (Bulfin) (the 75th Division) on our left will move up to conform. Some Yeomanry crowd are to watch the gap on our left between the Corps.

The 10th (Irish) Division is attacking in two portions. Right attack by 30th and 31st Brigades, direction N[orth] E[ast] objects, Attara[34] Ridge and Kalrawany and the long spur running N[orth] W[est] towards Ajul[35] village. The left attack by 29th Brigade, direction N[orth] on Neby Saleh[36] and Deir Es Sudan.[37] Our (30th) Brigade attacks with two battalions, 1st Royal Irish Regiment on the right and 6th Royal Munster Fusiliers on the left, 6th RDF in support.

The two attacking battalions are to pass through our outpost line by 05.30 on Saturday morning (9th) and all our companies will concentrate [...] by 06.30. We will then follow the general direction of the attack, in artillery formation. [...]

---

30  About 6 miles north of Ramallah.
31  Stanley Fielder Mott, 1873–1959 (*The Times*, 6 Feb 1959, p. 15).
32  Major General Eric Girdwood, 1876–1963 (*The Times*, 25 May 1963, p. 10).
33  Major General John Raynesford Longley, 1867–1953, who commanded the 10th (Irish) Division from Dec 1915 to June 1919 (*The Times*, 14 Feb 1953, p. 8).
34  Now 'Atara.
35  Now Ajjul.
36  Now Nabi Salih.
37  Now Deir as-Sudan.

There was a good deal of fog on Thursday and Friday and, on Saturday morning when we started the advance visibility was down to 100 yards, but later in the morning, it cleared away and the day was delightfully hot. The attack was very prettily carried out and we had a fine view as we strolled along about half a mile in the rear. The first phase was over by noon, and the Turk put up no sort of a decent show. We could have held his positions against twice the numbers. There was a good deal of badly aimed rifle fire and his MGs were well-served, but our casualties were slight, and his artillery gave him no decent support. I don't recall seeing a single shell falling among us as we marched placidly along in rear of the attack. We are to have our turn tomorrow. We stayed on the south slope of Kalrawany until dark as there was intermittent shelling going on, we had therefore plenty of time to have a good meal and study orders and maps for tomorrow. The 30th and 31st Brigades again form the right attack of the 10th (Irish) Division, but we (6th RDF) and the 1st Royal Irish Regiment do the star turn.

[…]

I had a look at the place this evening and it reminded me of going to have a tooth out – you must get it done but you don't like going there. It would be no mean feat climbing up the north side with full kit without any fighting, but if the Turk chooses to dispute each terrace with bombs dropped on the heads of those lower down, we will have a nasty time. It was too dark to see any details of sangars or strong points, but photos showed the upper part was covered with them, so sited that they all fired to a flank and thus obtained cross fire over the whole wadi, leaving no dead ground anywhere. Late in the evening, the arrangements were slightly altered, and the Royal Irish were ordered to dribble up men during the night, and to secure strong points as far up as possible. We start moving down from ATTARA before daylight and act in support of the Royal Irish Regiment as found necessary.

An unfortunate incident occurred during the night. Battalion orders had been sent out and Luke had to make some preliminary move with his Company. I don't know exact details but he didn't move and when sent a chit by the CO he refused to turn out. I can't imagine what demon possessed him but can only surmise that his rum ration was in proportion to his own size. However, there was nothing for it but to put him in arrest, and as C Company were in reserve for the next day, Luke was put under charge of the unfortunate Duggie English.[38] The whole incident is damned unpleasant, but, fortunately, very few knew of it at the time. Bill Whyte seemed very upset at having to take such a step, and no wonder, when an officer who had served pre-war in the Regiment, had so little regard for himself or the Blue Caps.

## Week ending Saturday 16 March 1918.
## Wadi El Jib/Jiljilia[39]

Sunday, 10th. Both the 74th Division and the 53rd on their right were very sticky yesterday and did not get their objectives until after dark. Our objectives today have been revised. It was originally intended that the Ghurabieh Ridge[40] [...] should be taken, but it was found that this would be a difficult place to stay on, and the flanks would be unsafe. It was therefore decided that the line should stop at the highest point on the north side of the Wadi Jib at Abwein and Jiljilia, and that we should not cross the Wadi Gharib.

We got to a move on about 02.00, I think it was, and made a very easy march along a good track, almost a road in fact, to Attara village where it petered out, or possibly turned off east. We could hear spasmodic fighting, apparently deep down below us in the wadi bed and the constant thud of grenades, and we could see them bursting with a tiny yellow sparkle, just like fire-flies. We made our way down a few hundred feet, clambering over huge boulders, falling into holes and getting tied up in scrub and undergrowth. I expected many broken rifles and lost ammunition. We got the men disposed under cover as far as possible and waited for daylight or a message from the Royal Irish. We had the [...] 5th Royal Inniskilling Fusiliers, 31st Brigade [...] on our right and Major French, who was commanding them, had a scheme of his own for getting across the wadi and up the other side. His objectives were principally the two hills (2,650 and 2,675 feet) on each side of the Wadi Et Tiyur which runs

---

38 Captain Robert Douglas English, born in 1880 and practising as a solicitor in Dublin (though with a home address in Dromore, Co. Down) when he volunteered in Sept 1914, immediately seeking a commission. Had previous service with the 13th Battalion, Imperial Yeomanry in South Africa in 1900–01. Prior to the 6th RDF, served with the 8th RDF in France. See WO 339/10583.
39 Now Jiljilyya.
40 High ground a few miles north of the battalion's eventual target.

south west to the Wadi Jib from Khurbet Aliuta.[41] He was keeping all his machine guns on the south side of the Wadi Jib and going to use them for overhead fire. Each section had a white flag or piece of tin, which showed exactly how far up they had climbed, and he hoped to be able to keep down the Turks in their sangars until he had enough men close enough to rush the enemy.

We had no news from our Brigade and for considerable periods there was no sound of firing or bombing. When full daylight came, we could fully appreciate the tremendous obstacle which the Wadi Jib forms naturally, and it didn't seem possible to capture the opposite mountain if the Turk put up any sort of scrap. On the other hand, if we bent him here, he was down and out and couldn't show his face again. We could at first see no signs of our troops, but, after a while, we made out a few parties in small numbers about a quarter of the way up and rather more to the left than we expected. [...] the Royal Irish seemed to be [...] held up and a lot of them must have come back down, as we could only see about twenty or so altogether.

Meanwhile the Royal Inniskilling Fusiliers started dribbling across in ones and twos, keeping well-separated and making fine climbing of it, one group standing fast till the next had arrived up. We could see their flags quite easily with glasses and they were keeping a good alignment. There was a good deal of MG and rifle fire but I did not see any of them hit. What worried us particularly was that the 74th Division on our right who ought to have been showing up or even have taken their hills 3038 and 2972 near the Nablous road, were nowhere to be seen, and we could see both hills swarming with Turks who had a lot of MGs and light guns there which could enfilade our front. There was nothing for us to do, however, except wait. It was a very hot day and no wind, and as I had not had any sleep since 04.00 on Saturday morning, I had a couple hours shut eye.

A show like this is, of course, extraordinarily slow, for no human beings could keep on moving fast up such a place – you're left gasping after five minutes hauling yourself up and then pulling up the next behind. I really lost all count of the time as I had no occasion to send any messages which needed timing, but I should say it was about 14.00 when we decided it was time for us to chip in, as the Royal Irish didn't seem to be doing anything, although they hadn't asked for help, and it was essential to get the whole battalion to the top before dark.

41   5 miles north-west of Tell 'Asur.

The Royal Inniskilling Fusiliers were making great progress and French's attack was a delight to see, well-planned and carried out; but, with no sign of the 74th Division on his right, and no Royal Irish on his left, he couldn't hang on to his bit on his lonesome if counter-attacked, as he was sure to be. A few of our contact planes were over during the day but I doubt if they could see anything at all. Our guns were firing but we could see no bursts anywhere so I suppose they couldn't reach the sangars belonging to the Turks and were doing some counter battery practice.

We started scrambling down towards a spot where there seemed a little cover at a place where the wadi takes a pronounced twist southwards. How we got the MG and ammunition mules down there beats me, but the more difficult the climb, the easier they seem to do it. We all got down eventually with only a few casualties, but found that our 'dead ground' was being simply sprayed with bullets. There was a small pool of water in the wadi bed near me, about ten feet long by three feet wide and it looked exactly like as if there was a shower of hail falling into it.

I found that Hudson,[42] my groom, had arrived with my horse. I couldn't be angry with him but how he imagined I could ride anywhere I don't know. The poor pony was wounded rather badly in the shoulder and in two places in the flank while I was trying to haul him up into a sheltered spot, but I don't think they are really serious. I will lose him, worse luck, and I will be lucky if I get another as good and sure-footed.

We had a pow-wow at the bottom of the wadi and settled the objectives which were the rows of sangars and MG posts [...]. Having secured this which seemed to be the key of our hill, we would stretch out right and left to get in touch with the Inniskillings and the RMF respectively.

I'll never forget that climb. It was impossible to see over any terrace to the one above, and every moment we expected a shower of stick grenades on our heads. We pushed up in as uneven formation as possible, every man either pushing up his pal first or pulling him up from above. How the mules got up, I don't know and can't imagine, as I was away ahead of them. Anyway, we pressed on up and up, seeing no Turks but hearing their MGs chattering away aloft, and the bullets zipping and pinging off the rocks. We had hardly any wounded, which is surprising.

At last, we got in sight of the sangars and could see German officers running backwards and forwards between them. We got everyone collected on a fair frontage and gave them a breather for five minutes, discarded

---

42  Too many men named Hudson served in the RDF to identify this individual.

our packs and haversacks and fixed our bayonets. When the whistle blew, away we went with a 'screech' like only Irishmen can give (it reminded us of 15th August, 1915 on the 'KTS' ridge at Suvla Bay, Gallipoli). When the Turk saw us coming, he never waited till we were within range, but just bunged every grenade he could lay hands on, in our direction, and even some of their rifles and FLED! What a scene! We arrived at the sangars puffing and blowing like grampus-es (or is it grampi?) and laughing a little shamefacedly as if our little bit of sword rattling had been rather overdone. We were sure Johnny Turk would have waited for us and put up some, and everyone was disgusted to find we had only to say 'Boo' and he ran away. When we got up to what we thought was the top, we found it was only a false crest. There was a slight hollow of comparatively smooth ground about 300 yards wide and then the crest proper. This ran slightly diagonally across our front [...] and just covering the village of Jiljilia. We could see the Turks holding this crest strongly and they seemed to have a good many MGs going.

The Colonel allotted the attack to A and D companies and they lay down under a terrace in shelter and sorted themselves out into proper order. The MGs had by this time arrived up behind us and we got them on each flank to give cross fire. The two companies were as keen as blazes to see which would get to the other crest first, as Bill Whyte in the good old style stood between them and sang out 'Are you ready, A Company?' Cheers and shouts of 'Blow the whistle, sir'. The same with D Company. 'Away you go' yells the CO and away they certainly did go 'hundred yards speed', bayonets glinting in the last rays of the sun, and no gear to hamper them. The Turks looked like sticking this time, but no, before our men got halfway across, old Johnny Turk broke and ran as hard as ever he could leg it, throwing away his rifles and equipment and bombs, and just clearing out – vamoosing – for all he was worth. We bagged a few with rifle fire, but it was impossible to fire steadily after a sprint like that, and to have really caught them meant following them down into the Wadi Gharib in front and this would have been the height of folly with darkness coming on fast.

We were not long arranging the line for the night and having picquets[43] posted. I went off to examine the village of Jiljilia and we found that we had just missed capturing four 77 mm guns which had been posted just south of the village immediately behind the crest [...]. They had cleared out in a hurry leaving everything except the guns, limbers and

---

43  A variant of picket or sentry.

ammunition. Their tents and shelters were there with bedding and officers' clothing, food and waste of all kinds. I did not see any signs of shell fire, so I suppose our planes did not spot them and our guns never engaged them. This must have been the battery that was making it pretty hot for us at Attara, which is only 3,500 yards away. There was a track on the map running east from Jiljilia to Sinjil on the Nablous road, marked 'reported fit for wheels', and we could see by the wheel tracks that the battery had got away by this route, and not long before we arrived, as their camp fire was still hot.

[…]

On Monday, 11th, we had a chance to examine the ground to our front more thoroughly, and we got out a proper system of defence which consists of a picquet line along the forward (North) slopes of the ridge, held by two companies. This line is only manned by night (and is the line of resistance) and, in daytime, only observation posts are manned, and the remainder of the troops are withdrawn behind the crests for rest and food. The third, or support, company finds the patrols at night.

I spent a good deal of Tuesday going over the line of Turk defences and found that all the sangars and rifle pits and MG posts were cleverly sited, so that every spot of the Wadi Jib and the north side of its banks was under fire from somewhere. Nearly all the positions were linked with telephones led to a central command post. Can't imagine why they ever let us take the place, as they had had very few casualties. We saw no wounded anywhere and they must have managed to get these away when they scooted. […]

[…]

## Week ending Saturday 23 March 1918. Jiljilia/Ajul[44]

We have had nothing to do […] except make the line impregnable. We have seen little of the Turk, and even at night, we hardly ever see or hear any of his patrols. […]

On Sunday 17th, St Patrick's Day, we had arranged for the Padre O'Carroll (RC) to hold a service at midday, but it poured such a drench

---

44 See Figures 17 and 18.

of rain all day, without stopping, that we cancelled the parade as we didn't want any more men soaked through than was absolutely necessary. On Tuesday, 19th, we received operation order No 42 [...] saying that we would be relieved on Wednesday by the 5th Royal Irish Fusiliers of the 31st Brigade, and that we would go into Brigade reserve near the bottom of the wadi at Ajul [...].

The Irish Fusiliers came along early and we were not long handing over our positions and telephone lines and giving them all the information we had about the front. On relief, the companies proceeded independently to our new camp, where we found a beautiful spot under trees (beech, plane, olive and fig) close to the bed of the Wadi Jib where it bends sharply round the spur on which is the very picturesque village of Ajul. Although there is now no running stream in the wadi, there is a fine pool just at the bend, and we found an excellent small spring for drinking water, about 100 yards upstream from our camp, on the north bank. There was a fall across the wadi bed beside us and from it there is a road being made up to Kalrawany along which the 30th and 31st Brigades will be fed.

[...]

We are to have two important jobs while here in Brigade reserve – one is to do road making down from Kalrawany and the other is to help to train a newly-formed Indian battalion which have arrived here. They are the 1st Kashmir I.S. (Indian Service) Rifles, and there have also arrived here the 38th Dogras and the 46th Punjabis. These troops are hardly trained at all and have never seen a bomb nor a machine gun, and we have to help their own officers to teach them. They have a native Indian Colonel, who isn't a soldier at all and some other officers, but there is an English second-in-command, and an Adjutant, and each company has one or two British officers. Our lot look rather like hill men and have a Mongolian type of face, looking something like Gurkhas. They are likely-looking fellows.

[...]

We have just heard on a very big attack by the Bosch in France, principally on the 5th Army on the Somme.[45] There is practically no

---

45 The German Spring Offensive which began on 21 March 1918, and eventually came within about 50 miles of Paris before being pushed back.

news available, but a serious view seems to be taken 'higher up' of the state of things.

[…]

## Week ending Saturday 30 March 1918. Ajul

From the scrappy news here, it seems that the Bosch attack in France is a serious affair pushed with enormous numbers of men liberated from the eastern front by the 'steam roller' going off the boil. We are all debating if we will get a shift to France, but I don't want to get stuck in trenches again. These open fights here are much finer business with plenty of elbow room, and a chance to work out your own little show.

[…]

An awful thing occurred one day which made men the men wild. The 7th RDF who are up the hill at Abwein found a young woman in an outlying hut, lying nearly naked and starving and with both her Achilles tendons cut right through and therefore unable to walk for the rest of her life. So far as we could make out, a Bosch officer had assaulted her and did this to her when leaving. We sent a mule up the hill with Paine and a couple of his stretcher bearers who brought her down. Paine cleaned the wounds as well as possible from the awful state they were in, but told us afterwards he was afraid she would lose both feet. I don't believe the Turk had any hand in this, or would do such an awful thing.

[…]

## Week ending Saturday 6 April 1918. Ajul/Abwein

[…]

On Tuesday, 2nd April, we moved up into the line in relief of the 7th RDF in what might be called the Abwein sector. As in other places, it consists of posts and strong points with MGs disposed for mutual support fire. […]

It is simply lovely up here, streets ahead of being down in the wadi at Ajul. Everything is in flower and leaf and the air is warm and fresh. Better than all – there is a grand view all round and we can get a good look at the old Turk. There seem to be a lot of them about the village of Amurieh[46] (2,208 feet) which is 3,500 yards from us and on the hill (2,628 feet) which has the tomb of Sheikh Tarutieh on it.

Since we have seen the front, the Turk has done a large amount of work on it and there is a great deal of heavy wire up now, so that at last he seems determined to put up a fight.

[…]

The Bosch gunners here with the Turks are most unenterprising. They will start each day at a certain hour and shell all up and down one of the small wadis running down from our positions to the Wadi Jib. After a spell of this they will switch over a quarter of a mile to the next one and dose it the same way and so on along our front. They never put any shells behind the crests where we live. Our gunners, however, sweep all the back slopes of their crests as well as the wadis and we can often see the Turks running wildly about looking for some shelter. [ … ]

[…]

We are out raiding and patrolling every night but so far have caught no Turks. They have an MG post somewhere [ … ] below Amurieh which we haven't located. It can fire into Abwein and is very annoying, so we must find it. We are now going to have the Indians (Kashmir Rifles) up with us in the line and will probably put a platoon in at a time till they get accustomed to shelling.

## Week ending Saturday 13 April 1918. Abwein

[…]

There was a horrible sight here of one of our observation sausages [balloons] being set on fire by a Bosch plane firing incendiary bullets into it. When the observer jumped out, his parachute did not open and the poor fellow crashed down a couple of thousand feet. I had my glasses on him at the time watching the Bosch. It is strange how far away one can see these incendiary bullets in brilliant daylight. The Bosch planes hardly ever venture over now, and then only at enormous height. One can only just detect them as a tiny dot.

---

46  Now Ammuriya.

## Week ending Saturday 20 April 1918. Abwein

We heard the result of the Luke court-martial and he has been acquitted[47] – so that's that.

[…]

The weather is getting very hot but the air up here is delightful, although patrolling at night is mighty hot work as no movement of the air gets down to the bottom of these tremendous valleys.

We got a Turk officer one night and found the poor fellow literally starving and was surreptitiously plucking leaves of trees and bits of grass as we marched him up here from Abwein. He was an European Turk, quite a gentleman and well-educated, and was wearing a strange medal ribbon which he told us was 'The Gallipoli Medal'. He had been fighting on our front near Anafarta Sagir and Suladzik and said if they only had guessed the weakness of our line there, they would have had us into the sea. This is probably true as we only had about one man to three yards of front including reserves. This Turk said that his battalion had been very short of food and only had as much for three days as they should have had for one. This explained to us what the Turks were doing whom we saw in the distance strolling about singly over the hill sides looking for something on the ground and now and then stooping to pick up something. They were looking for herbs and roots to eke out their rations.

[…]

Early this week it was announced that the line we are now on would be held for some time and that limited leave might be given to Cairo or Alexandria, so I put in my name and hoped to have a few days off. On Saturday my leave was granted for seven days from Ludd on the 23rd, Tuesday, to Tuesday, 30th, also back at Ludd.

## Week ending Saturday 27 April 1918. Going on leave/Cairo

I found I was to take down a party of NCOs and men and I put them in charge of Company Quartermaster Sergeant Stone[48] with their rations

---

47  WO 339/7840.
48  It has not been possible to locate a man with that name and rank in the RDF.

and told them to get off as soon as they liked and meet me at the railway station at Ludd at 18.00 on Tuesday evening. [...]

[...]

I started off after a good breakfast for Ludd and was simply astonished at the changed appearance of the country. I couldn't recognise any of it even when the driver told the names of the places. Camps, dumps, good roads everywhere made the places unrecognisable. We arrived in time for lunch at the rest camp, Ludd, having passed my fellows in a lorry on the way. I got my driver some food and sent him off after the heat of the day.

[...]

The train didn't start until dark and we had fairly decent sort of carriages with shelves fitted up to sleep on and a blanket or two apiece. I slept solidly all night and never awaked till we arrived at Kantara military siding. Went off to our Base depot and had a wash and shave and breakfast and got a lift through the base camps and across the swing bridge to the main station on the Port Said line, where I got the tickets for my men and arranged seats for them. [...] When we got to Zagazig, I noticed a peculiarly shabby-looking fellow mouching along in an officer's tunic but without badges or regimental buttons, unshaved and with long hair. He looked such a disgrace that I was on the point of speaking to him when one of the 10th Divison staff with whom I was sitting said to me 'Don't you think you might think first before blazing at him, and don't you know who it is?' I said I didn't and he replied 'That's Colonel Lawrence.'[49] He was probably just back from one of his wonderful stunts with the Arabs and had picked up any old gear to take him to Cairo.

[...]

Next morning I met Alan Beard (1st Connaught Rangers)[50] who arrived here a short time ago with the 3rd Indian (Lahore) Division, and we spent most of our leave together. One evening we drove out by motor to Mena House[51] for dinner and then climbed the big pyramid by night which was a wonderful experience. The noise which is called the

---

49   T.E. Lawrence 'of Arabia'.
50   Captain Alan Stephen Beard (WO 372/2/58011). See Figure 19.
51   A hotel near the pyramids.

silence of the desert could be heard better at the top than anywhere and we could hear the faint far-off hum of the teeming life of Cairo.

[...]

## Week ending Saturday 11 May 1918. Abwein

[...]

This week we started a pigeon service from the front line to 10th (Irish) Division HQ and we have been sending trial messages, training the birds, and the men who are looking after them.

We shot down an enemy plane with our Lewis guns into the Wadi El Kub in front of us. Both sides made a dash down into the wadi to get to it and quite a nice little scrap started in which we beat off the Turk and got the pilot alive and not much damaged but the observer was killed. Got all the gadgets, maps and plans out of the plane before destroying it.

Everything quiet in front of us. The Turk never does anything except dig and build sangars. These valleys and mountains are too big for the ordinary raid, so we never see him when we patrol.

## Week ending Saturday 18 May 1918.
## Abwein/Attara

Most poisonous luck. My eyes began to get sore again and in a couple of days I couldn't stand daylight at all so had to chuck my hand in. Went off on Saturday morning on a mule to Attara to the 30th Field Ambulance (Lieutenant Colonel Elvery)[52] and was just handed on to the 74th Casualty Clearing Station where I stayed the night. Sometime next day these people were sending an ambulance (horse) to Beitin or somewhere about there and I was shoved off to the next Casualty Clearing Station, the 66th.

---

52  Philip Gordon Moss Elvery (WO 372/6/203739).

# Week ending Saturday 25 May 1918. Hospital

On Monday I was pushed on to the 76th Casualty Clearing Station at Jerusalem where I was to stay. Was put in a sort of school where everything was at sixes and sevens. No food to be had – no washing water and one or two wretched nurses trying to cope with things. My eyes were rotten but I could not get anyone to look at them, so had to lump it. Next morning the hospital Medical Officer came round and saw me and said there was no eye doctor there and I must go to Ramleh that afternoon. We had a terrible drive to Ramleh. I was in the middle of a convoy of about twenty ambulances and therefore lived in a solid atmosphere of white dust. Our eyes, ears and mouths were useless when we got to Ramleh. There I found myself in the 36th Stationary Hospital in EP tents[53] in the middle of orange groves, with lovely shade and green grass and leaves. A Medical Officer bathed my eyes with something which eased them a lot but said I would not be allowed to stay there and would have to go to Alexandria. Pushed off early in the morning from the hospital siding at Ramleh and arrived at Deir Sineid near Gaza in the afternoon. Didn't see anything of the scenery. On Thursday morning we got another train to Kantara and so on to Alexandria. Here I found myself sent to the 17th General Hospital at Sidi Bishr.[54] Very nice, with Gippy waiters and attendants. Medical Officer very nice. He said I had the same trouble as before: corneal ulcers and inflammation of the iris, the latter being specially painful.

# Week ending Saturday 22 June 1918. Sidi Bishr

Had a rotten time these last few weeks with my eyes and I had two bouts of fever as well. However, nearly well now. Had a great surprise when Bill Whyte walked in today. The battalion is at Kantara under orders to France and he and a few others had a few days leave to Cairo and Alexandria. This looks like a repetition of my departure from Salonika.

---

53  More widely called 'EPIP' tents, the meaning of which is debated, but they were circular with a tall peak. For a discussion, see https://www.greatwarforum. org/topic/252797-british-and-empire-tents-and-shelters-of-the-great-war/ [accessed 7 April 2020].
54  Part of Alexandria.

## Week ending Saturday 29 June 1918. Sidi Bishr

I have been trying to get the Medical Officer to let me go, telling him that I will certainly be left behind if I don't get to Kantara, before they are made up to strength. Its no good – he won't let me go. [...]

[...]

## Week ending Saturday 6 July 1918. Sidi Bishr/I desert/HMT 'Malwa'

When Bill Whyte was here last week, I arranged with him to send me a wire as soon as he knew when the battalion was under orders to move, and, if by any chance, they were to sail via Port Said, to make that clear in his wire. On Tuesday morning, 2nd July, just after breakfast, a wire arrived from Kantara, 'Meet me three thirty morning of third – Whyte'. By arrangement with him I knew this meant at the docks, Alexandria, so I dashed off to the eye carpenter and to the ward Medical Officer and cajoled them both into signing my discharge, and then I went to the CO of the hospital (Lieutenant Colonel James Godding, Royal Army Medical Corps)[55] and tried to get him to let me go straight to the boat, but he wouldn't hear of it, said I must be sent in due course to the Sidi Bishr command Depot and go from there with the next draft to Kantara. It was useless to argue any more as he got quite snotty, so I pretended to be resigned to my fate and asked to be sent to the command Depot that morning, and he agreed to this. I then went back to the hospital and collected my kit and arranged for a pal to apply for leave during the afternoon and bring my kit to the Hotel Continental, Alexandria. Then I walked over to Mustapha Camp which was quite close to the hospital and reported to the Camp Commandant. Here I had a bit of luck as I was promptly transferred to No 2 Infantry Base Depot, Kantara and provided with a ticket for that evening's train. I therefore applied for leave to go into Alexandria in the afternoon for some clothing, which was graciously permitted. I had lunch in No 1 mess (for which I didn't pay) and then took the electric tram [...] and arrived at Alexandria about 4pm. I met my pal at the Continental and deposited my kit in a room which I booked, and then having bought some books to read, I locked

---

55   Also served in London Regiment (WO 372/24/24061).

myself in and decided not to appear in public till the next morning. Before retiring, I took the manager into my confidence and arranged that anyone making enquiries for me should be told that there was no such person in the hotel. I also told him to have a good meal for me at 02.30 next morning, and a gharry[56] at the door at 03.00. I spent a miserable evening wondering whether the battalion's timetable might be altered and whether the Assistant Provost Marshal might come nosing after me, when I didn't report back at the command depot.

Next morning, the hotel man was as good as his word and a jolly good supper (or breakfast – which?) was sent up to my room. I then slunk quietly down into the hall with my kit – jumped into the gharry which was waiting at the door and drove off to the docks. It was just beginning to be daylight and hardly anyone was to be seen. I had a bundle of papers with which I hoped to bluff the guard at the dock gates, and when we got near them, I made Jehu[57] drive furiously up to the gate. Without giving the sentry time to challenge, I yelled for the sergeant of the guard to have the gate opened as I had special papers for the Dublin Fusiliers who were just going to embark. He saw I was an officer and saying that the second train load had just arrived, swung open the gates and we galloped up to the side of a large transport where I saw troops embarking. To my great delight I found our people and they recognised me arriving, gave me a rousing cheer that was worth anything to hear. It was grand to be back in the bosom of the family again and we all had news to impart. I wasn't long on board before everyone knew I had 'deserted' and among Irishmen that's a great qualification as a notability, but I thought Bill Whyte was a bit worried about something and this turned out to be the question of whether I was officially on board or not. The Battalion was only allowed to leave Egypt at its exact establishments in officers and men and equipment and not a single man, animal, or cartridge extra might be taken, so that if he put me on the battalion strength I would be spotted and hauled off to jail. Stuffer Byrne then chipped in and said that unless I were taken on the strength, I would get no rations (officially). Eventually it was arranged that I should not appear in orders as rejoining until the morning after we sailed.

---

56  A horse-drawn vehicle.
57  A reference to Jehu or Yehu, of the Old Testament Books of Kings, commander of the chariots for the 9th-century BC King of Israel, Ahab, and later king himself.

We were on the transport 'Malwa' which was very comfortable and as there were several single cabins, I secured one but gave it up later as it was on the lower deck and the port holes were not allowed to the open even by day. This made the cabin so fearfully hot that I was glad to shift to a higher level where I could get some air. I found everyone looking remarkably well and the men all as fit as could be, so Duggie Haig[58] should be proud to get such reinforcement.

During the forenoon of the 3rd, we sailed out of the harbour but when we got just past the outer breakwater a launch came alongside with both naval and military officers on board, and I thought I was certainly stellenbosched, but, to my great relief, they only brought orders to anchor in Mex bay and await other transports which were to make up a convoy – nobody might go ashore except field officers and no bum-boats were to be allowed to trade with the troops.

Next day, Bill Whyte went ashore to the club and saw one of ours who is King of the Bobbies in Alex – Garvice[59] I think it was – and told him to make it all right about me if any enquiry were made.

We sailed from Mex Bay at noon on Friday, 5th, further exemplifying our fate of always making our 'major' moves on a Friday. We had I think, nine other transports and three destroyers manned by Japanese who handled their boats very smartly. We had a lovely sail in very hot weather but a fresh breeze from the west kept the ship pleasantly cool.

---

58  Field Marshal Douglas Haig.
59  Probably Major C. Garvice, Staff Intelligence, Alexandria (WO 372/24/23055).

# 9

# France, July–11 November 1918

As the 6th Royal Dublin Fusiliers travelled from the Middle East to France, Drury continued to be dogged by malaria.[1] That also affected many others in the battalion and in their initial weeks in France they were treated with ample doses of quinine. Meanwhile, with the 10th Division formally remaining in the Middle East (though without any of its Irish battalions and therefore minus its 'Irish' nomenclature), Drury's battalion joined 197th Brigade in the 66th (2nd East Lancashire) Division in late July. Alongside them were their 10th (Irish) Division comrades, the 5th Connaught Rangers. However, both units were moved within the Division in August,[2] by which point brigades were down to three battalions each: the 5th Connaught Rangers went to 199th Brigade and the 6th Royal Dublin Fusiliers to 198th where they served with the 5th Inniskillings and the 6th Lancashire Fusiliers.[3] Drury visited Rouen on leave[4] but found himself again suffering from the eye problems he had had in the past. He was confined to hospital for much of August before a period of leave home to the UK (some of which was spent in Ireland and some visiting friends in Scotland).[5] He eventually rejoined his battalion on 16 September 1918 in the Somme area just under 40 miles west of Arras.[6] By this stage of the war, Allied progress was rapid. The German attempt at a decisive advance in March–April had been resisted and

---

1   Diary entry, 15 July 1918.
2   Diary entry, 20/27 July 1918.
3   https://www.longlongtrail.co.uk/army/order-of-battle-of-divisions/66th-2nd-east-lancashire-division/ [accessed 20 April 2020].
4   Diary entry, 3 Aug 1918.
5   Diary entries, 10 Aug–14 Sept 1918.
6   Diary entry, 21 Sept 1918.

instead German forces were 'doomed by the summer'.[7] The Allied offensive launch at Amiens on 8 August began the 'Hundred Days', which saw first a series of probes into German position and then, from late September, a more general allied offensive. Some of this rested on superior fighting strength: the Allies' 1,672,000 infantry in the field by August were over a quarter of a million men more than German forces. These additional numbers were coordinated effectively with aircraft and artillery, plus the allies were vastly superior in tanks. To cap all of this, German morale collapsed.[8] However, to make the most of these opportunities, it was necessary for the infantry to be able to advance rapidly in a changing situation, and as Peter Simkins points out, 'The average British division', in contrast to the Germany Army during their 1918 spring offensive, had 'the capacity to keep up the pressure on the enemy over much of the three-month period of the Hundred Days'.[9] That was especially the case when fighting moved too fast for the heavy artillery to keep up.[10]

Consequently, once deployed, the 6th Royal Dublin Fusiliers were regularly on the move, sleeping where they could in the ruins of buildings. In late September Drury noted 'The billets were in ruined houses, in fact the whole place was in ruins. My billet had a cellar full of dead Bosches, but we were too cold and tired to mind and rolled up in the driest corner we could find and went to sleep.'[11] Moving south-east towards Villers-Bretonneux in early October they traversed areas which had seen much hard fighting during the war, and Drury described 'Enormous belts of barbed wire everywhere and nothing but mud or clay and shell holes.'[12]

The battalion was involved in fighting around Le Catelet, about 15 miles south of Cambrai, on 7 and 8 October as the British broke through the Hindenburg Line.[13] Drury noted, 'The enemy are now driven into the open country and those of us who have been accustomed to open fighting feel much more at home than in the trenches.'[14] After

7   Alexander Watson, *Ring of Steel: Germany and Austria-Hungary at War, 1914–18* (London: Allen Lane, 2014), 523.
8   Watson, *Ring of Steel*, 523–8; Gary Sheffield, *Forgotten Victory, The First World War: Myth and Realities* (London: Headline, 2001), 237–57.
9   Peter Simkins, *From the Somme to Victory: The British Army's Experience on the Western Front 1916–1918* (Barnsley: Praetorian Press, 2014), 205.
10  Sheffield, *Forgotten Victory*, 259.
11  Diary entry, 28 Sept 1918.
12  Diary entry, 5 Oct 1918.
13  Johnstone, *Orange, Green & Khaki*, 415–17; diary entries 7–8 Oct 1918.
14  Diary entry, 8 Oct 1918.

further movement until 11 October,[15] including 'the easiest day's fighting I ever had'[16] (it could be difficult to maintain contact with the retreating enemy),[17] the battalion took part in an attack on Le Cateau as part of the Battle of the Selle[18] on 17 and 18 October, facing gas shells from German lines.[19] Also at Le Cateau, as part of the 50th (Northumbrian) Division, were the 2nd Royal Dublin Fusiliers, who had fought there once before, in 1914. Among their ranks, Sergeant 14017 Horace Curtis, a Cornishman once of the 7th Royal Dublin Fusiliers, won the Victoria Cross for taking on a machine gun post.[20]

Late October saw Drury's battalion resting (and Drury given command of his former company, 'B' Company, to his great delight).[21] While at Prémont, Drury noted with some satisfaction a message from the 198th Brigade Commanding Officer saying that in twelve days the brigade 'have advanced 13¾ miles, on 10½ of which they were actually in touch with the enemy, have captured 484 prisoners, 23 field guns, three heavy howitzers, and a large number of machine guns in addition to inflicting heavy casualties on the enemy'.[22] The 6th Royal Dublin Fusiliers withdrew a few miles behind the front to Prémont and then Honnechy in the last week of October and into November. But they were again on the move forward on 5 November eventually towards Dompierre-sur-Helpe (just under 20 miles east-north-east from Le Cateau).[23]

However, with the war having now become one of 'pursuit' as the Germans retreated rapidly,[24] the battalion saw no more serious fighting. When news came at around 9am on 11 November of the armistice to take effect at 11am, Drury could scarcely believe it. The men displayed mixed emotions when Drury shared the news: 'they just stared at me and showed no enthusiasm at all. One or two just muttered "We were just getting a bit of our own back." They all had the look of hounds whipped off just as they were about to kill.'[25]

---

15  Diary entries, 10–16 Oct 1918.
16  Diary entry, 9 Oct 1918.
17  Sheffield, *Forgotten Victory*, 258.
18  Johnstone, *Orange, Green & Khaki*, 417–20.
19  Diary entries, 17–18 Oct 1918.
20  Grayson, *Dublin's Great Wars*, 266–7; Johnstone, *Orange, Green & Khaki*, 417–20.
21  Diary entries, 20–31 Oct 1918.
22  Diary entry, 21–31 Oct 1918.
23  Diary entries, 3–10 Nov 1918.
24  Diary entry, 8 Nov 1918.
25  Diary entry, 11 Nov 1918.

## Monday 15 July 1918. Serqueux

The 6th Royal Dublin Fusiliers arrived in France from Egypt, at a place called Forges-les-Eaux twenty miles from Rouen. We travelled overland from Taranto in the south of Italy via Brindisi, Turin, Genoa, Bordighera, Lyons and Tours. It was a tiresome journey and I had malaria most of the way.

Forges is a quiet little spot near Serqueux, and no sound of guns can be heard, so that we might be at home in the UK. We belong nominally to a Division which was almost wiped out during the fighting in March of this year. It is the 66th and it is in the process of reorganising, so we don't know yet how we stand. It is an enormous pity that the good old 10th (Irish) Division could not have come over complete and with our own staffs, whom we know and who know us.

We are to do light training here for a while, and have a special course of treatment to get rid of the malaria which a great many of us have.

## Week ending Saturday [20 or 27] July 1918[26]

We are in the 197th Brigade 66th (2nd East Lancashire) Division (Brigadier-General Wheatley)[27] which consists of:

6th Royal Dublin Fusiliers
14th King's Liverpool Regiment
5th Connaught Rangers
10th Black Watch (Royal Highlanders)

This arrangement may not be permanent and the whole Division will probably be reorganised when the troops have become acclimatised.

The French front certainly is a good place for supplies for we have only to ask for an extra marquee for the mess, or sheet iron for cook houses, or timber for goal posts, and it arrives within a few hours of the indent going in. A Royal Engineers officer often comes round to see we have all we want. They even give us a ration of fire wood and we have fresh bread and meat every day.

---

26   This entry is dated 13 July in Volume 4 of the diary but that makes no sense in terms of the running order and the events it records. Either side of it are entries for 15 July and the week ending 3 Aug.

27   Leonard Lane Wheatley, 1876–1954 (*The Times*, 12 June 1954, p. 8).

Our timetable is laid down something like this, –

| | |
|---|---|
| 07.30 | PT (Jerks) |
| 08.00 | Breakfasts. |
| 09.00 | Company and CO Orderly Room. |
| 09.15 | Quinine parade – all ranks five grains. |
| 09.30 to 11.00 | Platoon and company drill. |
| 11.00 to 12.00 | Musketry, bombing, MG training, signalling, etc. |
| 13.00 | Dinners |
| 13.30 | Quinine parade – all ranks – five grains. |
| 13.30 to 15.00 | Rest. Everyone lie down |

It has been most unusual for anyone to have any money on them at all, and now one has to try and dissuade the men from spending too much.

[…]

Everyone is bucking up in fine style and putting on flesh here. We have lashings of good food and we can buy eggs, milk and butter from the farm beside us. The owner is in the French Army and the place is being run in his absence by a competent staff composed as follows: his wife of about thirty – one daughter of about ten and another eight – an old man of seventy – and a couple of dubious looking screws used for carting. They start work at 05.00 and keep hard at it till nearly 20.00. Our fellows often wander down in the afternoon or evening and give a hand, to the great astonishment and delight of the family who seemed to think that the Allied troops must be the next worst to have to do with, to enemy troops. It's really astounding how well the men get on with the local people – neither knows a word of the others' language yet they get on like life-long friends, chopping wood for the fire and tidying up, milking the cows, etc. and laughing and joking all the time and then being invited into the house for a cup of coffee. We have been issued with pamphlets containing all sorts of instructions as to how to behave to the people on whom we are billeted, but it is evident that the compilers can never have been with an Irish battalion behind the lines. I daresay it is the same with the Scotch and English regiments, particularly the former.

Occasionally, Hun planes come over at an immense height but no notice is taken of them, and sometimes we hear bombing squadrons passing in the night.

One day, we had a most amusing footer match of officers versus sergeants at soccer, at which the speed of the officers roughly balanced the science of the sergeants. I unfortunately came into the limelight by committing an unpardonable mistake in soccer. I forgot I was not playing rugby and, seeing a favourable chance, seized the ball and sprinted for the goal. I didn't realise that the shouts were not those of applause until I grounded the ball behind the goal, and only then I realised that the whole crowd were convulsed with laughter – even the players were hardly able to continue for some minutes. No more soccer from me.

## Week ending Saturday 3 August 1918. Rouen/Serqueux

Got leave to go to Rouen for 48 hours to 'buy clothing' and started off with RD English from Serqueux Station at 21.00. As the train came into the station, we noticed two English nurses waving at us from the front carriage. Neither of us knew them but they called to us to come into their carriage. They told us a queer yarn. They had been in a General Hospital at Saint Omer for a year past, and recently had been so bombed and harassed every night that they had nearly had a breakdown and were being sent to [Le] Havre for a change. They had only been warned late the previous night about their transfer and had entrained about 07.00 that morning – no proper directions how to travel – no rations – in fact, no arrangements of any kind made for them. All the day they had been pestered by drunk poilus and civilians trying to get into their carriage. Both girls were almost fainting from fatigue and hunger, so we made them lie down on the seats and sleep. There was a breakdown on the line about halfway to Rouen and the train was stuck for about an hour. The Railway Transport Officer was a Meath man and he bustled around and got some tea made for the nurses. I really think it saved their lives – I never saw girls so done in, and the tea revived them a little. He made them go asleep again on the seats and Duggie English and I sat on the floor facing each other, with our backs against the doors. The trains simply crawled to Rouen which we reached about 01.30. There was nobody to meet the nurses and no vehicles to be had, so English got them into a filthy waiting room with no light and I started off to look for some Nurses' Hostel or a hospital where they could go to. After a lot of hunting, I failed to find any place and had almost decided to take them to our hotel in spite of Mrs Grundy when I spotted an ambulance lower down the street just turning a side street. I was feeling fairly tired and sleepy by this time but managed to do a record ¼ mile sprint and managed to make the driver hear my shouts. It turned out to be a WAAC and I got her to go back to the station with me and drive the two nurses to the place she stayed at. It was after 02.00 when we reached the station and rescued the wayfarers. The WAAC said she would arrange to drive the nurses down to the place at Havre they were bound for, the next morning.

Duggie and I went after the Hotel de la Poste in the Rue Jean[ne] D'Arc where the good dame gave us a fine supper 'and so to bed'. Next morning I felt rotten, seemed like fever again, so got a good whack of quinine from a chemist who seemed scared when I asked for twenty grains. We bought the various things we wanted and visited a few places of interest but I could hardly drag myself round. We got the return train at the Rive Gauche Station at 21.00 on Monday 29th, and arrived in camp about midnight.

Had bad go of fever for the next few days but resisted Paine's endeavour to send me away, as I was afraid the Regiment might move in my absence.

## Week ending Saturday 10 August 1918.
## Serqueux/Rouen

On Monday 5th, my eyes began to get bad again, damn rotten business, and off I had to go to the No 8 General Hospital at Rouen. Went via Ambulance waggon and was put in a large hut in the grounds under fine trees. Very efficient and very diminutive Canadian nurse from Saskatoon in charge. Felt rotten all week and bright sun for once proved anything but pleasant. Couldn't stand opening even the good eye. Air raids and bombing nearly every night – sometimes two or three raids in one night. Got nearly done in one night when a large nose cap came through the tin roof and fell on my bed and bounced onto the floor.

# Week ending Saturday 24 August 1918.
## No 8 General Hospital, Rouen

Got discharged from No 8 General on Tuesday, 18th and was ordered to report to the Base depot. Several of us were driven across the town in an ambulance driven by a nice girl from the North of England. I got beside her and asked her if she could manage to drive me straight to my regiment at Serqueux if I could wangle leave to rejoin at once. She said it was an extraordinary coincidence that she had to bring up medical stores to the Indian Hospital at Forges les Eaux, just beside Serqueux. At the Base Depot I found the usual red tape, 'No, quite against regulations, must go and drill for a week on the square, etc. and do courses!' I couldn't stand this, so sought out the OC and found him playing tennis, about 10 o'clock in the morning. Insisted on seeing him and presented my papers for signature and said I had a car at the door. With many maledictions on my head for putting him off his game, he signed everything like a lamb and I dashed off before he could change his mind. The girl driver invited me to lunch at her depot and I was astonished on arrival to find her CO was Miss Shaw of Edinburgh whom I often met at the Lethems. Spent a very pleasant hour and then drove to Serqueux in afternoon where she dropped me at our camp gate.

Great news when I got back. My name had been sent in while I was away, for leave to the UK and it was expected to come through any day. Found nearly half the officers and men away. They told me at Brigade HQ that we were not expected to go up to the line for several weeks yet as things were to ease down a bit for road making and getting forward supplies before another big forward movement.

My leave papers came in on Friday and I started at 17.00 on Saturday with leave till 7th September. […]

Submarine alarm on way to Folkestone and a lot of shooting and poofing off of depth charges.

# Week ending Saturday 31 August
## 1918. Leave to UK

On leave in Ireland. Lot of heavy fighting in France, and still there are crowds away on leave. […]

# Week ending Saturday 7 September 1918.
## Leave to UK

On leave to UK. Still great accounts from France. Haig still pushing hard. [...] Reported to [...] War Office on Saturday and boldly asked for a bit more leave. A dear old man about seventy years old was sympathetic and gave me five more days.

# Week ending Saturday 14 September 1918.
## Leave to UK/Boulogne

Spent a few days at Dunbar (Berwickshire), with the Lethems. Left in evening by GNR for King's Cross and had train stopped at Dunbar by stationmaster. Did it in style and had a sleeper engaged. [...] Had no excitement crossing to Boulogne, sea smooth and boat crammed. Everyone looks and, I am sure, feels like condemned criminals being led to the cells. Still, I had a good spell of leave and in a sort of way felt glad to be getting back. People have a rotten time at home and never know what is really happening. People in London don't look very healthy but the country people are OK.

Arrived at Boulogne, the Railway Transport Officer said he thought the Regiment had moved up to the line and spent a lot of time wiring to find out. [...]

Left by train on Saturday afternoon, and went by a military line specially laid for our use. Stayed the night at Gueschart with Colonel Paterson,[28] 5th Royal Inniskilling Fusiliers, as it was too far to Maison Ponthieu where the RDF are, to go straight on.

# Week ending Saturday 21 September 1918.
## Maison Ponthieu

On Monday, I borrowed a horse after breakfast and rode across to Maison Ponthieu, a beautiful little village with very pretty cottages with gardens in front. Enquired for the Orderly Room to report and going up the garden path, I ran into a man I used to race with in the Isle of

---

28  A.W.S. Paterson, formerly Somerset Light Infantry. WO 372/24/48546; *Monthly Army List*, Sept 1918, col. 1158.

Man named Little. I clapped him on the back and asked what on earth he was doing there. At that moment, Esmonde put his head out of the door and looked so scandalised that I wondered what was wrong. He introduced me to 'our new Colonel'. You could have knocked me down with a feather as the saying goes. What on earth had happened to Bill Whyte and what was wrong with Luke or Shadforth, or Wodehouse[29] for the job? Colonel Little evidently noticed my chagrin and said he saw I was upset but felt sure we would get on together. It seems that his battalion was practically wiped out and when it was decided to give Bill Whyte a rest for a while at home, Little was sent to us. He has an MC and bar and DSO and bar, so he must be a useful chap.

I was also very upset to hear that Stuffer Byrne had gone home too, and a miserable little rat called Unwin[30] sent instead of him. However, it was delightful to get back into the bosom of the family again and I spent the day looking up everyone in their billets and finding out where my men were. Everyone is looking in top-hole form now and ready for the Hun at any time. The rest of the week was spent in various training schemes, marches, etc. [...]

We have an American Doctor now instead of Paine who has gone home. He seems a capable man and is hard working. He was one of several who came over early in the war from the USA to volunteer for service with our RAMC. He has most peculiar table manners, and at breakfast he takes bacon, eggs, toast, marmalade, butter, or whatever else there may be, of and he chops the whole lot up together into a terrible looking mess, and then uses a spoon to feed himself. This fellow is quite pleasant and we all like him, but badly miss our old friend Paine who has been when us ever since September 1915 when he joined us near ALI BEY CHESME, Suvla Bay, Gallipoli.

---

29 Major Arthur Hugh Wodehouse, born in 1879 in Whitehaven, Cumberland, and educated at Bedford Grammar School. Began his military career in 1899 in the 5th Royal Dublin Fusiliers and Served in the South African War with the 1st Royal Dublin Fusiliers. In the Special Reserve from 1909 to being called up in Aug 1914. Served most of the war in the 5th Royal Dublin Fusiliers but went overseas in late 1917 to join the 6th battalion in the Middle East, remaining with them until the end of the war. See WO 374/76182.
30 Lieutenant George Frederick Unwin, formerly Cambridgeshire Regiment (WO 372/20/127184).

# Week ending Saturday 28 September 1918.
## Liencourt/Corbie

[…] On Friday, we heard that the 1st and 3rd armies had started a big attack on Cambrai and the Hindenburg line. Movement Order No 5 came round for the battalion to move to Corbie on the Somme, and that settled all the speculation as to our destination in the line. Most of us imagined we were going in near Arras, but now we know that we are to move south and operate on the famous Somme battlefield. The orders said we were to march from Liencourt at 07.15 and entrain at Petit Houvin at 11.25 arriving at Corbie probably about 15.30. All baggage is to go off today and I believe will travel by road. To our huge disgust, Saturday morning dawned with streaming skies and we had no greatcoats. We were all absolutely soaked through when we arrived at the station and I could feel the water trickling down my back and chest. There was no train when we arrived and the stationmaster hadn't the foggiest idea when it would arrive and didn't seem to care either.

The battalion squatted down in a field overlooking the railway cutting and waited. We all got as cold as blazes and in desperation we took some old sleepers and other refuse and lit fires for the men to warm themselves at. The blessed train didn't arrive until about 17.30 or 18.00 and it was a most remarkable affair. The carriages were shaped like a series of old horse coach bodies mounted on a long truck. There was no glass in the windows and those who had carriages with cushions were worse off than those with none!

We travelled very slowly and haltingly via Frévent, Doullens, Vignacourt to Amiens, where the train waited for a long time. We then went out via Longueau and up the valley of the river Somme, past where the river Ancre joins in, and finally ended up at Corbie about 23.00, still in the pours of rain. We had some distance to go from the station to the far end of the village and we had an awful time floundering about in shell holes full of mud and water which we couldn't see in the dark. Machine guns, rifles and ammunition all got soaked and filthy but as we were already wet through we only added mud to our already heavy equipment.

The billets were in ruined houses, in fact the whole place was in ruins. My billet had a cellar full of dead Bosches, but we were too cold and tired to mind and rolled up in the driest corner we could find and went to sleep.

## Week ending Saturday 5 October 1918.
## Corbie/Harbonnières/Guillemont/Ronssoy

Sunday morning was fortunately fine and we marched off at 09.30 past a big British cemetery up the road to Warfusée – Abancourt. The scene of desolation was terrible. I have never seen any of the French line where there has been heavy fighting for so long as here.

As we climbed the bare scarp of the ridge on which runs the main Route Nationale from Amiens to Vermand and Peronne, we could see on our left-hand the remains of some woods which had been so smashed by shell fire that at first glance one would not know what they were. The tree trunks were just masses of big splinters sticking up about five or six feet out of a dense mass of rotting vegetation and worse. It looks as if nobody had lived in the district for years and I'm sure nobody will for years to come. Warfusée itself is just a heap of bricks and timber, with only the skeleton of a house here and there to show that this was not a scrap heap but had been a good-sized main road village.

We had a considerable delay at Warfusée waiting while a lot of troops marched past on the main road and we have plenty of time to look about and see the scene of the Australians' fighting.

We resumed our march in an hour and went through Bayonvillers to Harbonieres [Harbonnières] where we got billets for the night. We had a good choice as no other troops were in the place which is a nicely situated village with a fine view over undulating country. Harbonieres is not so badly smashed as other places we saw, and most of the houses are undamaged.

The Hun had used the tower of the village church, which had a big spire, as an artillery observation post for a great many batteries. There were scores of wires connected to a sort of conning tower in the spire where map tables and instruments were fitted. These wires ran down to the inside of the church where an enormous dugout was made underneath, with an entrance and stairway in the floor of the chancel. All the furniture had been smashed and the pulpit was lying away in one corner. A large telephone exchange was fitted up in this cellar about twenty feet below ground, and living and sleeping quarters were fitted up.

On Tuesday, 1st October, we left Harbonieres and marched via Proyart across the Somme to Bray-sur-Somme to Suzanne […]. We saw the same desolation everywhere. Close to Proyart there was a Hun plane standing on its head with the tail vertically in the air, only just brought down. Colonel Little entertained me with stories of the great March retreat when he was in command of the Durhams and was across this area. He did remarkably well in that show, and in the end had collected over a battalion of troops representing dozens of regiments, in place of his own which was shot to pieces. They took a heavy toll of the Hun as did all the other units and their advance was finally stopped just at Villers-Bretonneux. After a slow march with many delays, we arrived in the evening at Suzanne and dossed down in the remains of houses or cellars.

[...]

The next couple of days were spent in doing a silly practise show round the neighbourhood of Guillemont – Ginchy – Montauban and Longueval, the same sort of thing which we have done dozens of times before and never will do in reality to the Hun.

I was glad, however, to see those terrible places where many fellows I know had been fighting. Delville Wood, High Wood and Bernafay Wood are shocking places. The whole place is a mass of rotting vegetation and stinking, slimy pools and bones and equipment lying about everywhere. The woods are almost impassable except on duck boards here and there, and if you slipped off you would never get out again.

Guillemont where we stayed in the remains of some army huts has completely disappeared. There is not one complete brick even. Everything is shattered and scattered to the winds. The only thing that would indicate that the village had ever existed here is the tangled remains of the metal parts of a sugar factory. The place is absolutely alive with enormous rats as big as cats and we could get no sleep with them crawling over one. [...]

On Saturday, the 5th, we marched out of this pestilential spot for Moislains, via Bouchavenes where we bivouacked in a fairly clean spot where good water was available. We crossed the main Peronne–Bapaume road near Sailly-Saillisel and through Templeux-La-Fosse and Villers-Fauçon [...] to a spot near Ronssoy [...] where we bivouacked for the night.

## Monday 7 October 1918.
## Le Catelet/Hindenburg Line/Beaurevoir

Battalion moved up towards Le Catelet in the Hindenburg Line, marching all night. Found a safe spot for the men with deep dugouts and cover from view where they could lie about in the air. I went off with the Divisional (66th) Intelligence Officer to spy out the land. [...] Our troops are now practically through the line which is extraordinarily strong, with masses of wire such as I have never seen before. We soon got into the open but saw no signs of the Bosch, in fact, we saw no signs of our troops except an occasional sentry post. I don't know where they have hidden all our troops, as I couldn't see any. We made our way very carefully up to a farm on a slight hill (the farm was called Villers Farm). We had to walk like Agag,[31] as the Bosch were only just beyond and had only just left the farm building, as fires were still warm. Got a very good look at the country in front where we will attack tomorrow. The ground is very bare and slopes gently down for a mile and then rises again to a ridge running along the front with a farm on it with a huge barn in the trees. Couldn't see any signs of work going on and I don't think there are any regular trenches at all – just small sections spitlocked out here and there. I took all the compass bearings I could for future reference. I thought it was time to get back after we had spent an hour there, so that I could get my report in to the Brigade Headquarters in good time.

Arrived back at 15.30 feeling very hungry and tired and was damned fed up to find a message from Brigade that I was to go out again at 17.00 with an NCO and six men to lay the Brigade line and approach tapes after dark and then guide the Brigade up to their positions during the night. I had been marching all the previous night and walking all the forenoon and early afternoon while everyone else was asleep. The Colonel, however, had had a good dinner got ready for me so I had a wash, feed, and then started off about 17.30 with several dozen reels of tape carried between the men slung on rods. The 198th Brigade[32] are to attack with the South African Brigade on their right with 199th Brigade in Divisional reserve. The 198 Brigade will have 6th RDF on the left and the 5th Royal Inniskilling Fusiliers on the right with the 6th Lancashire Fusiliers in support. The Brigade objective to be a line between and including Marliches Farm – Hamage Farm and then exploit N[orth] E[ast] as far as possible to the Walincourt–Audigny line. [...] 6th RDF two companies in line on 500 yard frontage, one approach tape to be laid to centre of each battalion, and the companies on approaching front will turn one to right and the other to left and company commanders will

---

31 A Biblical reference which means walking delicately.
32 The 6th RDF were transferred from 197 to 198 Brigade on 21 Aug while Drury was on leave. See http://www.longlongtrail.co.uk/army/order-of-battle-of-divisions/66th-2nd-east-lancashire-division/ [accessed 6 Jan 2020].

see that no bunching occurs and that the line is evenly held. Barrage will start 25 yards out.

I got my party up as far as possible while it was light and waited under cover till darkness came. The Divisional Intelligence Officer was sent out with us for some reason, but he was a hindrance rather than a help. He was in a regular funk and didn't know one end of a compass from the other. He didn't even know what I meant by 'setting the map'. As soon as it was dark we started off for Guisancourt from where the line was to run off to the right across the hollow ground up to the next rising ground towards Beaurevoir. I sent three of the men out as a screen and started with Corporal Alderton[33] and the other three men carrying the tapes. A damp mist was lying low on the ground and the going was very heavy with the long grass and occasional shell holes, and progress was slow. After we had been working for some time the Bosch must have got some idea of what was going on as we had a lot of rather unaimed rifle fire in our neighbourhood, but nobody was hit. Soon, however, I began sending over shrapnel which got the range to a yard. Time after time, the tape was cut behind us and we had to trace it back in the dark and knot it.

The worst misfortune happened was when a machine gun opened and fired a lot of bullets through the coils of tape, cutting it into one foot lengths. We had to tie each of these in the dark and still keep our proper line on the compass. It would have been the very devil if we had got it skew to the line of attack for the morning, as the troops would have got all bundled up to one flank – the one thing the tapes were intended to prevent. Sometime about now, the 'Intelligent' Officer disappeared and I was delighted to see the last of him as he wouldn't believe I was laying the tapes on the right bearing and wanted to lay on a bearing nearly at 90° different to mine! We were all fearfully hot and tired as we were all wearing our coats and equipment which we were afraid to dump in case we never saw them again, but we had to keep going hard as I was afraid we would not get finished when the battalion arrived about 03.30.

The shelling was getting worse and a lot of HE was coming over as well as shrapnel, but nobody was hit and the men were simply grand – didn't pay any more attention to it than if it had been a shower of rain.

We had got about three-quarters of the line taped when there was a tremendous burst beside us and I got an awful crack in the back and went down badly winded and nearly knocked out, for a minute I lay almost afraid to move as I thought there must be a devil of a hole in my back or

33  Probably 27808 Walter Alderton (WO 372/1/401778).

else my back was broken. Horrible thoughts flashed through my head, but soon I got courage to move an arm – OK so far, – then the other arm – again OK – then my legs. Thank the Lord, OK again, so saying to myself 'Get up, you silly ass' I pulled myself together and whispered to the others to know whether they were OK. They said none of them was hit and that they were looking for the remainder of the rolls of tape, also for the end of that which we had already laid which had blown goodness knows where. I found I had been hit by a piece of shell case which had opened out flat about twelve inches square. This had hit exactly on my pack which was stuffed with woolly waistcoat, spare socks and towel, etc. and had done me no damage at all. I felt very small then at my fright of trying to move lest I should find my back broken.

At last the front tape was laid and we overhauled it all along the front, finding two or three more breaks where shells had burst on it. The approach tapes gave us no trouble but we all felt used up.

I posted my men at the junction of the two approach tapes with the front, one at each end of the front, and one at the end of each approach tape. By this time, the battalion was nearly due and I went off to meet them. Suddenly the shelling increased to a tremendous barrage which fell behind me and somewhere about where the battalion would be. I decided to wait a while where I was as I was sure the Colonel would not bring up the troops through the barrage as he had plenty of time before Zero hour. I must've sat there for nearly half an hour smoking under the lee of a bank, when the barrage eased off and then moved back over our back areas. Zero was at 05.20 and it was now about 04.30 so no time was to be lost. After going on a bit, I found the battalion hidden about under banks and in shell holes. We had lost nearly 100 men by the shelling. The first casualty I saw was poor Carruth whose whole abdomen was carried away. We could do nothing for him but give a cigarette which he asked for. He didn't seem in pain but we knew he couldn't last long. Poor old chap, I was awfully sorry about him as we all liked him immensely.[34]

General Hunter[35] thought that the men would have lost their nerve after such a bad handling and so many casualties, but the Colonel assured him

---

34  Lieutenant John Carruth did not actually die until 10 Oct 1918: https://www.cwgc.org/find-war-dead/casualty/255254/carruth,-/ [accessed 7 April 2020] & WO 372/4/30030. At his death, his wife was working at a school in Cumberland but gave her permanent address as being at her parents in Stewartstown, Co. Tyrone, although she was living in Rathmines, Co. Dublin in 1919. See WO 339/43825.

35  A.J. Hunter, formerly King's Royal Rifle Corps (WO 372/24/32019).

that the RDF were not made of that kind of stuff and would soon show the Bosch whether they were shaken or not. At last I got the battalion on to the line and the 5th Inniskillings on to theirs and left them in an atmosphere of dead silence, not a round being fired.

## Tuesday 8 October 1918.
## Beaurevoir/Marliches Farm/Petit Verger
## Farm/3rd line taken

The enemy are now driven into the open country and those of us who have been accustomed to open fighting feel much more at home than in the trenches.

After seeing the troops on to the alignment tapes, I went back to see about communications with Brigade Headquarters. I fortunately found Sergeant Fay[36] and some signallers and runners. He had used his common sense and had been to Brigade HQ and seen where they were and had a lamp working with them from a position about 200 yards behind our front where there was the last of the Bosch concrete dugouts we saw. There seemed the most uncanny silence, we knew there were many thousands of men all round and behind as well as hundreds of batteries of all sorts but not a sound was to be heard nor a light seen. We kept eyeing our watches for Zero time and suddenly a battery some distance behind us fired four rounds quite deliberately 1 – 2 – 3 – 4 while you would count slowly. Then the air was rent with a snap and crash of sound such as I have never heard before – one almighty deluge of sound poured over us as made it difficult to breathe. I could feel the air pulsating and almost buffeting the breath out of my body. After the first moments of almost stupor, I could hear the crack and bang of our guns going as fast as the roar from the exhaust of a racing car. In a few seconds the Bosch guns opened fire in reply. I have no clear recollection of what happened. Shells of all kinds fell round us, knocking us over and over and unfortunately smashing our only signalling lamp. Sergeant Fay, who always looks so smart and clean, had all his clothes cut and torn. I was not in much better plight so I grabbed at all the party I could see as no voice could be heard, and scuttled down into Mr Bosch's dugout, 30 feet underground where at least we could breathe comfortably. We got a candle lit and waited for the strafe to blow over. We could hear the heavy thuds of big shells

---

36  Sergeant 16716 William Fay (WO 372/7/32280).

hitting the ground far over our heads, but, beyond clay dropping down from between the boards of the ceiling, we were undisturbed. I could not help pitying the poor Hun who must have been getting a couple of tons per minute of various sized shells poured on his head.

Soon the Hun barrage shifted and we emerged into early daylight and messages began to arrive for the Colonel that the line was pushing on tight behind the barrage and very few Bosches were to be found. We decided to push on after them and not worry about Brigade HQ whose job was to keep in touch with us and not us with them.

We found there was very little real fighting and, after the barrage had got to the limit line, the firing stopped and we went on across fairly open country to capture Beaurevoir Farm and Villers-Outreaux. We had a fair number of casualties but nothing like what I thought probable. I was very sorry to find Captain Gaffney killed.[37] He was a very fine officer who had been in the Canadian Mounted Police – a very charming fellow in every way. Someone told me that Tony Shadforth was killed, but I met him soon after hale and hearty, thanks be to goodness.

The Bosch was putting up a poor fight and we captured a good many and a fine a lot of equipment. […]

It was most surprising how little damage was done by the bombardment and we found comparatively few dead Huns. One fellow I came across looked in the distance to be standing in a hole with his head and shoulders above ground. When I got near, I found he had been cut in two at the waist by a shell and the upper part of his body was sitting upright on the ground with his legs about 100 yards away.

All the forenoon we pushed slowly along at a most leisurely speed, keeping in touch with the people on each side of us, but doing practically no fighting. We were all itching to get on fast but were told we must conform to the other troops, who were not used to open fighting. I was able to stroll about in the open going from one company to another and looking after communications generally. We found the Brigade signallers useless. We tried them with a lamp and later with both helio and flags but could get no answer. I therefore sent a party of four men under a corporal to find Brigade HQ and keep with them and remain in touch with us. This scheme worked OK. At the same time, they had not much to do because Brigade were not anxious about us and Colonel Little had practically no messages for them.

---

37   Captain James Gaffney: https://www.cwgc.org/find-war-dead/
     casualty/587858/gaffney,-james/ [accessed 15 April 2021].

When we got to Petit Verger Farm, we had to wait a good while for the Division on our left to clear the town of Villers-Outreaux, which had a lot of Bosches in it. This farm had an enormous barn and we got the two reserve companies of HQ into it and had a bit of something to eat. We then relieved the two companies in the line, and brought them in for a rest. While we were there one of our 8″ howitzers started shelling the farm and actually put one shell through the roof and out through the side wall without bursting. What an escape. We flagged a message of protest to our men at the Brigade saying we thought the battery doing the damage was somewhere north of Le Catelet [...]. Eventually they were stopped without doing us any harm, although another smaller battery shelled us with what looked like phosphorus shells which put up a dense white smoke screen just when we most wanted a clear view. Late in the forenoon we saw the Bosch streaming away N[orth] E[ast] from Villers-Outreaux and saw that it was captured by the 50th Division.

We had a small wood or spinney of oziers or sally trees in front of us and the Bosch had a good many men in it and several machine guns. Tony Shadforth with B Company was told off to discover them with A Company and D Company on the left and right respectively. There was a sunk road running across its front about 50 yards from the wood, so we lined up along the bank and gave the Bosch such a fusillade that we kept him looking to his front while B Company advanced round the Bosch right flank by section rushes. Most of the Bosch skedaddled before we got into the wood but we did get a bit of bayonet work on them before they went, and then hurrying the machine guns through the wood, we gave them a few salvoes across the open at long range. I captured one fellow with one of the new anti-tank rifles. It was useless of course for any sort of fighting as it is far too heavy and slow, and he had no other weapon. [...]

During the afternoon, we pushed on past the Marliches – Henage line to what was marked on our maps as the Bosch reserve line, Malincourt – Audigny line, but this had never been dug and the Bosch never stayed there but trekked away back towards Clary.

This most leisurely battle would not have suited Allenby if he were here. The Bosch are given plenty of time to clear off and take all their gear with them.

Once we got away from the Hindenburg line and the Canal de Saint Quentin we have seen very little gear left behind. The guns we captured today were all old ones pushed up near the front with a supply of ammunition dumped beside each of them. The gunners fired until we got within rifle range of them and then vamoosed leaving the guns behind. We should have harried good and proper instead of letting them get their troops and supplies away in good order to make a stand somewhere further on. If we could have rushed on and got to the railways radiating from Le Cateau, we would have crippled their retirement.

We bivouacked for the night in a sunk road and the cookers followed us up and we all had a good square meal with fresh meat. Bosch planes over in the night bomb dropping, but we had no casualties.

I was surprised to find nobody in the farms we took during the day. They must've left quite recently, as everything was in order.

## Wednesday 9 October 1918. Elincourt

We kicked off at 08.00 the 198th Brigade being in support to the 66th (2nd East Lancashire) Division with the 25th Division on our left as before. Our right is the line of the Roman road (Chausee Romaine) running away N[orth] E[ast] past Le Cateau and on to Bavai, where four or five of these old straight roads meet, and on the right of the 66th (2nd East Lancashire) Division comes the 1st (?) American Division between us and the French Army. I haven't seen much of the Yankee Army yet, but they look a smart, well-set up lot, but very young looking and rather pallid in face. Their march discipline is atrocious, or rather it is non-existent.

The 198th Brigade objectives today are the villages of Elincourt, Serain, Maretz and Bertry taken in three bounds. [...]

This was the easiest day's fighting I ever had, I don't think we fired a single round all day. Just marching along in support of the attacking line who had matters all their own way. There have been rumours floating around that the Bosch have been suggesting peace terms and we had a chit round from the Divisional HQ to pay no attention. It's just like the Hun to want to stop playing as soon as the game begins to go with us.

[...]

## Thursday 10 October 1918. 'The Culvert'

We moved on today to a position astride of the road from Cambrai to Le Cateau at the point where it crosses the Roman road. The Cambrai road has a steam tramway running along the side of the road like the

Dublin & Blessington Steam Tram and at this point passes through a cutting in the fields to avoid a change of gradient, and then passes along an embankment about 200 yards long and 35 or 40 feet high with a well-built stone culvert under the embankment about 4' high and 100' long. This was ready for blowing up, being packed with explosives and great quantities of HE shells of all calibres. We were just in time to prevent the damage as two Bosch engineers were caught just as they were about to blow whole thing up.

We have had a lot of shelling today and a good deal of it was gas, both Phosgene and tear gas.

[…]

When the cookers arrived about 19.00, the Bosch put down a tremendous shoot with Phosgene shells and everyone had to don their respirators and stand-to, expecting an attack. There was our dinner spoiled. The mules were galloped away up the Roman road where there was no shelling and we hoped they were all right.

I went off during the night down the main road to Le Cateau to see how the line stood there. I met some Connaught officers and they said they didn't think there were any Bosches in the main part of the town at all but that they were holding the railway triangle and embankments with a lot of troops. We walked down across the light railway embankment and got into the town by a partly broken bridge. Several of the streets look very well-built but it was too dark to see much. There were very few people to be seen but one or two poked their heads out of their doors and seemed to think we were Bosches. I heard that there were a couple of Inniskilling officers in the town too, but as it was too dark to see much, we were afraid of being scuppered and left the town about 02.00.

## Friday 11 October 1918. The Culvert/Reumont

The shelling at the road junction of the Roman road and the Cambrai road lasted on and off all night till daylight. We had a few casualties. […]

About 09.00 the General (Hunter) came round to have a decko round and seemed rather surprised to see all the men shaving and washing and togging up a bit after the shelling last night. Seemed to think our morale was pretty good and so it is. It's a good thing to boast a little on suitable occasions, and we told him he would have to be up very early to catch the Blue Caps dirty or unshaved.

Esmonde showed me where the 2nd Battalion passed near here in the Retreat from Mons and some of them are buried near Inchy a mile or so up the Cambrai road. I had not got time, however, to go and look for the graves.

I had a damned nasty trick played on me today by a Hun plane while I was walking across the open on the north side of Le Cateau towards the Le Cateau–Montay road. The blighter swooped down out of the clouds and started machine gunning me and my orderly from about 200 or 300 feet up. He was using some tracer bullets and we could see the damned things flicking down on us. He didn't hit either of us although only missing us by a few feet. We threw ourselves down in a most lifelike representation of a casualty and, after circling round, the fellow sheared off into a mist.

It seems that we have been getting too far out in front of the general line, as the other troops don't know anything about running a moving battle and they feel lost if they get the least gap between sections or platoons. Our men on the other hand are quite happy with a couple of hundred yards between sections of machine guns and give each other cross fire along their front to help them forward, as a matter of course.

## Tuesday 15 October 1918. Reumont

We were issued with a wonderful town plan[38] [...], showing all the streets of Le Cateau, principal houses, factories, stores and who lives in them. It also shows the wonderful system of cellars which are in many cases three deep down to 90 feet below ground, the first on the 30 feet level, the second on the 60 feet level and the third on the 90 feet. Most of them are really the quarries out of which was taken the sandstone for building the houses which stand on top of them.

There are a number of springs in the town and 450 of the houses have their own wells, which vary from 60' to 200' deep.

The principal person in Le Cateau is Madame Seydoux who owns the Seydoux spinning and weaving mills which are the largest in France.

---

38  Drury included a copy of this booklet in the diary. Its cover says 'Issued by General Staff Third Army' and carries the title *Notes and Town Plan of Le Cateau*. The imprint says 'Printed in France by Army Printing and Stationery Services', and it is dated October 1918. It has eight pages and a fold-out plan.

This book [the town plan] is a wonderful tribute to our Secret Service and it is hard to imagine how all this up-to-date information has been obtained. It was only printed this month.

There are a lot of cavalry collected near here to take advantage of any chance but to judge by the maps, the country in front of us towards Landrecies and the Forest of Mormal is so closed in with hedges and fences, they won't get much chance of doing anything.

[…]

## Wednesday 16 October 1918. Reumont/Le Cateau

I got word today that I am to stay out of the show, damnation to them, and to act as Liaison Officer between the South African Brigade HQ and the 198th Brigade HQ.

The Battalion moved down the Le Cateau road about dusk and [...] assembled at our old spot 500 yards west of the Four Valleys Bridge.

Operation order No 15 was issued at 22.55 by Colonel WB Little which set out in detail that Le Cateau is to be attacked by the South African Brigade who will have the 25th Division on the left flank and the 50th on the right. The attack will not be made on the town direct, but will move around on each side of it, having as the first and main objective the main railway on the embankment to the east of the town and the railway triangle south-east. The Dublin Fusiliers will attack the town and mop it up. B & C companies under Captain Shadforth and Major Luke are to do the attack and established posts along the east bank of the River Selle, and B and C will move out through them to start the mopping up. Later A and B Company will move further east and maintain touch with the other two companies, supporting where necessary and helping to form other posts along the railway when it has been taken. My job promises to be an unpleasant one wandering about among shells and bullets to see where people are. Anyway, I should see more of the battle than most of the others.

## Thursday 17 October 1918. SA Brigade/Le Cateau

A special order [...] was issued as 01.17 this morning, giving Zero as 05.20.

[…]

At Zero, a fairly heavy bombardment was opened by us on the railway triangle and the big curved embankment and also on the back areas. The Bosch also started shooting with a very large number of guns, mostly directed on the town itself but partly on the approach roads. Battalion HQ were in a cellar of a cottage on the road side [...] about 500 yards from the Selle bridge and the South Africans were [...] in some dugouts in a steep reverse slope where they were safe from most of the shell fire.

I found the General Commanding the South African Infantry Brigade a most charming man, who knew every inch of his job and who was most thoughtful for the comfort of his men. I noticed that when a runner came with a message when the shelling was particularly hot he brought the man down into his own dugout and gave him a tot of rum and made him rest awhile before sending him back.

The South African attack went on fast and up to time, and they got to their objectives quickly although the Bosch put up a stiff fight. The River Selle is a great barrier as it is too wide to jump and too deep to ford. The plans said it was four feet deep but at the part near the Seydoux factory where I saw it, the river was about 25 feet wide and about ten feet deep and the water was only eighteen inches below the level of the meadow. Pontoons have been ordered up to bridge the river at some points including this, but ours had been burst up by shell fire. Presently some tanks appeared and one was driven down into the river and the men were able to run over on its back which was like a half-tide rock. I heard that another tank was driven over the river on the back of the sunken one.

I saw Madame Seydoux's chateau which had been for some time the headquarters of the German 2nd Army commander, General Von der Marwitz, but it was badly damaged by the Hun artillery. The big weaving factory was also smashed but the Huns had taken all the plant out of it and carted the whole lot into Germany.

During the fighting today troops belonging to seven different Bosch divisions were identified, one of them being a Marine Division from Wilhelmshaven.

A train-load of troops actually steamed down towards Le Cateau from the eastwards but the troops were shot to blazes before half of them were out of the train.

Later in the day, the General of the South African Infantry said he didn't want me any more as his men were in their positions and I might be more use to my own battalion for a while, but I could come back and spend the night at his Headquarters.

I got down into Le Cateau about 15.00 and found that the mopping up was a tremendously difficult business and it seemed to me that at least two battalions would have been required. The main difficulty was the inter-connected cellars. As soon as we had cleared one street and driven all the Huns out of it and started down the next street, machine gun fire would be opened on us from the very houses we had first cleared. The big Church […] was cleared three or four times and yet the Hun fired from the tower (which is 180 feet high). John Luke was having the devil of a time clearing the street leading from the church out under the railway towards Bazuel. Bullets were whizzing about from all directions and it was not a bit safer under the walls than in the middle of the road. Afterwards, I went along towards the north end of the town where Shadforth was, and found that he had also had a good many casualties and a party of one platoon Inniskillings with two Vickers guns had all been wounded on the way to him as reinforcements. Shadforth was then pushing out towards the railway and some of his men were in touch with Luke's C Company […].

I found it was impossible to do any signalling scheme of any use. It was too dark to helio – we had no electric lamp and laying of wires was out of the question as the shelling would have ripped them to pieces, besides we had not enough wire, so I left the bulk of the signallers with HQ to act as runners and work the Brigade line, sending the remainder to the companies.

[…]

I got back to the South African HQ about 20.00 feeling dead beat, then I realised I had neither eaten nor drunk since dawn. They had an excellent meal ready for me and I felt mightily refreshed. I shared a small dugout with the Staff Captain and scrounged a couple of blankets hoping Providence would be kind and not pull me out in the middle of the night.

I wasn't fated to spend much of a night as the Hun decided to counter-attack in the force and turned every gun that would bear on to the town and surrounding district.

I had no sooner dossed down for a sleep than I was waked up by an orderly and told that the Hun had changed to phosgene and mustard gas shells and to get on my respirator 'Eck Dum'.

There was a regular rain of shells most of the night and as we had no gas curtains, it was a case of wearing our respirators all night and until about 06.30 this morning. All shelling then stopped but it wasn't safe to walk about in the hollows which were still drenched with gas.

Several messages came in during the night that the Hun counter-attack was easily beaten off and a good many prisoners taken. I got also a copy of a 198th Brigade order saying that the 6th RDF would be relieved by the 6th Lancashire Fusiliers about dawn and [...] would concentrate [...] in Brigade reserve. This means that the mopping up has been completed OK. At 07.20 I got a message from Lieutenant WO Parish by Private Norris[39] (runner) that the battalion was moving further back [...], so I had breakfast with the South Africans and said goodbye to the General, and rejoined the battalion.

I found we had a good many casualties but not nearly as many as I thought likely from my promenade yesterday. There were, unfortunately, a good many gas cases of men's respirators being shot through and inhaling the gas before they realised it. Our American doctor got a rather bad dose off the clothing of the men he was attending.

I heard a lot of complaints of the bad organising of the forward station of the Field Ambulance. They were much too far back – several miles – and the stretcher bearers took hours to carry men so far and they were utterly done in by the evening, so that men had to be taken out of the firing line to assist. The Advanced Dressing Station for us was a way back up the Reumont Road [...].

## Friday 18 October 1918. Le Cateau

There were some very sad cases of gas poisoning among inhabitants of Le Cateau. Most of the people took refuge in the cellars from the shell fire and MG bullets and many of them forgot to shut their doors and others had their roofs blown off. The gas being heavier than air, found its way down the cellars and many were gassed in this way, including some children. We collected all the respirators we could find and sent to Divisional HQ for more and distributed them among the houses. We also took the respirators from casualties as soon as they were out of the danger zone.

When I had a look through the town today, I was amazed at the damage – the Hun fired all day and most of the night with every gun which could bear on the town and had completely ruined it. The fine streets near the Town Hall and the church were filled with the debris of

---

39  Too many men named Norris served in the RDF to identify this individual.

the houses and shops. The Palais Fenelon was also in ruins, as also was Chateau Seydoux. When I was in town on the night of the 10th October, there was not a pane of glass broken and now the town is all smashed up.

[...]

We marched today back to Maretz and have billets there for the night.

## Sunday 20 October 1918. Le Cateau

Battalion resting and cleaning up. Got orders in the evening that the 66th (2nd East Lancashire) Division is to go into reserve and we are to move back further to Prémont.

## Monday 21 October 1918. Prémont

The battalion marched off this morning in fine weather to the village of Prémont about three miles away and a mile the other side of the Roman road from Serain.

[...]

To my unbounded delight I was given command of my old Company, B Company, Shadforth having been given a staff job at the 66th (2nd East Lancashire) Divisional HQ.

## 21 to 31 October 1918. Prémont

I was glad to find a lot of the men I still knew with the Company and they all seemed glad to see me again. I wasn't long getting over to my new billets and was soon immersed in Company Rolls, pay sheets, lists of equipment, etc. I found everything in good order and the next morning had a full strength, full dress, parade of the Company.

I made a very minute inspection of every man and his gear, and purposely kept them a long time. But no body stirred – all were as steady as guards on parade, and they had evidently done an extra turn of spit and polish for the occasion and my benefit.

The men looked very fit indeed and I told them, before dismissed, how pleased I was to be back with the famous old B Company and how their smart turnout and bearing on parade upheld the old tradition.

[...]

I saw something of the American Army during these days. They have been working on the right of the 66th (2nd East Lancashire) Division between us and the French Army to the south of the British line. Their discipline is very bad. It is quite a usual thing to see fully loaded limbered and GS waggons with half a dozen men reclining on the top of the load. The same thing with their artillery. I often saw officers and men in the back area going about unshaved and dirty looking and the men seemed seldom to have their proper equipment.

There was one place near Busigny which they (the Yankees) attacked with tanks and they had chucked all their training to the winds, so that the mopping up parties just buzzed off after the first wave and never did their job at all, with the result that the Bosch lugged their machine guns up out of the cellars after the troops had passed on and blazed at them from behind. The Yankees were caught between two fires and had fearful casualties. Some say they lost eight thousand out of the division in that one small scrap. As well as that, they left a whole lot of our tanks unprotected with the result that 25 of them were shot to pieces by close range artillery fire.

[...]

We have recently had allotted to us a RC padre named Burns.[40] He is a Franciscan, I think, and was educated and trained at St Joseph's Monastery at Mill Hill. He has for years been a missionary up country in Uganda. He is a tall, thin, lantern jawed man who says very little but is a real good fellow. He marches along with a big looping stride which he can keep up all day. He says he has often walked 40 miles in a day. He is very kind and thoughtful and always marches at the rear of the battalion so as to help anyone who falls out. He carries in his pack wherever he goes a beautifully made Communion service in a specially made box which prevents damage.

The Company is at present organised in three platoons with four sections in each. [...] but they are now being reorganised with three sections, two of Lewis gunners and one rifles, as now that we are out of

---

40  It has not been possible to identify this chaplain. In the diary entry, Drury wrote 'Burn' but then later in the diary twice wrote 'Burns' and gave the initials 'JS'. However, there appears to have been no JS Burns serving as a Catholic chaplain at this time, not any other variations (Burn, Byrne or Byrnes). There are three possible candidates: F.S. Burns, P.J. Burns, and J.H. Byrne (*Monthly Army List*, Dec 1918, col. 1795c), but the personal records of none have survived.

trench warfare, bombing has greatly diminished in importance and good machine gun work will be chiefly relied on.

What a contrast this makes with 1915 when we had only two machine guns in the battalion compared with 24 now. Then, the MGs were a separate unit attached to HQ and used separately by the CO or even taken over by the Brigade. Now, eight guns belong absolutely to each company and the brigade has a separate company of the heavy Vickers guns to use as required.

[...]

An interesting letter as set out below has been circulated and read out to the men on a ride from Brigadier-General Hunter, DSO commanding the 198th Brigade.

The BGC wishes to congratulate the Brigade on their performances of the last 12 days.

During that period they have advanced 13¾ miles, on 10½ of which they were actually in touch with the enemy, have captured 484 prisoners, 23 field guns, 3 heavy howitzers, and a large number of machine guns in addition to inflicting heavy casualties on the enemy. Their final effort was to clear the town of Le Cateau east of the river Selle thus liberating over 1,000 French civilians who have been under German domination for over four years.

This result has been obtained by the hard work and unselfishness of all ranks, coupled with a determination to do their duty and get to grips with the enemy in spite of all deterrents. The BGC regrets the casualties sustained in fighting a stubborn enemy, but he knows that now the brigade has got the measure of the enemy, and that he can rely on them in future operations to do equally good work in bringing the war to a speedy and victorious conclusion.

I have just got a new officer sent to me, Lieutenant AJ Carrigg,[41] late International footballer, a huge chap who looks a bit sleepy.[42] [...]

---

41 Austin Joseph Carrigg. Born 1884 and was working at the National Health Insurance Commission when he volunteered in Jan 1916, immediately applying for a commission, while living at Booterstown, Co. Dublin. He served with the 7th RDF from Feb 1916 and was sent to Salonika in Sept 1916. See WO 339/54105; *Monthly Army List*, Nov 1916, col. 1552.

42 There is no apparent evidence that Carrigg was an international footballer, whether in the Association or Rugby Union codes.

## Sunday 3 November 1918. Honnechy

Battalion moved to Le Cateau starting at 15.45 and marching via Reumont, beastly wet, muddy march, with many stoppages owing to traffic. [...] We billeted in some battered houses in Le Cateau and the people were most hospitable, making hot coffee, ad lib. They seem very badly off and have very little food so I gave strict orders that the men must not accept food of any kind. There was nothing to prevent them, however, giving cigarettes away and this they did liberally.

## Monday 4 November 1918. Honnechy

Orders issued to march from Le Cateau at 11.00 were subsequently altered to read 16.00 and we marched to Pommereuil where we had horrible filthy billets, with bad roofs and we spent a very cold night.

We got orders to move forward at 06.30 – breakfasts at 05.30, but later altered to 08.15. We are now heading N[orth] E[ast] and seemed to be going straight to the wood called Bois L'Eveque, after which comes the big forest of Mormal which is about ten miles long by six miles wide. This looks like some heavy fighting in front of us, but I think we have much more experience of wood fighting than the Bosch. We have just received operation order No 19 for tomorrow accompanied by notes by Colonel Little reminding everyone of the dense close country ahead, and saying that compasses will have to be used to keep direction. Bill hooks will be issued for hacking a way through hedges and even machine gun fire can be used for this purpose. He says that the Bosch are sure to rely mainly on their machine guns so we must work our guns in pairs so that one may engage an enemy gun while the other attacks from a flank.

[...]

## Tuesday 5 November 1918. Landrecies

We marched this morning at 08.15 to [...] north of Landrecies down in an orchard to await the results of the first phase. It poured a regular torrent of rain from dawn and everyone is damned miserable tonight. My Aquascutum 'three decker' coat with the oiled silk lining let me down badly and I was soaked through before midday. It seems that the Hun is getting the wind up and won't stand and fight and the 25th Division are finding it very difficult to keep in touch with him owing to the heavy mist which makes observation impossible and the awful enclosed country where the widest field is only twenty yard. across. Orders came out tonight authorising the issue of 'Hooks-bill, per man, one' which seems an amusing way of describing a slash hook.

Nothing happened and we got no news all day. The dense fog and damp prevented us hearing if there were any firing and no aeroplanes were about, so the battle so far is a very peaceful affair. This damned rain will ruin everything, I'm afraid, as it will be impossible to put up a decent fight under such circumstances. The men today presented a most comical appearance, they were all sitting around on their tin hats and their waterproof sheets over their heads and shoulders, looking like some sort of gigantic glistening grey mushrooms.

At 17.00 we got orders to move down to Landrecies which took only half an hour. We got some poor billets with leaky roofs and an awful smell of which I discovered later was due to the remains of several Bosches in the cellar. However, I was too cold and wet to move. I managed to scrounge some coke and wood at the station and got the men's clothes somewhat dried. At any rate they got warm which is something to be thankful for and I insisted on foot drill for fifteen minutes. Each man rubbing the other's feet like blazes with a towel until good circulation is caused. I['ll] have no trench feet in B Company if I can help it.

The 4th Army appear to be going to attack along each side of the Forêt de Mormal without doing any very serious fighting in it because the Bosch seems to be getting back fast and is not likely to be in strength in the forest.

[…]

## Wednesday 6 November 1918.
## Landrecies/Noyelles

[…]

It took us 5½ hours to march about 10,000 yards to Noyelles[43] via Maroilles. We moved about 500 yards and then waited half an hour and then repeated this ad lib. The roads were ankle deep in mud and

---

43  Noyelles-sur-Sambre.

the traffic congestion was terrible, waggons in continuous streams and ammunition, guns going up to new positions, etc. and the PBI (the 'poor bloody infantry') struggling on against the ditches. It was far more tiring than a 30 mile straight away march. The men are carrying a big load and my shoulders are weary tonight with all the stuff I have to carry, besides all my own gear, glasses, revolver, etc., I have bundles of company papers, books, etc., until it is so heavy that I have to get someone to lift my equipment up on to my shoulders. Got to Noyelles to very decent billets at 22.00 and it didn't take the men long to get dossed down. [...]

## Thursday 7 November 1918. Dompierre

We had the morning free to rest and clean rifles and ammunition and get mud off clothing and equipment.

We marched off again in the rain at 15.00 to Dompierre[44] via Taisnieres.[45] The roads were in a terrible state and the bridges over the Grande Helpe Rau were blown up so we had to wade in. There has been great talk of the Germans asking for peace terms and as we were passing Divisional HQ we were told that envoys from the Hun has been allowed to pass through our lines today to state their case. They must feel that we have beaten them definitely now that all the coast of Belgium up to the Dutch frontier is ours and we here are only about 25 miles from Mons where we started the war. It looked then as if the Hun was bound to win, and yet here we are again but with the Hun in full retreat. I hope the Bosch won't be let off now just as we are getting a bit of our own back.

The Bosch rearguards are fighting very cleverly – holding us up a lot but never getting to close quarters. [...]

We got very comfortable billets in Dompierre. The people looked better off and they did everything to make the men comfortable. I had a very good billet with my officers and the house was well-furnished and they have huge blazing wood fires for us.

A mail arrived in the evening and I got a welcome cake from Winifred and a letter from Jack – the first for many months. After I had seen all the men fed and dossed down and the horses fixed up, I went back to find a great supper ready and the good woman and the husband and children beaming away and jabbering French to the batmen who, of

44  Dompierre-sur-Helpe.
45  Taisnières-en-Thiérache.

course, didn't understand a word, but smiled back at them and all well. I divided up the cake among them and they seemed astounded at such a thing. They said the Bosch would never do such a thing and turned them out of the rooms to live in the outhouses. The poor children had not seen a cake I suppose since the Bosch came there in 1914 and they clapped their hands and squealed with delight. The old man produced a bottle of red wine from some secret store and we drank each other's healths until we fell asleep through fatigue and the hot fire. We all slept round the fire on the floor of the little sitting room and felt that we hadn't had such luxury for ages.

## Friday 8 November 1918.
## Dompierre/Les Trois Pavées/Maubeuge road

Received orders at 04.05 issued 03.40 that we must be prepared to move about 06.00 'breakfasts to be prepared and issued now'. Lewis guns and battle equipment to be removed from transport which will not accompany the battalion.

This was followed by operation order No 20 at 04.30 saying that our line now ran somewhat diagonally to our line of advance, the left being a bit further forward than the right. The Hun are holding the spur [...] and the farm La Croisette with a lot of machine guns: 'The 198 bde. with the 199 bde. on the right and the 150th bde. of the 50th Div. on the left will continue the pursuit at 07.30 today 8th inst.' This is the first time this word 'pursuit' has appeared, and it just fairly expresses the character of the battle.

The general objective is a line on the west side of the Bois de la Vilette 4,000 yards east of the Maubeuge–Avesnes road and when this is taken, cavalry patrols will pass through us and examine ground in front. The attack on the Avesnes road is to be done by the 5th Inniskilling Fusiliers with 6th Lancashire Fusiliers in support and 6th RDF in reserve. When the Royal Inniskilling Fusiliers get their line, the Lancashire Fusiliers will go through them, the RDF coming into support and leaving the Royal Inniskilling Fusiliers in Brigade reserve.

We had an early start today, the battalion being formed up at Dompierre Church ready to move at 06.00, the order today being B company leading D-A-C HQ, [...] we moved on a 2-company front, B Company directing on the left with D Company on the right. If artillery fire was experienced, companies were ready to open out into artillery formation, but most of the time we marched close up, as no firing was going on there. We moved slowly on till about 10.00 where we halted [...] at a house [...]. I had had no reports from 150th Brigade so I sent Corporal Emm[46] and two men to get in touch with the supports of this brigade. They went through [...] but could see no one. They heard no rifle nor gunfire and the inhabitants said they thought our troops had moved on eastwards. The patrol returned at 10.53. The Red Line was captured by the Royal Inniskilling Fusiliers about 13.00 and the 150th Brigade on our left were also reported through our Brigade HQ to be on their line.

About noon, I was ordered to withdraw pickets [...] and to advance to, but not beyond road running north and south [...].

The country here is more open and should be very pretty in summer time with nice woods here and there. C Company on my right appear to have edged away to the south a bit as I found it hard to keep in touch with them. I am the directing company and their job is to keep in touch with me.

At 13.10 I got an order that the advance would be continued on a two-company frontage with two platoons of each company in front and the third in reserve to its own company. B Company on left and directing as at present. A Company in centre and D Company on the right. The resistance of the Hun rearguards seems to be stiffening up and there are a lot of machine guns about, but very little artillery. I didn't notice any of our guns firing and I don't think they were needed. We stayed at the road [...] until 13.30 when the advance from this position was ordered to commence at 14.00 and companies not to get closer to the 6th Lancashires' reserve company than 400 yards.

We reached the Maubeuge road about 16.30 and found ourselves rather close to the 6th Lancashires who didn't seem to be advancing. I was just going up myself to see what they were doing when Colonel Little came along and said that the Lancashires had got very sticky, and to help them if necessary. I said I was nervous about our left flank which appeared open and a sudden counter-attack down the Sars-Poteries road might cause trouble and suggested putting a strong post at Les Trois Pavées. He agreed, so I sent Lieutenant Carrigg with No 6 platoon to this point and to report if the Lancashires were in front of him. I also sent word to Lieutenant Byrne to proceed with one NCO and three men north along the main Maubeuge road from Les Trois Pavées to ascertain actually the position of the 150th Brigade. The King's Own Yorkshire Light Infantry

---

46   14935 Arthur S. Emm (WO 372/6/207469).

were said to be holding the Maubeuge road from the Trois Pavées but Carrigg could not find them. He was also to find out if any cavalry or other troops had passed out through them.

At 16.38 I received the message from Purcell No 8 platoon that as A Company on his right had moved forward, he had done so too, so as to keep the required distance. He [...] reported the Lancashires as being held up by heavy MG fire on their left. A few minutes later, I got word from Booth No 6 platoon that the Lancashires' right had cleared a small farm and were moving forward and were asking was he to follow. I replied 'no, return to me at roadside house [...]'. At 17.10 Carrigg reported that the Lancashires' left was still held up by heavy MG fire from a large farmhouse surrounded by outhouses and large trees marked on map as 'Fme. a Jonquiere NE'. I told him to remain under orders of Captain Ridler of the 6th Lancashire Fusiliers and assist as far as possible.

At 18.00 I also called in Byrne No 5 platoon as I was afraid that they would get too scattered in the night for quick concentration and I must have some troops under my hand for immediate use. Byrne's report on his patrol came in at 20.45. He found the Scottish Horse dug in along the Maubeuge road with their right about 300 yards from our left. Their Colonel said they were badly held up by fire from their right [...]. He also said that the 2nd RDF had pushed out to and captured the village of Floursies. It is evidence that the Hun strong point at the farm opposite us is holding everything up so I wrote to Battalion HQ that I intended organising an immediate attack on this farm in conjunction with Ridler. I got Carrigg's platoon, and the Lewis gun section from No 5 and a good supply of smoke rifle grenades. We crept through the trees and farm buildings in the dusk and plugged dozens of smoke grenades into the upper windows, completely blinding the Hun, who didn't see Carrigg and his men working round the back. By this time, it was quite dark and it was very hard to see what was happening. The Bosch suddenly got the wind up and started to clear out, leaving everything behind. We got a good many of them with Lewis gun fire but took no prisoners.

I then went myself up the Sars-Poteries road to find what was holding up the Scottish Horse but this post was evacuated too, and we only got some long range bursts of fire down the road, hoping to wing some of them. Finally, ordering Carrigg to remain astride the road on Ridler's left with two Lewis guns well-sited, I took the remainder of the Company back to my cottage, and everything remained quite peaceful.

[...]

I called for an ammunition return and sent an indent in for our requirements with the ration party. We actually got a cooker up and I had a good, hot meal sent up to Carrigg's platoon, but it had to be carried a good, long way and I'm afraid won't be very hot. The rest of the Company are under cover in a couple of houses nearby.

There is no doubt now that the Hun is clearing out with no intention of returning as there are numerous big explosions of dumps going up and the glare in the sky speaks of big fires in various places. One perfectly colossal explosion occurred about midnight which shook the house badly and burst in a lot of windows. This occurred behind us somewhere and must be caused by the delay action fuses which the Bosch uses.

## Saturday 9 November 1918. Maubeuge road

Had a quiet night and some sleep. Visited Carrigg and the 6th Lancashires about 02.30 and found everything quiet and the men resting. They had a fire in the farm and were taking turns at drying themselves. [...]

During the night it became evident that the Bosch was clearing right out, and an urgent message came for Company Commanders to go to HQ for conference. Zero was then altered to 06.00 and hurried arrangements made for the men's breakfasts. [...] The Lancashires will push out from their present positions and we will follow.

B Company were out promptly at 06.00 and into position behind the 6th Lancashires. [...] At 09.40 was ordered back to billets but to be ready to move when required.

I sent an urgent message that at least fourteen pairs of boots already indented for were urgently required and asking the CO to expedite delivery in every way possible.

The weather is still bad with thick misty rain and very cold and Colonel Little visited me during the morning and said that the Bosch were going away so fast that the cavalry were pursuing and that we would not move forward today. I went over to the farm we captured last night and found the place was a huge dump of ammunition, Very lights and pistols, artillery cooperation flares and grenades, so I arranged a little 'diversion' for the men tonight.

A lot of cavalry – 12th and 17th Lancers and others – passed going east during the day, also the South African Scottish marched past. I turned out our guard to them and the men in the billets turned out and cheered them, at which compliment they seemed very pleased. [...]

News in the afternoon said the cavalry are already fifteen miles ahead, and the 50th Division are forming a mobile column to help in the chase. I wonder where the Bosch intends to stand. I suppose on the river Meuse if he gets the chance.

At dusk I let the whole company go down to the farm and each man was given a Very pistol and a pile of ammunition. We had a lot of the artillery flares, the kind we used to see in the trench lines sailing slowly upwards like coloured balls on a string, sometimes two reds and a green. Others were three reds or two yellows and a green. They were made up in a cardboard case shaped like an 18lb. shell and are fired from a metal pot or mortar stuck upright on the ground by means of a long spike with a plate on it, like an exaggerated shooting stick. As soon as tattoo was sounded, up went a perfect barrage of flares, signal lights and rockets like Brock's benefit at the Crystal Palace.[47]

Soon we had messengers running up from all the units round asking for a supply. We had more than we could possibly use, so gave all they could carry. We even had a limber sent up from Brigade Headquarters with a note from General Hunter asking for some.

It was a great night and the men were like school boys and enjoyed the show hugely. After about an hour, I ordered the 'cease fire' and they all knocked off and trooped back to billets for supper and a long night's sleep.

[…]

## Sunday 10 November 1918. Dompierre

We marched off from the Avesnes–Maubeuge road at 09.00 back to the outskirts of Dompierre where my company had billets just east of the railway on the road over the railway. The billets were very good and had wooden framing fitted up with wire mesh to make beds. These had been made and used by the Hun so we burned the straw and put in a fresh supply. I had a good room with a decent bed in the farmhouse and the poor people in the house were awfully kind to us.

We all turned out in the afternoon to start filling in a huge mine crater at the crossroads just to the east of us. It was a huge hole in which two or three tram cars could have been buried.

---

47  A reference to public displays of fireworks by the manufacturer Brock's Fireworks.

I had a note saying that the boots I indented for could not be got for the present but that the regimental shoemaker was placed at my disposal to effect repairs.

I got the barber to work in the evening and everyone had a haircut as we may not get a chance for some time again.

[...]

There is any amount of Bosch flares, signal lights and ammunition here too. The men started a sing-song in the evening but didn't keep it up long as we are all dog-tired. I don't think there was a sound after 20.00. [...]

## Monday 11 November 1918. Finis la guerre

The Company turned out for work on the filling of the mine crater at 08.30, as we are trying to get a road through, fit for wheels by tonight.

About 09.00, Colonel Little came along and after saying 'Good morning', casually remarked 'Well, we stop today', so I replied 'Thank the Lord, we could do with a spell of a few days'. So he smiled and said 'Oh, but we stop altogether, the old war's finished'. I thought he was pulling my leg so I asked him was I to tell that to the men? He said 'Yes, certainly, an Armistice has been signed and all fighting will cease at 11.00 exactly'. He then handed me the official order, – 'OC B Coy 6th Royal Dublin Fusiliers. Hostilities will cease at 11.00 hours today, Nov. 11th. Troops will stand fast on the line reached at that hour which will be reported by wire to Advanced Army Headquarters. Defensive precautions will be maintained. There will be no intercourse of any description with the enemy until receipt of instructions from Army headquarters. Further instructions follow' – 16th Corps HQ, 07.00, 11th November 1918.

I can hardly believe it. I don't know what I feel, but somehow it's like when one heard the death of a friend – a sort of forlorn feeling.

I went along and read out the order to the men, but they just stared at me and showed no enthusiasm at all. One or two just muttered 'We were just getting a bit of our own back.' They all had the look of hounds whipped off just as they were about to kill.

The French people are fairly off their heads, laughing and crying and singing, and clasping everyone round the neck and kissing them. The Lancashire Fusiliers have a good band and they played popular tunes in the town all the afternoon.

Dumps and delay action mines are still going off in every direction. The men got up a little better spirits in the evening and we had another firework display after dark. More limbers arrived from other units asking for supplies of fireworks. A regular 'Brock's Benefit' resulted.

We got word that we are to move up nearer the final line reached at 11.00 in case the Bosch plays any tricks. The start is ordered for 09.30 tomorrow.

# 10

# Armistice, 12 November 1918– 11 March 1919

On the day after the armistice the 6th Royal Dublin Fusiliers moved a short distance to Avesnes-sur-Helpe.[1] From here, they expected that they would eventually push on into Germany as part of the Army of Occupation. However, they would get no more than 80 miles towards Germany. Their final location from December was the Belgian town of Jemelle, about 70 miles short of the German border.[2] During their progress towards Jemelle the battalion took part in parades[3] and also carried out road repairs,[4] finding that there were delay action mines still causing damage.[5] Drury encountered damage to property caused by Germans and 'wished there were no armistice and that we could get the dirty hounds with the bayonet.'[6] However, he did manage to get temporary use of an abandoned Renault car with German number plates, and he used that to see the countryside.[7] Encounters with the local population were not always positive. In Hemptinne in Belgium, Drury noted: 'The people are unpleasant, and I suppose treat us as they did the Bosch – as interlopers.'[8] At Hastière, Drury found a 'tremendous display of Union Jacks'. These, it seemed, had been bought from Germans who had told the Belgians 'that the British were awful savages and would beat and

---

1   Diary entry, 12 Nov 1918.
2   Diary entries, 13 Nov–31 Dec 1918.
3   Diary entries, 13–14 Nov 1918.
4   Diary entry, 15 Nov 1918.
5   Diary entries, 13, 15, 24, 30 Nov 1918.
6   Diary entry, 23 Nov 1918.
7   Diary entry, 30 Nov 1918 and Jan 1919.
8   Diary entry, 21 and 22 Nov 1918.

burn all before them if each house did not show a flag'. The Germans had 'browbeat the people into buying an enormous stock of flags which were brand new and made in Germany specially for the occasion!'[9] By this time, of the thirty-two officers in the battalion, Drury was one of only two who had been in the original unit, the other being Captain G.Y. Loveband (see Appendix 3).

Drury had leave to Paris in the early half of December.[10] It was to be his last piece of tourism. After spending part of Christmas Day with the people with whom he was billeted, Drury noted with joy that the battalion was to be presented with colours and much preparation went into practising for the ceremony. However, the colours were not awarded (for reasons which are unclear) and, when the battalion learned of the city of Dublin accepting enemy guns captured by New Zealanders, this all added to a feeling of 'the slights which were constantly being put on us'.[11]

Drury secured leave home at the end of January 1919 not then knowing that he would not return to his battalion. However, he found both his brother and his sister-in-law suffering from influenza. Across 1918–19, nearly three thousand people in the city and county of Dublin died from the 'Great' or 'Spanish' flu.[12] As Drury was in London returning to Belgium his brother became more ill and the War Office granted him extra leave. He reached home hours after his brother died. Heading back to London, Drury went to the War Office and explained the position at home. He was allowed to return on 24 February.[13] By 11 March, his demobilisation had come through and he closed his diary entries by noting simply 'Doffed uniform and turned civilian again.'[14]

9   Diary entry, 24 Nov 1918.
10  Diary entry, 14 Dec 1918.
11  Diary entry, Jan 1919.
12  Grayson, p. 269.
13  Diary entries, Jan and 23 Feb 1919.
14  Diary entry, 11 March 1919.

## Tuesday 12 November 1918. Avesnes

The battalion moved to Avesnes[15] at 09.30. The roads are still filthy but the rain has stopped. The regiment looks very spruce again and everyone stepped well out on the Short March.

This town is practically undamaged and there are still fair stocks in the shops. One of the chief Hun army commands was living here during the war.

I climbed up the church tower and had a very fine view of the town and the country round. The town is packed with troops and I saw Argyll & Sutherlands – Dorsets – cavalry units – MG companies and lots of gunners.

A complete Hun artillery park and an ammunition train was captured here a couple of days ago, also a lot of cars and lorries.

I had a very comfortable billet with clean bed and sheets actually. I slept the sleep of the just and was waked by the old dame at 08.00 with a cup of coffee.

## Wednesday 13 November 1918. Sars-Poteries

We marched off this morning and 09.30 for Sars-Poteries which is on the main road to the Belgian frontier which is about five miles further on. We had great delay by a delay action mine which blew a big hole in the road half a mile north of Avesnes and broke the bridge over the Grande Helpe river.

[…]

We […] got a message from the 13th Corps Commander, Lieutenant General Sir TLN Morland[16] KCB,[17] DSO, saying that during the period 3rd October – 11th November, we have advanced 50 miles, meeting and beating sixteen different enemy divisions and captured 8,300 prisoners, representing 28 divisions, 250 guns and enormous quantities of stores of all sorts. He also expressed to the 66th (2nd East Lancashire) Division, on our leaving his Corps for the 9th Corps, his 'high appreciation of their gallant

---

15  Avesnes-sur-Helpe.
16  Thomas Lethbridge Napier Morland, 1865–1925. Commanded the British Army of the Rhine in 1920–22.
17  Knight Commander of the Order of the Bath.

and distinguished service during these operations which have resulted in complete victory. To each individual of the British, Irish and South African troops comprising the Division my hearty thanks for his splendid efforts.' Tonight I had a great honour. General Sir T Morland arranged to have a farewell parade tomorrow in Solre le Chateau of 100 men from each brigade in the 66th (2nd East Lancashire) Division and I am in orders tonight to take our 100 men.

I had the whole battalion paraded and sized and picked my 100 men and also one subaltern from each company. There was great work all evening and into the night polishing up and repairing clothes, changing over equipment, etc.

## Thursday 14 November 1918.
## Sars-Poteries/Guard of Honour

The guard of honour paraded this morning after breakfasts and they were all sized and dressed off when I came on parade. I felt like cheering when I saw them, – they looked magnificent and tremendously proud of themselves and why shouldn't they? Representing the oldest regiment in the Army (first records dated 1621). The remainder of the battalion, including officers and transport, crowded round to look. The band looked very smart too, and I had a word of congratulation for old Bryan, our band sergeant.

We had a great march for the five miles. The roads were dry for a change, but each man had a bit of rag in his pocket to clean his boots with when we arrived. They were in battle order and steel helmets, but, to our great surprise, the other parties were wearing caps and had only 50 rounds of ammunition. I was flabbergasted and, as I had no copy of the order with me, I dashed into the Corps mess and saw one of the staff and told him what had happened. He said I was perfectly right, but, in order to have the parade all the same, he would send a car back to collect our caps and bring them on. There was fortunately plenty of time to do this, and he promised that we should get credit with the general if he noticed anything.

We formed a three-sided square in the market square the town and General Morland came round each party in turn. He had with him the 4th Army Commander Sir Henry Rawlinson,[18] whose brother 'Toby'

---

18  General Henry Rawlinson, 1864–1925, 1st Baron, and commander of the Fourth Army in 1916 and 1918 (*The Times*, 28 March 1925, p. 17).

Rawlinson, I have met motor racing. They shook hands with each of the officers and spoke to many of the men. Finally, he presented decorations to the men which have been recently awarded, and six of my men got the Military Medal. We ended with a march past which went magnificently, the 'Old Toughs' going like the Guards and looking much more like veterans than any of the others.

The General had kindly arranged for a good dinner for all the men in a big building which used to be a Bosch hospital, and the officers had a 'slap up' lunch in the Corps Mess. Everything very jolly and the General in great form.

I collected my party and the Band, and having got equipment, etc. just right, we marched right through the town with the band giving tongue in great style. The Corps guard turned out to us as we passed. After we had gone about a mile, a staff car overtook us and stopped about 100 yards on. An officer in it held up his hand and beckoned me over, so I halted the party in fours and went over to find Sir H Rawlinson and General Morland returning home. They asked me who we were and remarked on the height and size of the men, Morland remarking 'There aren't men like that now, why didn't they send you out long ago?' to which I replied 'We left home on 30th March, 1915, and have been out ever since.' They got out of the car and walked along the men again and said a few words which bucked the men up no end. When they went on, we resumed our march but found them waiting round a turn to see us go by. By Jove, it was worthwhile going a long way to see the men swanking along with chests out and chins down and a good straight glance of the eye on the word 'Eyes left'. A great day altogether.

Received a circular from 4th Army HQ signed by Major General AA Montgomery[19] dealing with discipline and behaviour to the inhabitants now that we are going forward with the first troops to Germany. Regulations forbidding the use of cameras are now withdrawn and the censorship is to be relaxed, men being permitted to say where they are and to describe their surroundings.

19  Archibald Armar Montgomery, 1871–1947, from Fivemiletown, Co. Tyrone, became Montgomery-Massingberd in 1926 when his wife inherited family estates, and served as Chief of the Imperial General Staff in 1933–36 (*The Times*, 14 Oct 1947, p. 6).

# Friday 15 November 1918. Sars-Poteries

Worked hard on the roads, mending mine craters, etc. [...]

# Saturday 16 November 1918.
## Sars-Poteries/Solre le Chateau

We marched to Solre le Chateau today at 09.30. It's a most gentlemanly proceeding, these 9.30 starts after so many Zero hours at 05.00 and thereabouts. I got a draft of 44 men representing, it seemed, every regiment under the sun. We have started a serious reorganisation for the march to the Rhine. Men whom the doctor says are not fit for long marches must be left behind, poor devils. I have the Company now in four platoons of four sections each as of yore and five officers (one second in command and four platoon commanders). The Lewis gun establishment is reduced and the ammunition to be carried is less. Officers returned their web equipment to store and resume wearing Sam Brownes. Wire cutters, 'hooks, bill'[,] bombs and bomb dischargers are all handed in. It is ordered that all ranks take five grains of quinine daily for the next three weeks. [...]

# Sunday 17 November 1918. Rance

The weather has suddenly changed to hard frost and it is most invigorating after the perpetual rain and drizzle we have had.

We paraded today at 09.30 to Rance crossing the frontier into Belgium about a mile west of Sivry. It was very cold and heavy clouds were hanging about like a threatening of snow.

Arrived at 15.00 and we billeted in a Bureau for distributing food, run by the Americans. A Hun general has been living here for some time and has only left a few days.

# Tuesday 19 November 1918. Hemptinne

Marched at 08.00 to Hemptinne via Cerfontaine – Senzefille and Philippeville. We had ¾ hour halt at noon for a snack. There was a band playing in the square of Philippeville when we passed through, and a great crowd of troops principally cavalry. It was a heavy march of about sixteen miles on very slippery roads with half frozen mud. 6th RDF our advance guard today with C and D companies providing the van guard.

[…]

## Thursday 21 and Friday 22 November 1918. Hemptinne

[…] My billet is the coldest place possible and I have to sleep on a tiled floor. The people are unpleasant, and I suppose treat us as they did the Bosch – as interlopers. Orders came tonight for a move tomorrow at 07.30.

## Saturday 23 November 1918. Rosée chateau

We marched off at 07.30 to Rosée along the main road to Dinant on the river Meuse. We billeted in a very large fine chateau just on the east of the town. It must have been a very beautiful place before the war. It belonged to an officer in the Belgian Cavalry who was called up in 1914 leaving his wife and children in the chateau in charge of an old family butler. When the Bosch came, they commandeered the place and made the lady clear out to Brussels. The Bosch systematically stripped the house of every single thing in it. Furniture, pictures and silver. They even stripped away every bit of lead and copper off the roofs and took away all the ornamental railings. The old butler stuck to the place, however, like a man, although he was knocked about and beaten to make him tell of secret stores of any kind. The only thing left was a fine grand piano which was in a drawing room on the second floor. The day the Bosch left last week, they ran the piano across the floor, smashing the window frame out of the wall and sending the piano crashing down twenty or thirty feet into the area below, where we saw it all smashed to pieces – a mass of tangled wire and wood. When we arrived, we found the whole lawn in front of the house, several hundred yards long by one hundred wide, covered over with mess left by the last party of Huns who had stopped there on their retreat. Any remaining bedding had been piled in the hall and set fire to, and the poor old butler and his wife and another very old man had struggled to prevent the house being burned down.

Although nearly dead with fatigue, they had managed to smother the fire although, when we arrived, it was still smouldering. We turned a couple of hundred men on to cleaning up the awful mess and putting things to rights and gave our cards to the old butler to show to his lady if she still survives.

What brutes these Huns are. It's possible sometimes to excuse burnings and damage at the front on military grounds, but when we found such wanton looting and damage to property such as this and at Madame Seydoux' chateau and factories at Le Cateau, I wished there were no armistice and that we could get the dirty hounds with the bayonet.

## Sunday 24 November 1918. Hastière

The battalion marched off at 08.45 for Hastière on the Meuse going as far as Anthée on the main road and then turning south-east down a by-road. The order of march was HQ – B Company – C – A, and D doing rearguard to the Brigade under Major Wodehouse. We had a very pleasant march in a fine bright day with a brisk breeze. The country is very pretty and well-wooded with slight undulating hills.

When we got down to the river and marched to the town we were astonished to see the Main Street profusely decorated with Union Jacks. Two large larch trees had been planted bodily one on each path and a huge banner slung between with 'Welcome to our deliverers' on it. Several others spanned the main street in places with 'Honour to the Heroes', 'Greetings to the Conquerors', etc. Every man, woman and child had turned out to greet us, and the Mayor or whatever he is called turned out in a frock coat […] and a tri-colour sash round his waist to present us with an Address. Everyone of the inhabitants were fearfully affected by his Address and most of them were crying with joy at being liberated at last from the heel of the Hun. Most infectious all these hysterics and I felt most uncomfortable.

The people explained the tremendous display of Union Jacks by saying that the Bosch came along a couple of days ago in a motor lorry full of them and told the people that the British were awful savages and would beat and burn all before them if each house did not show a flag. So they browbeat the people into buying an enormous stock of flags which were brand new and made in Germany specially for the occasion!

I had a fine billet in a beautiful house with fine gardens and green-houses and, on looking round was astonished to find an enormous dump of machine guns in an outhouse. There were 487 light guns – 50 heavy – 38 spare locks – 400 stands at 100 waterproof gun covers. The men have very comfortable billets and the people can't do enough for them. It is rumoured that there will be a halt here for some days as it is getting increasingly hard to get up rations. We have been short for some time now and these damned delay action mines keep going off and blowing up roads and railways.

## Week ending Saturday 30 November 1918. Hastière

There is some doubt when we will move forward as there is the greatest difficulty in getting supplies forward over the battle area, as all the roads are smashed up – bridges broken and rivers diverted or overflowed. The railways, too, are out of commission and even when sections are repaired and ready for use, delay action mines keep going off and blowing everything up again.

It is rumoured that half of the Rhine Force is to go on now, and the other half will wait for a while until communications are better and join the others later.

A scheme of educational classes has been worked out for the purpose of keeping the men's spare time occupied and with a view to helping them when they are demobilised.

When we got to Hastière, we found a very long German goods train abandoned in the station and among the things were a two-seater car and a sectionised chassis. I had a look over the car and found it was a French make with a Renault type of bonnet, and radiator on the dash. It appeared in perfect order except that there was no carburettor and no tyres. I had arranged for a party to come down in the evening and we unshipped the car after a fearful struggle. The truck on which it was fixed had solid sides about two feet high and was about the middle of the train. There were very few planks to be found but with the help of some of the boards out of other trucks and a few pieces of rope we got it safely down on to the siding and pushed it out of the station to a shed whose owner I had squared to say nothing about it. Next morning I was surprised to get a memorandum from the Brigade HQ saying that 'sanction has been obtained for the temporary use of the German motor car at present on a railway truck, etc. for instructional purposes' and ordering the 6th RDF to detrain this car and arrange for its storage. The sectioned car was a <u>German</u> make and was on the next truck to the one I had just rifled, so I decided to say nothing about the French one (which had German numbers) which was not mentioned in the order. After some trouble, I managed to get four tyres of the right size (815 × 105) from a motor transport man I knew and stole a carburettor from a Bosch motor dump which had a lot of spares. The carburettor was large lorry size but with the help of the armourer staff sergeant I got it faked to suit the car and it ran really well. After so long foot-slogging, it seemed incredibly fast, and I got great value out of it, hoping the Powers-that-Be would not hear of it.

There is quite a good photographer here and we have all had photographs taken, singly and with companies and platoons, also all the officers together, and the NCOs and the band.[20]

[…]

## Two weeks ending Saturday 14 December 1918.
### Hastière/Namur/Charleroi/Valenciennes/ Douai/Arras/Paris/Amiens/Jemelle

I had a glorious week and quite an adventurous trip. A message came round that leave might be given for three days to Paris to officers and senior NCOs but they would have to pay their own way and get there and back as best they could. I put in my name and expected a rush of 'entrants' but was astonished to find that none of our officers wanted to go. I went by train in the afternoon of Saturday, the 14th from Hastière to Namur […].

[…]

After dinner in the hotel facing the station, I returned in good time for the train – the station was packed with shabby starved-looking Belgians. Presently I noticed a woman sitting on the platform with her back to the wall and thought she looked very ill, so I asked her if I could do anything for her. To my amazement, she answered me in English in a very weak voice and said she was all right but tired. On questioning her further, I found she was trying to get back to France so suggested she should come

---

20  See Figures 20 and 21.

along with us as we had a seat to spare and no foreigners could come in. She seemed delighted at this. I had to lift her up off the low platform into the carriage while one of the NCOs helped from above. It turned out that she was a married Englishwoman who had gone to Germany in 1914 before the war to act as holiday governess to a family. In July 1914, they had been away in some quiet farm and she heard nothing of the war rumours, and it wasn't until the war actually started that she knew anything of it. She was shamefully treated – told she was a prisoner and would be put in jail if she did not do as she was told, and was made to do servant in the farm all the war, being abused and starved and not allowed to write or receive letters. She told me she had a daughter aged ten or twelve years, in a school in London, but had never heard a word from her nor anyone else since May, 1914. When the Hun retreat started and the Armistice was signed, she was turned out at a moment's notice and told to clear out. She had no warm clothes nor gear of any kind and had started to tramp westwards hoping to meet some British troops, but finding the main roads blocked with retreating Huns, she had gone by byroads and at last got a farmer to give her a lift as far as Namur. The unfortunate woman was nearly dead, and I was afraid to give her too much to eat in case it finished her.

It was an awful journey, the train ran at about ten miles an hour for fifteen minutes and then stopped for ten minutes and repeated this performance ad lib. I got one of the sergeant-majors to go up to the engine for some boiling water and we made tea for her and gave her a little bread and jam, and, when she had finished this, I made her lie full length on the seat and sleep, while we sat on the floor. The poor woman seemed so grateful for anything we did for her that she could hardly thank us at all but nearly broke down.

We got to Charleroi about 23.00 and were told the line was pretty safe as far as Mons, so on we went the same way – no lights in the carriage, of course, except a candle end which I had in my haversack. At Mons, they said we could go on to Valenciennes. We made the lady some more tea and gave her some cake which she ate greedily as she was still starving. She was so weak I began to feel frightened about her and so decided to put her off the train at Valenciennes. We arrived there early in the morning while it was still dark and leaving her in the carriage with orders to the sergeants to let no one in, I went off to see if there were a Railway Transport Officer about. Found him at the other end of the station and he turned out to be an Irishman, I think, named Longfield. He was the right sort and turned out of his warm hut and got his bed ready for our lady and made his batman get some cocoa heated. He promised to keep her there till the morning and then got her on to a hospital train going down to the Base. I felt quite safe leaving her here as I knew she would be looked after. We carried her along the platform between us and to the Railway Transport Officer's bed and that is the last I saw of her. I forgot to ask her name and I hope to goodness she gets safely home to her daughter. She was evidently a lady and, although her clothes were mended and patched to the last, they were evidently expensive London clothes originally.

[...]

We arrived in Paris about 23.00 (Sunday 15th) and I got a doss down in a very disreputable looking small hotel by the Gare du Nord. Next day (Monday 16th) I spent the morning hunting round nearly all the hotels in Paris I could find but they were all full. Finally, I was walking along the Rue St Georges off the Rue Lafayette when I saw an American officer come out of a hall-way. I asked him if he knew of any place near, and he said this was the Hotel St Georges, and he was just leaving and perhaps I might get his room. The old dame said she had promised it several times over, but at last agreed and I dumped my pack and haversack in the room which was clean but small.

I found some extremely nice American ladies of the Red Cross and YMCA were living there and I was interested to find that one of them was the daughter of the American Consul in Bergen (Norway) when I was there in 1905.

I spent the next three days going about with some of these people who happened to be off duty – one fellow in particular I liked, a doctor called Summerling.

I had been given some money by the Division when I left Hastière to buy a lot of gear for a theatrical party they were getting up for Xmas and I had a most comic time in the Galeries La Fayette buying ladies' hats and garments of various kinds which a mannequin obligingly put on to let me see the effect! Most comical business altogether – the assistants being in screams of laughter, with the shopwalkers threatening to interfere.

I had an awful journey home again with all this gear. [...] Finally got a lumbering train going through to Namur, a single line having got going the last few days. Arrived at Namur about 18.00 the next evening in company with the General Staff Officer 2 of the 66th (2nd East Lancashire) Divisional staff who said he had a car to meet him. No car was to be seen but enquiries led us to a garage where the driver was struggling with a burnt out magneto. He had wired for another car to come out with a new magneto, so we waited and had tea. Presently the second car arrived saying there was no magneto to be had so we bundled all my gear and parcels into the broken down car and started to tow it with the good one. The rain was pouring down in torrents and the towing car boiled like blazes and finally stopped at the first decent slope, when we had to get out and push behind the towed car to help take some of the weight off. We got mightily wet and mightily heated by the time we arrived at Divisional HQ which we found had now gone forward to Rochefort. They gave me a jolly good supper in the mess and got me a decent billet for the night. I heard the 6th RDF were in a small town called Jemelle about three or four miles off and I got a message through on the phone for my groom to meet me in the morning.

Jemelle proved to be a very nice little town with important railway repair shops and engine sheds. Our job is to guard a lot of German mechanics who have to repair the engines they damaged when retreating.

My billet is in a private house where I am very comfortable.

## Notes up to 31 December 1918. Jemelle

We now know definitely that we are not going on to Germany, the difficulties of supply are too great to permit the original numbers of troops to go forward. So a line was drawn north to south through the Ardennes and the troops east of that line moved on and those of the Rhine Army west of it stay where they are as reinforcements.

The office work has become most laborious, as the men are all applying for demobilisation and the preference is given to men whose employers give guarantees that their jobs are open for them. The whole day is spent reconciling men's pay books and allotments to families, and the most scandalous mistakes are constantly coming to light on the part of the Record people at the Base. One Sergeant of mine who has drawn hardly any of his pay during war and his book showed well over £150 in credit, was billed with over £100 owing to the Paymaster. Many other cases like this but not so bad had occurred.

Day by day, men dribble off and it is not easy to keep things going smoothly. However, the men are marvellous, they still keep good discipline and personal smartness, just like any time they were out behind the line.

[…]

We have been making what preparation we can for the men's Xmas dinner but rations are short and it is impossible to buy much locally. However, what with presents from home and various supplies secured by the officers, we had a very decent show. Each Company made their own arrangements, so I can only speak for my own. We secured a large school room near the station and pinched a lot of coal off a dump there (the weather was very cold with some snow and hard frost) and had big fires going. I found an abandoned German field oven, a queer flat oval affair with four wheels which turned out magnificent roasts and also roasted potatoes. We backed this up against a side door of the hall and gave everyone a great feed. After dinner, the tables were cleared and everyone sat about smoking and enjoying quite a good scratch concert, while everyone could have beer to drink. Later on, all the people in the houses we were billeted were asked in for dancing. There was an infernal organ in the school played by putting in pennies so someone found how to make it play without pennies and kept it going full blast for the dance. The whole show was A1 and the Belgians were greatly pleased at being entertained.

The officers' dinner was held in a house where the Colonel lived which had two large rooms with folding doors between them. When these were opened back, there was plenty of room for a long table to seat about 30. We had a pleasant but sober evening and everyone seemed rather subdued, I thought. It seems miserable to think that we all will soon be breaking up and going our own ways and perhaps never meeting again. It's like the prospect of leaving school and college.

I had a pleasant afternoon with the people in my billet. They invited me to bring my officers and take tea, or whatever they call such a meal, during the afternoon. We all assembled with about six or seven friends of the family, sitting round a large dining table which was covered with piles of a curious sort of cake made with a pattern like rubber matting. It is really a sort of wafer and is called 'Gaufrette'. The proceedings opened with the host passing round a bottle of Hock. Everyone toasted everyone else and nibbled bits of gaufrette. Then another sort of wine was sent around, everyone taking about a liqueur glass full – more toasts, more gaufrette, a third and a fourth kind of wine, each different, was similarly sampled and then someone went to the piano and sang songs. We were simply forced to sing every sort of Irish song we could remember although they knew no English whatever. Young Byrne sings quite well and I managed to vamp some sort of accompaniment and when we ended the applause was deafening. I can't understand how these people live. They seem quite well-off – the man does no work but tidies his garden and gossips with similar people in the village. I could not find out anything about him but rumour says that he and many like him profiteered off the Bosch by selling corn and fodder. However, it doesn't seem to fit in with what we have heard of the Hun's methods.

## Notes for January 1919. Jemelle/Home

I have been getting great value out of my Bosch car. General Hunter offered to get me all the petrol I want if I were to teach him to drive, so I often go across to Rochefort and give him a lesson in the afternoon and then stay to tea, or, sometimes, I go over earlier for lunch. The General has a most marvellous collection of war curios, and samples of every sort of Hun rifle or pistol, also bombs and ammunition. It is easy of course for him to cart these about, and pack them safely. Paid a visit to the grottos at Han.

On the 8th January, there was a very interesting rugby football match with the South African Infantry Brigade at their place at Marche. A big crowd went over, on horses, bicycles, mess carts and car, my freight being Colonel Little and Esmonde. They ran the show, as usual, in great style, and the officers were entertained to tea afterwards. We have had two or three other matches with them and we like them very much. They are all South African Scotsmen of first or second generation. They are fine soldiers and good pals. Our men like them very well too. We don't see much of the 6th Lancashire Fusiliers, who are quite near us at a place called 'On' but I have been over once or twice to call and the compliment was not returned.

During the month, we got word that King's Colours were to be presented to us by the Prince of Wales. The whole Brigade started practising Trooping the Colour but we are the only unit who know what to do. I had the great honour of supplying the whole of the Colour Party and the officers [...].

We did the final practice so well that the General asked us to repeat it for the benefit of the other regiments as an illustration of how it should be done. We used the colours themselves (cased) which we had already been sent by the Ordnance Dept.

The day of the ceremony was fixed and then came a couple of postponements and finally we were told officially that we were not to have Colours after all. It's a most damnable shame; nothing would have been a fitter wind up for a purely <u>Volunteer</u> Battalion, who were the first Service Battalion of the Regiment in the first Kitchener Division – one of the First Hundred Thousand, and now disappointment and grumbling from the men. To make matters worse, we heard that the other Brigade, the South African Infantry, had had their colours presented by the Prince, who said official goodbye to them on their return to South Africa. About this time, I drafted a letter to the 'Irish Times' protesting against the arrangement announced in the last copy to hand, of sending to Dublin a present of some enemy guns captured by the <u>New Zealanders</u>, saying it was considered a gratuitous insult to Dublin's own Regiment. Surely a selection could have been made from the numerous guns captured by the Royal Dublin Fusiliers, battalions of which have been fighting in France, Belgium, Gallipoli, Serbia, Bulgaria, Greece, Turkey, Egypt and Palestine. The letter, however, was not sent, but it shows how much everyone felt the slights which were constantly being put on us.

On the 31st January, I left for ten days' leave to the UK […].

Spent most of the leave in Ireland. Found Jack and his wife both laid up with 'flu. Everything at home much as usual, and somehow the leave felt a bit flat.

Went to the War Office on February 14th and they gave me an extension from the 16th to the 25th, which I arranged to spend in Scotland and booked a sleeper for the 17th. On the evening of the 17th, got on wire that Jack was very ill, so cancelled the sleeper but was too late for the Irish train. Left London by the day mail on the 18th but was too late to see Jack who passed away at 3.30pm from septic pneumonia.

## Sunday 23 February 1919. London

Crossed to London by night and saw War Office on Monday morning. Explained the altered circumstances at home. They gave me two weeks' special extension, and, if the General agrees meanwhile, they will demobilise me.

## Tuesday 11 March 1919

Doffed uniform and turned civilian again.

# Appendix 1

# 6th Royal Dublin Fusiliers leaving home for service overseas, 10 July 1915[1]

D = Died
K = Killed
M = Missing
S = Sick
W = Wounded

## Officers

|  |  | *Status* | *Former service* |
|---|---|---|---|
| *Headquarters* |  |  |  |
|  | Lieutenant Colonel Patrick GA Cox | Commanding | Rifle Brigade |
| K | Major JG Jennings | Second in Command | 66th Punjabis |
| S | Captain H Anthony Shadforth | Adjutant | 1st RDF |
| D | Lieutenant Ronald BC Kennedy | Machine Gun Officer |  |
|  | Lieutenant NE Drury | Signal Officer |  |
|  | Lieutenant RC Byrne | Quartermaster | 1st RDF |
| *A Company* |  |  |  |
| K | Captain A John D Preston | Commanding | 1st RDF |
| W | Captain WS Lennon | Second in Command | Royal Irish Constabulary |
|  | Lieutenant WJ Arnold |  |  |

---

1   D1, pp. 42–3.

| | | *Status* | *Former service* |
|---|---|---|---|
| S | Second Lieutenant MG Corbet-Singleton | | |
| K | Second Lieutenant WHG Mortimer | | |

*B Company*

| | | *Status* | *Former service* |
|---|---|---|---|
| W | Captain WH Whyte | Commanding | RDF |
| W | Captain JJ Carroll | Second in Command | Royal Irish Constabulary |
| K | Lieutenant J Stanton | | |
| K | Lieutenant WR Richards | | |
| K | Second Lieutenant J McGarry | | |

*C Company*

| | | *Status* | *Former service* |
|---|---|---|---|
| W | Captain John Luke | Commanding | RDF |
| S | Captain JM Tittle | Second in Command | |
| K | Lieutenant Charles A Martin | | |
| K | Second Lieutenant FB O'Carroll | | |
| W | Second Lieutenant RW Carter | | |
| K | Second Lieutenant Wm. C Nesbitt | | |

*D Company*

| | | *Status* | *Former service* |
|---|---|---|---|
| S | Captain PTL Thompson | Commanding | 79th Carnatic Rifles |
| K | Lieutenant JJ Doyle | Second in Command | |
| K | Lieutenant DR Clery | | |
| W | Second Lieutenant CE Healy | | |
| W | Second Lieutenant DB Gilmore | | |
| | Second Lieutenant Arthur A Cullen | | |

*Details of Battalion*
28 Combatant officers
1 Medical Officer attached
6 Warrant officers
45 Sergeants
8 Lance Sergeants
34 Corporals
42 Lance Corporals
788 Privates
952 all ranks

# List of Signallers leaving home for Gallipoli

*Headquarters*

|   | 13904 Sergeant Johnson |
|---|---|
|   | 11903 Corporal Fay |
| W | 13537 Lance-Corporal Forbes |
| W | 12717 Private McGinn |
| W | 18393 Private Booth |
| W | 13400 Private Crosbie |
| W | 12331 Private Dunne |
|   | 11805 Private Dunne |
|   | 15346 Private Elston |
| W | 13370 Private McCafferty |
| K | 12581 Private Shevlin |
| W | 13433 Private Wright |
|   | 13264 Private Ferrie |

*A Company*

| W | 14343 Private Major |
|---|---|
|   | 11838 Private Perryman |
|   | 13360 Private Percival |
| W | 13427 Private Hart |

*B Company*

| W | 14379 Private McDonnell |
|---|---|
| W | 14331 Private Janes |
| W | 14383 Private Taaffe |
|   | 14342 Private Blackford |

*C Company*

|   | 13039 Lance-Corporal Currie |
|---|---|
|   | 13082 Private Bolger |
| W | 13038 Private Higney |
| W | 13113 Private King |

*D Company*

|   | 13204 Private Gourly |
|---|---|
| M | 13147 Private Fox |
|   | 13180 Private Watters |
|   | 13049 Private McMillan |

*Company messengers with HQ*

|   | A Company | Private Kavanagh |
|---|---|---|
|   |   | Private Purtell |
|   | B Company | Private Cahill |
| K |   | Private Magee |
|   | C Company | Private Brogan |
|   |   | Private Gorman |
|   | D Company | Private Wynne |
| K |   | Private Fairclough |

# Appendix 2

# The Effects of the Gallipoli Campaign on the 6th Royal Dublin Fusiliers[1]

## Officer Casualties on the Gallipoli Peninsula *Total 24*

*Killed 6*
Captain AJD Preston
Captain WR Richards
Lieutenant JJ Doyle
Second Lieutenant WC Nesbitt
Second Lieutenant FB O'Carroll
Second Lieutenant WF McGarry

*Wounded 10*
Captain WH Whyte
Captain PTL Thompson
Captain RBC Kennedy
Captain J Luke
Captain JJ Carroll
Captain WS Lennon
Lieutenant CA Martin
Second Lieutenant RW Carter
Second Lieutenant CF Healy
Second Lieutenant M Moloney

*Died of wounds 1*
Second Lieutenant WLC Mortimer

*Missing believed killed 3*
Major JG Jennings
Lieutenant DR Clery
Second Lieutenant R Stanton

*Sick 4*
Captain JM Tittle
Second Lieutenant AA Cullen
Second Lieutenant DB Gilmore
Second Lieutenant MG C-Singleton

*Mentioned in Despatches*
Lieutenant Colonel PGA Cox
Major WH Whyte
Captain Preston
Captain Thompson
Captain Richards
Lieutenant Byrne Quartermaster
Regimental Sergeant-Major Campbell
Corporal E Bryan

---

1   D1, pp. 152–3.

# 'B' Company 6th R. Dub. Fusiliers
*Original commander Captain WH WHYTE (late 1st RDF)*

*Original strength*
5 officers
1 Regimental Sergeant-Major
1 Regimental Quartermaster Sergeant
1 Company Sergeant-Major
1 Company Quartermaster Sergeant
9 Sergeants
3 Lance Sergeants
7 Corporals
14 Lance Corporals
213 Fusiliers
————
5 officers 250 other ranks

| | | |
|---|---|---|
| Strength at home | | 250 other ranks |
| Struck off strength | 10 | |
| Transport men left in England | 15 | |
| Left at Alexandria Record Office | 1 | |
| 1st Reinforcements left at Mudros | 38 | 64 |
| *Total landing* at Suvla, Aug 7th 1915 | | 186 |
| Reinforcements joined | 38 | |
| Rejoined from hospital | 7 | 45 |
| | | 231 |
| *Casualties*, viz:- | | |
| Killed | 40 | |
| Wounded | 84 | |
| Missing | 1 | |
| Sick | 27 | 152 |
| *Total leaving* Gallipoli Oct 1st 1915 | | 79 |
| | | |
| Disposed of as follows | | |
| at Battalion Headquarters etc | 25 | |
| attached to 31st Field Ambulance | 1 | |
| Serving with the Company | 53 | 79 other ranks |

# Nominal Roll of Officers of the 6th R. Dub. Fus. who landed at Suvla Bay 7th August 1915

| | | | |
|---|---|---|---|
| Lieutenant Colonel PGA Cox | In Command | OK | |
| Major JG Jennings | Second in Command | Killed | |
| Captain WR Richards | Acting Adjutant | Killed | Note Captain HA Shadforth left in Alexandria. Sick. |
| Lieutenant NE Drury | Signals | OK | |
| Lieutenant RBC Kennedy | Machine Guns | Wounded | |
| Lieutenant RC Byrne | Quartermaster | OK | |
| Captain AJD Preston | Commanding A Company | Killed | joined later |
| Captain WS Lennon | Second in Command A Company | Wounded | |
| Lieutenant WJ Arnold | A Company | OK | |
| Second Lieutenant WLC Mortimer | A Company | Killed | |
| Captain WH Whyte | Commanding B Company | Wounded | |
| Captain JJ Carroll | Second in Command B Company | Wounded | |
| Second Lieutenant R Stanton | B Company | Killed | |
| Second Lieutenant W McGarry | B Company | Killed | |
| Second Lieutenant CE Healy | B Company | Wounded | |
| Captain J Luke | Commanding C Company | Wounded | |
| Lieutenant CA Martin | Second in Command C Company | Wounded | |
| Second Lieutenant FB O'Carroll | C Company | Killed | |
| Second Lieutenant RW Carter | C Company | Wounded | |
| Second Lieutenant WC Nesbitt | C Company | Killed | |
| Captain PTL Thompson | Commanding D Company | Sick | |
| Lieutenant JJ Doyle | Second in Command D Company | Killed | |
| Lieutenant DR Clery | D Company | Killed | |
| Second Lieutenant DB Gilmore | D Company | Sick | |
| Second Lieutenant AA Cullen | D Company | Sick | |

*Joined later with reinforcements*

| | | |
|---|---|---|
| Captain Tittle | C Company | Sick |
| Lieutenant Corbet-Singleton | A Company | Sick |
| Second Lieutenant Moloney | A Company | Wounded |

# Appendix 3

# Officers of the 6th Royal Dublin Fusiliers at Hastière-sur-Meuse, Nov 1918[1]

Original 6th Battalion marked *

Lieutenant Colonel WB Little DSO (bar) MC (bar)

| Major AH Woodhouse | D Company |
| Major W Vance MC | Second in Command |
| Captain HJ Hayes MC | A Company |
| *Captain NE Drury | B Company |
| Captain RD English | C Company |
| Captain J Esmonde | Adjutant |
| Captain JI Watson MD | Medical Officer in charge |
| *Captain GY Loveband | Second in Command A Company |
| Lieutenant HJ Oliphant | |
| Lieutenant GE Larkin | A Company |
| Lieutenant WO Parish | D Company |
| Lieutenant AJ Carrigg | B Company |
| Lieutenant CW Booth | B Company |
| Lieutenant J McGaghy | A Company |
| Lieutenant GF Unwin | Quartermaster |
| Lieutenant Rev JS Burns RC | Padre |
| Second Lieutenant J McCann DCM | C Company |
| Second Lieutenant Millar MC | D Company |
| Second Lieutenant Manley | C Company |
| Second Lieutenant Rooker | C Company |
| Second Lieutenant O'Hea | C Company |
| Second Lieutenant GT Swayne | B Company |
| Second Lieutenant W Harney | B Company |
| Second Lieutenant WR Wade | A Company |

1  D4, p. 68.

| | |
|---|---|
| Second Lieutenant Scales | D Company |
| Second Lieutenant PP Purcell | B Company |
| Second Lieutenant JJ Byrne | B Company |
| Second Lieutenant McMillan | D Company |
| Second Lieutenant Young | D Company |
| Second Lieutenant Livingstone | D Company |
| Lieutenant WF Hannin | D Company |

# Biographies

**Allenby, Edmund Henry Hynman.** Born Nottinghamshire in 1861. Educated Haileybury College and Royal Military College. Lieutenant in May 1882, Captain in January 1888, Major in May 1897. Served in 6th (Inniskilling) Dragoons in South African war (1899–1902). Lieutenant Colonel in November 1900, Colonel in August 1902. Commanded 5th (Royal Irish) Lancers after the war before promotion to Major General in September 1909. Initially with the British Expeditionary Force on outbreak of war in 1914 steadily moving from divisional command to command of the Third Army in October 1915. Given command of the Egyptian Expeditionary Force in June 1917. Famous for walking into Jerusalem on foot after its capture in December 1917. Promoted to Field Marshal and made Viscount in 1919. High Commissioner of Egypt 1919–25. Died 1936.

**Byrne, Richard Charles.** From Lucan, County Dublin, and a military family. He served in the South African War. During the First World War, Quarter Master of 6th RDF and Honorary Lieutenant (later Honorary Captain) from August 1914. Died in November 1939 aged 60 in Twickenham in London as a Lieutenant Colonel and Chairman of the London Branch of the RDF Old Comrades' Association and chief of the Corps of Commissioners in London. Awarded the MC and OBE.

**Cox, Patrick Godfrey Ashley.** Known as 'Paddy'. First commissioned in February 1894, became Captain in August 1900 and Major in August 1902. Retired in February 1911 to Reserve. Lieutenant Colonel, commanding 6th RDF from late October 1914 until September 1917. Previous and later service with Rifle Brigade.

**Cullen, Arthur Armstrong.** Born in 1893 in India. Attended school at Christ's Hospital then studied at Oxford University and was serving in King Edward's Horse at the outbreak of war. Applied for a commission in December 1914 naming a preference for the RDF or Royal Munster Fusiliers. Lieutenant in 6th RDF. Served in the Royal Flying Corps from

1917 then in the RAF. Reported dead in August 1918, with his effects sent home, only to appear in Constantinople in January 1919 having been held captive in a Turkish prison. See WO 339/17769.

**Drury, Kenneth Kirkpatrick.** Drury's brother, born 18 May 1889. Educated at Tipperary Grammar School and Trinity College Dublin where he had been in the Officer Training Corps as an Acting Staff Sergeant. Worked at the Stewart Institute, Chapelizod, before the County Asylum, Warwick, where he was when war broke out and applied for a commission on 31 August 1914. Served throughout the war in the Royal Army Medical Corps and worked as a doctor post-war. Died in 1984.

**Esmonde, James.** Captain in 6th RDF. Formerly Drill Sergeant in the 2nd RDF, with the service number 10695. Commissioned in November 1915 and joined 6th RDF. Adjutant from May 1916 to the end of the war. Not to be confused with another RDF officer, John Lymbirck Esmonde, Irish Parliamentary Party MP for North Tipperary.

**Jennings, John Gilderdale.** Known as Jack. Commissioned in the Indian Army in August 1896, Lieutenant in November 1898, Captain in August 1905, and promoted to Major in August 1914. Served in 6th RDF attached from 66th Punjabis. Missing presumed killed at Gallipoli aged 37 (according to Drury on 9 August but noted by CWGC as 10 August). Son of General Sir Robert Melvill Jennings and husband of Adeline Braund Jennings of 1 Hyde Park Terrace, London.

**Kennedy, Ronald Bayley Craven.** Lieutenant in 6th RDF. Born 1895. Educated at Clifton College. Living at Kilmacthomas, County Waterford, on application for a commission on 25 September 1914. Wounded in the neck and shoulder, with partial paralysis, at Gallipoli on 27 September 1915 and did not fully recover until July 1916. He was deployed the next month to the 5th Corps Headquarters in France where he contracted tuberculosis in December. Sent home for treatment, he died at Fitzwilliam Nursing Home in Dublin's Upper Pembroke Street on 10 August 1917 and was buried in his family plot at the Church of Ireland Church in Stradbally.

**Little, William Benjamin.** Began war as 2nd Lieutenant in 9th Durham Light Infantry seeing action in France. Took over command of 6th RDF in September 1918. Post-war moved to East Lancashire Regiment and served with them in the Second World War. DSO (and bar), MC (and bar).

**Loveband, Arthur.** Lieutenant Colonel. Born 1865. Lieutenant in August 1885, Captain in December 1894, served in the South African War. Major in April 1907. Briefly commanding officer of the 6th RDF on its formation in August 1914 before being promoted to Lieutenant Colonel in September 1914 and transferred to command of the 2nd RDF arriving in France on 21 October 1914. Joined the regiment in 1885 and served in South Africa in 1902. Wounded at Ypres and died on 25 May 1915.

**Loveband, Guy Yerburgh.** Born 1892. Living at Ifield Vicarage, Crawley, Sussex, and was a student when he applied for a commission on 7 September 1914. He requested to join the RDF, stating that his uncle, Colonel Arthur Loveband, was to command a new battalion. Ended war as a Captain.

**Luke, John.** Born Faversham House, York, Western Australia, 1891. Educated at Merchiston Castle School, Edinburgh. Joined RDF in April 1911 after Sandhurst. Resigned commission in 2nd RDF in 1912 after charge of drunkenness but rejoined at the outbreak of war and became a Captain in the 6th RDF in September 1914. Promoted to Major in February 1917. Acquitted at court-martial of disobeying a lawful command in May 1918 and ended service briefly as second in command of 7th/8th Royal Inniskilling Fusiliers from July 1919, though left the army later in the same month. Found guilty of having been drunk and riotous in London in November 1922. Wrote to the War Office from Lambeth in November 1924, 'Hearing that the Socialists are going to try to break this government in the near future, I herewith offer my services in any capacity should it be found necessary to form a Defence Force. I am prepared to go anywhere & do anything and am free to start right away.'

**McClean, Richard Arthur.** Reverend Canon and Church of Ireland Rector of Rathkeale. Studied at Trinity College Dublin, graduating in 1891, then held posts in parishes in Sligo, Western Australia and Ballymacarrett in Belfast. He had been Rector for about ten years prior to volunteering soon after the outbreak of war, having previously been Curate of the same parish. He served as Protestant Chaplain to the 6th RDF when in his late fifties at Gallipoli and on the Salonika Front before being invalided home, to be appointed as Senior Chaplain in the Royal Barracks and Portobello Barracks in Dublin. Awarded CBE in 1922 and resigned his Rectorship in 1924 due to ill health. He died in 1948 aged 90. In some items he appears as Mclean or Maclean. The format used here is from his army service record and his death certificate.

**Mahon, Bryan Thomas.** Born in Belleville, County Galway, in 1862. Began his army career in the 8th (King's Royal Irish) Hussars in 1883 and serving in the Sudan Lieutenant from January 1883, Captain from April 1888, Major in October 1897 and was Lieutenant Colonel (from November 1898) by the start of the South African War (promoted to Colonel in March 1900), taking part in the Relief of Mafeking. Major General from December 1906 and Lieutenant General from September 1912. Commanded the 10th (Irish) Division at Gallipoli, later taking command of the British Salonika Force from September 1915 to May 1916. He briefly commanded the Western Frontier Force in Egypt in mid-1916. As General Officer Commanding in Ireland from late 1916 until May 1918 he was seen as a more conciliatory figure than his predecessor, John Maxwell. From October 1918 to March 1919 he was military commandant at Lille and retired from the army in 1921 to his home in County Kildare. Mahon was briefly on the privy council in the abortive Senate of Southern Ireland and was elected to the Seanad of the Irish Free State in 1928, remaining in office until his death in 1930.

**Martin, Charles Andrew.** From Monkstown, County Dublin. Lieutenant in 6th RDF. Wounded and missing on 8 December 1915 aged 20. On 1 January 1916, knowing that he was missing but hoping for better news, his mother, Mary, began writing a diary which she hoped he would one day read. She continued it until 25 May 1916. During 1916 there were still hopes that Martin was a prisoner, but in September 1917 Lieutenant W.E. Gilliland's August 1917 account of Martin's death, written as a prisoner of war, was sent by the War Office to his mother. This described how a Bulgarian medical student had been involved in treating Martin after he was found by Bulgarian troops on 9 December 1915, paralysed from the hips downward. It was thought he probably died on 10 December. His body was never located.

**Nicol, Lewis Loyd.** Brigadier General of 30th Infantry Brigade from late September 1914 and at Gallipoli. Commissioned February 1879, Lieutenant in June 1881, Captain in March 1890, Major in July 1897. Served in the Zulu War of 1879 and in the expedition against the Mahsood Wuzeerees in 1881. Began his army career in the Connaught Rangers but served the bulk of it in the Rifle Brigade, including its 7th battalion when it was established after the war's outbreak, prior to commanding 30th Brigade. Died in May 1935 aged 77, at Saint-Jean-de-Luz where he had lived for the previous fifteen years.

**Preston, Arthur John Dillon.** Born in Huddersfield in 1885 into a military family (his father was then a Major in the Duke of Wellington's Regiment). Captain in 6th RDF. Previous service in 1st RDF. Killed in action on 15 August 1915. Married in London in March 1914, but a son was born in Dublin in January 1915. At his death, his parents lived in Kilmessan, County Meath, and wife in Greystones, County Wicklow.

**Richards, William Reeves.** Known as Billy. Born in 1891. Lieutenant then Captain in 6th RDF. Killed in action on 15 August 1915. Drury succeeded him as battalion Adjutant. Parents lived in Greystones, County Wicklow, and in Dublin.

**Shadforth, Harold Anthony.** Known as Tony. Served in army from February 1912, was made Second Lieutenant in Sept 1913 and became first Adjutant of the battalion at the outbreak of war. Promoted to Captain in November 1914. Took on a staff role in 66th (2nd East Lancashire) Division in October 1918. Later served in the Egyptian Army and the Palestine Police Force, and as HM Consul in Aleppo. Awarded MC, OBE and King's Police and Fire Service Medal. Died in June 1983 at Hermanus, South Africa.

**Whyte, William Henry.** Known as Bill. Had served in South African War and came from a long-established County Down family, whose home was at Loughbrickland House. First commissioned in May 1901 and promoted to Lieutenant in May 1906, retiring in that rank in October 1909. Returned at the outbreak of war, initially a Captain in 6th RDF, rising to take command as Lieutenant Colonel in September 1917 for the next year. Awarded DSO. He died in 1949 after a varied life including rubber planting in Malaysia. His son, John Henry Whyte (1928–1990) was well known as Professor of Politics at University College, Dublin, and was an authority on the Northern Ireland Troubles.

# Bibliography

## Archives

National Archives of Ireland, 1901 and 1911 Census (http://www.census.nationalarchives.ie)

National Army Museum, London: Diaries of Noël Drury

The National Archives, Kew
  AIR 76: RAF Service Records:
    AIR 76/251/29: Jackman, Cecil Davies
  WO 95 First World War and Army of Occupation War Diaries
    WO 95/4296, 4583 & 4836: 6th Royal Dublin Fusiliers
    WO 95/4831: 67th Brigade, Royal Field Artillery
    WO 95/4836: 30th Infantry Brigade Headquarters
  WO 339: Army Officers' Service Records
    WO 339/744: Turner, Richard
    WO 339/901: Moloney, Michael
    WO 339/910: McKenna, James O'Neill
    WO 339/2380: Gaffney, James
    WO 339/4895: Nesbitt, William Charles
    WO 339/6748: Preston, Arthur John Dillon
    WO 339/7840: Luke, John
    WO 339/10583: English, Robert Douglas
    WO 339/10632: Goodland, Herbert Thomas
    WO 339/10955: Drury, Kenneth Kirkpatrick
    WO 339/13039: Doyle, John Joseph
    WO 339/13071: Martin, Charles Andrew
    WO 339/13084: Richards, William Reeves
    WO 339/13484: Lennon, William Sherlock
    WO 339/19084: McCreery, Mona James Nathaniel
    WO 339/20588: Watt, Gerald Allingham

WO 339/20715: Loveband, Guy Yerburgh
WO 339/21452: Kennedy, Ronald Bayley Craven
WO 339/25769: Carter, Robert Wellington
WO 339/25819: O'Carroll, Francis Brendan
WO 339/29007: Vance, William
WO 339/32747: Drury, Noël Edmund
WO 339/40044: Clay, Robert Angus
WO 339/43825: Carruth, John
WO 339/45707: Jackman, Cecil Davies
WO 339/54073: McClean, Richard Arthur
WO 339/54105: Carrigg, Austin Joseph
WO 339/103070: Pearce, William Hugh
WO 372: Index to Medal Rolls
WO 374: Army Officers' Service Records
WO 374/1936: Anstruther, Robert Abercrombie
WO 374/8842: Brewer, Alexander Hampton
WO 374/76182: Wodehouse, Arthur Hugh

Trinity College Dublin Archives, Admissions Records, 1877–1910

## Newspapers and periodicals

*Irish Times*
*The Motor Cycle*
*The Times*
*Weekly Irish Times*

## Secondary publications

Bowman, Timothy, Butler, William, and Wheatley, Michael, *The Disparity of Sacrifice: Irish Recruitment to the British Armed Forces, 1914–1918* (Liverpool: Liverpool University Press, 2020)

Cooper, Bryan, *The Tenth (Irish) Division in Gallipoli* (London: Herbert Jenkins, 1918)

Dungan, Myles, *Irish Voices from the Grear War* (Dublin: Irish Academic Press, 1995)

Ennis, Mervyn, *The Story of Swift Brook Papermill* (Dublin: South Dublin County Council, 2016)

Falls, Cyril and Becke, A.F., *History of the Great War: Military Operations Egypt & Palestine From June 1917 to the End of the War, Part I* (London: HMSO, 1930)

Fitzpatrick, David, 'The Logic of Collective Sacrifice: Ireland and the British Army, 1914–1918', *Historical Journal*, XXXVIII (1995), 1017–30

Grayson, Richard S., *Dublin's Great Wars: The First World War, the Easter Rising and the Irish Revolution* (Cambridge: Cambridge University Press, 2018)

Hanna, Henry, *The Pals at Suvla Bay: Being the Record of "D" Company of the 7th Royal Dublin Fusiliers* (Dublin: Ponsonby, 1917)

Harris, H.E.D., *The Irish Regiments in the First World War* (Cork: Mercier Press, 1968)

Hughes, Matthew, *Allenby and British Strategy in the Middle East, 1917–19* (London: Routledge, 1999)

Hughes, Matthew, ed., *Allenby in Palestine: The Middle East Correspondence of Field Marshal Viscount Allenby* (Stroud: The History Press for the Army Records Society, 2004)

Jeffery, Keith, *Ireland's Great War* (Cambridge: Cambridge University Press, 2000)

Johnson, Rob, *The Great War & the Middle East* (Oxford: Oxford University Press, 2016)

Johnstone, Tom, *Orange, Green & Khaki: The Story of the Irish Regiments in the Great War, 1914–18* (Dublin: Gill and Macmillan, 1992)

Kitchen, James E., *The British Imperial Army in the Middle East: Morale and Military Identity in the Sinai and Palestine Campaigns, 1916–18* (London: Bloomsbury Academic, 2014)

Macleod, Jenny, *Great Battles: Gallipoli* (Oxford: Oxford University Press, 2015)

Orr, Philip, *Field of Bones: An Irish Division at Gallipoli* (Dublin: Lilliput Press, 2006)

Sandford, Stephen, *Neither Unionist nor Nationalist: The 10th (Irish) Division in the Great War* (Sallins: Irish Academic Press, 2015)

Sheffield, Gary, *Forgotten Victory, The First World War: Myth and Realities* (London: Headline, 2001)

Simkins, Peter, *From the Somme to Victory: The British Army's Experience on the Western Front 1916–1918* (Barnsley: Praetorian Press, 2014)

Stanley, Jeremy Stanley, *Ireland's Forgotten 10th: A Brief History of the 10th (Irish) Division 1914–1918, Turkey, Macedonia and Palestine* (Ballycastle: Impact Printing, 2003)

Ulrichsen, Kristian Coates, *The Logistics and Politics of the British Campaigns in the Middle East, 1914–22* (Basingstoke: Palgrave Macmillan, 2011)

Ulrichsen, Kristian Coates, *The First World War in the Middle East* (London: Hurst, 2014)

University of Dublin, Trinity College, *War List, February, 1922* (Dublin: Hodges Figgis, 1922)

Wakefield, Alan and Moody, Simon, *Under the Devil's Eye: The British Military Experience in Macedonia 1915–18* (Stroud: Sutton, 2011; Barnsley: Pen & Sword, 2017 edition)

Watson, Alexander, *Ring of Steel: Germany and Austria-Hungary at War, 1914–18* (London: Allen Lane, 2014)

Wylly, H.C., *Crown and Company, 1911–1922: The Historical Records of the 2nd Batt. Royal Dublin Fusiliers* (London: Arthur L. Humphreys, 1925)

Wylly, H.C., *Neill's Blue Caps*, vol. III (Aldershot: Gale and Polden, 1925)

# Index